CHOCOLATES AND CONFECTIONS

CHOCOLATES AND

Formula, Theory, and Technique
for the Artisan Confectioner

Peter P. Greweling, CMB

The Culinary Institute of America

THE CULINARY INSTITUTE OF AMERICA

THE WORLD'S PREMIER
CULINARY COLLEGE

SECOND EDITION

CONFECTIONS

WILEY

John Wiley & Sons, Inc.

This book is printed on acid-free paper. ∞

Photographs © 2013 by Ben Fink

The Culinary Institute of America

President	Dr. Tim Ryan '77
Provost	Mark Erickson '77
Senior Director, Educational Enterprises	Susan Cussen
Director of Publishing	Nathalie Fischer
Editorial Project Manager	Lisa Lahey '00
Editorial Assistants	Shelly Malgee '08
	Erin Jeanne McDowell '08

Published by John Wiley & Sons, Inc., Hoboken, New Jersey
Published simultaneously in Canada

For general information on our other products and services or for technical support, please contact our Customer Care Department within the United States at (800) 762-2974, outside the United States at (317) 572-3993 or fax (317) 572-4002.

Wiley also publishes its books in a variety of electronic formats. Some content that appears in print may not be available in electronic books. For more information about Wiley products, visit our web site at www.wiley.com.

Cover and interior design by Vertigo Design NYC

Library of Congress Cataloging-in-Publication Data:

Greweling, Peter P.
  Chocolates and confections : formula, theory, and technique for the artisan confectioner / Peter P. Greweling ; the Culinary Institute of America. -- 2nd ed.
    p. cm.
  Includes index.
  ISBN 978-0-470-42441-4 (cloth)
  1. Chocolate candy. 2. Confectionery. I. Culinary Institute of America. II. Title.
  TX791.G786 2012
  664'.153—dc22
                        2009041248
Printed in China

10 9 8 7 6 5 4 3 2 1

CONTENTS

ACKNOWLEDGMENTS

This book bears my name, but at no point was I alone in making it a reality. Many individuals and organizations contributed generously to this work, and without each of them, the book in your hands would have been a lesser one.

I remain indebted to those who worked with me to create the first edition of this book, and undertaking the second edition has added to the long list of people with whom it has been my pleasure and good fortune to work.

The administration, faculty, staff, and students of The Culinary Institute of America all touched and influenced this book. I thank the administration for agreeing to join me in producing what I hope will be an important textbook, professional reference work, and contribution to the field of confectionery. My friend Tom Gumpel deserves special credit for providing me with the impetus to begin work on this book. Without his encouragement, I would never have undertaken the project. Were it not for the ongoing support of Dean Thomas Vaccaro, completing the second edition would have been considerably more arduous.

My colleagues in the Baking and Pastry Department supported my efforts, shared their opinions and expertise, and abided the wake of this project for long enough to have earned congressional commendations. In lieu of those, they have my unending gratitude.

The staff of the publishing department at The Culinary Institute of America had a great deal to do with the production of this volume, in particular Lisa Lahey, Maggie Wheeler, Nathalie Fischer, Erin McDowell, and Shelly Malgee. This book would not be anything close to what it is without their talents and hard work.

CIA students are a constant source of inspiration, enthusiasm, and creative energy, and so many have contributed in various ways that I could not possibly mention them all. Sune Naude, Karys Washburn, Adam Harvey, and Matt Plaza worked so many nights with me on formula development as to become slightly vampiric. Kelly O'Neil, Samantha Ramirez, Bryan Graham, and Susan Hemphill also played meaningful roles in formulation for the second edition.

Many individuals and companies outside of The Culinary Institute of America also made important contributions to bringing this volume to life. The stunning photography of Ben Fink graces the pages of this book; working with Ben is always both a joy and a privilege. For sharing their knowledge and enthusiasm, I thank Mel Warnecke of Warnecke Associates, Mark Heim of Hershey's, Thalia Hohenthal of Guittard Chocolates, Bob List and the artisans of Hammond's Candies, Anil Rohira of Albert Uster Imports, and so many others in this small candy world who selflessly share for the betterment of all. For their help in providing equipment for this project, I thank the Waring Company, Ohaus Scales, Jack Marshall of Pastry Chef Central, and Tom Elsinghorst and Brian Donaghy of Tomric Plastics. And, as always, I thank my wife, Kyra Greweling, for listening to countless hours of confectionery geek-speak during the creation of this book and for supporting me throughout this and all of my endeavors.

INTRODUCTION

The history of American confections follows a route parallel to that of many other traditional foods: born of artisans, adopted by regional producers, and captured by manufacturers. With each step in this process, the products tend to lose a little bit of their identity, becoming less unique, less diverse, more anonymous, and further removed from their artisan and geographic roots. Up until the early twentieth century, artisan foods were made by skilled craftspeople in small family-owned businesses in every town and village, with the trade handed down from generation to generation or learned through apprenticeship. Bread bakers, brewers, cheese makers, and, of course, confectioners produced relatively small quantities of fresh, unique products for their customers, who were also their neighbors. This is the tradition of artisan confectionery. Improvements in automation and transportation led to the rise of regional confectioners who prepared unique specialties in larger quantities with the aid of machinery and who distributed their products throughout a larger area than local artisan confectioners could supply. However, these regional confectioners still made candy that was traditional to the location and distributed it within that area, thereby contributing to the food culture of the region. Some examples of these products are pralines in the southern United States, sponge candy in western New York State, fudge throughout the Midwest, taffy at the seashore, buckeyes in Ohio, and maple candies in New England.

Further advances in automation, along with improved systems for distribution and the natural progression of capitalism, led to the rise of a few corporate producers, who today manufacture and distribute the vast majority of the candies consumed in America. Most of their products were artisan confections that were altered so that the manufacturers could produce thousands of pounds of them per hour for national or global distribution. Mass-produced confections are made using ingredients designed to provide a minimum shelf life of six months and to save the few cents that equate to profit when millions of units are produced. Due to their sheer size and economic advantage, these corporations have led to the near demise not only of the local artisan confectioner and his or her unique products but also of the regional confectioner. Although manufacturers are able to produce confections with great uniformity and economy of scale, the artisan aspect of handmade confectionery using ingredients of the highest quality has nearly been lost.

In recent years, however, a segment of the American market has grown weary of manufactured food products that are more about shelf stability and inexpensive ingredients than quality, flavor, and freshness. The revolution that has occurred in bread baking is a prime example of the backlash against manufactured food and the return to traditional ingredients and techniques.

Similar revolutions are under way in brewing, cheese making, winemaking, and farming, to name only a few areas of the American culinary landscape. Chocolate and candy making stand today where bread baking stood twenty years ago: poised for a renaissance in status and public awareness and ready for a revival in the use of traditional techniques to produce world-class products.

Artisan confections will never replace mass-produced candies in the marketplace, nor should they. Instead they will remain a niche market for those who are passionate about freshness, quality, and flavor. It is my hope that this book will fuel the artisan confectionery revolution by helping people who share this passion to understand and create confections that truly provide a feast for all the senses: the sight of perfectly tempered chocolate or beautifully striped handmade hard candies; the scent of chocolate, freshly roasted nuts, and caramel; the feel of chocolate melting in the mouth; the sound of crisp toffee cracking; and, of course, the taste of freshly made confections created with the best-quality natural ingredients.

Vive la revolution!

About the formulas

All of the formulas in this book are presented using three units of measure: metric, U.S., and percentage of the whole, uncooked batch. I have chosen metric for the primary units of measure for several solid reasons: grams allow for great ease of use; there is no need for fractions of ounces or conversion to and from pounds, as occurs when U.S. measurements are used. Also, being a smaller unit of measure, grams have a greater level of inherent accuracy. Most users of this book already work with digital scales that easily read either metric or U.S. measurements, so new equipment is not required. Finally, the United States remains the only country on the globe that has not embraced the simpler, more logical metric system; I believe that the change is long overdue.

For those who prefer them, U.S. units of measure are provided along with the metric. Regardless of the unit of measure chosen, the quality of the results from these formulas will be the same.

Percentages are provided primarily for those wishing to greatly increase or decrease the yields of the formulas and for those who want to make changes in the formulas in order to slightly alter the results or to compensate for ingredient substitutions. I have opted to represent percentages of the total, uncooked batch. Remember that in confectionery the weight of the uncooked ingredients is often vastly higher than the yield of the cooked batch, as a result of the removal of water during cooking.

Classic flavor profiles dominate the formulas in this book. The formulas recognize global influences and modern taste preferences but do not bow to fads, which are likely to be short-lived. By using the information on formulation and methods in each chapter, users can successfully create their own flavor profiles to meet the needs of their markets.

I have eschewed the use of nonfood additives in the formulas. Lecithin, sorbitol, glycerin, and other additives are not uncommon ingredients in confectionery, and although they are not intrinsically detrimental, I have formulated the products in this book without them. Even the use of colors and manufactured flavors has been limited to confections such as hard candy, where such additives are traditional and nearly essential.

The yields given for the formulas are likely to be appropriate for use in a restaurant, hotel, catering operation, or small confectionery shop. However, the formulas can easily be scaled up or down by using the percentages given, whether the desired outcome is a few dozen pieces or dozens of pounds.

The dark chocolate used in the formulas is 64 percent cacao with 38 percent cocoa butter content. The milk chocolate is 38 percent cacao, 24 percent cocoa butter, and 38 percent total fat. The white chocolate is 30 percent cocoa butter and 35 percent total fat. The heavy cream used is 40 percent butterfat. While it is not mandatory to follow precisely these specifications, results may vary, and some formulas may require adjustment when vastly different ingredients are used. Such adjustments can be made successfully by reading and understanding the discussions of ingredient functions in each chapter. The sugar-cooking temperatures given are for sea level; adjustments will be required for formulas cooked at altitude.

About the theory

A long-standing tradition among craftspeople who have learned their trade through apprenticeship or trial and error is knowing exactly how to do a job, but not necessarily knowing exactly why it is done as it is. Many extremely skilled workers fall into this category. The theory presented in this book is an attempt to help confectioners understand more about how confections work so that when conditions or ingredients change, they can adapt, and when the results are not as expected, they can create new formulas or adjust existing ones. The confectionery theory provided in this book is written for nonscientists, and is presented in an approachable fashion. There is nothing about confectionery that cannot be easily understood by the average person with an interest in the subject. Virtually all of confectionery is governed by three basic concepts: (1) understanding and controlling the crystallization of sugars and fats, (2) manipulating water content, and (3) creating stable emulsions. Whether the confectioner is mass-producing thousands of pounds of candy bars in an automated facility or producing a few dozen truffles by hand, these are the vital concepts that apply.

About the techniques

The majority of the techniques represented in this book are traditional for the confections in which they are used. In a few cases, I have applied theory and altered the technique for the sake of quality, efficiency, or both. Each technique is followed by the theory behind it, which is essentially an explanation of why each step in the technique is important and what the avoidable pitfalls are.

Excellence in artisan confectionery rests in the triumvirate of formulas, theory, and techniques; any confectioner needs knowledge in all of these areas to be consistently successful. I trust that the information in this book will supply a sound foundation in these three foundations for anyone who cares to use it, regardless of his or her experience or goals.

A word about conversions

All measurements in this book are presented in both metric and U.S. measurements, with the metric units displayed first. All units of measure have been rounded off to a degree that is appropriate for the confectioner using them under that circumstance. For instance, in most formulas the confectioner would not need to scale heavy cream or sugar to a quarter-of-an-ounce measurement but would use single-ounce increments; so when converting from grams to ounces, the units are generally rounded to the nearest ounce. Only when the amount of an ingredient is extremely crucial, as with baking soda or spices, is the ounce measurement given with greater accuracy.

Because of this rounding off, the yields of the metric formulas will naturally differ slightly from the yields of the formulas in U.S. measurements. Either version of the formulas can be used to make the confections, with only a slight (less than 10 percent) difference in yield.

Temperatures and linear measurements too have been rounded off to a logical standard of accuracy. When the temperature is critical, as in tempering and working with chocolate, temperature conversions are made to the nearest degree Fahrenheit. When the temperature is a guideline, and not truly critical, as when cooling fudge on a marble, it is more logical to convert to a rounded number that a confectioner would normally use. In this scenario, it makes more sense to refer to 50°C as 120°F because it is not a highly critical measurement. Millimeters provide a high degree of precision when describing linear measurements. In most U.S. measurements, units are in sixteenths, eighths, quarters, or halves of an inch. That standard has been honored here, even where it may not precisely concur with the metric measurement from which it is being converted.

The percentages listed in the formulas are percentages of the total batch prior to cooking. These too have been rounded off to the nearest percentage point. Some ingredients are significantly less than one percent of the total batch and are simply listed as "<1."

This book has been written by a confectioner for other confectioners to use. It has been written with a level of accuracy appropriate for those wishing to use the formulas, understand the theory, and employ the techniques.

Enjoy!

1

Confectionery is arguably the most demanding of the culinary arts, requiring a degree of precision and accuracy unequaled in other areas of the kitchen.

CONFECTIONERY INGREDIENTS AND EQUIPMENT

A batch of confectionery centers is not as forgiving as a batch of bread or cake. Because confections themselves are smaller than pastries or baked goods, a typical batch of confections uses smaller increments of each ingredient. When scaling and handling small quantities, slight errors translate as sizable percentages of the total. In addition to this basic requirement of precision in the amounts of ingredients, confectionery art demands precise handling techniques. Cocoa butter will crystallize in a desirable form only under specific conditions; if the temperature is a few degrees off, or the amount of agitation is not adequate, the chocolate will bloom, resulting in a ruined product. Sugar too requires exact control over percentage, temperature, and handling in order to achieve the desired result, whether that is the prevention or formation of crystals. These are just some of the factors that the artisan confectioner must deal with every day. By understanding the ingredients commonly used in confectionery, knowing the proper use of confectionery tools, and mastering the basic processes, the artisan confectioner can bring to fruition any creative inspiration.

CONFECTIONERY INGREDIENTS

As compared with cooking or even baking, confectionery involves relatively few ingredients. It is how those ingredients are handled and the relative quantities of each that makes each confection unique. Understanding the basic properties of each ingredient and how ingredients interact enables the confectioner to succeed in creating precisely the results desired. The importance of this cannot be overstated: when a professional truly understands ingredients, there is nothing that he or she cannot accomplish in formulation.

Sweeteners

Sweeteners are the heart of confectionery. One of just five tastes that the human tongue can detect, sweetness is a defining quality of confections. So, naturally, sugars are essential ingredients in confectionery. In addition to providing flavor, sweeteners play a number of roles in confectionery, including acting as a preservative, doctoring and bulking agent, humectant, and source of crystallization. The sweeteners most commonly used in confectionery are sucrose and glucose syrups, but many other sweeteners are also employed for their unique flavors and functionality.

SUCROSE

While the word *sugar* may rightfully be applied to a variety of nutritive carbohydrate sweeteners, when the term is used without any modifiers, it refers to sucrose. Sucrose is a disaccharide made up of one molecule of fructose, also known as levulose, bonded with one molecule of dextrose, also known as glucose. (To avoid confusion between *glucose* and *glucose syrup*—a starch-derived product—the term *dextrose* is used in this book to refer to that monosaccharide.) The sucrose commonly used in confectionery is one of the purest food substances available—at least 99.8 percent pure sucrose.

Commercially, sugar is obtained from sugarcane or sugar beets. Although the refining methods are different, there is no difference between the sucrose derived from either source, thanks to excellent processing technology. While artisan confectioners typically purchase sugar in dry crystalline form, mass-production manufacturers are more likely to buy liquid sugar, a syrup consisting of approximately 67 percent sucrose dissolved in water, because it is easier to handle in large quantities.

A defining feature of sucrose is its tendency to crystallize at high concentrations. Understanding this tendency and knowing how to control it are two of the most fundamental concepts in confectionery. (See Saturation and Supersaturation, page 218.) Crystalline sucrose and noncrystalline (amorphous) sucrose behave very differently in terms of their hygroscopicity, stability, water-activity reduction, and flavor release. (See Sucrose Qualities table below.) At common room temperatures, sucrose is soluble to approximately 67 percent solids—that is, 67 percent sugar and 33 percent water. In order to be shelf stable, sugar confectionery must have a dissolved-solids content of approximately 75 percent or higher. If the product is to remain noncrystalline, as is essential in hard candies and brittles, sucrose alone is not usually acceptable as a sweetener, and doctoring agents must also be added in order to promote stability and prevent crystallization. Glucose syrups are the adjunct sweetener most commonly used to prevent crystallization and increase the solids content.

Sucrose is available in a wide range of crystal sizes and in powdered form with various particle sizes. Powdered sugar, referred to in this book as confectioners' sugar, is categorized by its degree of fineness, specified by a number, with the highest number indicating the smallest particle size. The confectioners' sugars categorized as 6X and 10X are the ones most commonly used, but others are also available. American-made confectioners' sugar is an exception when it comes to the purity of sucrose; it contains approximately 3 percent cornstarch to prevent caking.

SUCROSE QUALITIES

AMORPHOUS SUCROSE	CRYSTALLINE SUCROSE
Exhibits a high level of hygroscopicity	Exhibits a relatively low level of hygroscopicity
Reduces A_w	Has little effect on A_w
Holds fat in emulsion	Expels fat
Dissolves quickly in the mouth	Dissolves more slowly in the mouth
Is chemically reactive	Is not chemically reactive
Releases flavor relatively rapidly	Releases flavor more slowly

A_w = water activity; see pages 42–43.

MOLASSES

A thick brown syrup that is a by-product of the sugar-refining process, molasses is used in confectionery primarily for its distinctive flavor and its doctoring properties. Because it contains a significant amount of invert sugar, minerals, and amino acids extracted during the refining process, it has a tendency to brown during cooking as a result of the Maillard reaction (see page 231) and to increase the hygroscopicity of products that contain it.

Molasses is available in varying degrees of darkness and flavor intensity. When it is obtained early in the sugar-refining process, it is relatively light in color and flavor; molasses from the later stages of refining has a darker color and a more intense flavor. The darkest molasses, known as blackstrap molasses, is used primarily in the distilling industry, in yeast manufacturing, and for animal feed, although a small percentage of it is sold for use in human food. All molasses used for human consumption comes from sugarcane, not sugar beets.

BROWN SUGAR

The most common form of brown sugar is made by fully refining sucrose and then restoring a measured amount of cane-sugar molasses to the refined sugar. The result is sugar crystals that have a thin molasses coating and a soft, moist texture. The added molasses provides flavor and increases the sugar's hygroscopicity and its propensity for browning when heated. Producing brown sugar by this method affords the manufacturer control over the product, permitting greater consistency from batch to batch. Brown sugar is available in several grades, depending on the type of molasses and other ingredients added to it. Commercially, brown sugar is given a number to indicate how dark it is, with the highest number indicating the darkest sugar. The grades of brown sugar most commonly found are 6, 8, 10, and 13.

Turbinado sugar is a type of brown sugar produced by leaving some of the molasses in during the refining process rather than fully refining the sugar and then adding molasses back to it. Because the molasses in turbinado sugar is inside the crystal rather than on its surface, this sugar is not soft and moist like the commonly produced brown sugar but consists of hard crystals with a golden hue. Whether it deserves it or not, turbinado sugar has developed a reputation as a more natural alternative to fully refined white sugar. It is available in various crystal sizes.

INVERT SUGAR

Invert sugar is made by splitting disaccharide sucrose into its two component monosaccharides, fructose (also known as levulose) and dextrose (also known as glucose). (See Inversion, page 216.) Commercially, inversion may be accomplished by exposing disaccharide sucrose to an acid, usually hydrochloric acid, or treating it with the enzyme invertase. Invert sugar is valued by confectioners for its doctoring capacity, which is its most common function in confectionery formulation. It is sweeter than sucrose, more hygroscopic and, unlike sucrose, it readily contributes to Maillard browning. (See Maillard Reaction, page 231.) Because sucrose alone is soluble only to approximately 67 percent at room temperature, and invert sugar is soluble to approximately 80 percent, invert sugar is frequently added to sugar confectionery to increase the dissolved-solids content, lower water activity, and extend shelf life. Invert sugar is most commonly found as a creamy liquid paste containing approximately 80 percent solids.

GLUCOSE SYRUP

Glucose syrup is the legal name for nutritive sweeteners made by the hydrolysis of edible starch. The name of the source starch may replace the word *glucose* in the name of the syrup; for example, *corn syrup* is a permissible name for glucose syrup derived from cornstarch. Glucose syrups are made by hydrolyzing the long dextrose chains (polysaccharides) contained in starch and converting them into shorter chains of dextrose molecules. The process of breaking the bonds between dextrose molecules during syrup manufacture is called conversion, and it is accomplished with the use of acids or enzymes, or both. (See conversion

Starch

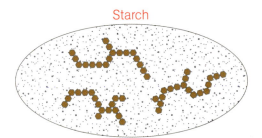

Plus Acid &/or Enzymes

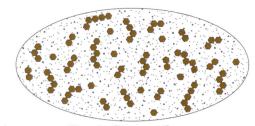

Equals Glucose Syrup

LEFT: *Starch is a polysaccharide. Each molecule is made up of thousands of dextrose molecules bonded together.* RIGHT: *When treated with acid or enzymes, the starch molecule is broken down or converted into shorter sugar chains. Glucose syrup is a blend of short and long chains in a small amount—about 20 percent—of water.*

diagrams above on page 4.) Most American glucose syrups are made from cornstarch because of its wide availability and low cost and are commonly known as corn syrup. In Europe most glucose syrups are made from wheat or potato starch, but there is effectively no difference among syrups made from the starches of corn, wheat, or potatoes.

One of the most important factors to consider when selecting a glucose syrup is the syrup's DE, or dextrose equivalence. DE is the specification used to describe how much the starch molecule has been broken down into simpler sugars. Starches are examples of compounds called polysaccharides—that is, thousands of dextrose molecules chemically bonded together. While it is not exactly chemically accurate, the DE of glucose syrup may be considered roughly the percentage of the starch that has been converted to sugar. For instance, unhydrolyzed starch has a DE of zero; that is, none of the bonds has been broken; all of the thousands of dextrose molecules are still bonded into one large unit. Pure dextrose has a DE of one hundred, meaning that 100 percent of the bonds from the original starch molecule have been broken, resulting in 100 percent single dextrose molecules.

The DE of glucose syrup profoundly influences the syrup's characteristics. High-DE syrups are sweeter, more hygroscopic, less viscous, and more prone to Maillard browning than low-DE syrups are. (See comparison table below.) By definition, glucose syrups are required to have a DE of at least 20. The glucose syrup most commonly used in confectionery has a DE of approximately 42. When a formula calls for glucose syrup or corn syrup without specifying the DE, this is the syrup that should be used. Other commonly available syrups include those of approximately 27 DE and 63 DE, each with its own degrees of viscosity, reactivity, sweetness, and so on.

Understanding the concept and ramifications of DE is only the beginning of selecting a glucose syrup. Some specialty glucose syrups that are widely available include high-fructose syrup and high-maltose syrup, which are produced by the action of enzymes that create a particular carbohydrate profile. Each syrup has its own unique qualities. Of most interest to artisan confectioners, though, is high-maltose syrup. It resists browning at high temperature and so is useful in hard-candy applications. Compared to the glucose syrup most commonly used in confectionery, high-maltose syrup has lower viscosity when hot, making it easier to work with, and its lower hygroscopicity protects finished candy from damage due to humidity. Many of the European-made glucose syrups are high maltose, and American manufacturers also make a range of high-maltose syrups.

Glucose-syrup manufacturers produce a variety of syrups of varying DEs and carbohydrate profiles, as well as other specifications, for a wide range of applications. When special syrups are

Characteristics of Glucose Syrups

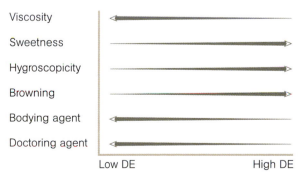

Viscosity
Sweetness
Hygroscopicity
Browning
Bodying agent
Doctoring agent

Low DE　　　　　　　　High DE

The DE of a glucose syrup greatly influences many of its characteristics. The table illustrates some of the differences between lower- and higher-DE syrups. The arrows indicate an increase in the given quality as the DE number changes. For instance, viscosity increases as DE decreases, and sweetness increases as DE increases. While these are good general guidelines, specialty glucose syrups such as high-maltose syrup and high-fructose syrup may exhibit slightly different qualities.

desired, it is advisable to ask the manufacturer to recommend a product for a specific application and to supply a sample for trial use. Specification sheets that list the DE, conversion process, and carbohydrate profiles for syrups are available from manufacturers and on their Web sites.

HONEY

Honey is the substance that bees produce naturally from gathered plant nectar. Chemically, honey bears considerable resemblance to invert sugar; the sugars in it are mainly fructose and dextrose in nearly equal proportion, with a moisture content of approximately 17 percent. In addition to these main components, honey contains smaller quantities of other sugars as well as proteins and acids that provide its characteristic flavor and color. The flavor and color of honey is greatly influenced by the types of flowers from which the bees gather the nectar. Therefore, honeys can range from the dark, richly flavored buckwheat honey to the lighter orange blossom honey. Many other honeys are available, each with a unique flavor profile. Although it possesses the same doctoring and humectant properties as invert sugar, honey browns more readily during cooking and is used in confectionery mainly to impart its flavor.

MAPLE

Maple syrup and maple sugar are both made by concentrating the sap from the sugar maple, or black maple, tree. Sap from maple trees typically contains approximately 2 percent sugar, nearly all of which is sucrose. To concentrate the sugar, the sap is boiled in open evaporators in order to remove the desired quantity of water. Maple syrup is boiled to a dissolved-solids content of just over 66 percent. At this concentration the syrup is saturated but will not crystallize easily. Maple sugar is made by removing more water and inducing crystallization of the sugars. In addition to removing water, boiling causes Maillard browning and some inversion. Maillard browning, in particular, is crucial to the development of maple syrup's and maple sugar's characteristic flavor, so the time and temperature must be carefully controlled for optimal results. (See Maillard Reaction, page 231.) The flavor of maple syrup and sugar is also influenced by environmental factors such as climate, soil type, and the point in the season when the sap is harvested. The highest grade of maple syrup is the lightest in color and flavor; the lowest grade is the darkest, which has a less subtle, more robust flavor and may therefore be better suited to confectionery applications.

ALTERNATIVE SWEETENERS

A wide range of alternative sweeteners is available, with still others in development all the time. These range from the polyols, or sugar alcohols, such as sorbitol and maltitol, to aspartame and sucralose. These sweeteners unquestionably have applications in the marketplace. For example, they are suitable for consumption by those with diabetes or those wishing to avoid simple carbohydrates. Working with alternative sweeteners is a discipline in and of itself; such sweeteners behave very differently from traditional carbohydrate sweeteners, and each has its own unique properties. This book focuses on the creation of artisan confectionery using traditional ingredients and methods, so alternative sweeteners are not used in the formulations or addressed in the discussions of theory.

Fats

Fat plays a vital role in many types of confectionery, from chocolate to caramels and nougat, improving viscosity, texture, flavor, and mouthfeel. Many different fats are available to the confectioner, including hydrogenated and/or fractionated fats manufactured for specific confectionery applications. Although these fats have something to offer, they are generally designed to act as low-cost replacements for the fats used in traditional formulations, such as butter, cocoa butter, and coconut fat. The formulations in this book use traditional fats and do not include the hydrogenated alternatives.

COCOA BUTTER

Cocoa butter is the most important fat in confectionery; it is also among the most expensive and most difficult to control. One unique quality of cocoa butter is its narrow melting range, which is just below normal human body temperature; cocoa butter remains solid up to a temperature very close to its melting point, and then melts rapidly. This is why even at a warm room temperature, chocolate remains crisp, yet melts rapidly in the mouth. Cocoa butter is capable of setting in several different crystal forms, making it relatively difficult to work with. (See Polymorphism of Cocoa Butter, page 55.) It is also costly because it must be pressed from cocoa beans, themselves an expensive commodity. Aside from its use in chocolate, cocoa butter may be added to some confection centers to improve shortness and firmness.

BUTTER

Butter is the second most frequently used fat in artisan confectionery. It may be added to confections either directly or through the use of dairy products containing butterfat. Butter used for confectionery should always be unsalted sweet cream butter.

Butter is obtained by churning cream, agglomerating the fat, and then separating the butter from the remaining buttermilk. Butter is not a pure fat, but an emulsion of water in fat; it also contains milk solids and lactose. (See Emulsions, page 96–97.) Because of the presence of protein from the milk solids and the reducing sugar lactose, butter contributes to Maillard browning when it is cooked in confectionery formulas. Butterfat may be isolated from the water and other components in butter by boiling the butter to separate the emulsion. This results in pure butter oil that contains no moisture. This anhydrous form of butter is sometimes used in manufacturing chocolate.

One of the primary functions of butter in confectionery is to combine with cocoa butter to create a softer fat that melts at a lower temperature than pure cocoa butter does. This is desirable both for centers such as ganache and sometimes for chocolate manufactured with the addition of butterfat. (See Eutectics, page 411.)

LAURIC FATS

Lauric fats are occasionally used by the artisan confectioner, primarily for the powerful eutectic effect they have when combined with cocoa butter. (See Eutectics, page 411.) Examples of lauric fats are coconut fat and palm kernel oil; of the two, coconut fat is more commonly used by the artisan confectioner. When it is combined with cocoa butter, the resulting eutectic often has a melting point that is lower than either of the original fats, resulting in a meltaway center.

At room temperature coconut fat is a relatively hard fat, one that may be fractionated and/or hydrogenated to provide specific desired melting points. RBD (refined, bleached, deodorized) coconut fat that is not hydrogenated has a melting point of 25°C (76°F), is widely available, and is well suited to the formula applications in this book. Deodorized coconut fat should be used to avoid contributing undesired coconut flavor to confections. In certain applications, such as taffy and nougat, coconut fat may be a lower-cost alternative to cocoa butter and can contribute to the shorter, less chewy texture desired in these confections. When deciding whether to use lauric fat, the confectioner must take into account flavor, texture, and reactions with other ingredients like cocoa butter.

Dairy products

Dairy products play several important roles in confectionery, including providing moisture, amino acids, and lactose for Maillard browning; contributing to confections' fat content; and acting as an emulsifier. Dairy products are available to the artisan confectioner in many forms, each with its own advantages. One dairy product can often be substituted for another, depending on the fat, water, and milk-solids content of the choices available.

FRESH DAIRY PRODUCTS

Fresh dairy products include nonfat milk, whole milk, half-and-half, and cream. The single primary difference among them—fat content—is the property by which the FDA defines and classifies each of these fresh dairy products. Fresh dairy products are valued by the artisan confectioner for their flavor, and they are, when practical, the dairy products of choice.

The main drawbacks of fresh dairy products are storage requirements, high water content, and cost. Dairy storage seldom presents a large obstacle to the artisan confectioner, who purchases such products frequently and in small enough quantities that storage does not become an issue. Water content can be a problem, though, when making confections such as caramels, which use a large quantity of dairy product and require long cooking to remove moisture.

Although it is possible to use all fresh dairy products to make such confections, the prolonged cooking times required not only makes them less efficient to produce but could also cause the milk solids to curdle. For these confections, therefore, processed dairy products can be used. They provide all the milk solids necessary and far less water to remove during cooking. A combination of fresh and processed dairy products can provide some of the advantages of each. For making ganache, however, fresh dairy products are always the ingredients of choice.

PROCESSED DAIRY PRODUCTS

The processed dairy products commonly used in confectionery include sweetened condensed milk, evaporated milk, and dry milk. Each has its own characteristics that make it suited to particular applications.

Sweetened condensed milk, which is frequently used in the production of caramels, is made by adding approximately 18 percent sugar to whole milk, then removing the water under vacuum to half the milk's original volume. Sweetened condensed milk must contain 8 percent milk fat, 28 percent total milk solids, and, since it is not heat-treated during canning, sufficient sugar to prevent spoilage. Sweetened condensed milk is more resistant to curdling during cooking than either evaporated milk or fresh dairy products. This stability, combined with the milk's low moisture content, makes it the dairy product of choice in many caramel formulas. Sweetened condensed milk is also available as a fat-free product.

Evaporated milk is whole milk that has had a substantial portion of its water removed. It contains at least 6.5 percent milk fat and at least 16.5 percent nonfat milk solids and may contain emulsifiers and stabilizers. Evaporated milk is heat treated to prevent spoilage and must be refrigerated after opening. The reduced water content of evaporated milk, as compared with fresh dairy products, makes it well suited to caramel production, although it is more prone to curdling than sweetened condensed milk.

Artisan confectioners seldom use dry milk in cooked mixtures. One of the few applications for dry milk in artisan confectionery is in making nougats, which are designed to crystallize during storage. Dry milk helps to seed the nougat, promoting crystallization, and it adds flavor and fat. Dry milk is available as nonfat dry milk and dry whole milk powders. Whole milk powder is less commonly available, as it is prone to rancidity from the butterfat content.

CULTURED DAIRY PRODUCTS

Cultured dairy products, such as yogurt, sour cream, and buttermilk, are seldom used in artisan confectionery because of their tendency to curdle when heated. One minor exception is crème fraîche, which can be used to make ganache provided it is not heated to a temperature sufficient to cause curdling.

Flavoring and coloring agents

FLAVORS

Flavors used in artisan confectionery are most often aromatic food ingredients such as spices, nuts, extracts, and purées. In certain cases—when making hard candies, for example—it is difficult and impractical to use these ingredients, so manufactured flavors must be employed. These may be either "natural flavors" or "artificial flavors." Apart from the labeling, there is little difference between the two. Each category is created by combining various organic compounds to replicate a naturally occurring item. The only difference between natural and artificial flavors is the source of the chemicals used to make a flavoring.

The FDA has precise guidelines for the way flavorings can be labeled. In order for a flavoring to be called "natural," its components must be derived from plant materials, meat, dairy, or seafood sources, by any of a number of processes, including extraction, distillation, fermentation, and hydrolysis. "Artificial" flavors are those whose components do not come from these sources. All natural and artificial flavors used in a product must be declared on its label. Natural flavorings typically command a higher price because deriving components from the allowable food and plant sources is more expensive than obtaining them from other sources and because consumers value the term "natural" and often turn away from anything containing the word *artificial*. Artisan confectioners should be extremely judicious in the use of manufactured flavors, adding them to only products that cannot practically be flavored with food ingredients.

Other types of flavoring occasionally used by artisan confectioners are organic acids such as citric acid, naturally occurring in lemons; malic acid, naturally occurring in apples; and tartaric acid, naturally occurring in grapes. When used as flavoring agents, these acids balance sweetness and more realistically mimic fruit flavors. Each type of acid has its own flavor-release profile and affects a confection's flavor differently. These same acids may be used as components in confectionery reactions such as sugar inversion, starch hydrolysis, and pectin gelling. Because of acids' reactivity, exercise caution with regard to the amounts used and the stages at which they are added. These ingredients can also be harmful to skin and eyes and therefore must always be handled with care.

COLORS

In certain areas of confectionery, the addition of color is normal and expected. It is difficult to imagine hard candies without added color, and truly striking effects can be obtained by coloring chocolate and using color-lined molds to make confections. It is part of the philosophy of artisan confectionery, however, that when possible, no unnatural color or flavor should be added.

Colors for confectioners are divided into two categories: fat-soluble and water-soluble. Fat-soluble colors are used for coloring chocolate or cocoa butter. They are designed to dissolve in fats and so are ideally suited for use in chocolate. Fat-soluble colors are commonly found either in a liquid form that is predissolved in oil or cocoa butter or in a powder form that must be dissolved. The predissolved form is slightly more convenient to use, but similar results can be obtained from either variety. When dry colors are used, they must first be dissolved in a small quantity of cocoa butter, which is then mixed into chocolate or more cocoa butter for application. Dry colors are often difficult to dissolve fully and can require agitation and grinding. For this reason it is advisable to prepare a quantity of colored cocoa butter in advance that can simply be melted and used when needed.

Another colorant that has become widely used in artisan confectionery is colored cocoa butter. Many of these colors are opaque rather than transparent, and, as a result, when they are brushed or spread into a mold before the chocolate lining, the mold takes on the color of the cocoa butter rather than the color of chocolate. These opaque colors have been a decided trend in chocolates in recent years; they are the colorant used to create the very brightly colored shell-molded chocolates that have become popular in the upscale chocolate market.

Another type of colorant approved by the FDA for food use is interference colors. These mica-based powders can be brushed dry onto set chocolate to provide a unique surface quality. Unlike many of the dry-powder colors, interference colors are approved for food use up to 1.25 percent of the weight of the finished product. They are typically slightly metallic, and their hues vary with the angle from which they are viewed, giving them a striking appearance. Interference colors are not effective when mixed with chocolate; they should always be brushed on after the chocolate has set or brushed into a mold prior to lining with chocolate.

Water-soluble colors are used to color hard candies and other aqueous systems. These colors are available in liquid, paste, gel, and dry forms. Dry colors should be hydrated before being added to a mixture. Whatever form of color is used, it should be as concentrated as possible, so as not to add excess water to the confection, thus softening it. This is particularly important for hard candies if they are colored after cooking. To minimize water content, it is advisable to use paste and dry colors, which are more suitable than liquids and gels for most sugar confectionery.

Nuts and seeds

Nuts and seeds are commonly used in confectionery for their flavor, texture, and fat content. Various nuts may be used by the artisan confectioner; these include hazelnuts, almonds, pecans, and macadamias. While they all differ botanically, their general qualities and handling requirements are virtually the same. Their common trait is a high fat content, and the fat they contain is prone to rancidity. For that reason, nuts and seeds should always be stored in a cool place, away from anything that can contribute to the onset of rancidity: light, oxygen, and reactive metals such as cast iron or copper. The flavor of most nuts is improved from toasting prior to their use. Different nuts reach their peak flavor with different degrees of toasting, and it is up to the confectioner to determine the level of toasting that best complements each variety of nut. The oil content of nuts is a double-edged sword; oil is responsible for much of nuts' appeal, but it does not store well and can be responsible for fat migration, resulting in softened chocolate and fat bloom. The more finely ground the nuts in a confection are, the more fat is released, and the more pronounced these effects can become. Seeds such as sesame seeds, pumpkin seeds (pepitas), peanuts, and cocoa nibs are all similar to nuts in their storage and use requirements.

Water

Water is probably the most overlooked ingredient in confectionery, and yet it is among the most important. Almost every confection contains water, and it serves vital functions in confectionery, including controlling texture and influencing shelf life. It also acts as a solvent to dissolve sugar and as a medium in which reactions such as Maillard browning can occur.

Controlling the amount of water in products is one of the most fundamental steps in confectionery. Water content directly affects the consistency of all finished products, from ganache to marzipan to hard candy. Along with affecting a confection's firmness, excessive free water can also lead to spoilage. The total water content of confectionery is controlled by cooking to remove the desired quantity of water; the amount of free water is controlled by the dissolved-solids content, which binds water, preventing spoilage. (See Water Activity, page 40.)

In confectionery it is often necessary to dissolve sugar, regardless of whether the end results are to be crystallized, as with fudge and fondant, or amorphous, as with toffee, caramels, and hard candies. Water acts as a solvent for sugar. It is also the medium that permits the myriad reactions that regularly occur in confectionery. Maillard browning, inversion, and emulsification are a few of the common reactions and processes that benefit from or require water.

Water in confectionery may come from dairy products, fruit purées, or fruit juices, or, more commonly, it may be added to formulas directly. Potable tap water is perfectly adequate for confectionery use, but there are occasions when differences between various sources of water may become apparent. The most common differences are in pH and mineral content.

Most tap water is somewhat acidic; the more acidic the water, the more inversion occurs when that water is used to cook confections. Although a small difference, it may be noticeable with sugar confectionery such as hard candies, where excessive inversion can make the candies soft and sticky, and with fondant or fudge, where excessive inversion can inhibit crystallization and result in a softer product. Water with a high mineral content can also contribute to sugar inversion. Because of the generally excellent quality and purity of American drinking water, the confectioner's water source is seldom a problem; however, due to variations in pH and mineral content in water from different sources, a disparity in results can occur from one location to another.

CONFECTIONERY EQUIPMENT

Confectionery is a highly specialized discipline that requires the use of appropriate equipment, some of which is not commonly found in pastry kitchens. Precisely what equipment a confectioner requires depends on the size of the operation and the types of confections being produced: a hard-candy operation, for example, requires entirely different facilities and equipment from those needed for making and enrobing ganache centers. The confections made in a hotel's pastry shop require much different equipment from that used to produce wholesale shell-molded chocolates.

General tool requirements are listed in the paragraphs that follow. They are given in tiers, from the most basic requirements in tier one, to automated production equipment in tier three.

Tier one

The tools and equipment in tier one are intended for the production of relatively small batches of the wide range of confections represented in this book, such as might be produced in a restaurant, hotel, or catering operation.

CHOCOLATE MELTERS: Having a supply of melted chocolate on hand saves valuable time. A variety of melters are available. The most important factors in choosing one are temperature control and size. The right melter is one that accurately controls the temperature for proper melting and maintains the crucial temperatures of different types of chocolates. Its size should be appropriate for the production requirements.

CLOCKWISE FROM TOP LEFT: *Silicone stencil, caramel cutter, dipping tools, refractometer, infrared thermometer, praline cutters, bars for creating confectionery frames*

CLIMATE CONTROL SYSTEM: A climate-controlled environment is quite possibly the most fundamental element of the confectionery process. Temperature must be controllable, and humidity must be kept to a minimum for the successful production of all confectionery, including chocolate and sugarwork.

CONFECTIONERY FRAMES: Metal bars of varying thicknesses or one-piece frames are used for slabbing (i.e., spreading) centers on a stone slab. The formulas in this work are made using metal frames with 12-in cm bars of three depths: ¼ in, ⅜ in, and ½ in. Other sizes may be used to achieve confections of different thicknesses, but the formula yields may require adjustment. In addition to the frames used for slabbing centers, a larger set of bars surrounding the stone slab can be helpful for containing large batches of hot mixtures, such as fudge or hard candy, while they cool.

DIPPING FORKS: For the small-scale chocolatier, these are absolutely essential tools for dipping centers. Dipping forks are often sold in sets of ten or twelve, but most chocolatiers find that two or three forks receive 90 percent of the use.

FONDANT FUNNEL: This tool is essential for depositing fondants, caramels, jellies, and other liquid centers into molds or shells. Automatic funnels permit greater accuracy and control than old-fashioned stick funnels do.

FOOD PROCESSOR: A professional-grade food processor is indispensable for the production of small batches of marzipan and gianduja, as well as for the myriad other tasks it performs. Hand tools: A selection of basic hand tools for stirring, cutting, and working with chocolate—scrapers, spoons, brushes, knives, palette knives, and so on—is required for basic confectionery production. Plastic stirrers are preferable to wooden implements because they do not harbor moisture or bacteria.

MIXERS: Depending on the confections and the batch sizes, 5-qt, 12-qt, or 20-qt and larger planetary mixers are valuable in confectionery, particularly for producing aerated confections such as nougat and marshmallow.

PLEXIGLAS SHEETS: Plexiglas sheets are convenient flat surfaces on which to place just-dipped confections to crystallize. They are also useful for slabbing ganache, allowing portability as the ganache crystallizes. The size most convenient for confectionery work is 30 by 41 cm by 5 mm/12 by 16 by ³⁄₁₆ in.

POLYCARBONATE CHOCOLATE MOLDS: These durable plastic molds for producing shell-molded confections are available in many styles.

SCALE: Accuracy in scaling is essential to confectionery success. A digital scale that reads in single-gram increments and also displays U.S. units is recommended. A scale with a capacity of 5 kg/11 lb is adequate for production of small batches of confectionery.

STAINLESS-STEEL BOWLS: An assortment of bowls for mixing ingredients and working with chocolate is mandatory in the confectionery shop.

STANDARD COOKWARE: Small batches of confections do not require special cookware; standard stainless-steel saucepans are adequate for the job. Untreated aluminum is unacceptable because it can catalyze the inversion of sugar, resulting in excessively soft candies.

STANDARD GAS STOVE: For small-scale production, a professional-output gas stove with four or six burners is adequate for cooking batches of confectionery.

STONE SLAB: A marble, granite, or another nonporous stone slab is vital for cooling sugar confectionery and for chocolate work. Stone is ideal for its heat conductivity and thermal mass; it quickly draws heat out of substances without becoming significantly warm itself. To possess the best thermal-mass properties, the stone for confectionery use should be as thick as possible and large enough to easily hold the largest batch size made in the shop.

THERMOMETERS: Digital thermocouples are the most useful all-around thermometers, as they can be used both for high-temperature sugar boiling and for chocolate and ganache. Alcohol-filled glass thermometers are reliable instruments that never run low on batteries, but separate thermometers are required for different temperature ranges. Bimetal thermometers are slower to react, and are not as accurate as thermocouple technology. Surface-reading infrared thermometers are excellent for monitoring the temperature of chocolate. The same thermometer should be used each time; small differences between individual thermometers can cause inconsistent results.

Tier two

Used together with the tier-one tools, these will assist the confectioner in producing any of the confections in this book more expeditiously and will allow for more efficient work and the production of larger batches.

MAGNETIC MOLDS

Magnetic molds have become a popular way to gain all the advantages of both shell molding and transfer sheets. These are two-piece molds consisting of a body and a base plate, made of polycarbonate plastic. Magnets embedded in the plastic firmly hold the two parts together for molding, but the parts may be separated for the insertion of transfer sheets and for unmolding. Transfer sheets are available custom fit to the molds, or larger sheets can be cut to fit. As with any use of transfer sheets, many stock designs are available, suiting general use or special occasions. Or, for a small investment, custom designs, including business logos, can be made to create unique signature items that announce their origin and advertise a business. Using transfer molds provides the confectioner with the nearly perfect uniformity and high-gloss shine of shell molding, along with the striking designs available in transfer sheets.

Transfer molds are used exactly as any other polycarbonate mold would be, but with the additional steps of inserting a transfer sheet into the mold before use and removing the base prior to unmolding. The temperature and degree of temper of the chocolate is doubly important when transfer molds are used, as chocolate that is too cool or is overseeded when deposited will not pick up the design from the transfer sheet. Once the filled and sealed molds have set, they should be refrigerated briefly, just as other molds are, to liberate the latent heat of crystallization, to contract the chocolate, and to ensure the maximum shine from the transfer sheet. Removing the base plate of the mold makes unmolding extremely simple. (For more information on working with molds, see pages 77–85.)

CANDY KETTLES: Copper kettles with rounded bottoms, designed to fit into candy stoves, greatly increase the efficiency of cooking. The copper conducts heat extremely well; the rounded bottom provides the maximum surface area for heat transfer; and the large surface area ensures the most rapid evaporation of water. Care must be taken not to cook anything in these untreated kettles that could react with the copper and form toxins.

CANDY STOVE: For larger-scale sugar confectionery, a candy stove is indispensable. Candy stoves have tremendous heat output and are designed for rapid and efficient heat transfer when used with candy kettles. Fast cooking not only makes a confectionery operation more profitable, but also prevents excessive inversion and Maillard browning.

CARAMEL CUTTER: The multiple wheels of this device allow caramel and other sugar confectionery to be cut into squares.

GUITAR: Also known as a confectionery cutter, a guitar cuts ganache, jellies, marzipan, and other softer centers quickly and perfectly.

HEAT GUN: A heat gun such as those used for removing paint is valuable for such tasks as maintaining the temperature of tempered chocolate and warming molds.

IMMERSION BLENDER: An immersion blender can be used to restore separated ganache, agitate chocolate for tempering, and remove lumps from mixtures.

PANNING MACHINE: This rotating drum machine is essential for producing any of the panned items such as chocolate-coated nuts and dried fruits discussed in this book.

PRALINE CUTTERS: These specialized tools are used to cut shapes from a precoated slab of center, such as marzipan. They are sold in sets of six, with various shapes included.

REFRACTOMETER: This tool measures the sugar content of syrups. It is valuable for use in candying fruit and producing jellies, as it can determine the solids content to ensure consistency from batch to batch. A refractometer is superior to a saccharometer or hydrometer for this purpose.

SHELL-MOLDING MACHINE: Several hand-operated machines are available to fill chocolate molds and thus increase efficiency.

SPRAY GUN: A spray gun can be used to spray chocolate for decorative purposes or to bottom large numbers of individual centers at a time. Some spray guns rely on a separate compressor; others generate their own pressure.

STORAGE FREEZER: When proper procedures are followed, a freezer permits longer storage of confections in anticipation of the busiest seasons.

TEMPERING MACHINE: A wide range of tempering machines is available, from small tabletop units that temper only one kilo of chocolate, to units that continuously temper hundreds of kilos. For larger-scale confectionery shops, a larger tempering machine greatly streamlines production.

UPGRADED FOOD PROCESSOR: Larger, more powerful processors, called "Stephan Machines" some with vacuum pumps, are helpful when making large quantities of high-quality marzipan and gianduja and emulsifying ganache.

VACUUM-PACKAGING EQUIPMENT: This equipment prepares confections for prolonged storage in a freezer.

Tier three

Machinery is available to handle virtually every aspect of candy production. The following equipment allows a relatively high-yield artisan confectioner to produce larger quantities with greater accuracy and speed, for increased volume and profitability. Any one of the following pieces of equipment for large-scale production of confectionery represents a substantial investment and is intended for very specific production needs.

BATCH WARMERS, PULLERS, SIZERS, CUTTERS: Every artisan hard-candy operation requires this equipment in order to be economically viable.

DEPOSITOR: This item portions large batches of centers to be enrobed.

ENROBER WITH COOLING TUNNEL: Nothing increases production capacity like an enrober. (See page 16.) This machine eliminates the need for hand-dipping and greatly enhances production. Properly set up cooling tunnels help to ensure perfect crystallization of the chocolate surrounding the centers.

FIRE MIXER: A mixer with a burner under the bowl is ideal for the production of caramels and other confections that require long cooking with constant stirring.

FONDANT MAKER: This item beats cooked sugar into fondant and is designed for confectioners who require large quantities of fondant for use in centers.

PACKAGING EQUIPMENT: This is particularly important for presenting and preserving individual pieces such as unenrobed caramels, hard candy, and taffy.

REFINER (MÉLANGEUR): Two-roller refiners can be used to make excellent-quality marzipan and gianduja in large quantities.

SHELL-MOLDING EQUIPMENT: Various parts of shell-molding production can be partially or fully automated for efficiency. Vacuum cooker: A vacuum cooker removes water at lower temperatures than open cooking does and ensures rapid production and less caramelization in hard candies.

WATER-ACTIVITY METER: This unit is especially important if the products being made are ganache, marzipan, or other high-moisture centers. A water-activity meter allows the confectioner to adjust formulas for maximum shelf life and for compatibility when two or more types of centers are combined in one confection.

SPECIAL EQUIPMENT

Confectionery operations with a focus on specific types of centers or processes must be equipped accordingly. The following are three different types of operations, or parts within an operation, and the equipment that would be needed for a moderate level of production

ENROBERS

An enrobing line is the heart of most artisan confectioners' production facilities; without this vital piece of equipment, it would simply not be possible to produce enough enrobed chocolates for the confectioner's output to be economically viable. An enrobing line represents a substantial investment, and there are several brands and models with various features from which the artisan confectioner may choose. Among the factors influencing the choice of enrobers, potential output is of prime consideration. An enrober that is too small for current and future needs will create a bottleneck in production. Buying an enrober that is too large is a waste of both money and space. The potential output of an enrober is based on two factors: the width of the belt, and the length of the cooling tunnel.

The width of the belt determines how many centers can be loaded per linear foot of belt. Most artisan confectioners are likely to use an enrober with a belt from 18 to 25 centimeters/ 7 to 10 inches wide. To determine the pieces per linear foot, multiply the number of rows per row across the belt by the number of pieces that can be loaded lengthwise on a foot of the belt. For instance, on an 18-centimeter/7-inch belt, enrobing a typical-size center, 3 centers will fit across the width of the belt, and 7 centers will fit in a foot length. Therefore, in a linear foot of belt, there are 7 rows of 3, or 21 centers. The wider the belt is, the more centers can be loaded on a linear foot and the greater the potential output of the enrober.

The speed of the belt is determined by the required cooling time and the length of the cooling tunnel. For most chocolate applications (not compound coating) the requisite cooling time is approximately 8 minutes; this is the desired cooling time that will be used in the following example. Regardless of the length of the tunnel, the belt must move at a speed that will travel the length of the cooling tunnel in those 8 minutes. To determine the speed of the belt in feet per minute, divide the length of the tunnel in feet by the desired cooling time in minutes. For example, if the desired cooling time is 8 minutes, and the tunnel is 3.7 meters/12 feet long, 12 feet divided by 8 minutes = 46 centimeters/1.5 feet per minute. The longer the tunnel, the faster the belt can move and the greater the potential output.

in each. While bigger, faster, and more expensive machinery is always available for a price, the hypothetical operations shown here demonstrate a more moderate approach. In none of the scenarios is automation taken to an extreme, thus preserving the artisan aspect of the business and limiting the investment. Additionally, the equipment requirements listed are for production only. Each of these scenarios assumes proper storage, including refrigeration, as well as warehousing and packaging facilities.

Panning operation

Assorted chocolate panned nuts and dried fruits are the items produced in this operation. Because these centers have different weights, the potential output varies according to which centers are being produced. An average nut weight is used for the calculation below. In this scenario, two machines are operated simultaneously on a daily basis to engross centers and also to polish and glaze the centers that were engrossed the day prior. Each day of this operation sees 113.4 kilograms/250 pounds of centers engrossed in each of the pans, and the same quantity of centers are polished and glazed in each.

To determine the number of enrobed centers produced per minute of enrober operation, multiply the number of centers per linear foot by the feet per minute (fpm) of the belt. In the example given above, there are 21 centers per linear foot. Multiplying that number by 1.5 fpm = 31.5 centers per minute potential output from the enrober. Multiplying this number by 60 will yield the number of centers per hour—in this case 1,890.

The complete formula for enrober yield may be expressed as follows:

(centers in a row across belt × rows of centers per foot of belt)

×

(length of tunnel ÷ desired cooling time)

×

60 =

number of finished enrobed confections per hour

This information can easily be converted to weight as well as used to determine the amount of tempered chocolate required.

The weight of the finished product is determined by multiplying the number of products by the weight of an individual finished piece. Fourteen grams, or ½ ounce, is a typical weight for a finished confection of this sort. Using the example above, 60 finished enrobed confections per hour multiplied by 14 grams/ ½ ounce give an hourly output in weight of approximately 26.4 kilograms, or 59 pounds.

The amount of chocolate required depends on the size and shape of the pieces produced as well as the viscosity of the chocolate, but if 40 percent of the finished weight is enrobing chocolate, then, in this example, approximately 10.5 kilograms, or

23 pounds, of tempered chocolate are required per hour of enrober operation.

Of course, potential output is not the only factor to consider when choosing an enrober. Different machines have various features such as bottomers and cold plates, blowers, detailers, and packing tables; longer cooling tunnels may feature two- or three-zone cooling. Availability of service and price point are always legitimate concerns when investing in equipment as well.

For an illustrated guide to the setup of a moderate-size enrobing operation, see Appendix B, page 515.

ITEMS PRODUCED

Chocolate-coated nuts, dried fruit, coffee beans, cereals, and blends

APPROXIMATE OUTPUT

226.8 kg/500 lb per day, depending on the centers

EQUIPMENT REQUIREMENTS

- ✦ Two revolving pans, each approximately 107 cm/42 in wide
- ✦ Fans and ducting for blowing air on pans
- ✦ One chocolate melter, with capacity of 136 kg/300 lb; tempering not required
- ✦ Six rolling racks with sheet pans
- ✦ Stainless-steel work tables
- ✦ Small goods: scales, ladles, scrapers, measures, thermometers, humidity meter

ENVIRONMENTAL REQUIREMENT

Climate control that maintains 15°C/59°F and less than 60% relative humidity in panning area

For an illustrated guide to the setup of a moderate-size panning operation, see Appendix B, page 515.

Shell-molding operation

In this operation, shell-molded chocolates with ganache and caramel-based fillings are produced. The scenario assumes that an operator is able to complete 40 molds per hour for 6 hours of each day. An average mold yields 340 grams/12 ounces of finished product, so the output from this operation is approximately 81.7 kilograms/180 pounds per day.

ITEMS PRODUCED

Shell-molded filled chocolates; ganache and caramel fillings

APPROXIMATE OUTPUT

81.7 kg/180 lb per day

EQUIPMENT REQUIREMENTS

- ✦ Chocolate melter-temperer, with capacity of at least 45.3 kg/100 lb
- ✦ Polycarbonate chocolate molds; a minimum of 15 of each variety used in the operation (a total of at least 80 molds)
- ✦ Vibrating table
- ✦ Hand-depositing machine for fillings
- ✦ Stove for cooking ganache and caramel
- ✦ Warming cabinet
- ✦ Refrigerator capable of maintaining 10°C/50°F
- ✦ Stainless-steel work tables
- ✦ Rolling racks and sheet pans
- ✦ Wire screens
- ✦ Cookware for ganache
- ✦ Small goods: scales, ladles, scrapers, measures, thermometers, humidity meter

Climate control that maintains 21°C/70°F and less than 60% relative humidity in workroom

For an illustrated guide to the setup of a moderate-size shell-molding operation, see Appendix B, page 515.

Enrobing operation

This operation produces assorted enrobed centers. Assuming adequate cooking, cooling, and cutting facilities, the limiting factor on production is the size and speed of the enrober. (See Enrobers, page 16.) This example uses a small enrober fitted with an 18-centimeter/7-inch belt and a 3.7-meter/12-foot cooling tunnel that a small-scale artisan confectioner might employ.

ITEMS PRODUCED

Enrobed centers of ganache, gianduja, nougat, marzipan, butter ganache, and jellies

APPROXIMATE OUTPUT

158.8 kg/350 lb per day

EQUIPMENT REQUIREMENTS

✦ Convection oven for toasting nuts

✦ Stove

✦ Refrigerator capable of maintaining 10°C/50°F

✦ Candy stove

✦ Large stone cooling table

✦ Confectionery frames

✦ Guitar

✦ Twenty-qt planetary mixer

✦ Stephan machine

✦ Food processor

✦ Chocolate melter, appropriate size for operation

✦ Enrober with 18-cm/7-in cooling belt and 3.7-m/12-ft cooling tunnel

✦ Warming cabinet

✦ Rolling racks and sheet pans

✦ Candy kettles

✦ Cookware

✦ Small goods: scales, ladles, scrapers, measures, thermometers, humidity meter, palette knives

ENVIRONMENTAL REQUIREMENTS

Cooking area separate from cutting and enrobing area

Climate control that maintains 20°C/68°F and less than 60% relative humidity in area for cutting and enrobing

For an illustrated guide to the setup of a moderate-size enrobing operation, see Appendix B, page 515.

2

Chocolate is without question the most complex ingredient that confectioners use. Because of the complexity of chocolate, a confectioner could work with and study it for a lifetime and still not learn all of its secrets.

CACAO AND CHOCOLATE

Each step of the transformation, from cacao pods growing in a tropical forest to perfect crisp chocolate shells on finished confections, is marked by care, attention to detail, and a bit of alchemy. The body of knowledge about chocolate is constantly growing and evolving as researchers learn more about cacao genetics and agriculture, manufacturing techniques, cocoa butter crystallization, and the intricacies of chocolate as a system. Even with these advances, parts of chocolate manufacturing, such as conching, are still not fully understood. Although only a handful of artisan confectioners manufacture their own chocolate from beans, a basic knowledge of that process can help the confectioner to better understand the material and to select the right chocolate for each application.

More relevant to artisan confectioners than chocolate manufacture is the complex subject of cocoa butter crystallization. Every time a confectioner tempers chocolate—a truly fundamental procedure—he or she is controlling both the form and quantity of cocoa butter crystals present in that chocolate. Failing to produce either the right form or quantity of these crystals, which cannot be seen by the naked eye, will end in a failed product. Understanding the basic physics of working with chocolate is vital to the success of the artisan confectioner. Knowing some of the prerequisites and processes that lead to high-quality products is beneficial to selecting chocolate for a given purpose and to marketing artisan confections to an increasingly sophisticated audience.

CACAO VERSUS COCOA

The term *cacao* is used in the chocolate industry to indicate the tree *Theobroma cacao*, its cultivation, and the raw products that come from it. The name commonly used for the products made from the tree, once the cacao pod is opened and the beans are fermented, becomes *cocoa*—as in cocoa beans, cocoa butter, and so on. In this book, that guideline is honored, with one exception: when referring to a manufacturing process that may affect a number of different products (e.g., cocoa butter, chocolate liquor, cocoa powder), the term *cacao* is used to denote the range of cacao products that may be affected by that process.

FROM BEAN TO BAR: CACAO AGRICULTURE

Chocolate manufacturing bears several similarities to winemaking: like wine, chocolate starts out as an agricultural product. Like winemaking, chocolate production requires fermentation and uses only a few ingredients; and in both winemaking and chocolate making, these few ingredients can produce an infinite range of products with unique flavor nuances, characteristics, and qualities, from the pedestrian to the exquisite. The ultimate outcome is dependent on the raw materials used and, to a great extent, the skill of the producer.

Unlike winemakers, however, chocolate manufacturers seldom have control over the cultivation, harvest, and fermentation of their raw materials. The majority of the world's cacao crop is grown not on large corporate plantations but on small plots of land by individual or family landowners, who often cultivate their cacao alongside other crops. Also, two other vital processes occur before the beans even reach the manufacturer: fermentation and drying. Each of these steps is critical to the quality of the chocolate that can be made from the beans, and each must happen immediately after harvest, at the location where the cacao is grown. This fact, combined with the remote nature of cacao agriculture, means that these crucial steps usually happen beyond the control of the chocolate manufacturer. The only control the manufacturer can exert is to evaluate the beans when they arrive at the manufacturing facility and decide whether or not to buy them based on the manufacturer's specifications.

Beans

Cacao agriculture and production is an enormous topic, worthy of volumes in its own right. The References section (see page 524) lists several resources with extensive information on this topic. For the present discussion, it is sufficient to say that there are essentially three varieties of cacao grown commercially: Criollo, Forastero, and Trinitario. Criollo cacao is generally regarded as the finest quality, but it is low yielding and prone to damage from disease. Criollo constitutes a very small portion of the world crop; most estimates put it at around 10 percent of the annual cacao harvest. Forastero is a hardier variety that produces better yields but tends to lack the flavor complexities of the Criollo bean. Forastero constitutes the majority of the world's cacao harvest, approximately 70 percent of the annual production. Trinitario is a hybrid of Criollo and Forastero, a crop that exhibits some of the advantages of each of the parent varieties and makes up some 20 percent of the world harvest.

While generalizations can be made about quality and flavor profiles, they are far from foolproof. Like any crop, cacao is profoundly affected by the vagaries of terroir; the same variety of cacao can produce vastly disparate results when grown in different locations. In addition, a Forastero grown and fermented under ideal conditions may well be a superior bean to a Criollo grown and fermented under poor conditions. Perhaps a better way to look at the world cacao crop is to divide it into "bulk" beans, which constitute some 95 percent of the harvest, and "flavor" beans, which make up the remaining 5 percent of the crop. This ratio is a profound illustration of just how little of the cacao harvest is deemed to be the highest quality, and why premium-quality cacao commands a high price.

Fermentation

After the pods are harvested, the cocoa beans and pulp are removed from the shell and fermented, either in wooden boxes or in a wrapping of banana leaves. Fermentation takes an average of five days. During the first days of fermentation, the temperature of the beans rises significantly, killing the live bean and preventing germination. The primary function of fermenting cocoa beans is to produce the flavor precursors that allow the development of the chocolate flavor produced when the beans are roasted.

While fermentation itself does not result in chocolate flavor, unfermented beans do not contain the compounds necessary to produce chocolate flavor during roasting; fermentation creates these flavor precursors. Without fermentation, chocolate flavor cannot exist. Cacao fermentation is carried out by native yeasts, bacteria, and enzymes and results in liquefaction of the pulp, allowing it to run off of the beans. More important to the chocolate producer, though, are the changes that occur within the bean itself: many complex compounds, such as polyphenols, proteins, and polysaccharides, are broken into smaller compounds, a process that reduces their bitterness and astringency and provides the raw materials for Maillard browning, which results in chocolate flavor when the beans are roasted. (See Maillard Reaction, page 231.)

The proper degree of fermentation is critical to the quality of the bean and to the resulting chocolate; unfermented or even underfermented beans simply do not contain flavor precursors, and therefore cannot provide chocolate flavor, even when roasted. Excessive fermentation, however, can cause loss of quality and spoilage.

Fermentation of cacao is an extremely complex process involving various yeasts, anaerobic and aerobic bacteria, and diverse enzymatic processes. The full extent of the reactions that occur during fermentation are not fully known or understood. Still, fermentation remains one of the most crucial steps on the path from bean to chocolate.

Drying

After fermentation is complete, the beans must be dried. The immediate result of drying is to stop the fermentation process, but the major objective is to make the beans stable for shipping and storage. Beans that are not dried to approximately 8 percent moisture are prone to mold formation, which can result in severe loss of quality. Various methods can be employed for drying beans, depending on climatic conditions and the availability of energy. Ideally, the beans are spread out in a layer a few inches deep to dry in the sunshine. Periodically throughout the day, the beans are raked in order to expose all their surfaces to the sun and air; at night they are covered either with a roof on wheels or with tarps, to protect them from dewfall. If the climate permits, this method of drying is ideal, as it requires no machinery and no energy source other than the sun, and it dries and cures the beans slowly and evenly, resulting in a superior product.

Other methods of drying involve the use of fire for heat, either with or without additional convection. As a group, these methods are called "artificial drying." There are several drawbacks to artificial drying, the most severe of which is the danger of contamination from smoke, resulting in a smoky flavor in the beans. Smoky flavor notes are not necessarily present in artificially dried beans, but such a risk is to be avoided. Other negative effects of artificial drying include producing "case-hardened" beans, in which the outside of the bean dries very rapidly, hardening and preventing the moisture and acids inside the bean from escaping. A final problem with artificial drying is the potential for overdrying the beans, which results in brittle beans that break easily during shipping.

INGREDIENTS IN CHOCOLATE

Chocolate contains very few ingredients, yet varieties of chocolate vary widely with respect to flavor, texture, and viscosity. In the United States, the FDA closely regulates the ingredients—and the quantities of those ingredients—that may be present in various cacao products in order for those products to meet the FDA's definition for chocolate. (See Cacao Product Standards of Identity table, page 35.) European regulations and nomenclature for chocolate are slightly different but are also closely regulated. An overview of the ingredients permissible in chocolate and related products follows.

Chocolate liquor

Chocolate liquor is the name used for cocoa beans that are ground into a paste; it is the ingredient in dark and milk chocolate that provides chocolate flavor. *Chocolate liquor* is also a legally permissible name for unsweetened chocolate.

Roasted cocoa beans are approximately 55 percent fat; when they are ground, the cell walls rupture, releasing the cocoa butter. The result is a system consisting of solid cacao particles surrounded by fat (cocoa butter), which yields chocolate liquor. Due to its high fat content, chocolate liquor is liquid when warmed above the melting point of cocoa butter. In the parlance of chocolate specifications, chocolate liquor is 100 percent cacao and 50 to 60 percent cocoa butter. (See Chocolate Percentages, page 35.)

IS CHOCOLATE HEALTH FOOD?

There is a growing body of evidence that some of the naturally occurring compounds in chocolate may have health benefits. Like most emerging research that touts the nutraceutical aspect of foods that we know and love, there are some valid claims as well as much unfounded hype on the subject.

A brief Internet search on the health benefits of chocolate will reveal a wide range of claims, including that eating chocolate releases endorphins in the brain, mimicking the feeling of love and acting as a pain reliever; that chocolate consumption reduces the risk of heart disease and cancer; that chocolate is actually good for the teeth; and the perennially popular claim that chocolate is an aphrodisiac. The list goes on from there. Just how valid most of these claims are is somewhat unclear. Most studies cite research that backs up their assertion, but research is only as good as the methods that produce the results. Many studies supposedly demonstrating the salubrious effects of cacao are funded by companies with substantial gains to be made from the positive results, creating motivation to arrive at the desired outcome rather than performing good science to arrive at an honest result, whatever it might be.

It is certain, however, that cacao is a very complex substance, containing many different types of naturally occurring compounds, including caffeine, theobromine, polyphenols, pyrazines, tannins, phospholipids, and so on. The list of multisyllabic chemical compounds is hundreds long. The cacao research that is creating the most excitement focuses on certain types of polyphenols, namely the flavanols that are found in cacao. Flavanols are types of flavonoids, which are phenolic compounds high in antioxidants, and have been shown to reduce damage due to free radicals that can lead to heart disease and cancer. The research on cacao flavonoids has consistently shown that their consumption increases antioxidants in the bloodstream, and offers other cardiovascular benefits including lowered blood pressure and improved circulation. Good-quality, valid research has demonstrated this correlation almost beyond question: This is the good news. The bad news is that, while cacao is high in these flavanols, processed chocolate may not be. Polyphenols such as these are among the compounds that are broken down during fermentation of cacao, and with good reason: polyphenols themselves are astringent in flavor, and it is the broken-down compounds that contribute to the development of chocolate flavor during roasting. Roasting also no doubt further diminishes the flavanol content, and Dutch processing, if employed, all but removes flavonols. The result can be chocolate that contains very few of these desirable compounds. Only through careful minimal processing are the maximum amounts of cacao flavanols preserved. The presence of milk in chocolate may inhibit the absorption of these antioxidants, so milk chocolate likely has negligible health qualities, and white chocolate, containing no cacao solids, has none.

To maximize the gains from chocolate consumption, eat dark chocolate of a high-cacao content, or better yet, consume cocoa powder that is not Dutch processed. Chocolate is necessarily high in fat and sugar, and therefore high in calories. Consuming large doses of chocolate will add many calories to the diet, leading to weight gain that will negate any benefits from the flavanol intake.

So is chocolate health food? Not exactly, but the consumption of a moderate amount of high-cacao, good-quality dark chocolate may benefit the body as well as the spirit.

TOP: *A pyramid of white chocolate, milk chocolate, and dark chocolate surrounded by* (LEFT TO RIGHT) *cacao pods, cocoa nibs, cocoa powder, and cocoa butter*

Cocoa butter

Cocoa butter is the naturally occurring fat in cocoa beans. It is extracted from chocolate liquor by pressing and is generally filtered and deodorized before use. The function of cocoa butter in chocolate is to suspend and lubricate the cacao and sugar particles. Cocoa butter lowers the viscosity of melted chocolate but does not itself significantly contribute to chocolate flavor, having little flavor of its own. Cocoa butter has several unique qualities that make it a very desirable fat:

+ Cocoa butter has a narrow melting range that is just below normal human body temperature. It tends to stay hard until it is very close to body temperature, and then it melts rapidly, carrying and releasing flavors on the palate.

+ Cocoa butter sets to a brittle consistency at normal room temperature. If cocoa butter were not brittle, chocolate would not have its characteristic snap.

+ Cocoa butter contracts significantly upon setting. It is the contraction of cocoa butter as it crystallizes that makes it possible for the confectioner to release chocolate easily from molds once it is set.

Along with this unique combination of desirable traits, however, cocoa butter possesses some more problematic aspects:

+ Cocoa butter is expensive. Cocoa butter is easily the most expensive ingredient in most chocolate.

+ Cocoa butter can be difficult to work with. Cocoa butter is the ingredient in chocolate that makes it necessary to temper the chocolate prior to use.

In spite of the drawbacks of cocoa butter, it is a crucial part of chocolate for the mouthfeel it provides and for its working characteristics. Most chocolate contains not only the cocoa butter present in chocolate liquor but additional cocoa butter as well. In order to obtain the extra cocoa butter for chocolate production, manufacturers must press it from chocolate liquor.

There is less disparity in the quality of cocoa butter from various beans than there is in the solids of those beans. As a result, manufacturers tend to press the chocolate liquor made from lower-quality beans to extract cocoa butter, leaving the solids to be sold as cocoa powder. Cocoa butters are not all identical, however; their differences lie most noticeably in their melting points. Cocoa butter from beans grown near the Equator, such as those from Malaysia, tends to have a slightly higher melting point than cocoa butter pressed from beans grown in more moderate climates, such as Brazil. As a result, chocolate made from beans grown nearer the Equator requires slightly higher temperatures for tempering and handling than chocolate from cooler climates does.

Sugar

Sugar is typically the second most prevalent ingredient in dark chocolate and makes up an even more substantial part of many milk and white chocolates. Its purpose is simply to provide sweetness to the bitter cacao. Although FDA regulations permit the use of any nutritive carbohydrate sweetener in chocolate manufacture, crystalline sucrose from sugarcane or sugar beets is by far the sugar most commonly used in chocolate. The sugar in chocolate is not dissolved but is refined to very small particles to create a smooth mouthfeel. The crystalline sugar may be pulverized prior to being mixed with the batch or may be fully refined together with the chocolate liquor. Either way, the particle size must ultimately be reduced to less than 25 microns so that the chocolate will feel smooth in the mouth.

Milk solids

Milk solids are a defining component of milk and white chocolates and are permissible in American dark chocolate in quantities up to 12 percent, although they are seldom added to dark chocolate. (See Cacao Product Standards of Identity table, page 35.) Milk solids contribute a creamy, smooth flavor to milk and white chocolates. Several different forms of dry milk may be used in manufacturing, including spray-dried milk, roller-dried milk, and milk crumb. Each product has its own unique flavor profile and advantages. Manufacturers select a milk product based on the flavor profile they want a chocolate product to have. The milk solids added to some chocolates are treated with lipase, a fat-degrading enzyme, resulting in a sort of controlled rancidity of the fat in the dry milk. This is done to increase the buttery flavor of the milk solids in order to obtain the signature flavor profile the manufacturer seeks.

Dairy fat

Milk solids also contain butterfat, which has pronounced effects on cocoa butter: with the presence of butterfat, the rate of cocoa butter crystallization slows, and the temperature at which the various crystals form is depressed. Because of these phenomena, milk and white chocolates must be handled and used at a lower temperature than dark chocolate. (See Tempering Chocolate, Time, page 56.)

Milk fat or butterfat is a permissible ingredient in American dark chocolate. When used as an ingredient in dark chocolate, milk fat is added to inhibit the potential for bloom and to soften the chocolate slightly, resulting in a less brittle product and a faster melt in the mouth. Milk fat is less expensive than the cocoa butter it displaces, so it also lowers the cost of the chocolate. Although it is permissible, not all American-made dark chocolate contains butterfat; the highest-quality dark chocolates do not contain any fat other than cocoa butter. As with any of the ingredients used in manufacturing chocolate in the United States, if butterfat is present, it must be declared on the label.

Flavoring

Vanilla is the standard flavor adjunct used in manufacturing chocolate. It adds floral, creamy flavor notes that complement the bitterness of cacao and round out the flavor of the chocolate. Manufacturers may use vanilla beans or vanillin, a manufactured flavor compound found in vanilla beans. Vanilla and vanillin are the flavors most commonly added to chocolate, but FDA regulations allow the addition of many other flavors, including spices, nuts, salt, and natural or artificial flavors, provided that they do not imitate the flavor of chocolate and that their presence is indicated on the label.

Lecithin

Almost all chocolate contains trace amounts of lecithin. Lecithin is extracted from soybeans and is well known as an emulsifier. Because chocolate contains no water, it is not an emulsion, but rather a suspension of solid particles in fat. The function of lecithin in chocolate is not to emulsify but to reduce viscosity; a very small amount of lecithin improves melted chocolate's ability to flow. Lecithin reduces viscosity only up to a point, however. When the lecithin in chocolate exceeds about 0.3 percent, viscosity begins to increase again, so adding more lecithin to chocolate will typically make it thicker, not thinner. Chocolate manufacturers usually add the amount of lecithin that will give them the maximum advantage in viscosity.

FROM BEAN TO BAR: AT THE MANUFACTURER

Chocolate manufacture is not the immediate concern of the artisan confectioner. It is logical, however, that any culinary professional who uses chocolate frequently should have an essential knowledge of how that product is made. The steps in the manufacturing chart on page 30 can be performed in different orders by different manufacturers.

Cleaning and blending cocoa beans

Cocoa beans arrive at the manufacturer containing an assortment of impurities, such as stones, pieces of metal, twigs, and every type of foreign matter imaginable. Obviously these items must be removed prior to further processing. Cleaning takes place in stages and is accomplished by several methods, including sieving, the use of magnets, and the removal of dust to ensure the purity of the chocolate.

Historically, the blending of several varieties of bean at the manufacturer is another important step in chocolate production. In recent years, there has been a marketing effort emphasizing single-origin chocolate made from beans from one country, region, or even plantation. Opinions regarding single-origin chocolates vary. Some claim this chocolate to be of highest quality; others maintain that the best chocolate is made by mixing beans with different characteristics to create a chocolate with the most complex flavor. A case can be made for either argument, but, as with all things taste related, opinions on this matter are highly subjective. Each confectioner must choose chocolates based on their flavor profile and working characteristics and on economic realities.

Roasting

The primary function of roasting is to develop chocolate flavor. Fermented, unroasted cocoa beans exhibit little or no chocolate aroma but contain the precursors to create chocolate flavor. Just as coffee may be roasted to varying degrees for different results, cocoa beans may also be roasted to different temperatures for specific flavor profiles, depending on the desired outcome and the beans used. Roasting may be performed at different points in manufacturing. There are three main methods of roasting in common use: whole-bean roasting, nib roasting, and liquor roasting. Each method has its unique advantages and challenges, but excellent results can be obtained from any of these methods. In all cases, the object is to roast the beans to develop optimal flavor without roasting them too much, which can overshadow flavor nuances. Lower-roast chocolates often exhibit a reddish color, while darker-roast chocolates are a deeper brown. In addition to developing flavor, roasting removes most of the remaining moisture from the beans, making them more friable for further processing. When roasting is completed, the cacao has developed its chocolate flavor but still has a decidedly sour aroma due to the volatile acids that are by-products of fermentation. These acids are not removed until near the end of processing, during conching. (See page 26.) Due to naturally occurring differences between varieties and batches of beans, it is desirable to roast varieties of beans independently of one another in order to ensure optimal flavor development. Only then are the varieties of beans blended.

Micronizing

Micronizing is the process of breaking the beans into pieces. This step may occur at one of two points: when the beans are already roasted, if whole-bean roasting is employed, or before

Beans
↓
Cleaning
↓
Roasting
↓
Blending
↓
Micronizing
↓
Winnowing
↓
Dutching —Optional→ Grinding
↓
Chocolate Liquor → Pressing → Cocoa Powder
↓
Vanilla, Sugar, Lecithin, Milk Solids → Mixing ← Cocoa Butter
↓
Refining
↓
Conching
↓
Tempering
↓
Molding & Cooling
↓
Chocolate Blocks, Pistoles, Chips

Chocolate processing, from cacao bean to finished product

roasting, when nib roasting or liquor roasting is used. Once broken, the bean consists of two parts: nib and shell. During micronizing, it is important that the shell be completely detached from the nib so that the two parts may be sifted apart. For the manufacturer, it is also desirable to have all of the nibs a homogeneous size to ensure even roasting, particularly if nib roasting is employed. Micronizing the cocoa beans permits the next steps in processing.

Winnowing

Manufacturers separate the shells from the nibs through a process called winnowing. It is carried out by a series of sieves combined with airflow. By FDA standards, chocolate liquor may contain no more than 1.75 percent cocoa shell. Regulations aside, it is important to remove as much of the shell as possible, as it can contribute off flavors to the chocolate, and the fat it contains has a softening effect on cocoa butter.

Grinding (milling)

Grinding, or milling, is the process of crushing the nibs to create chocolate liquor. (See page 24.) In chocolate manufacturing, chocolate liquor may be used in one of two processes: either it is pressed in order to separate it into cocoa butter and cocoa powder or it is mixed into a batch of chocolate.

Mixing

During mixing all the ingredients in a batch of chocolate—chocolate liquor, sugar, cocoa butter, vanilla, lecithin, and sometimes milk solids—are combined to create a homogeneous blend. Although lecithin is an integral part of most chocolate, it is likely that only a portion will be added during mixing. The rest will likely be incorporated at the end of conching, because lecithin's hydrophilic quality—its tendency to hold moisture—diminishes the efficacy of conching.

Refining

Refining is the vital step of reducing the particle size of the mixed chocolate. Chocolate liquor can be a relatively coarse product, with a discernable grain to it, and the sugar used in chocolate manufacture is crystalline, so when these ingredients are mixed together to make chocolate, the blend has a coarse texture. The objective of refining is to reduce the particles of all components to a size that cannot be felt on the palate. About 25 microns is the generally recognized size under which particles cannot be felt in the mouth, but fine-quality chocolate has a particle size in the neighborhood of 15 to 20 microns, resulting in a delightfully smooth mouthfeel. Refining is usually accomplished by running the batch through a series of steel or stone rollers, which crush and shear the particles to their final size.

Conching

Although all the ingredients in chocolate are now present, and the particles are reduced to the proper dimensions, the product still bears little resemblance to the chocolate that confectioners work with every day. It is a thick, crumbly paste that does not flow. Also, although it has a chocolate aroma, it still contains the volatile acids that were present in the fermented beans and therefore has a pronounced sour aroma. During conching, a process accomplished by long-term exposure to heat, oxygen, and agitation, the volatile acids and most of the remaining traces of water are evaporated, and the viscosity of the chocolate is improved. Dark chocolate is usually conched at approximately 70°C/158°F, for a period ranging from 3 to 96 hours. Removing the traces of water in the chocolate helps to improve the viscosity, and evaporating the lactic, acetic, and other organic acids removes the sour smell and flavor. Conching also coats all of the particles with a film of cocoa butter, allowing them to move within the system more freely, thus improving viscosity.

The full range of reactions that occurs during conching—and exactly how conching contributes to flavor development—are not totally understood, so some of the mystique of the process remains. A persistent myth holds that longer conching necessarily produces a higher-quality chocolate. Like any cooking process, however, more is not necessarily better. In cooking, it is up to the chef to decide when a preparation has reached its full potential and when further cooking will actually diminish quality. The same is true of conching: it is up to the manufacturer to decide at what point the chocolate has reached its optimal quality for use and when further conching will result in diminished quality rather than in an improvement.

Tempering, depositing, and cooling

Just as the artisan confectioner must temper the chocolate to be used in enrobing, manufacturers must temper the finished chocolate before molding or depositing it in order to ensure proper gloss and snap upon setting. This is usually accomplished by tempering machines that agitate and seed the chocolate continuously so that it can be deposited or molded. Chocolate tempered in this way will set with the expected degree of shine, hardness, and uniformity. The only freshly manufactured chocolate not tempered before shipping is liquid chocolate, which is transported in tanker trucks to confectionery manufacturers.

When chocolate is to be sold in blocks, bars, pistoles, or some other solid form, it must be deposited and then cooled to promote proper crystallization. Cooling is accomplished in a cooling tunnel, which gradually decreases the temperature, setting the chocolate, and then slowly returns to a more ambient temperature to prevent any thermal shock or condensation, which could result in sugar bloom. (See Bloom, page 33.)

Dutching and pressing

An optional step in chocolate manufacturing, Dutch processing is accomplished by treating the cacao with an alkali, usually potassium carbonate. Dutch processing may be carried out at various stages by the chocolate manufacturer, including treating the whole beans, nibs, chocolate liquor, or cocoa powder, although it is most often the nibs that are treated. The primary function of Dutch processing is to reduce the acidity of cacao; it also noticeably darkens the color. Dutch processing is not frequently used in the manufacture of chocolate. It is, however, frequently applied to cacao that will be pressed to separate the cocoa butter from the cocoa powder. Manufacturers press chocolate liquor because they need extra cocoa butter to manufacture chocolate. In a manner of speaking, then, cocoa powder is a by-product of the chocolate-manufacturing process and is not likely to be made from the highest-quality cocoa beans—those used to make chocolate. Usually the lower-quality, more acidic cacao is used for pressing. Dutch processing removes excess acidity and sour flavors and gives the cocoa powder a darker color, increasing its visual appeal. Most people would agree that while Dutching makes cocoa powder look more like chocolate and makes it less sour tasting, it does not make the cocoa powder *taste* more like chocolate. Any chocolate or cocoa powder that is Dutch processed must indicate on the label that it has been treated with an alkali.

USE AND HANDLING OF CHOCOLATE

General guidelines

While detailed knowledge of chocolate manufacturing is not essential for confectionery success, knowing how to handle and store chocolate is. The basic guidelines for handling chocolate are rather simple: always keep chocolate away from moisture and excessive heat; these are the two factors that destroy chocolate more rapidly than all others. Also, chocolate should be stored in a cool, dark place, away from strong odors that can taint its flavor.

A very small amount of moisture in chocolate noticeably increases its viscosity, making it unacceptable for dipping or enrobing. When melting chocolate, be careful not to allow excess steam to develop, which will interface with the surface of the chocolate, moistening it and increasing the viscosity. When working with chocolate, always be certain that all utensils and surfaces are dry. Chocolate that has been exposed to moisture may still be used in some applications, such as chocolate caramels or chocolate fudge, but it should not be used for dipping or enrobing.

Excessive heat causes chocolate to form grains and to thicken. Dark chocolate should not be heated above 50°C/120°F. Milk and white chocolates are especially vulnerable to damage from heat due to the milk solids they contain; to prevent damage, do not heat them above 40°C/104°F. When melting small quantities of chocolate, it is important to chop it finely, melt it over a warm water bath, and stir it as it melts. The chocolate must be chopped in order to ensure that it melts evenly and quickly without overheating. The water bath should be warm, not boiling. A boiling water bath not only introduces the hazard of steam but also overheats the chocolate in the bottom of the bowl. Stirring ensures that the chocolate melts evenly without overheating. An alternative method for melting chocolate is the very gentle dry heat of a melter. These devices can be set for the desired temperature, and the chocolate left overnight to melt, without having to be chopped beforehand or stirred while melting—making melters the easiest way to melt large quantities of chocolate. (See Confectionery Equipment, Tier One, page 11.)

Work environment

All work with chocolate should be carried out in a temperature-controlled, low-humidity environment. Although various steps of confectionery production may be best accomplished at different temperatures, most artisan confectioners do not have the luxury of having more than one temperature-controlled room for their work. For general chocolate work, including crystallization of finished pieces, an ambient temperature of 20°C/68°F is appropriate.

BLOOM

In confectionery, bloom refers to the gray cast, streaks, or spots that appear on poorly handled chocolate. There are two types of bloom: fat bloom and sugar bloom. Fat bloom is the visible crystallization of fat on the surface of chocolate. It is caused by improperly tempered or stored chocolate. (See Polymorphism of Cocoa Butter, page 55.) Chocolate that has been allowed to set without proper tempering will immediately form fat bloom. Chocolate that has been precrystalllized with the wrong form of crystals will form fat bloom during storage. If, during storage, the chocolate melts and then recrystallizes, it will also exhibit fat bloom.

Sugar bloom is the formation of sugar crystals on the surface of chocolate. It is caused by the exposure of chocolate to high humidity or other moisture. When exposed to moisture, the sugar particles on the surface of the chocolate absorb the moisture, and dissolve. When the moisture subsequently evaporates, the sugar recrystallizes in larger crystals, resulting in sugar bloom.

It is difficult to distinguish sugar bloom from fat bloom by sight alone, but there is a simple test to determine the source of the bloom: gently rub a sample of the bloomed chocolate on your lip or wrist. If the chocolate feels smooth, the bloom is fat bloom. If there is a noticeable rough texture to the chocolate, it is sugar bloom.

LEFT: *The result of sugar bloom.* RIGHT: *The result of fat bloom.*

Temperatures significantly higher than this causes tempered chocolate to crystallize too slowly. Temperatures that are much lower will result in rapid cooling and an increase in viscosity as well as the formation of unstable cocoa butter crystals, causing poor gloss and snap, and the formation of bloom during storage. (See Tempering Chocolate, page 54.)

Chocolate storage guidelines

Because chocolate contains virtually no moisture, it has a very low water-activity level and is not prone to bacterial spoilage during storage, resulting in a long shelf life. (See Water Activity, page 40.) The factor limiting shelf life for chocolate is rancidity, the breakdown of fats that can create off flavors. Although cocoa butter is relatively resistant to rancidity, chocolate should be stored protected from exposure to oxygen, light, heat, and moisture. In addition, when working with chocolate, do not expose it to reactive metals such as copper and iron. All of these factors shorten the potential shelf life of chocolate products by increasing the likelihood that rancidity will develop. When stored under ideal conditions, dark chocolates have a shelf life of approximately twelve months, while milk and white chocolate have a shelf life of approximately six months. These are the maximum times suggested for storing chocolate. The artisan confectioner is well advised to turn over his chocolate inventory much more rapidly to ensure the highest-quality products with the freshest flavor.

VARIOUS CACAO PRODUCTS

The table on page 35 compares U.S. government standards for commonly used cacao products. These standards represent the minimum legal requirements a product must meet in order to be allowed to go by the name given. Many of the permissible ingredients for products are not necessarily used in the manufacturing of the highest-quality products. For instance, butterfat is a permissible ingredient for making semisweet chocolate. It is added to inhibit bloom and to soften the chocolate slightly. The highest-quality dark chocolate, however, whether made in the United States or elsewhere, is made without adjunct fats, including butterfat. In all cases, a product's ingredients must be indicated on its label.

Coating

A commonly available cacao product is coating. Compound coatings may not legally be labeled as "chocolate," but must be labeled as coatings. These are chocolate-like products that contain additional ingredients not permissible in chocolate, most commonly vegetable fats (usually hydrogenated) and bulking agents. The primary advantage of coatings is the vegetable fat they contain, which makes it unnecessary to temper them. Chocolate coatings are often less expensive than fine-quality chocolate, but they do not have the same melting characteristics or flavor that chocolate does. European varieties of coatings are labeled as *pâte à glacer*.

Couverture

A common term in chocolate marketing, the French word *couverture* translates roughly as "covering." Couverture is recognized in European Union nations and controlled by EU regulations, but the term has no legal standing in chocolate manufacturing in the United States. European dark chocolate labeled as couverture is subject to guidelines very similar to those that regulate chocolate in the U.S., except that it must contain at least 35 percent cacao and 31 percent fat; dark couvertures nearly always contain a much greater cacao content than the minimum required. In dark chocolate couverture, the fat is almost always 100 percent cocoa butter, although the addition of 5 percent vegetable fat is permitted under EU guidelines, provided that it is clearly stated on the label. Much like the allowable butterfat in dark chocolate in the U.S., this optional fat is not added to the highest-quality products from Europe. The fat content of milk and white couvertures consists of the combination of cocoa butter and the milk fat found in the dry milk in those products.

CACAO PRODUCT STANDARDS OF IDENTITY[1]

Note: X = impermissible ingredient; O = optional ingredient; R = required ingredient, the quantity of which is not regulated. Percentages denote the ranges required to meet the Standard of Identity.

	CHOCOLATE LIQUOR[2]	SEMISWEET/ BITTERSWEET CHOCOLATE[3]	SWEET CHOCOLATE	MILK CHOCOLATE	WHITE CHOCOLATE	BREAKFAST COCOA[4]	COCOA[5]	LOW-FAT COCOA
CHOCOLATE LIQUOR	R	≥35%	≥15%	≥10%	X	X	X	X
COCOA BUTTER	50%–60%	O	O	O	≥20%	≥22%	10%–22%	<10%
COCOA POWDER	O	X	X	X	X	R	R	R
SUGAR[6]	X	R	R	R	≤55%	X	X	X
MILK SOLIDS	X	<12%	<12%	≥12%	≥3.5%	X	X	X
BUTTERFAT	O	O	O	≥3.39%	≥14%	X	X	X
ALKALIZER	O	O	O	O	X	O	O	O
SPICES, FLAVORS, NUTS, SALT, ETC.[7]	O	O	O	O	O	O	O	O
EMULSIFIER (LECITHIN)	X	<1%	<1%	<1%	<1.5%	X	X	X

[1] United States Government Standards of Identity as of April 4, 2011. http://www.accessdata.fda.gov/scripts/cdrh/cfdocs/cfcfr/CFRSearch.cfm?CFRPart=163%20

[2] Chocolate liquor may also be called unsweetened chocolate.

[3] The FDA does not differentiate between bittersweet and semisweet chocolate; this product may go by either name.

[4] Also known as "high-fat cocoa."

[5] Also known as "medium-fat cocoa."

[6] May include any nutritive carbohydrate sweeteners.

[7] May include spices, nuts and natural and artificial flavors, provided they do not imitate the flavor of chocolate.

CHOCOLATE PERCENTAGES

Much of the dark and milk chocolate sold indicates a percentage on the label. While a great deal has been made of this number in recent years, surprisingly few professionals seem to understand the number, its significance, or what it does and does not tell us about the chocolate.

Simply put, the percentage listed on a label describes the portion of the chocolate that came from the cacao tree. In the case of dark chocolate, virtually all of the remaining ingredients consist of sugar. The percentage of chocolate represents the combination of chocolate liquor and cocoa butter but fails to differentiate between them. As a result, two chocolates, each of them labeled 65 percent, can be radically different from each other. One of those chocolates may contain 65 percent chocolate liquor and no additional cocoa butter. That chocolate would be strongly flavored and would have a high viscosity. The other might contain 50 percent chocolate liquor with 15 percent cocoa butter added. That chocolate would be less intensely flavored and of a much lower viscosity.

The percentage provided on the label gives the confectioner an idea of the relative sweetness of the product but says nothing of other aspects of the flavor profile. Currently there is great interest in high-percentage chocolates. Considering their potential for having very full cacao flavor, this is understandable. However, the percentage tells the confectioner nothing about the quality of the cacao in the chocolate. Therefore, it is entirely possible to have a poor-quality 75-percent chocolate that doesn't exhibit the flavor of a fine-quality 60-percent chocolate.

The cocoa-solids content of milk chocolate is an even more nebulous area because in milk chocolate, there are milk solids in addition to the sugar, cocoa butter, and chocolate liquor. In selecting chocolate for various uses, the confectioner must always let his palate be his guide.

SELECTING CHOCOLATE

In the United States, the manufacturing and labeling of chocolate is closely controlled by government regulations, and labels can provide a good deal of information for those who know how to interpret them. No label, however, has ever defined the flavor or quality of the chocolate the package contains; this crucial step is up to the confectioner. Years ago, it was virtually impossible to find American-made world-class chocolate; it simply did not exist. Happily, this situation has changed, and several American manufacturers are now making chocolate that equals the best-quality couverture from anywhere in the world.

Scharffen Berger and Guittard are two examples of American companies that are manufacturing fine-quality chocolate on traditional machinery with great attention paid to the beans used and to flavor development in processing. While there will always be a large market for ordinary-quality mass-produced chocolate, Scharffen Berger and Guittard are demonstrating that American manufacturers have both the capability to produce, and the market to sell, chocolate that is among the finest in the world.

The selection of chocolate for specific uses in artisan confectionery is based on balancing several criteria, primarily flavor, viscosity, and economics. The number of chocolates that a confectioner chooses to use in his or her repertoire can vary widely, but most artisan confectioners are no longer satisfied to have simply one dark chocolate, one milk chocolate, and one white chocolate. Instead, most use several different chocolates for specific applications.

Flavor

The flavor of chocolate is of primary concern to the artisan confectioner. However, it is not enough to decide if a chocolate tastes good. In matching a chocolate to a specific use, flavor nuances must also be taken into account. A chocolate with fruity flavor notes might be more appropriate with a fruit-flavored ganache, while a dark-roasted, earthy chocolate might better complement a hazelnut gianduja. Although high-percentage chocolates have an important place in confectionery, a lower-percentage, lower-roast chocolate might be just right to make a delicately infused lavender ganache in order to allow the light, floral aroma to shine through. That high-percentage chocolate might be better used to stand up to the bold impact of a liquor cordial. Matching the right chocolate to individual flavors is an important step in fine-tuning confections and can be an effective marketing tool with knowledgeable consumers. As Americans become savvier about chocolate and food in general, more information about the percentage and origin of the chocolate being used becomes a powerful selling point for artisan confections.

Viscosity

The viscosity of chocolate is determined primarily by its fat content. Viscosity is a crucial consideration for dipping or enrobing chocolates. For this purpose, the confectioner generally chooses a low-viscosity chocolate, which sets up to provide a thin shell with well-defined corners. Low-viscosity chocolate helps maintain a low ratio of chocolate to center and prevents the chocolate covering from overpowering the center. A chocolate being used for making ganache or for flavoring fudge does not require the cocoa butter content that a dipping chocolate needs. In fact, a lower cocoa butter content is often desirable for this type of application. Cocoa butter does not contribute chocolate flavor, is expensive, and can lead to separated emulsions due to excessive fat.

Economics

In any business, economics plays a major role in every decision, and confectionery is no exception. By the very nature of their business, artisan confectioners tend to use higher-quality ingredients and charge correspondingly higher prices for their products than mass-production manufacturers do. Artisan confections are true luxury items, so it behooves the confectioner to use the highest-quality chocolate he or she can afford. Successfully choosing which chocolates to use in confectionery requires some knowledge of manufacturing and labeling and a great deal of experimentation: the artisan confectioner must judge the qualities of different chocolates—their flavors and working characteristics—in light of economic realities. Understanding the differences among chocolates and choosing the right chocolate for each application is one more aspect of the artisan confectioner's art.

3

By definition, confections have a long shelf life; the word *confection* is derived from the French *confit,* meaning "preserved." It is fair to say that unless an item can be stored safely at room temperature, it is simply not a confection.

PACKAGING AND STORAGE

Throughout history, one of the goals of confectionery has been preservation by sugar content, and to a large degree this is still true. The typical shelf life of confections ranges from approximately three weeks for ganache centers to a year or longer for hard candies. When properly stored, most of the products made by artisan confectioners will not suffer a significant loss of quality for approximately three months. (See Water Activity of Confections table, page 42.) The factors that limit shelf life may be the intrinsic qualities of the center such as water activity, pH, or fat content, or environmental factors such as handling, temperature, humidity, or exposure to oxygen.

Loss of quality in confections may occur when the confections' surfaces become scuffed or scratched during improper handling; they develop bloom (in the case of chocolate); their amorphous sugar centers crystallize; they dry out or become too moist; or—in the worst-case scenario—they develop microbial spoilage from molds, yeast, or bacteria. Most of these factors are controllable to a large degree through proper formulation, handling, packaging, and storage. One of the greatest strengths of the artisan confectioner over the large-scale manufacturer is the ability to use the highest-quality ingredients and to offer fresh products to be enjoyed promptly rather than ones that have spent months in distribution and storage. The creation of fresh, high-quality products should always be the primary objective of the artisan confectioner.

INTRINSIC FACTORS AFFECTING SHELF LIFE

Factors that lead to deterioration and spoilage of confections can be divided into two major groups: intrinsic and environmental. Intrinsic factors relate to water activity, internal moisture migration, fat migration, and a confection's pH level. Production conditions also fall under this category, since poor production systems can lead to food contamination by bacteria and the like.

Water activity

The same amount of total water can have widely varying amounts of free water depending on sugar content.

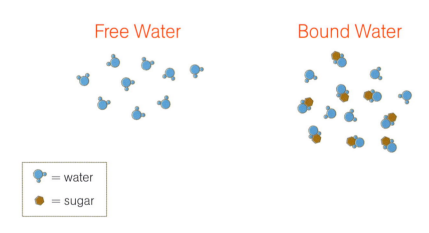

Free Water   Bound Water

= water
= sugar

EQUILIBRIUM RELATIVE HUMIDITY

Equilibrium Relative Humidity (ERH) is another method used to express water activity. While water activity is expressed as a decimal, ERH is expressed as a percentage. To translate from ERH to A_w, divide by 100, or simply move the decimal point two places to the left. For instance, pure water has an ERH of 100 percent and an A_w of 1.00. A soft caramel might have an ERH of 55 percent, corresponding to an A_w of 0.55. The two methods of assessing water activity—ERH and A_w—express exactly the same thing: the unbound water in a product. ERH is defined as the relative humidity at which a substance will neither gain nor lose weight due to moisture migration. Free water always moves from a system of higher water content into a system of lower water content. If a center has a high ERH and is exposed to

an atmosphere in which the relative humidity is low, the moisture in the center will evaporate into the air, resulting in a dried center. Conversely, when a center with a very low ERH is exposed to an atmosphere with higher relative humidity, the water in the atmosphere may migrate into the center, resulting in a softened center that, in the case of hard candies or toffees, is likely to crystallize during storage. The only confections that are not prone to moisture migration are those that are fat systems—gianduja, for example. Because these are fat-based products, they are impervious to moisture migration and will neither pick up nor lose moisture to the atmosphere even when there is a large discrepancy between their ERH and the relative humidity of the atmosphere. Enrobing in chocolate, wrapping, and pack-

aging are all methods that effectively protect confections from the moisture migration that can result from disparities between relative humidity of the environment and the ERH of confections. Chocolate enrobing creates a layer of fat (the cocoa butter in the chocolate) that is impervious to moisture migration. Wrapping individual pieces tightly in plastic wrap or wax paper accomplishes exactly the same thing, except that the barrier is not designed to be eaten with the confection! Packaging such as boxes creates and contains a micro-atmosphere, which quickly reaches the ERH of the confections contained in the box. Once this equilibrium is reached, there is no further moisture migration between the atmosphere in the box and the confections.

The most profound intrinsic factor limiting the shelf-life potential of confections is water activity (A_w). The principle of water activity is the availability of moisture for the growth of bacteria, yeast, or molds or for the enzymatic or chemical reactions that can degrade the product. With regard to shelf stability, the total water content alone does not tell the whole story; the water contained in confectionery is in two forms: "free" water and "bound" water. It is the amount of free water that is the determining factor for shelf stability.

Certain substances, such as sugars, salt, and alcohol, chemically bind with water, making that water unavailable for other uses, such as the growth of mold or bacteria. Such water is said to be bound, and, because it is attached to other substances, it is not a factor in reducing shelf life. Water that is not chemically attached to other ingredients is unbound water, or free water. Because it is available for reactions, including biological growth and enzymatic activities, free water is a major factor in limiting the shelf life of a confectionery product.

Water activity (A_w) is a measurement of the amount of unbound water in a product. The water activity of a product is always compared to the water activity of pure water. Pure water has a water activity level of 1.00; it is 100 percent free water. A product with absolutely no unbound water has a water activity level of 0.00; there is no free water. Because virtually all confectionery products contain some unbound moisture, the water activity is expressed as a number that falls between these two extremes; the less free water there is in the product, the lower the A_w number, and the less perishable the product is.

Water activity is measured by using a water activity meter or by sending a sample of the confection in question to a lab to be measured. Knowing the water activity of confectionery centers helps the confectioner determine the potential for storage and the proper shelf life of the products. (See Water Activity of Confections table below.)

Although understanding the basics of water activity and spoilage is worthwhile for the artisan confectioner, it is not necessary to know the precise water activity of all of the confections in the shop; a general understanding is enough to ensure that the shop has fresh products that are not being stored longer than they should be.

No confection is more susceptible to spoilage than ganache. Not only is it high in total moisture, it is also relatively low in the sugars that bind that moisture. As a result, it has a fairly high water-activity level and a potential for spoilage if it is not formulated and handled properly. Marzipan and fudge are two other examples of confections that have a relatively high water activity level and therefore some potential for spoilage. Caramels, on the other hand, are lower in total moisture, and much higher in sugar, which binds the moisture, resulting in a low level of free water and a longer shelf life.

WATER ACTIVITY OF CONFECTIONS

A_w	CONFECTIONS TYPICALLY WITHIN THIS RANGE	ORGANISMS THAT CAN THRIVE	APPROXIMATE SHELF LIFE
1.00–0.95	None	Many bacteria, including pathogens	Highly perishable; requires refrigeration
0.80–0.85	Ganache	Nonpathogenic bacteria, all molds	3 weeks
0.75–0.80	Marzipan, fudge, fondant	Many molds, halophilic bacteria	2 to 3 months
0.60–0.75	Jellies, marshmallows	Osmophilic yeasts, a few molds	3 months
> 0.60	Toffee, hard candy, brittle, hard nougat, gianduja	No microbial proliferation	>3 months

Internal moisture migration

Moisture migration can be an intrinsic factor in mitigating the shelf life of confections, particularly when two or more types of centers are mixed within an enrobed confection. (Moisture migration can also affect unenrobed confections if they are not well protected by packaging. See Environmental Factors Affecting Shelf Life, page 44.) Under this circumstance, if the A_w of the centers is not equal, the free water can move from the higher-level center into the lower-level center, altering the texture of each. This scenario can lead to unwanted crystallization of amorphous centers; for example, caramel can crystallize if it absorbs moisture from an incompatible center. If, however, one of the centers is a fat system, like gianduja, it will not absorb moisture from the other center. Internal moisture migration may be prevented by creating a layer of fat, such as cocoa butter, between the two centers to act as a barrier to water movement.

Internal Moisture Migration

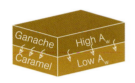

External Moisture Migration

60% RH in Atmosphere

Moisture migrates in   Moisture migrates out

Low ERH   High ERH
30   85
(caramel)   (ganache)

LEFT: *Moisture migrates from a higher A_w to a lower A_w until equilibrium is achieved. A barrier of fat between two layers can prevent this migration.* RIGHT: *Moisture migrates into or out of the confection from the atmosphere. Confections with low ERHs, like caramels, pick up moisture from the atmosphere, becoming sticky. Confections with high ERHs, like ganache, lose moisture to the atmosphere, becoming dry (see page 44).*

Fat migration

Fat migration is another intrinsic factor limiting the shelf life of confections. Nut centers, particularly those that contain ground nuts and therefore more released oil, are most subject to damage from fat migration. (See Fat Migration, page 410.) The effects of fat migration can be a softened chocolate shell, and therefore loss of textural contrast as the incompatible fats mingle, and fat bloom on the surface of the confection. Although it is quite harmless, bloom in any form renders confections unfit for sale.

Acidity and alkalinity (pH)

The pH of foods has an effect on their shelf life; lower pH levels generally extend the longevity of products. Because most confections are not highly acidic, pH is rarely a factor in their preservation. Rather than relying on pH, confectioners preserve their products by controlling water activity.

Production conditions

The conditions under which confections are produced also influence their shelf life. For this reason, following good manufacturing practices and adhering to strict sanitation standards are vital parts of artisan confectionery. Bacteria, yeasts, and mold spores are all ubiquitous, and many are not destroyed by common confectionery production methods. Therefore, care must be exercised not only to prevent bacteria, yeasts, and molds from multiplying but also to avoid introducing such microbes to begin with.

ENVIRONMENTAL FACTORS AFFECTING SHELF LIFE

External factors also profoundly affect shelf life; these are the environmental conditions to which the confections are exposed after they are made. External factors include physical damage, moisture migration, humidity, and temperature. Exposure to light and oxygen can also undermine the shelf life of confectionery products.

Physical damage

The simplest detrimental environmental defect in confections is scratching or scuffing of the chocolate shell of an enrobed confection due to improper handling. Even properly tempered chocolate is relatively soft for the first few hours after it has set. For days after a confection first sets, the cocoa butter in it continues to crystallize, and the chocolate continues to harden. It is in these first hours that chocolates are most susceptible to damage from improper handling. Touching chocolates at this stage, even with gloves, will almost invariably lead to unsightly bloom in the days ahead. A properly used cooling tunnel on an enrober will reduce, but not eliminate, the vulnerability of chocolate that has recently set. Even after the chocolate has had sufficient time to crystallize fully, it can still be easily damaged by improper handling.

Artisan confections are luxury items that command premium prices. Chocolates that are scuffed or that look as if they are old will not properly represent the skill and knowledge required to make them and will not be embraced by consumers. All that is required to prevent physical damage are careful handling techniques and respect for the product.

Moisture migration

Just as moisture migration may be an intrinsic phenomenon, it may also be environmental. While enrobed confections are protected from moisture gain or loss by their chocolate shell, those that are not coated with chocolate are very susceptible to environmental moisture migration. Confections may lose moisture to the atmosphere or may absorb it, depending on the ERH of the confection and the humidity of the storage environment. In general, noncrystalline sugar confections absorb moisture from the air, while crystalline sugar confections and ganache tend to lose moisture to the atmosphere. Fat systems such as chocolate and gianduja are not subject to moisture migration and therefore will neither absorb nor lose moisture.

Amorphous sugar confectionery, such as hard candies, brittles, and caramels, however, are extremely susceptible to absorbing water from the environment. Not only do they have a low A_w, but their noncrystalline sugar is hygroscopic. Once these confections have been exposed to humidity, that moisture will migrate through the entire piece, leaving crystallization in its wake. It is therefore imperative that these confections be protected from any exposure to humidity. This can be achieved by wrapping or enrobing them immediately after production.

DEW POINT

The atmosphere normally contains a certain amount of water vapor; this is humidity. Humidity is usually expressed as relative humidity—that is, the percent of moisture in the air as compared to the maximum amount of moisture the air can hold at a given temperature. Warm air can hold more evaporated water than cold air can. If the amount of water in the air remains constant and the temperature of the air decreases, the relative humidity increases until it reaches 100 percent (saturation), at which point the moisture in the air condenses into water droplets. The dew point is defined as the temperature to which air must be cooled in order to reach 100 percent relative humidity, or saturation, and for the water it contains to change from a vapor to a liquid state (condensation). The more water vapor the air contains, the higher its dew point is.

For the confectioner, the relevance of this discussion is the damage caused if confections are chilled below the dew point of the workroom. If confections are cooled to a point at which the air around them reaches its dew point, condensation will form on the products, resulting in sugar bloom. Under normal conditions, there are only two situations in which dew point affects the artisan confectioner: when refrigeration is used or when an automatic enrober equipped with a cooling tunnel is employed. When using chilling equipment for confectionery processing, the confectioner should be aware of the dew point in the room in order not to chill products below that critical temperature. Dew point calculators are available online and require only knowing the temperature and relative humidity of the room. In order to prevent condensation and the damage it causes, the artisan confectioner must carefully control temperature, humidity, and exposure to the atmosphere when using chilling equipment.

Crystalline confections such as fudge and fondant that are left uncoated with chocolate are also susceptible to environmental moisture migration. Because of their comparatively high ERH, barring extremely high humidity, these candies are much more likely to lose moisture to the air, resulting in dried-out products. This condition is also easily avoided by wrapping or enrobing immediately after production.

Chocolate-coated centers may also suffer from moisture migration if the integrity of the chocolate coating is breached. An inadequate bottom coat, bubbles on the surface of the chocolate, or a cracked shell will all allow the centers to suffer the effects of moisture migration, greatly diminishing the confection's shelf life. To prevent this type of damage, the integrity of the chocolate shell must be preserved.

Humidity

Excessive humidity is always to be avoided in the storage of confections. In addition to causing the crystallization of amorphous candies, a very humid storage environment can cause crystalline confections to absorb moisture, which raises their A_w and makes them likely to develop mold during further storage. Chocolate exposed to high humidity will form sugar bloom.

The ideal humidity for storing uncoated confections is precisely at their ERH, at a temperature above the dew point for that level of humidity. These precise conditions can be achieved by proper use of packaging. (See Packaging and Display, page 47.) Centers coated with chocolate should be stored at as low a humidity level as possible, one that reflects the low ERH of the chocolate coating.

Temperature

Temperature plays a vital role in the storage of confections. Excessive warmth not only causes fat bloom on chocolate but also increases the speed of various degrading reactions, such as enzymatic activity, sugar crystallization, and microbial reproduction. Cold storage, if not managed properly, can also lead to defects such as sugar bloom from condensation and cracking due to contraction. The best temperature for ordinary storage of confections is approximately 15° to 20°C/59° to 68°F.

Other factors

Both light and oxygen can contribute to rancidity of fats, and hence shorten the shelf life of confections. These factors are slower to cause deterioration than those mentioned previously and are typically not as large a concern to the artisan confectioner as they are to larger-scale manufacturers, who require a much longer shelf life from their products. Artisan confectioners, therefore, can present products in transparent packaging, while manufacturers must protect their products from light.

FREEZING CONFECTIONS

Most confections have a natural shelf life that is entirely adequate for the artisan confectioner. Confections with relatively short shelf lives, however, such as ganache, marzipan, and fudge, may present a challenge to the artisan confectioner, who must produce these items fresh and in adequate quantities during busy seasons. The ability to freeze products allows the confectioner to stockpile popular items for busy times. Following proper procedure, the confectioner can freeze confections without loss of quality, and thus build up inventory over time for use during the busiest seasons. Either enrobed or unenrobed confections may be frozen using this method.

| technique | theory | **CONFECTIONERY FREEZING** |

This technique allows the confectioner to successfully freeze products, including chocolates, without causing sugar bloom or excessive loss of quality.

1. **PACK CONFECTIONS IN A STURDY BOX, FILLING THE BOX WITHOUT DAMAGING THE PRODUCT.** The box should be strong enough not to collapse under vacuum pressure. It should be filled as much as possible, to use the space in the box efficiently and to limit the amount of air in it. The less air that is present in the box, the less chance there is that condensation will form, resulting in sugar bloom. In the case of enrobed centers, a desiccant such as silica gel may be placed in the box to absorb excess humidity. When freezing unenrobed confections, however, a desiccant should not be used, as it could draw moisture from the candies, resulting in unwanted drying.

2. **VACUUM PACK THE BOX WITH AIRTIGHT PLASTIC.** The vacuum should be a gentle one so as not to damage the chocolates. Aerated centers are particularly sensitive to vacuum packaging, and can burst under excessive vacuum pressure. The seal must be airtight to keep oxygen out of the package. If the seal is broken, the chocolates are lost.

3. **REFRIGERATE THE VACUUM-PACKED CHOCOLATES FOR 24 HOURS.** Twenty-four hours of refrigeration are required to prevent the sudden contraction and subsequent cracking that could occur if the chocolates were frozen without this acclimation step.

4. **MOVE THE CHOCOLATES TO A FREEZER.** Store at the lowest possible temperature until two days prior to intended use. The freezer should be as cold as possible to ensure the maximum benefit.

5. **TWO DAYS BEFORE THE CHOCOLATES ARE NEEDED, MOVE THEM TO THE REFRIGERATOR FOR 24 HOURS.** Forty-eight hours of defrosting time is required before the frozen chocolates are ready to be used. For the first 24 hours, the chocolates should be slow-thawed in the refrigerator, to prevent cracking from thermal shock.

6. **MOVE THE BOX OF CONFECTIONS—UNOPENED—TO ROOM TEMPERATURE FOR 24 HOURS.** During the second 24 hours, the still-sealed package should be returned to room temperature. To prevent condensation and sugar bloom, it is vital that the chocolates reach room temperature before the package is opened.

7. **OPEN AND USE AS DESIRED. THE SHELF LIFE CLOCK STARTS WHEN THE CONFECTIONS ARE REMOVED FROM THE FREEZER.** Freezing confections greatly slows, but does not stop, the deterioration of quality. Nor does freezing reverse any of the negative effects confections may have suffered while stored at room temperature. Once removed from the freezer, the confections must be used within the usual period of acceptable shelf life, which must include the time they were at room temperature prior to freezing. Confections can be frozen at −10°C/14°F for up to four months without loss of quality.

PACKAGING AND DISPLAY

Packaging: to protect and attract

Confectionery packaging serves two primary purposes: it protects the confections from environmental damage, and it presents them in an attractive manner for marketing. The best packaging achieves both goals. The minimum requirement for packaging is that it supply protection from physical damage, such as scratches on the surface of chocolate, and from the temporary fluctuations in temperature that might occur during transportation. The air surrounding confections packaged in an airtight container will very quickly reach the ERH of the confections, creating the ideal storage environment. This is especially important for uncoated sugar confectionery, whether crystalline or amorphous. It is less important that chocolate-coated confections be packaged in an airtight environment, since the chocolate coating is not easily damaged by normal humidity levels. The packaging must protect its contents but not interfere with the presentation and marketing function, as excessive packaging can do. Most artisan confectioners are not concerned with long-term storage in packages. More often the concerns are that the package protect its contents from mechanical damage and that it present the products in an attractive, inviting fashion.

Displays as marketing tools

Window and counter displays are invaluable tools for marketing confections. The style of the display can convey various impressions depending on the materials and techniques used. A minimalist display of modern-looking confections placed on mirrors and illuminated by high-intensity lighting gives a very different impression from a traditional-looking selection of chocolates displayed on ornate silver platters and surrounded by velvet and soft, warm lighting or one using rustic wooden boards and surrounded by burlap. Most confectioners choose a style of presentation compatible with the appearance and flavor profiles of their products, depending on whether these are venerable classics, rustic and simple candies, or sleek and modern confections.

Window displays are powerful marketing tools for retailers, and artisan confectioners are no exception to that rule. An attractive window display is a billboard that announces and advertises not only the presence of the business but the unique products and aesthetics of the

An appropriate display of modern confections is exemplified by minimal extraneous décor, modern presentation materials, and is likely to employ higher-intensity lighting. Sleek glass, ceramics, or plastic without unnecessary adornment are all appropriate to this sort of display.

shop as well. Properly designed and maintained window displays draw attention to the shop, attracting new customers, and keep the shop looking current, fresh, relevant, and enticing. In order to use window displays to their maximum potential, the confectioner should follow a few simple guidelines:

- ◆ **MAKE IT SIMPLE BUT ABUNDANT.** Remember that the primary objective of the window display is to highlight and promote the confections available inside the shop. Make the confections the focal point of the window. Excessive use of props or too many elements in a window display detract from the products being offered. Arranging single varieties of confections in straight lines generally draws in the eye more effectively than a more complex design does. Simplicity does not mean stinginess, however. The window should suggest abundance; it should never look meager.

- ◆ **INCORPORATE HEIGHT.** Store windows are well suited to creating several levels of height in a display; this is an important quality in an effective window display. Creating height not only increases the overall visual interest but also makes the window more visible from a greater distance, attracting more attention. A series of steps or risers can be used to add not only height to the display but depth as well. The risers may be draped with different fabrics to create different effects, or they may be left exposed for another unique look.

- ◆ **UP THE LIGHTS!** Brilliant lighting is mandatory for any effective window display. Even the best window looks dingy if the lighting is inadequate. A store window must be brightly lit to accentuate the products it contains. Lighting that does not generate excessive heat, such as LED's, is preferable—chocolate is notoriously heat sensitive—and fans and ventilation systems can help to dissipate the heat causes by lighting.

- ◆ **KEEP IT SCRUPULOUSLY CLEAN.** The window of a confectionery shop should represent the very best the shop has to offer in order to entice customers. The display itself must always look pristine and appetizing. Chocolates that are showing their age with bloom or a diminished shine will do nothing to promote the business. Crumbs or dust simply have no place in a window, and the window itself must be kept crystal clear to illustrate the management's commitment to quality and attention to detail.

- ◆ **CHANGE THE DISPLAY FREQUENTLY.** Window displays should be a continual source of stimulation to passersby. Once a window display has been seen repeatedly, it becomes just part of the scenery and loses its ability to pique interest. Each display is an opportunity to be timely; creating a window that suggests a seasonal or holiday theme is one way to make the display relevant. Frequently changing products, colors, layouts, and designs helps to project the innovative image for which artisan confectioners should be known.

- ◆ **MAKE IT YOUR OWN.** Each window display should represent the vision, products, and aesthetic of the confectioner. While there are guidelines for effective store window displays, there are few hard and fast rules. Originality and creativity in a store's window intimate that the same qualities will be found inside the store and serve to draw customers in. There is nothing wrong with traditional chocolate displays, but the use of unusual materials and props for displaying and accompanying chocolates can distinguish a confectioner as an original and entice customers who might otherwise pass the shop by.

- ◆ **CARRY IT BEYOND THE WINDOW.** An engaging window display is a great start toward attracting customers and increasing sales, but the window should be just the beginning. The appearance and atmosphere inside the shop should continue and develop the qualities that drew the customer to the window. It doesn't require a remodel each time the window changes, just some splashes of color and flair that tie it all together.

Matching the display to rustic confections such as fudge, brittle, and divinity permits the use of either less formal plates and platters, or even more unconventional rustic display materials such as wood, metal, or burlap.

Classical confections may be best displayed in a traditional manner to reflect their heritage. Formal platters suggesting old world elegance are appropriate for a classical display, with lighting and background to match.

4

Mastering the craft of artisan confectionery is a continual process of learning, creating, and improving techniques to upgrade both products and efficiency.

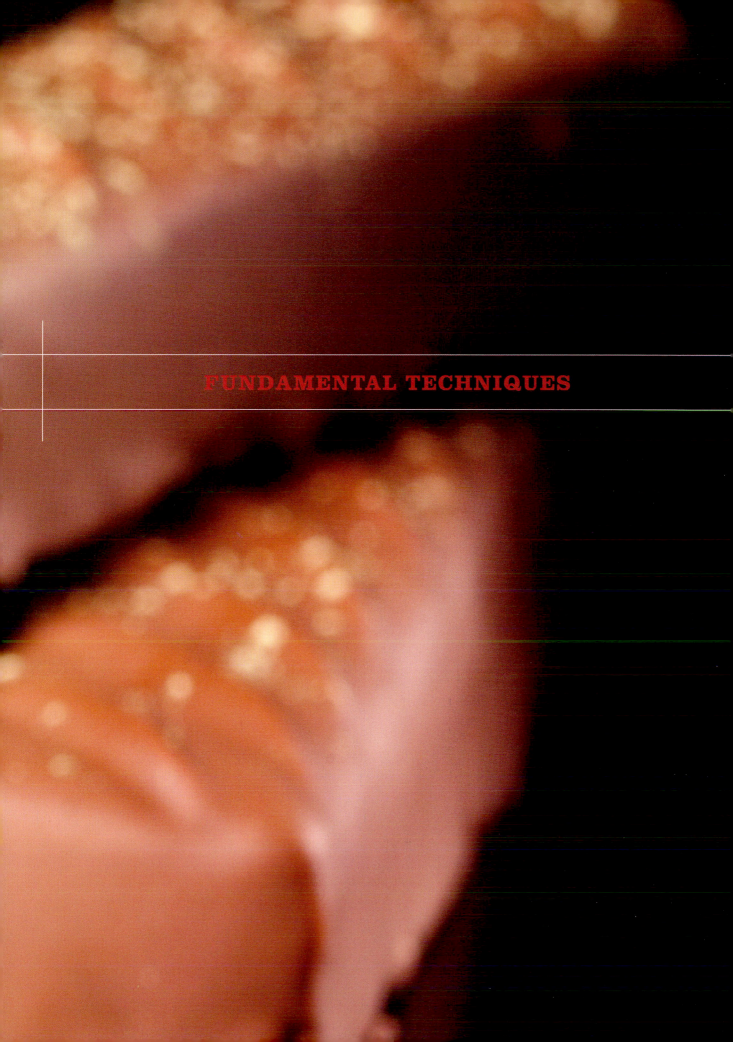

FUNDAMENTAL TECHNIQUES

The best formula is of little use without knowledge of the techniques required to make and finish it, and all of the knowledge in the world about ingredients is ineffectual without solid techniques for applying that knowledge to making marketable products. Techniques may vary slightly depending on the operation, available equipment, and desired outcome, and savvy confectioners are always looking for ways to fine-tune techniques to best suit their businesses. To be sure, the artisan confectioner must be well versed in a wide variety of techniques—from the fundamental, such as various ways to temper chocolate, to the esoteric, such as aerating that tempered chocolate with nitrous oxide. Of all the techniques a confectioner might have in his or her repertoire, however, a number may be considered fundamental to the craft; they form the foundation for all the products the confectioner creates. These are the techniques that are used over and over and are applied to a wide range of confections; they range from tempering chocolate to precoating and dipping centers, to lining molds. Only when these fundamentals are mastered—when they have become second nature—can all the confectioner's creative inspirations come to fruition. Without that understanding and mastery, the confectioner cannot possibly be successful. A few of these essential techniques are explained and illustrated in this chapter.

TEMPERING CHOCOLATE

Chocolate to be used for enrobing or dipping—and for numerous other applications in confectionery—must be tempered prior to use. The organoleptic reason for tempering is to ensure that the chocolate sets with proper gloss and a brittle snap and does not develop bloom during storage. While the physics of chocolate tempering are complex, the actual process is simple. It can be successfully executed without any deep understanding of the theory involved, simply by following instructions for cooling, stirring, and warming.

The function of tempering is to precrystallize a small percentage of the cocoa butter, in stable Form-V crystals, so that when the remainder of the cocoa butter crystallizes, it, too, will crystallize in Form V, resulting in good contraction, gloss, snap, and shelf stability. Both the quantity and the form of precrystallization are important factors for a proper temper.

Tempering may be accomplished by any of a number of methods, but in all cases the three requisites are the same: temperature, agitation, and time. Understanding the crystallization of cocoa butter will greatly enhance the artisan confectioner's ability to consistently achieve excellent results with chocolate. Following the set of instructions given in Tempering Techniques, page 58, will enable anyone to successfully temper chocolate, with or without understanding the crystallization of fats.

LEFT: *Incorrectly tempered chocolate with spots.*
CENTER: *Incorrectly tempered chocolate with streaks.*
RIGHT: *Correctly tempered chocolate.*

POLYMORPHISM OF COCOA BUTTER

Polymorphism is the ability of a substance to crystallize in several distinctly different forms. When discussing polymorphism, carbon is often cited as the classic example: pure carbon may crystallize in one form to create graphite, a soft, black substance used for making pencils. Pure carbon may also crystallize to create diamonds, one of the hardest, most brilliant substances known. Both of these substances are composed of pure carbon, but the crystal forms are different, and because of that, the substances are vastly different. Polymorphism is a defining quality of cocoa butter: the fact that cocoa butter can crystallize in various forms is the reason chocolate must be tempered prior to use. Properly tempered chocolate crystallizes as a hard, stable, shiny substance, like diamonds.

Chocolate that is not well tempered is soft and lacks shine, like graphite. Most current research indicates that there are six forms of commonly occurring cocoa butter crystals. While it is by no means necessary to grasp all the intricacies of polymorphism in order to be able to temper and use chocolate, an understanding of the basic physics involved will help the confectioner consistently produce the best possible results and remedy problems as they arise.

In some industries it is still common practice to refer to the forms of cocoa butter crystals by their Greek symbols: α, γ, β′, β, and so on. There are, however, some discrepancies among the names given when using this system. In the interest of clarity, then, in this book a simpler, more widely recognized system of numeric terms is used to refer to the crystal forms.

CRYSTAL FORMS

Of the six forms of cocoa butter crystals, only two of them—Form V and Form VI—are considered stable. Of these two types, only Form V can be practically formed during tempering. Research indicates that Form-VI crystals can be created only by the transformation of solid Form V to solid Form VI after the chocolate has set; they cannot be formed as seed crystals. All lower forms of cocoa butter crystals are considered unstable.

Unstable Crystals

Unstable cocoa butter crystals form and melt at lower temperatures, and transform to the next higher crystal form during storage. These crystals do not fit together tightly; therefore the chocolate in which they reside does not display good contraction upon setting or exhibit the characteristic snap of well-tempered chocolate.

An unstable crystal can also transform to the next higher crystal form over time. When this transformation occurs, the result is fat bloom. The length of time required for this transformation depends on the type of crystal and on the temperature of the chocolate. The lower the form of crystal, the more unstable it is: it melts at a lower temperature and transforms more rapidly to the next-higher crystal form. Form-I crystals have a life of only minutes before they transform to Form II, while Form-IV crystals may take weeks to transform to Form V, resulting in bloom.

Polymorphism of Cocoa Butter

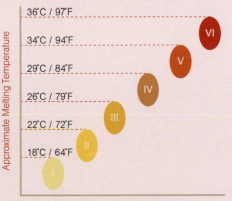

Approximate Melting Temperature

36°C / 97°F
34°C / 94°F
29°C / 84°F
26°C / 79°F
22°C / 72°F
18°C / 64°F

VI
V
IV
III
II
I

Forms of Cocoa Butter Crystals

Unstable cocoa butter crystals form and melt at lower temperatures than stable crystals do. The cooler the temperature, the more unstable the resulting crystals will be.

Temperature

Form-V cocoa butter crystals melt if the chocolate is above 34°C/94°F, so chocolate must be below this threshold in order to contain Form-V seed crystals. If the chocolate is used at a temperature below 29°C/85°F, however, it is likely to contain not only Form-V crystals but also the unstable Form-IV crystals, which can result in reduced gloss and snap and a tendency to develop bloom during storage. While the optimum temperature at which dark chocolate should be used is approximately 32°C/90°F, the reality of tempering is such that, in order to form crystals relatively quickly, the chocolate is usually cooled to well below 32°C/90°F during seeding. (See Dark Chocolate Tempering Curve, page 57.) At this reduced temperature, both stable and unstable crystals are formed. After the chocolate is adequately seeded, the unstable crystals can be melted out by warming the chocolate for use, to approximately 32°C/90°F. Of the three factors required in chocolate tempering, temperature is the most easily measured.

Agitation

Agitation promotes crystallization and is a fundamental concept for the confectioner. When making fudge or fondant, the confectioner agitates the supersaturated sugar solution constantly to promote the formation of many tiny sugar crystals. Tempering chocolate is no different, except that the crystals formed by the agitation are cocoa butter crystals. In any method used to temper chocolate, agitation plays a key role, as it results in the formation and distribution of many small cocoa butter crystals, which seed the chocolate and thus ensure proper setting and shelf life. The only way to observe whether the chocolate has been sufficiently agitated is to test a small sample of it to see if it sets quickly and without streaks.

Time

Time is the requirement for tempering chocolate that is most frequently overlooked by those with little experience. The function of time in tempering is to allow the seed crystals to form. Cocoa butter crystals do not instantly appear as soon as the chocolate is stirred at the right temperature; they require time to form.

The time that chocolate spends at the proper temperature for crystal formation during tempering is referred to as residence time. The amount of residence time required for the formation of seed crystals varies with the product (milk and white chocolates crystallize more slowly than dark chocolate does), the cocoa butter content, the temperature, and the type and amount of agitation performed. The longer the residence time at a given temperature, the more cocoa butter crystals form.

Just as it takes time for stable crystals to form for seeding, it also requires time for the unstable crystals to melt out when tempered chocolate is reheated. If, during tempering, chocolate is cooled to below 29°C/85°F, it will require not only warming to 32°C/90°F, but also residence time at that temperature to allow the unstable crystals to melt. As with agitation, the fulfillment of time in tempering chocolate can be measured only by testing a sample of the chocolate to observe if is has set properly.

Underseeding and overseeding

Proper tempering depends not only on the right type of seed crystals but also on their quantity. The ideal percentage of seed crystals present in chocolate depends somewhat on how that chocolate is to be used. Slightly more viscous chocolate may be desired for piping filigree, while thinner chocolate is required for dipping most centers. In general, the confectioner is likely to want tempered chocolate to contain the minimum percentage of cocoa butter

DARK CHOCOLATE TEMPERING CURVE

This is a typical tempering curve of the sort that might be found on the label of any block of dark chocolate. In Zone 1, the object is to melt out all cocoa butter crystals. If unmelted crystals remain in the chocolate, the viscosity of the chocolate will be increased. In Zone 2, the chocolate is cooling, but no crystals have yet been formed, as the temperature is still too high for crystallization. In Zone 3, Form-V cocoa butter crystals are being formed. While it would be possible to maintain the chocolate in this temperature zone and to continue agitation to temper it, the residence time required would be prohibitive, so it is more efficient to proceed to Zone 4. At this temperature, both unstable Form-IV and stable Form-V crystals are created. The low temperature enables rapid formation of crystals for efficient tempering. The warming that occurs in Zone 5 melts out the unstable Form-IV crystals, leaving only stable Form-V precrystallization. Zone 6 represents the temperature at which the dark chocolate should be used. It is important to remember that residence time is required not only to create crystals but also to melt the unstable crystals, in order to leave only Form-V crystals for proper tempering. It is therefore necessary not only to bring the chocolate into Zone 6 but also to hold it there for several minutes to remove the unstable crystals. The curve for milk and white chocolates would be identical, but with corresponding temperatures approximately 2°C/35°F lower than those shown above.

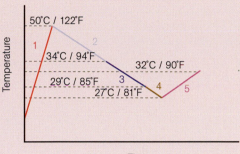

Dark Chocolate Tempering Curve

crystals necessary to promote proper setting. Research indicates that this number is very close to 1 percent of the total cocoa butter in the chocolate being precrystallized in Form V. If significantly less cocoa butter is precrystallized, there will be insufficient crystals to cause the chocolate to set evenly without forming fat bloom. If too much of the cocoa butter is precrystallized, the viscosity of the chocolate will increase, resulting in a thick coat of chocolate during enrobing, less contraction, and poor gloss and snap when the chocolate is set.

Temper meters accurately measure the degree of temper, but their cost puts them well beyond the range of most artisan confectioners, who are therefore left with no method to measure the quantity of seed crystals present other than to test the chocolate for proper setting and empirically evaluate its viscosity. Accurately determining the optimal viscosity requires experience working with the specific chocolate being used, as viscosity varies from chocolate to chocolate.

Keeping chocolate at the optimum working temperature still permits the ongoing formation of crystals, and periodic stirring accelerates this process. It is entirely possible, then, for chocolate to be at the ideal temperature, but to be overly viscous due to the presence of too many seed crystals. It is therefore necessary to remelt a portion of the existing crystals continually to prevent overseeding while the chocolate is in use. Various ways for the artisan confectioner to do this include gently warming the chocolate periodically by use of a burner, water bath, or heat gun; applying constant, gentle warmth from a low-heat source; and occasionally adding warm unseeded chocolate. In all cases, the confectioner must avoid melting too many seed crystals. If that happens, the chocolate will be underseeded, resulting in poor gloss and snap and the formation of fat bloom.

TEMPERING TECHNIQUES

On an observable level, the goal of tempering chocolate is to cause the chocolate to set rapidly, with superior gloss and hardness. This is accomplished by seeding the chocolate with the proper quantity of Form-V crystals. The artisan confectioner uses several methods to accomplish this. Each has its advantages and disadvantages.

| technique | **GENERAL TEMPERING** |

The general tempering technique involves four simple steps (see Dark Chocolate Tempering Curve, page 57).

1. Melt out all existing fat crystals.

2. Cool the chocolate, while agitating it, to a temperature at which both stable and unstable crystals form rapidly.

3. Rewarm the chocolate to melt out unstable forms, leaving only stable crystals to seed the chocolate.

4. Maintain at the proper temperature during use.

| technique | **TABLING** |

The tabling method is the most traditional, time-honored method for tempering relatively small quantities of chocolate. The tabling method has the advantage of being fast and efficient. The disadvantages of the tabling method are its requirement for a stone slab on which to work, the nearly inevitable incorporation of air bubbles, the generally higher skill level required as compared to other tempering methods such as seeding, and the practical limits on the amount of chocolate that can be tempered using the method.

1. **USING A WATER BATH, MICROWAVE, OR MELTER, MELT THE CHOCOLATE TO A SUFFICIENT TEMPERATURE TO REMOVE ALL EXISTING COCOA BUTTER CRYSTALS** (50°C/120°F for dark chocolate, 40°C/104°F for milk and white chocolates). Although melting the chocolate to this temperature is usually recommended, it is not absolutely necessary if the chocolate being melted is already tempered. Tempered chocolate contains stable cocoa butter crystals, and it is not absolutely necessary to melt them all out only to form them again. If, however, the chocolate being melted has been allowed to set in an untempered condition, it contains unstable cocoa butter crystals, and it is essential to bring the chocolate to this temperature in order to ensure that all unstable crystals have melted. This step corresponds to Zone 1 of the Dark Chocolate Tempering Curve, page 57.

2. **POUR HALF TO TWO-THIRDS OF THE MELTED CHOCOLATE ONTO A MARBLE SLAB, AND WORK THE CHOCOLATE WITH A SCRAPER AND PALETTE KNIFE UNTIL IT THICKENS SLIGHTLY.** Agitate the chocolate constantly to prevent any of it from completely solidifying and to form the requisite cocoa butter seeds. This step (illustrated in Zones 2 and 3 of the Dark Chocolate Tempering Curve) serves to create many Form-IV and -V crystals.

3. **RETURN THE THICKENED CHOCOLATE TO THE BOWL OF MELTED CHOCOLATE TO MAKE A UNIFORM MIXTURE OF THE CHOCOLATES.** This is the equivalent of Zone 4 of the Dark Chocolate Tempering Curve, wherein the unstable Form-IV crystals are melted out, leaving only stable crystals to seed the chocolate.

4. **TEST A SAMPLE OF THE CHOCOLATE TO OBSERVE IF IT SETS QUICKLY AND WITHOUT STREAKS.** If it sets properly and is at the correct temperature, it may be used. If it is too cool, it should be warmed slightly before use, and if it does not set properly, a portion of it should be tabled again.

LEFT : *Agitating the chocolate on a marble or granite slab until it thickens slightly (see step 2 of the technique).*
RIGHT: *Returning the thickened chocolate to the bowl of melted chocolate to make a uniform mixture of the chocolates (see step 3 of the technique).*

CAVEATS ON TABLING

The tabling technique is effective for relatively small quantities of chocolate and is commonly used in confectionery operations, but several precautions warrant mention:

+ Sanitation is of paramount importance in confectionery. Any surface onto which chocolate is poured must be thoroughly cleaned and sanitized. This may be accomplished by wiping with any type of sanitizing solution, such as chlorine, iodine, or alcohol, but the marble must be completely dry before pouring chocolate onto it. For drying, use clean, unused paper towels.

+ Tabling the chocolate on a marble slab for too long results in lumps of crystallized chocolate that must then be melted prior to use. This is one of the most common errors that novices make when tabling chocolate. Once the chocolate on the marble begins to thicken, the crystallization reaction proceeds quickly. Often the tabled chocolate can solidify before it can be returned to the bowl. Should the chocolate solidify on the marble, there may not be sufficient heat in the bowl to melt the solid portion, resulting in lumpy chocolate. To avoid this, do not allow the chocolate to overthicken on the marble, and return it to the bowl quickly once it is seeded.

+ If repeated tablings are required, it is advisable to table successively less chocolate each time and to leave it on the marble slab less time with each repetition. Every time the chocolate is tabled, its temperature falls, and with each successive tabling, there is less heat in the chocolate to melt out excessive and unstable crystals. When the chocolate is very warm from the melter, fully half the chocolate can be tabled until it thickens. Once it is returned to the bowl of warm chocolate, it will soften and be incorporated into the melted chocolate, leaving behind seed crystals. If the temperature of the chocolate is proper, but it is not setting properly due to insufficient seeding, as little as 200 to 250 grams/7 to 9 ounces of chocolate can be very briefly tabled and then returned to the bowl to provide the extra seed crystals that are needed.

+ When executed by inexperienced workers, the tabling method can be a messy proposition; it requires practice and experience to be executed well. Controlling melted chocolate on the marble while agitating and then returning it to the bowl requires skill if it is to remain contained. The tabling method is not the best choice for novices at chocolate work.

Seeding is a clean, efficient method of tempering chocolate in small or large quantities. The ability to temper much larger batches of chocolate than can be practically tempered by tabling is a major advantage of the seeding method. This technique relies on allowing the existing Form-V crystals in fully set chocolate to cool and seed the untempered chocolate. When tempering using the seeding technique, either small drops of chocolate, such as chips or pistoles, or a single large block may be used to cool and seed the chocolate. Each variation has its own advantages: a block may be easily removed when the chocolate is tempered, while chips cool the chocolate more rapidly. Regardless of whether the confectioner uses chips or a block, seeding, when executed properly, introduces only Form-V crystals and is therefore an excellent method for obtaining a superior temper.

1. **MELT THE CHOCOLATE TO A SUFFICIENT TEMPERATURE TO REMOVE ALL EXISTING COCOA BUTTER CRYSTALS (50°C/120°F FOR DARK CHOCOLATE, 40°C/104°F FOR MILK AND WHITE CHOCOLATES).** Although melting the chocolate to this temperature is usually recommended, it is not absolutely necessary if the chocolate being melted is already tempered. Tempered chocolate contains stable cocoa butter crystals, and it is not absolutely necessary to melt them all out only to form them again. If, however, the chocolate being melted has been allowed to set in an untempered condition, it contains unstable cocoa butter crystals, and it is essential to bring the chocolate to the temperature given above in order to ensure that all unstable crystals have melted. This step corresponds to Zone 1 of the Dark Chocolate Tempering Curve, page 57.

2. **SLOWLY ADD INCREMENTS OF SOLID TEMPERED CHOCOLATE TO COOL AND SEED THE MELTED CHOCOLATE.** The chocolate that is added may be in small pieces or a single block. This step corresponds to Zones 2 and 3 of the Dark Chocolate Tempering Curve. When using the seeding method, it is not necessary to overcool the chocolate, as it is when creating new cocoa butter crystals, although it often happens during the process, especially when a lot of seeding chocolate is added at one time.

3. **TEST A SAMPLE OF THE CHOCOLATE TO OBSERVE IF IT SETS QUICKLY AND WITHOUT STREAKS.** If it does, and if it is the correct temperature with proper viscosity and is free of unmelted pieces, it may be used. If it does not set quickly, or sets with streaks, more seed should be incorporated and stirred in. If the chocolate is too cool or contains pieces of unmelted seed chocolate, it must

be warmed to the correct temperature and the pieces melted out prior to use. Whenever the chocolate has been warmed, it must be retested to verify that it is still tempered.

Adding solid tempered chocolate to cool and seed the melted chocolate (see step 2 of the technique).

CAVEATS ON SEEDING

✦ Either small pieces of seed chocolate, such as pistoles, or larger pieces may be used. The smaller pieces cool and seed the chocolate faster, but the larger pieces have the advantage of easy removal after tempering. Regardless of which form of chocolate is used for seeding, it should be tempered chocolate. If untempered chocolate is used as seed in this technique, it will precrystallize the chocolate with unstable cocoa butter crystals, resulting in an inferior shine and snap and the formation of bloom during storage.

✦ If you are not using a single block, take care how much of the seed chocolate is added at any one time. When the bowl of chocolate is very warm directly from the melter, much more seed chocolate can be added at a time because the heat in the bowl of melted chocolate will melt all of the seeds. As the melted chocolate cools, however, less of the seed chocolate will melt and the danger of leaving unmelted chunks of chocolate in the bowl increases. When the temperature of the bowl of chocolate falls below about 32°C/90°F, seed chocolate is very slow to melt. At this temperature, if more seeding is required to temper the chocolate, very few pieces of seed chocolate should be added to provide the additional precrystallization that is required without leaving lumps in the bowl.

✦ It is not necessary to cool the chocolate much below 32°C/90°F when using the seeding method. Another major advantage of the seed method is that when performed properly, it introduces only Form-V crystals. Often during tempering, however, the temperature of the chocolate falls to a lower temperature than desired. If the temperature of the chocolate is too low, if the chocolate is overseeded, or if unmelted pieces of chocolate remain in the bowl, the chocolate must be carefully warmed. The chocolate may be warmed over a water bath, flashed on direct heat briefly, or heated in a microwave. Regardless of the method used to warm the chocolate, it must never exceed its maximum working temperature (32°C/90°F for dark chocolate; 30°C/86°F for milk or white chocolate) or the seed crystals will melt and the temper will be lost. After chocolate has been warmed, it should always be tested to verify that it is still in temper.

Using a microwave or warm water bath to melt and temper chocolate is also an acceptable method when small quantities are involved. Using this technique, about 80 percent of the chopped chocolate is melted, observing the usual precautions for exposure to heat and moisture. The bowl is then removed from the heat and the chocolate stirred. The unmelted pieces in the bowl become the seed chocolate, cooling and seeding the melted chocolate. This method is no different from the seeding method, except that it relies on incompletely melting out the stable crystals in the unmelted chocolate and using them to seed the melted portion of the chocolate.

1. **TEMPERED CHOCOLATE SHOULD ALWAYS BE USED FOR THIS TECHNIQUE TO ENSURE THAT THE CHOCOLATE IS PRECRYSTALLIZED WITH STABLE COCOA BUTTER CRYSTALS.** If untempered chocolate is used, it will precrystallize the chocolate with unstable cocoa butter crystals, resulting in an inferior shine, snap, and the formation of bloom during storage. Chop the chocolate to be melted finely so that it melts evenly without overheating. This step may be omitted if chips or pistoles are used.

2. **MELT APPROXIMATELY 80 PERCENT OF THE CHOCOLATE, USING EITHER A WARM WATER BATH OR SHORT APPLICATIONS OF MICROWAVE ENERGY.** When using a microwave, stir between each application. When melting the chocolate, do not allow the temperature of the melted chocolate to exceed about 36°C/97°F. Heating the chocolate significantly above this temperature will cause all of the remaining chocolate to completely melt, leaving behind no seed crystals.

3. **STIR TO INCORPORATE THE UNMELTED CHOCOLATE AND TO SEED THE MELTED CHOCOLATE WITH STABLE CRYSTALS.** The unmelted, tempered chocolate will cool the melted chocolate to the proper temperature zone and seed it with stable cocoa butter crystals, just as seeding chocolate does in the seeding method.

4. **TEST A SAMPLE OF THE CHOCOLATE TO OBSERVE WHETHER IT SETS QUICKLY AND WITHOUT STREAKS.** If it does, and if it is the correct temperature and viscosity and free of unmelted pieces, it may be used. If it does not set properly, it should be stirred more and retested for temper. If it does not set properly and all of the unmelted chocolate has melted, additional seed should be incorporated. If the chocolate is too cool, or if it contains pieces of unmelted seed chocolate, it must be warmed to the correct temperature and the pieces melted out prior to use. As always, it is imperative to test the chocolate after heating to verify that it is still tempered.

Water bath

It is possible to use a cool water bath to accomplish the cooling and seeding that occurs in Zones 2 and 3 of the Dark Chocolate Tempering Curve (see page 57). In order for this method to be effective, however, the chocolate should be in a round bowl to prevent it from solidifying in corners, as it would in a square or rectangular container. It is also of utmost importance that the water temperature remain above 26°C/78°F. The use of cold water or ice will create an abundance of Form-III and lower-level crystals, which can result in poor gloss, inferior snap, and the formation of bloom during storage. Since it is vitally important to return the chocolate to 32°C/90°F (for dark chocolate), and to keep it there for some time to allow the unstable crystals to melt out and transform to Form-V crystals, any time saved by using cold water is lost.

Tempering machines

A variety of tempering machines are available to confectioners. They range from very small tabletop models, which temper only about 900 grams/2 pounds of chocolate at a time, to very large machines suited to running enrobing lines. Most of these machines operate on the basic principles outlined in the Dark Chocolate Tempering Curve on page 57 and employ various methods to cool and agitate the chocolate during tempering and holding. When choosing a tempering machine, the confectioner should consider the volume of chocolate required, the relative speed of the machine, and its capacity to hold and maintain tempered chocolate.

CAVEATS ON INCOMPLETE MELTING

Always begin this technique with tempered chocolate so that the seed crystals left behind as the chocolate melts are stable crystals. Previously used chocolate that has set in an untempered state is not acceptable for this method because it will seed the chocolate with unstable crystals.

◆ As always when melting chocolate, the pieces should be small to ensure even melting without the risk of overheating. Small pieces of chocolate have the additional advantage of cooling and seeding the melted chocolate quickly once it is removed from the heat.

◆ When using a microwave, take care not to overheat the chocolate. Microwave ovens do not heat evenly, and long exposure without stirring will overheat the chocolate in some areas while leaving it unmelted in others. Always use short intervals in the microwave, and stir between exposures to equalize the temperature.

◆ Do not warm the chocolate much over 36°C/97°F during melting. Warming the melted chocolate past this temperature will melt all of the chocolate without leaving the requisite seed crystals to temper the chocolate. Should this happen, the chocolate will have to be tempered by another method— either by adding more seeding chocolate or by tabling.

◆ It is not necessary to cool the chocolate much below 32°C/90°F. A major advantage of incomplete melting is that when performed properly, it introduces only Form-V crystals from the unmelted tempered chocolate. Often during tempering, however, the temperature of the chocolate falls below the desired temperature. If the temperature of the chocolate is too low, or the chocolate is overseeded, or there are unmelted pieces of chocolate remaining in the bowl, the chocolate must be carefully warmed. The chocolate may be warmed over a water bath, flashed on direct heat briefly, or heated in a microwave. Regardless of the method used to warm the chocolate, it must never exceed its maximum working temperature (32°C/90°F for dark chocolate; 30°C/86°F for milk or white chocolate) or the seed crystals will melt and the temper will be lost. After warming chocolate, it should always be tested to verify that it is still in temper.

CHOCOLATE TEMPERING TROUBLESHOOTING

DEFECT	CAUSE	REMEDY
BLOOM, IN THE FORM OF STREAKS, SPOTS, OR GRAY CAST OCCURS WHEN CHOCOLATE SETS	Chocolate is undertempered	Seed chocolate more by agitation, adding seed chocolate, or tabling; test chocolate prior to use
BLOOM OCCURS DURING STORAGE	Chocolate is seeded with unstable crystals	Warm chocolate to proper temperature before using
	Chocolate is exposed to humidity, causing sugar bloom	Store chocolate in less humid environment
	Chocolate is exposed to heat, causing fat bloom	Store chocolate at proper temperature
CHOCOLATE SETS WITHOUT GLOSS AND WITH POOR SNAP	Undertempered chocolate	Seed chocolate more by agitation, adding seed chocolate, or tabling; test chocolate prior to use
	Chocolate seeded with unstable crystals	Warm chocolate to proper temperature before using
	Chocolate set in cold environment	Allow chocolate to crystallize at proper temperature

Note: All defects and remedies assume the proper ambient temperature for working with chocolate.

THINNING CHOCOLATE

There are times when it is advantageous to reduce the viscosity of the chocolate used for coating centers—for example, when a piped piece or a center with a nut or other garnish is meant to be plainly visible after the center has been dipped.

technique	theory	THINNING

When thinned chocolate is desired, melted cocoa butter can be added to reduce the viscosity and create a thinner shell. Cocoa butter should never be added to chocolate to make up for poor handling technique or overseeded chocolate.

1. **BEGIN WITH MELTED, UNTEMPERED CHOCOLATE AND MELTED, UNTEMPERED COCOA BUTTER.** By beginning with untempered chocolate and cocoa butter, the confectioner is better able to accurately judge the viscosity. If the chocolate is tempered, the degree to which it is seeded will affect viscosity, and it will be more difficult to achieve precisely the desired results.

2. **ADD THE COCOA BUTTER TO THE CHOCOLATE UNTIL THE DESIRED DEGREE OF VISCOSITY IS ACHIEVED.** The exact amount of cocoa butter to add varies widely depending on the initial viscosity of the chocolate and the desired final viscosity. A good general rule is to add a quantity of cocoa butter that is between 10 and 15 percent of the weight of the chocolate, but this is only a guideline. When it is properly tempered, chocolate will thicken only slightly, so there is no need to thin it substantially more than the viscosity at which it will be used.

3. **TEMPER THE CHOCOLATE BY ANY OF THE USUAL TECHNIQUES AND USE THE CHOCOLATE AS USUAL.** Chocolate with cocoa butter added to it tempers in essentially the same way as unthinned chocolate. The only noticeable difference is that when tabled on a stone, thinned chocolate tends to run very quickly, so care must be taken not to put too much on the stone at one time. When tempering by the seeding method, the viscosity will increase slightly due to the unthinned chocolate that is being incorporated.

4. **STORE SEPARATELY FROM UNTHINNED CHOCOLATE.** Thinned chocolate should not be added back to unthinned melted chocolate. Not only will it reduce the chocolate's viscosity and raise its cost, but the increased fat content could cause formulation difficulties, such as separated emulsions.

SLABBING

Slabbing is the process of creating a layer of chocolate of uniform thickness that can be precoated, cut, and dipped or enrobed. As with examples throughout this book, the confectioner uses metal bars to create a frame, which is then filled with the material that will be the center. The advantage of using bars, rather than other types of frames, is that they can be adjusted to fit different batch sizes.

Centers should always be slabbed on material such as parchment paper or plastic sheets, to facilitate handling and release after setting. Properly slabbed centers should be the same thickness as the frame enclosing them and should have a smooth surface.

With bars as a guide, layers are slabbed to a uniform thickness for later precoating, cutting, dipping, or enrobing.

PRECOATING (BOTTOMING)

Precoating a layer of soft caramel with chocolate will increase the center's shelf life and make it easier to handle as it is enrobed.

Precoating centers performs two vital roles: it makes the centers easier to handle, and it prolongs the shelf life of the finished product. Precoating a slab is also known as "bottoming," because it is always the bottom of the piece that is coated. Precoated centers are easier to handle because the bottom coat prevents a soft center such as ganache from sticking to the dipping fork, and it helps the center hold its shape. In addition, the product's shelf life is improved because the bottom coat prevents the center from settling through the chocolate before it sets, leaving a vector for moisture migration and allowing for exposure to oxygen. Moisture migration can cause drying, crystallization, and spoilage. Exposure to oxygen contributes to rancidity.

Before cutting a slab, the confectioner coats the entire bottom surface of it with a thin layer of tempered chocolate. Precoating truffles is simply a matter of applying by hand a thin coat of tempered chocolate to the entire surface of the center. Automated enrobers usually have a bottoming function that coats the bottoms of centers before they are enrobed.

CUTTING WITH A GUITAR

The guitar, or confectionery cutter, is the most efficient and accurate way to cut many soft slabbed centers. The guitar will cut jellies, ganache, marzipan, and gianduja; it will not cut caramels, most nougats, or other firm centers. Before being cut on the guitar, the centers must first be precoated to facilitate handling. The slab is transported and handled using the stainless-steel sheet provided with the guitar. For soft centers such as ganache, the slab is lined up on the near side of the guitar base. For harder slabs such as gianduja, the slab is positioned near the top of the base and held in place manually during cutting. Steady, consistent pressure is the key to cutting centers cleanly without breaking the guitar strings.

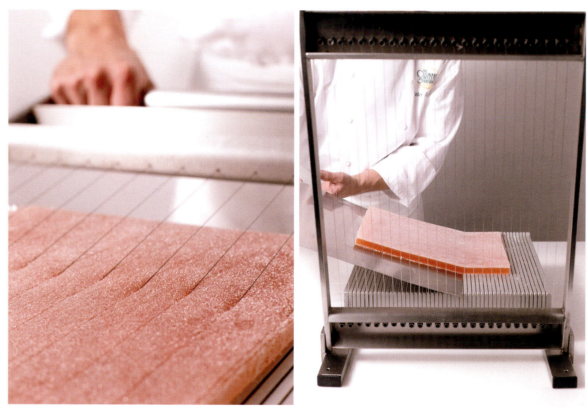

LEFT: *Jellies are cut with a guitar, or confectionery cutter, to ensure consistency in portion size.*
RIGHT: *Using the metal sheet that comes with the guitar, layers can be repositioned for a second cut, making them into small squares.*

DIPPING

Setting up a dipping station for ergonomics and efficiency is the first step in hand-dipping chocolates. For a right-handed confectioner, the work should progress from left to right (vice versa for a left-handed confectioner). The bowl of chocolate should be placed in the center and tipped toward the confectioner. This brings the chocolate to the edge of the bowl so that the fork can be held level, preventing the center from falling during dipping. Once dipped, the centers are placed on a receiving tray, beginning on the side farthest away from the confectioner. This keeps the confectioner from dripping chocolate on pieces that have already been dipped. Care must be taken during dipping to avoid defects such as air bubbles and feet. Maintaining the chocolate at its proper temperature and viscosity during dipping helps to prevent these problems. At the time of dipping, various finishing techniques may be employed, including marking confections with the dipping fork, garnishing their tops, and using a transfer sheet or textured plastic. After the chocolate has set, the confections may be decorated with a piped filigree or sprayed effect.

The front of the dipped confection is placed on the tray and the fork is slid out from under it.

When centers are hand-dipped, and therefore not run through the cooling tunnel of an enrober, they should be allowed to crystallize for 24 hours before any attempt is made to handle them. Although tempered chocolate sets quickly, it continues to crystallize for at least 48 hours after it first sets, becoming much harder in the process. If chocolates are handled immediately after setting, they will almost certainly incur damage that will result in diminished shine or the formation of fat bloom. Either condition will render the confections unmarketable.

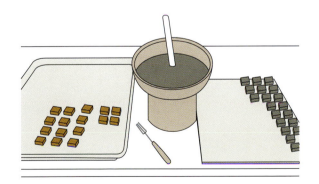

For a right-handed worker, work flows from left to right.

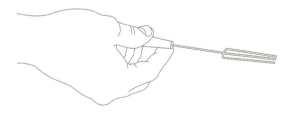

How to hold a dipping fork.

CRYSTALLIZING CENTERS

The process of crystallizing centers is a simple technique that adds yet another dimension to a confectioner's repertoire. It is most commonly used for ganache centers and candied fruit, but it could just as easily and effectively be applied to any number of confectionery centers like gianduja, butter ganache, and marzipan. The process itself involves little more than cooking a syrup to the proper density, allowing it to cool, and then immersing the desired centers in the syrup overnight so that a thin skin of crystals forms on the outside of the centers. The crystalline skin acts very much like a covering of chocolate might; it prevents moisture migration and exposure to oxygen, while adding visual and textural interest.

TOP, LEFT: *Ganache is piped into rosettes.* RIGHT: *The rosettes are placed on an icing screen in a crystallizing tray.*

BOTTOM, LEFT: *Cooled syrup is poured over the rosettes.* RIGHT: *After soaking in the syrup, the rosettes are placed on an icing screen to dry.*

1. **BOIL THE SUGAR AND WATER TO 72° BRIX. BRUSH THE SIDES OF THE POT WELL DURING COOKING.** Higher sugar concentrations will result in more, but smaller crystals. The syrup contains no doctoring agent because the object is for it to crystallize. The density of the syrup must be above 67° Brix, since that is the saturation point for sucrose at room temperature, and the solution must be supersaturated in order to crystallize. If the syrup is boiled to a higher density, it will crystallize too rapidly, creating an excessively heavy crystal coating, one that coats all the surfaces in the container as well as the centers. Good sugar-cooking technique is imperative to prevent premature crystallization, and removing sugar crystals from the sides of the pot is the most crucial step in controlling the process (see page 269).

2. **COVER THE SYRUP WITH A WET CLOTH, AND LEAVE UNDISTURBED UNTIL COOLED TO 21°C/70°F.** The syrup must cool to below the melting point of the center, which is often ganache. As it cools, it becomes supersaturated. It must not be agitated so as not to crystallize the syrup prematurely. The wet cloth over the syrup creates a high humidity microclimate over the syrup, helping to prevent the formation of crystals on the surface due to the evaporation of water.

3. **IF SUGAR CRYSTALS FORM ON THE SURFACE OF THE SYRUP WHILE IT IS COOLING, DISSOLVE THEM BY FLOATING A THIN FILM OF COOL WATER ON THE SURFACE OF THE SYRUP.** In spite of the wet towel, the syrup frequently begins to crystallize on the surface. If left unchecked, these crystals can seed the syrup, setting off premature and uneven crystallization of the sugar. When water is sprinkled onto the heavy syrup, it forms a film on the surface, dissolving any existing crystals and preventing the formation of new ones.

4. **PLACE THE CENTERS BETWEEN SCREENS IN A CANDYING PAN, AND GENTLY POUR THE COOLED SYRUP OVER THEM UNTIL THEY ARE COMPLETELY IMMERSED. COVER, AND LEAVE UNDISTURBED AT ROOM TEMPERATURE FOR APPROXIMATELY 15 HOURS.** The screens will allow the syrup to contact all sides of centers so that they will crystallize all the way around, protecting the entire center from future moisture migration. In addition, the screens prevent the centers from either sinking to the bottom of the tray or floating to the top of the syrup. Approximately 15 hours is required for the sugar to crystallize to the desired thickness on the centers. It is important not to agitate the tray during this time so that the sugar crystallizes evenly.

5. **REMOVE THE CENTERS FROM THE SYRUP, AND ALLOW THEM TO DRY ON AN ICING SCREEN AT ROOM TEMPERATURE FOR 24 HOURS.** Leave the centers on one of the screens so that the excess syrup can drain off. Overnight drying ensures that the crystalline shell is strong and crisp.

6. **THE SYRUP MAY BE REBOILED AND REUSED.** The syrup may be reused repeatedly as long as it is kept clean and is returned to 72° Brix before each use. After several uses, however, inversion will make the syrup unusable for this technique.

BASIC FORMULA FOR CRYSTALLIZING SYRUP:

3500 g/7.7 lb sugar

1500 g/3.3 lb water

METHOD:

Boil the sugar and water together following the sugar-cooking technique on page 219. Adjust the density of the finished syrup to 72° Brix using a refractometer.

PANNING

Panning is the process of placing centers in a rotating drum to build even layers of chocolate or sugar on them. There are three general types of panning—soft-sugar panning, used to coat jellybeans; hard-sugar panning, to make jawbreakers and Jordan almonds; and chocolate panning, for chocolate-covered nuts and dried fruit. On a dollar-per-hour return basis, most

TOP, LEFT: *Chocolate buildup inside the machine.* RIGHT: *Precoating nuts with polish and cocoa powder to prevent fat migration (see step 4 of the technique).*

BOTTOM, LEFT: *Chocolate is added during the engrossing step (see step 5 of the technique).*
RIGHT: *Polish is added to create shine (see step 8 of the technique).*

A small tabletop panning machine with attached blower.

artisan confectioners would find neither soft- nor hard-sugar panning economically viable options; so only chocolate panning will be considered here.

Although chocolate panning is time consuming, the batch size is usually large enough that it is, in reality, one of the most efficient ways for the artisan to produce prodigious volumes of product. Since the size of the batch does not directly influence the time required to produce it, larger pans are much more efficient than smaller ones, and so, when buying equipment, the largest pan practical should always be the choice. Although panning requires an investment in both machinery and climate control, it is not difficult to become proficient at the art, and, with a little practice and the right environmental conditions, anyone who works with chocolate regularly can turn out hundreds of pounds of attractive finished product in just a few hours.

Panning is a confectionery art in and of itself. Even in large-scale manufacturing, panning is still carried out by skilled workers, seldom by automation. The variables involved in panning are many, and, as with any craft, practice is the key to success. Although truly excellent panning requires patience and practice, it is well within the reach of artisan confectioners to make good-quality products in their first few attempts, and repeated efforts will pay off with increasing perfection.

For an illustrated guide to the setup of a small panning operation, see Appendix B, page 517.

---

technique | theory | **CHOCOLATE PANNING**

1. **WORK AT OPTIMAL TEMPERATURE/HUMIDITY LEVELS.** Chocolate panning requires specific environmental conditions, namely a room temperature of 13° to 16°C/55° to 60°F and relative humidity below 60 percent. Without these conditions, it is difficult to obtain good results. A room that is too warm allows excessive heat to build up in the pan, slowing the process, causing bare spots on the centers or preventing the chocolate from setting completely. A room that is too cold causes the chocolate to have a rough finish or to flake off during engrossing and causes an excessive number of doubles or clusters. Excessive humidity prevents polishes and glazes from developing and maintaining the proper shine and in extreme cases can lead to sugar bloom on chocolate. The temperature and humidity of the room must always be maintained within the proper parameters to achieve the desired results.

2. **SELECT THE PROPER CENTERS TO PAN.** Centers to be chocolate panned are most frequently either roasted nuts or dried fruits, although a range of solid centers may be used, including caramels, fondants, and jellies. The rounder and more uniform the center, the easier it is to obtain a smooth finished product; hazelnuts will result in a smooth finish with few doubles much more easily than dried cranberries will because the nuts are rounder and smoother to begin with. The most common cause of the formation of doubles or clusters during panning is centers that are not round. Peanut halves, dried cranberries, or whole coffee beans will

always have a tendency to join together because they each have a flat side, which naturally conjoins with other centers. When panning dried fruit, the moisture content must be sufficiently low to prevent the fruit from softening during the panning process. While it is not impossible to pan non-round centers with irregular surfaces, it is more difficult than panning round, regular-surfaced ones.

3. **USE CENTERS AT PANNING-ROOM TEMPERATURE.** Centers to be panned should be at the same temperature as the panning room. Cold centers causes flaking, formation of doubles, and a rough coat, just as an excessively cold room does. Warm centers cause bare spots and slow the engrossing process, much like a panning room that is too warm. Storing the centers in the panning room overnight before panning ensures that they are at the correct temperature for the process.

4. **PRECOAT THE CENTERS.** Load the centers into the pan, start rotation at 25 rpm, and apply a thin precoating of a gum or starch solution. Panning polish is often used for this step. Once the centers are moistened with the polish, apply a dusting of cocoa powder and/or confec-

tioners' sugar. The moist polish will affix the dry powder to the centers. The more irregular the centers are, the more heavily they should be precoated to fill in irregularities. Precoating reduces the incidence of fat migration from nuts (see Fat Migration, page 410), improves adhesion of the chocolate, and fills irregularities in the centers—thus reducing the time and amount of chocolate required to complete the process—resulting in a smoother finish.

5. **ENGROSS THE CENTERS.** Engrossing is the process of rapidly building up layers of chocolate on the centers by adding many charges of chocolate to the centers as they cascade in the rotating pan. To engross the centers with chocolate, rotate the pan at about 25 rpm, and ladle untempered chocolate (at approximately 32° to 35°C/90° to 95°F) into the pan in small increments. The exact amount of chocolate to add depends on the size of the batch and the size of the individual centers being panned. As a rule, enough chocolate should be added with each charge to lightly cover all of the centers with a thin, fresh coat of chocolate. Adding too much chocolate in charges increases the incidence of doubles. Allow each new addition of chocolate to set

LEFT: *Cold air creates a rough exterior (see step 1 of the technique).* CENTER: *Doubles or multiples are caused by adding chocolate too quickly (see step 5 of the technique).* RIGHT: *Polishing unsmoothed centers creates a rough exterior (see step 6 of the technique).*

on the centers before adding the next; this typically takes 3 to 5 minutes; setting is complete when the centers begin tumbling freely in the pan. During this time, cool air from the panning room should be blown into the pan to dissipate built-up heat and accelerate the crystallization of the chocolate.

The total amount of chocolate used depends on the desired results and the variety of centers used. Chocolate-panned coffee beans may require 4 or 5 parts chocolate to 1 part beans, while nuts may use as little as 1 part chocolate to 1 part nuts. Panned centers most commonly use chocolate in the range of two times the weight of the centers. It is always easier to obtain a smooth finish using more chocolate rather than less. At the end of engrossing, the centers should be entirely coated but have a slightly irregular texture on their surface.

(continued)

TOP, LEFT: *Properly precoated hazelnuts.* RIGHT: *Properly engrossed hazelnuts ready for smoothing.*

BOTTOM, LEFT: *Smoothed hazelnuts ready for polishing.* RIGHT: *Well-panned and finished hazelnuts.*

6. **SMOOTH THE ENGROSSED CONFECTIONS.** Once the centers are engrossed, they may be smoothed by adding more charges of warm chocolate without the addition of air, which permits heat to build up in the pan, softening the chocolate on the centers. Some pans have lids that help to hold heat in during the smoothing process. As the softened chocolate cascades in the pan, the tumbling action eliminates the irregularities that have formed on the surfaces during engrossing, resulting in a smooth, regular surface that will provide a uniform, high-gloss finish with no unpolished crevices. The important role smoothing plays in the final appearance of panned confections cannot be overstated. Centers that have not been adequately smoothed will not accept polish and glaze uniformly, will be covered with unpolished valleys, and will never achieve the desired appearance. Properly smoothed centers can be identified by a simple test: take one or two of the centers in the hand, and exhale deeply onto them to fog them. The appearance of the fogged centers approximates how they will look when polished; if irregularities are present, the centers should be smoothed further until all irregularities are eliminated.

7. **ALLOW THE CONFECTIONS TO HARDEN.** Once the centers are coated and smooth, they should be placed on trays in a cool area overnight to allow the chocolate to further crystallize, so that it is well hardened for polishing. Properly hardened centers will maintain their shape and smoothness during the polishing and glazing process.

8. **FINISH BY POLISHING.** Polishing is accomplished at a lower speed of the panning machine (18 to 20 rpm). Add a small quantity of polishing agent, usually a gum-arabic product, and tumble the centers while cool air is blown into the pan. To remove imperfections, apply several coats of polish. Continue this low-speed tumbling action of the rotating pan until the products are buffed to a high shine.

Because the polishing agent is water soluble, the shine developed by polishing will be destroyed by humidity if it is not protected by a glaze. The glaze used in panning is usually shellac based and is applied in a similar manner to the polish, but without the addition of air. Once the shellac is distributed over the centers, shut off the machine, rotating it only briefly (jogging it) every 1 to 3 minutes until the shellac has dried. Then run the pan slowly for a final few minutes to buff out any "kiss marks," where the candies have touched.

If a shiny finish is not desired, cocoa powder or confectioners' sugar may be applied in lieu of the polish and glaze. This finish saves labor and produces a more rustic-looking product.

Panning setup

A panned-goods operation is relatively simple to set up; there are not many discrete steps to the process, and therefore not many work stations are required. A panning operation does not have the linear flow of an enrobing process, but it does present a great opportunity for customers to view a very active process with lots of motion. Running two or more pans maximizes the efficiency of the operation by minimizing the amount of time that the operator is inactive, waiting for chocolate, polish, or glaze to be ready for another coat.

The racks are used mainly to tray engrossed products overnight, allowing them to crystallize and harden prior to polishing and glazing. The work tables are useful for scaling, blending panned mixtures, preparing chocolate for melting, and so on. All toasting of nut centers occurs outside of the panning room, which must be closely climate controlled.

PANNED CHOCOLATES DEFECTS

DEFECT	CAUSE	REMEDY
UNEVEN CHOCOLATE COATING	Air too cold during engrossing	Maintain panning-room temperature of 15° to 18°C/59° to 64°F
	Inadequate smoothing	Smooth without blowing air into pan; allow to tumble until properly smoothed
BARE SPOTS	Chocolate too warm	Centers should be at panning-room temperature
	Centers not adequately precoated	Seal centers with gum solution and precoat with sugar and cocoa powder mixture to ensure chocolate adhesion
	Centers have sharp edges or points	Select smooth-edged centers
CHOCOLATE FLAKING OFF DURING ENGROSSING	Soft centers	Precoat centers with sugar and allow to dry overnight before panning
	Cold centers	Keep centers at panning-room temperature
	Oily centers	Seal centers with gum solution and precoat with sugar and cocoa powder mixture to ensure chocolate adhesion
CENTERS STICKING TOGETHER, CREATING "DOUBLES"	Cold centers	Keep centers at panning-room temperature
	Concave surfaces on centers	Select centers with even surfaces
POOR SHINE AFTER POLISHING	Excessive humidity	Maintain humidity below 55% while polishing
	Rough surface	Smooth products more before polishing
	Insufficient polish	Apply more coats of polish, drying between coats
SHINE THAT DIMINISHES AFTER POLISHING AND GLAZING	Insufficient drying of polish before applying glaze	Allow polish to dry thoroughly before glazing
	Excessive humidity before glaze cures	Maintain relative humidity lower than 50% for 24 hours after glazing

SHELL MOLDING

Shell molding allows the confectioner to create chocolates with a high-gloss finish and uniformity unequaled by those produced using any other method. Because the chocolate shell is produced first and is then filled, fillings for these confections can be softer than the centers for dipping or enrobing can be. As a result, there is great potential to create a delightful textural contrast between the crisp shell and a soft filling. In addition, with a little extra effort, many eye-catching special effects can be efficiently created using molds. It is small wonder that shell-molded confections are so popular.

Shell molding may be totally manual, partially machine assisted, or fully automated, depending on the quantity of confections being produced. Artisan confectioners are likely to use manual methods of production, perhaps along with limited use of machinery to increase efficiency, as opposed to using the fully automated production lines favored by manufacturers. Regardless of the degree of mechanization, the fundamentals of shell molding remain constant.

Types of chocolate molds

Chocolate molds vary not only by design, size, and cost, but also by the material from which they are made. Molds may be made of metal or different types of plastics. Each type suits a particular production need and budget. All molds must be carefully used and cared for, as even minor scratches can ruin the look of a finished confection.

METAL MOLDS

For many years chocolate molds were all made of steel and lined with a thin coating of tin to protect them from rust and to provide a shiny surface for molding. These molds are not commonly made or used now; they have been replaced by lighter, less expensive plastics. Metal molds, including antique molds, can still be used to produce excellent-quality products, provided the interior of the mold is in good condition. When evaluating metal molds for use, look closely at the interior surface, inspecting it for scratches, dents, rust, pits, and cracks. Chocolate makes a mirror image of the surface it sets on. If the interior of the mold is shiny and smooth, the chocolate that comes out of it will also be shiny and smooth. If the interior of the mold is pitted, dull, or scratched, the chocolate that comes from it will also have a poor appearance. Metal molds have accrued value as collectibles, so their cost is inflated as compared to modern plastic alternatives. For production purposes, metal molds are not usually worth the price.

POLYCARBONATE MOLDS

Injection-formed polycarbonate molds are the state-of-the-art chocolate molds for today's production needs. They offer several advantages over metal molds, including lower cost, lighter weight, transparency, superior shine, and ease of use. Molds made from this material are extremely durable; they last indefinitely provided they are properly cared for. Polycarbonate molds may be transparent or translucent. In either case, the ability to see the chocolate as it contracts from the mold is a convenience for the confectioner, who must determine if the chocolate has contracted enough to be removed from the mold. Polycarbonate molds are available in a wide variety of styles, some modern and some made from actual antique metal molds, thereby coupling convenience and durability with traditional design.

OTHER PLASTIC MOLDS

Inexpensive thin plastic molds that are virtually disposable are also available. These molds are capable of turning out good-quality chocolates, but they are not durable and are not well suited to repeated use in a production setting. If one of these molds is needed for a special occasion, and is not likely to be used frequently, it is worthy of consideration. Inexpensive chocolate molds are also ideal for casting plaster imprinters for starch molding. (See Starch-Molding Technique and Theory, page 90.)

Regardless of what material the mold is made from, the technique for creating shell-molded confections is essentially the same: the prepared molds are filled completely with tempered chocolate, vibrated, and allowed to set for several minutes. The molds are then inverted to remove all of the chocolate except for the shell. This shell becomes the outside of the confection. The method described is for a completely manual procedure, but each step in this procedure also occurs in automated shell molding.

1. **CLEAN, DRY, AND POLISH THE MOLDS.** In order to obtain smooth, high-gloss chocolates from molds, they must be polished with a soft cloth to remove water spots, fats, and other defects that could affect the finish of the chocolate. Molds should be polished after each washing, but they need not be polished between uses, when they have not been washed.

2. **WARM THE MOLDS TO 25° TO 28°C/77° TO 82°F.** Warming the molds helps to prevent the chocolate from setting too quickly and unevenly when the molds are filled. Chocolate that cools rapidly in cold molds is very likely to trap air bubbles, which leave cavities in the chocolate's surface, and to exhibit uneven cooling spots upon unmolding. While it is desirable to warm the molds prior to filling them, warming them above 32°C/90°F is likely to take the chocolate out of temper. This makes it difficult to remove the chocolate from the molds and results in the formation of bloom.

3. **USE OPTIMALLY TEMPERED CHOCOLATE.** Successful use of chocolate molds depends on the contraction of tempered chocolate as it sets. Without sufficient contraction, the chocolate will not pull away from the molds, allowing for easy removal. Chocolate that is optimally tempered is neither overseeded nor underseeded. (For more information, see page 57.) Underseeded chocolate does not contain enough seed crystals to cause the chocolate to crystallize uniformly or to contract and thus pull away from the inside of the molds. Overseeded chocolate contains too much precrystallized cocoa butter, which has already contracted in the bowl, and will therefore not shrink sufficiently inside the molds to permit easy removal. The chocolate for shell molding should also be very close to its maximum working temperature to ensure optimal shine and contraction upon setting.

4. **APPLY DECORATIVE EFFECTS, IF DESIRED.** When using colored cocoa butter or a contrasting chocolate, apply them prior to adding the chocolate in step 5 (see page 83). (For decorative molding techniques, see pages 81–85.)

5. **LADLE OR DEPOSIT CHOCOLATE IN THE MOLDS.** Remove excess chocolate from the tops of the molds using a scraper or palette knife. The mold cavities must be filled to the tops with the tempered chocolate. In most artisan operations, this is accomplished by hand-ladling the chocolate over the molds to fill the cavities. Some operations use a metered filling machine to fill molds quickly and cleanly. Once the molds are filled, scrape the excess chocolate from the tops immediately, leaving the mold cavities filled evenly to the top.

6. **VIBRATE THE MOLDS AGGRESSIVELY ON A TABLE.** Vibrating the molds on a tabletop removes any air that may have become trapped. If not released, the air will mar the surface of the finished confection. In addition, vibration brings the chocolate into firm contact with the molds, resulting in optimal shine.

7. **KEEP THE FILLED MOLDS UPRIGHT AT ROOM TEMPERATURE.** Allowing the chocolate to sit in the filled molds for a few minutes allows a shell of chocolate to form inside the molds; the longer the molds sit, the thicker the shell will be. How long the molds sit depends on many factors, such as the ambient temperature, viscosity of the chocolate, size and shape of the molds, and shell thickness desired. The usual length of time is from 2 to 5 minutes. Once the setting time for the molds has been determined, it can be repeated from batch to batch to produce many shells of uniform thickness. In general, it is desirable to have a thin, delicate shell of chocolate surrounding a filling. A shell that is too thin, however, will be prone to breakage and will not produce sufficient contraction to allow the product to pull away from the molds.

8. **INVERT THE MOLDS OVER A BOWL TO REMOVE THE EXCESS CHOCOLATE.** Tap them with a wooden dowel to more thoroughly remove the chocolate, creating a thinner shell. Once the chocolate shell has formed, the excess chocolate is drained from the molds, leaving only the chocolate lining. Tapping the molds lightly with a wooden dowel removes more of the chocolate and results in thinner, more uniform shells.

9. **SCRAPE EXCESS CHOCOLATE OFF THE TOPS OF THE MOLDS.** Scrape to remove excess chocolate and to leave clean, uniform edges on the chocolate lining.

LEFT: *Ladle or deposit chocolate into clean, dry, polished molds, making sure to fill them to capacity (see step 5 of the technique).*
CENTER: *Remove the excess chocolate from the tops of the molds using a scraper or palette knife (see step 5 of the technique).*
RIGHT: *Vibrate the molds against a hard surface to remove any air pockets in the chocolate (see step 6 of the technique).*

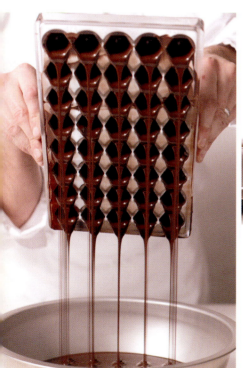

LEFT: *Invert the molds over a bowl to drain off the excess chocolate. This creates a thin outer shell (see step 8 of the technique).* CENTER: *Elevate the inverted molds slightly and allow the shells to set (see step 10 of the technique).* RIGHT: *Pipe the desired filling into the each shell, leaving about 3 mm / ⅛ in of room from the top for a cap (see step 12 of the technique).*

10. **PLACE THE MOLDS UPSIDE DOWN TO ALLOW THE CHOCOLATE TO SET.** Inverting the molds while the chocolate sets helps to create more uniform shells by preventing the chocolate from settling to the bottom of the molds.

11. **SCRAPE THE TOPS OF THE MOLDS AGAIN BEFORE THE CHOCOLATE SOLIDIFIES.** When the chocolate reaches a plastic state, scraping the tops of the molds one more time ensures a smooth bottom edge on the chocolate shell for uniformity and proper adhesion of the base.

12. **FILL THE MOLDS WITH THE DESIRED FILLING.** Fill to within 3 millimeters/⅛ inch of the top. The filling for shell-molded chocolates should be applied at both the proper temperature and the proper viscosity. The temperature of the filling should be 20° to 25°C/68° to 77°F and should never exceed 30°C/86°F, at which point the chocolate shells would soften. The viscosity of the filling should be such that, with vibration, it flattens to a uniform level inside the shells. Stiff fillings that do not flatten make it difficult to cap the molds with a coating of uniform thickness. Fillings that are extremely soft will not support the chocolate as the cap is applied.

The determining factor for the thickness of the cap is the distance between the top of the filling and the top of the shells. Ideally, the cap will be the same thickness as the shell; 2 to 3 millimeters/¹⁄₁₆ to ⅛ inch is an appropriate thickness. The fillings most commonly used in shell-molded chocolates are ganache, fondant, and nut- and caramel-based fillings, usually with a soft consistency to create a textural contrast.

13. **ALLOW THE FILLING TO COOL AND SET, IF REQUIRED.** Fillings that set as they cool should be allowed to do so before the molds are capped. Permitting the filling to set prevents it from becoming mixed together with the chocolate cap, which could cause leakage and moisture migration.

14. **SOFTEN THE TOP EDGE OF THE CHOCOLATE SHELLS.** Use a hair dryer or heat gun to slightly soften the edges of the chocolate shells. This helps the cap to bond to each shell. Care must be exercised not to melt the chocolate, which would take it out of temper, resulting in bloom and causing difficulty in releasing the chocolate from the molds.

LEFT: *Using a heat gun, soften the top edges of the chocolate shells slightly so that they will adhere to the caps (see step 14 of the technique).* CENTER: *Ladle tempered chocolate over the molds to cap each piece (see step 15 of the technique).* RIGHT: *Lightly tap or flex the inverted molds to remove the finished confections (see step 18 of the technique).*

15. **CAP THE MOLDS WITH TEMPERED CHOCOLATE.** The cap is applied in much the same way that the molds are filled in step 5; usually with a ladle. After capping the filled shells, the excess chocolate is once again scraped off, and the molds vibrated lightly and placed upright at room temperature to crystallize.

16. **ALLOW THE MOLDS TO CRYSTALLIZE AT A COOL ROOM TEMPERATURE.** The shell-molded chocolate must crystallize at room temperature for 15 minutes prior to refrigeration to ensure the formation of stable Form-V crystals, which might not develop if the molds were refrigerated immediately.

17. **REFRIGERATE THE MOLDS FOR APPROXIMATELY 15 MINUTES.** Refrigerating the molds facilitates the escape of the latent heat of crystallization, which is released as the chocolate sets. (See Latent Heat of Crystallization, page 89.) The larger and thicker the molded chocolate, the more heat is released and the more important this step is. Refrigeration also cools the chocolate, causing it to contract and pull away from the inside of the molds for easy release. When using polycarbonate molds, which are transparent or translucent, it is possible to see when the chocolate has pulled away from the inside of the molds sufficiently to allow easy release.

18. **INVERT THE MOLDS TO REMOVE THE CONFECTIONS.** Flexing or tap the molds lightly if necessary. Once the chocolate shells have contracted away from the molds, they will easily fall out when the molds are inverted. Place a support, such as a piece of stiff cardboard, on top of each mold, then invert the support and the mold together. Once the mold is inverted, remove the support. With this procedure there is less risk of damaging the confections, as might happen if the molds were simply inverted and the chocolates allowed to fall out.

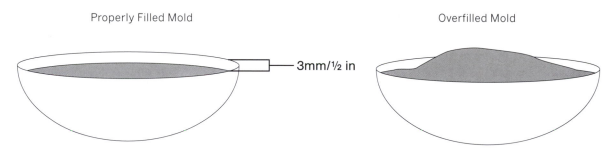

Properly Filled Mold   Overfilled Mold

—3mm/½ in

LEFT: *Properly lined and filled mold.* RIGHT: *Overfilled mold. Excessively viscous filling does not level out when the mold is vibrated, making effective capping of the mold impossible (see step 12 of the technique).*

Special effects for shell molding

Various special effects may be used with the basic shell-molding technique to enhance the appearance of the finished product. While the possibilities are endless, the technique is essentially the same: apply colors or transfer sheets to the inside of the mold before filling it. The result is high-gloss shell-molded pieces that exhibit contrasting colors and patterns. These are some of the most visually striking confections made.

USE OF TRANSFER SHEETS WITH MAGNETIC MOLDS

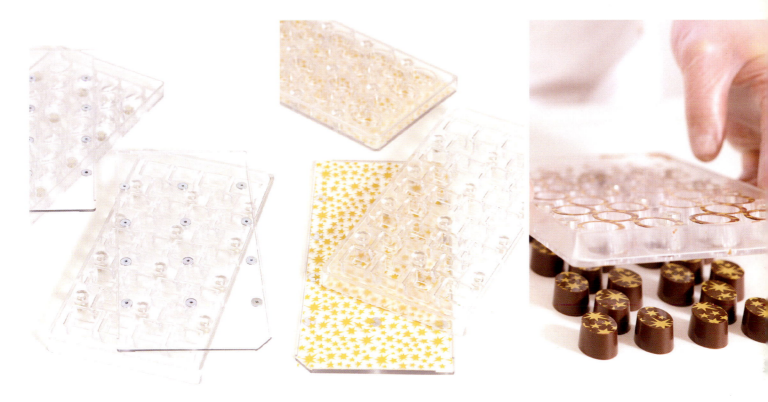

LEFT: *Two-piece molds with magnets embedded for use with transfer sheets.* CENTER: *Transfer sheets of the correct size fit perfectly into the molds.* RIGHT: *Once the chocolate has set, the transfer sheets are removed and the confections are unmolded.*

USE OF COLOR

Any color to be used with chocolate must be fat soluble. (Water-soluble colors thicken the chocolate and do not adhere properly.) Fat-soluble colors are available in liquid or powder form; either form can be used successfully, depending on the desired result. Chocolate colors are usually dissolved first in warm cocoa butter, then applied to the mold or mixed with chocolate. Powdered colors approved for use in foods, such as those used in gum paste work, are also useful in creating color effects in shell-molded chocolates. These may be used dry or mixed with cocoa butter before application.

Adding color is not the only way to provide flair to shell-molded chocolates; applying dehydrated fruit powders or chocolate of a contrasting color—such as white or milk chocolate—also creates contrast. Whatever materials are used, by applying colors unevenly and using several layers of different colors, a remarkable appearance of depth can be created. Shell-molded chocolates with color effects have great potential to create stunning signature items.

To add a decorative accent to chocolates, airbrush colored cocoa butter or chocolate into a mold before filling it.

APPLYING THE EFFECTS

There are three basic methods for adding effects to molded confections: airbrushing, brushing, and applying dry luster color. Airbrushing is a quick and efficient method, but it requires specialty products and equipment. Brushing is a more time-consuming technique, but it can yield different and interesting results depending on the tool used to apply the medium to the mold. Finally, applying luster color, a specialty product, creates a singular effect not achievable with any other product.

AIRBRUSHING

Either fat-soluble colors dissolved in cocoa butter, or chocolate itself may be airbrushed into molds prior to filling. When airbrushing chocolate, thin it substantially with cocoa butter to ensure that it will flow through the airbrush; approximately equal parts cocoa butter and chocolate are commonly used. Dissolve colors in enough cocoa butter to make them fluid. It is not necessary to temper either the chocolate or the cocoa butter that will be airbrushed into a mold; simply apply it at around 34°C/93°F or slightly cooler. The force of atomizing the color or chocolate as it passes through the brush—and the cooling that occurs in the process—is sufficient to precrystallize the cocoa butter and ensure proper shine and adhesion.

BRUSHING

A simple method for applying color to molds is to brush the dissolved color or tempered chocolate directly into a mold. Any number of tools may be used to do this, resulting in different visual effects. Brushes, sponges, piping cones, and gloved fingertips all may be used successfully to introduce a contrasting color to the inside of a mold. The same tools may be used to splash or spray tempered color into a mold to create a dramatic, random appearance. When brushing colors or chocolate into molds, temper the cocoa butter or chocolate in order to provide shine and adhesion to the chocolate shell. Care must be exercised not to allow the chocolate or cocoa butter to set during brushing, which would result in a diminished shine and a flaking finish during unmolding.

TOP, LEFT: *A variety of cocoa butter colors are available for use in molded chocolates.*
RIGHT: *Tempered, colored cocoa butter is applied to molds using a brush.*

BOTTOM, LEFT: *Tempered, colored cocoa butter is applied to molds using a finger.*
RIGHT: *Finished molded chocolates made using opaque colors.*

TOP, LEFT: *Various interference colors.* RIGHT: *Interference colors are applied to finished chocolates using a brush.*

BOTTOM, LEFT: *A small amount of color produces a dramatic effect.* RIGHT: *Different techniques produce different cosmetic results. Left to right: painted cocoa butter, dabbed interference color, transfer sheets, airbrushed cocoa butter, and brushed interference color.*

APPLYING DRY LUSTER COLOR

Dry colors approved for use in food may be dusted lightly into a mold before filling the mold with chocolate, or they may be mixed with cocoa butter and brushed in. When applied dry, these colors create an entirely different effect from the one created by liquid colors.

Dry luster color, when lightly dusted into an empty mold, adds a brilliant edible hue to the top of finished chocolates.

SHELL-MOLDED CHOCOLATE DEFECTS

DEFECT	CAUSE	REMEDY
POOR SHINE	Mold not well polished	Polish mold well after washing
	Mold in poor condition	Use mold with smooth, clean interior
	Chocolate over- or undertempered	Use optimally tempered chocolate
	Chocolate applied while too cool	Apply chocolate at maximum working temperature
	Brushed-in chocolate overcrystallized	Stop brushing chocolate before it crystallizes
DIFFICULTY RELEASING	Chocolate over- or undertempered	Use optimally tempered chocolate
	Chocolate not fully set	Allow chocolate to set longer
	Chocolate not cooled enough	Chill chocolate more to allow it to contract
	Shell too thin	Leave chocolate in longer before inverting mold to drain away excess
BUBBLES ON SURFACE	Chocolate overtempered	Use optimally tempered chocolate
	Molds too cold	Warm molds to 25° to 30°C/77° to 86°F before filling
	Chocolate too viscous	Use chocolate with higher cocoa butter content
	Mold not vibrated sufficiently	Vibrate mold well to remove air bubbles
DULL SPOTS ON SURFACE	Mold not warmed before use	Warm mold to 25° to 30°C/77° to 86°F before filling
	Mold not polished well	Polish mold well after washing
BLOOMED CHOCOLATE	Undertempered chocolate used	Use optimally tempered chocolate
		Do not refrigerate too long
	Excessive humidity	Work in low-humidity environment
	Latent heat of crystallization not released	Chill molds as they crystallize
OOZING CENTER	Overfilled mold	Fill mold only to within 2 to 3 mm/⅟₁₆ to ⅛ in of the top
	Shell too thin	Allow filled molds to sit longer before removing excess chocolate
	Inadequate adhesion of cap	Warm the mold slightly before capping
FLAKING SURFACE	Brushed-in chocolate overcrystallized	Stop brushing chocolate before it crystallizes
	Mold not well polished	Polish mold well after washing
CRACKED SHELL	Refrigerated too long	Remove from refrigerator sooner
	Shell too thin	Leave chocolate in longer before inverting mold to drain away excess

The use of foil cups lined with chocolate is very similar in both concept and technique to shell-molded chocolates. The major difference is that when using foil cups, the cups themselves are an integral part of the finished piece; only when the consumer is ready to eat the confection is the foil peeled away to reveal the filled chocolate within. Like shell molding, the use of foil cups permits soft fillings such as caramel cream, for textural contrast. The method for using foil cups to make filled chocolates is nearly identical the one for using molds, except that the cups must be handled one at a time and the chocolate is not unmolded.

1. **USING A DISPOSABLE PASTRY BAG FILLED WITH TEM-PERED CHOCOLATE, FILL APPROXIMATELY 10 CUPS AT A TIME TO WITHIN 3 MILLIMETERS/⅛ INCH OF THE TOP.** It is critical that the tempered chocolate be at its optimum temperature and viscosity to create a shell of the proper thickness. Filling substantially more than 10 shells at a time will cause a thick layer of chocolate to build up, creating overly thick shells.

2. **WORKING IN THE SAME ORDER IN WHICH THEY WERE FILLED, INVERT THE CUPS ONE AT A TIME** over a bowl and shake lightly to remove excess chocolate, leaving only a thin lining of chocolate in the cup.

3. **PLACE THE LINED CUPS UPSIDE DOWN ON AN ICING SCREEN.** To avoid dripping chocolate onto the cups already on the rack, place the inverted cups to the far right—if the confectioner is right handed—of the work area.

4. **WORKING IN THE SAME ORDER IN WHICH THE CUPS WERE INVERTED, PICK UP EACH CUP BEFORE THE CHOC-OLATE SETS, AND PLACE EACH UPRIGHT ON A CLEAN PAN.** It is crucial to pick the cups up off of the screen before the chocolate sets, which would make the cups adhere to the screen.

LEFT: *Invert the foil cups one at a time over a bowl and shake lightly to remove excess chocolate, leaving only a thin lining in the cup (see step 2 of the technique).* RIGHT: *Cap the filled foil cup by piping tempered chocolate over the entire surface (see step 6 of the technique).*

5. **ANY OF THE FILLINGS THAT ARE APPROPRIATE FOR SHELL MOLDING ARE ALSO APPROPRIATE FOR FOIL CUPS.** Soft textured fillings such as caramel cream or nut pastes are particularly well suited to these confections. Fill the cups to within 2 millimeters/1/16 inch of the top to allow room for the chocolate cap to seal the confection.

6. **CAP THE CUPS ONE AT A TIME,** using a paper cone to pipe tempered chocolate onto the top of the filled cup, and then vibrate each cup to remove irregularities.

7. **A GARNISH INDICATIVE OF THE FILLING,** such as nuts, may be applied when the chocolate begins to set. Decoration may be piped on after the chocolate sets.

FILLED FOIL-CUP CHOCOLATES DEFECTS

DEFECT	CAUSE	REMEDY
OOZING CENTER	Overfilled cups	Fill cups only to within 2 to 3 mm/1/16 to 1/8 of the top
	Excessively thin shell	Allow filled cups to sit longer before removing the excess chocolate
	Filling too cold	Apply filling at 20° to 25°C/68° to 77°F
SHELL CRUMBLES WHEN FOIL CUP IS REMOVED	Shell too thin	Leave chocolate in longer before inverting cups to drain away excess
	Undertempered chocolate	Use optimally tempered chocolate
THICK SHELL	Overtempered chocolate	Use optimally tempered chocolate
	Cup left too long before inverted to drain away excess chocolate	Fill fewer cups before inverting to drain away excess chocolate
CUP NOT FULLY LINED	Cups not filled sufficiently before inverted	Fill cups to within 2 mm/1/16 in of top before inverting

LATENT HEAT OF CRYSTALLIZATION

The latent heat of crystallization is the heat released as a substance like cocoa butter changes from an amorphous state into a crystalline state. Nearly all substances—including sugar and even water as it turns to ice—release latent heat as they crystallize. The release of heat as the cocoa butter in chocolate crystallizes is most likely to affect the confectioner when chocolate molds are being used. As the chocolate in a mold sets, the heat produced in the center of the mold slows the crystallization of the rest of the chocolate, resulting in the formation of fat bloom. Because plastic does not conduct heat well, the heat of crystallization tends to be trapped in modern plastic molds. The simple solution is to place the filled molds into a refrigerator to liberate the latent heat of crystallization. The larger and thicker the molds are, the more important it is to help diffuse the heat; thin or small molds have a greater surface area compared with their volume, and therefore lose excess heat more easily; large or thick molds have more of a tendency to retain heat and form fat bloom as a result.

Several precautions should be taken when refrigerating molds: the chocolate should already have begun to crystallize; if the chocolate is chilled quickly, before it begins to crystallize, it can form unstable crystals, resulting in poor contraction, poor snap, and the formation of bloom during storage. The refrigerator should not be too cold; a temperature of approximately 5°C/41°F is ideal. Temperatures significantly colder than this can result in the formation of unstable cocoa butter crystals. Never put filled molds in the freezer, as this causes unstable crystal formation and leads to excessive contraction, resulting in cracking. The refrigerator must not have high humidity, which can lead to the formation of sugar bloom. (For more information on sugar bloom, see page 31.) Finally, the molds should not remain in the refrigerator for an extended period; 15 minutes is usually appropriate. Molds left in the refrigerator too long are likely to form condensation when they are removed, resulting in sugar bloom; they can also crack due to excessive contraction.

STARCH MOLDING

The technique of starch molding is used in manufacturing to make many different confections, including gummy bears, gumdrops, candy corn, and various other molded candies. In smaller operations starch molding may be used for forming fondants, jellies, and cordials, among other things.

Starch molding is a simple and effective, if somewhat dusty, method of making confections. Anyone undertaking starch molding should be aware of one caveat: starch is flammable. Should a large quantity of it become airborne and be exposed to an open flame, the result could be a flash fire or explosion. Starch molding is not inherently dangerous, but caution should be exercised nonetheless to avoid having too much starch blown into the air, particularly when there are open flames present.

---

technique | theory | **STARCH MOLDING**

The steps in starch molding are simple: Make an impression of a desired shape in a shallow bed of dry starch. Deposit the desired soft medium into the impression and allow it to set. When the set confection is removed from the starch, it will have the shape of the impression originally made in the starch bed. The confection may be finished as desired.

1. **AERATE WELL-DRIED CORNSTARCH IN SHALLOW BOXES BY WHISKING OR SIFTING.** Level the starch flush with the top of the box. The box for starch molding should be shallow in order to contain the minimum amount of starch. The box should be a size that fits on convenient storage trays, often sheet pans. The starch can be simply cornstarch, although some confectioners prefer a mixture of different starches. In larger operations, starch marketed specifically for molding is treated with a small quantity of mineral oil to prevent it from absorbing liquid confections. In all cases, it is crucial that the starch be well dried. To do this, dry it in the box in a low-temperature oven (93°C/200°F or lower) for several hours. If the starch is not sufficiently dried, it will attract rather than repel the liquid deposited in it, absorbing it. If the starch box has been stored under ambient conditions for several days, it may be necessary to dry it before molding. Once dried, the starch is ready for use. Aerate the starch by lightly whisking with a whip, then level off the surface so it is flush with the edges of the box. The aerated and leveled bed of starch can now be imprinted and filled as desired.

2. **MAKE CAVITIES IN THE STARCH BED USING AN IMPRINTER.** Imprinters are easy tools to make. Making original imprinters allows the confectioner to create unique shapes for products. The simplest way to make an imprinter is to buy an inexpensive chocolate mold of the size and shape desired, spray it with a pan release, and then fill it with plaster of Paris. When the shaped plaster hardens, release it from the chocolate mold and allow it to cure overnight. Once the plaster forms are fully cured, glue them onto a wooden stick leaving 1 centimeter/½ inch or more between each form. Imprinters may also be made by sculpting clay that is subsequently cured in an oven, or even by using existing objects, such as toys, and attaching them to a stick.

3. **FUNNEL THE LIQUID CENTER INTO THE PREPARED STARCH CAVITIES.** Use a fondant funnel to deposit the fluid mixture into the prepared molds. In many cases it is important to keep the funnel warm during depositing.

4. **IF DESIRED, SIFT DRY STARCH ON TOP OF THE STILL-LIQUID CENTERS.** In the case of liquor cordials, starch should be sifted over the top of the centers to promote crystallization. When molding jellies in starch, this step may be omitted.

5. **ALLOW THE FILLING TO SET OR CRYSTALLIZE FOR THE REQUIRED TIME IN THE BOX.** The length of time the filling should be left in the starch varies with the product. Pectin jellies should be removed as soon as they have set; gelatin gummies should be left in the starch overnight. Liquor cordials must also remain in the starch overnight, but they should be turned over after 4 to 5 hours to allow an even skin of crystallization to form. Brush candies free of excess starch.

TOP, LEFT: *Make impressions of a desired shape in a level bed of dry starch (see step 2 of the technique).* RIGHT: *Funnel the finished syrup into the starch impressions, filling each one (see step 3 of the technique).*

BOTTOM, LEFT: *Remove the candies from the mold and gently brush them free of excess starch (see step 5 of the technique).* RIGHT. *Liquor cordials enclose a liquid center in a thin crystalline wall.*

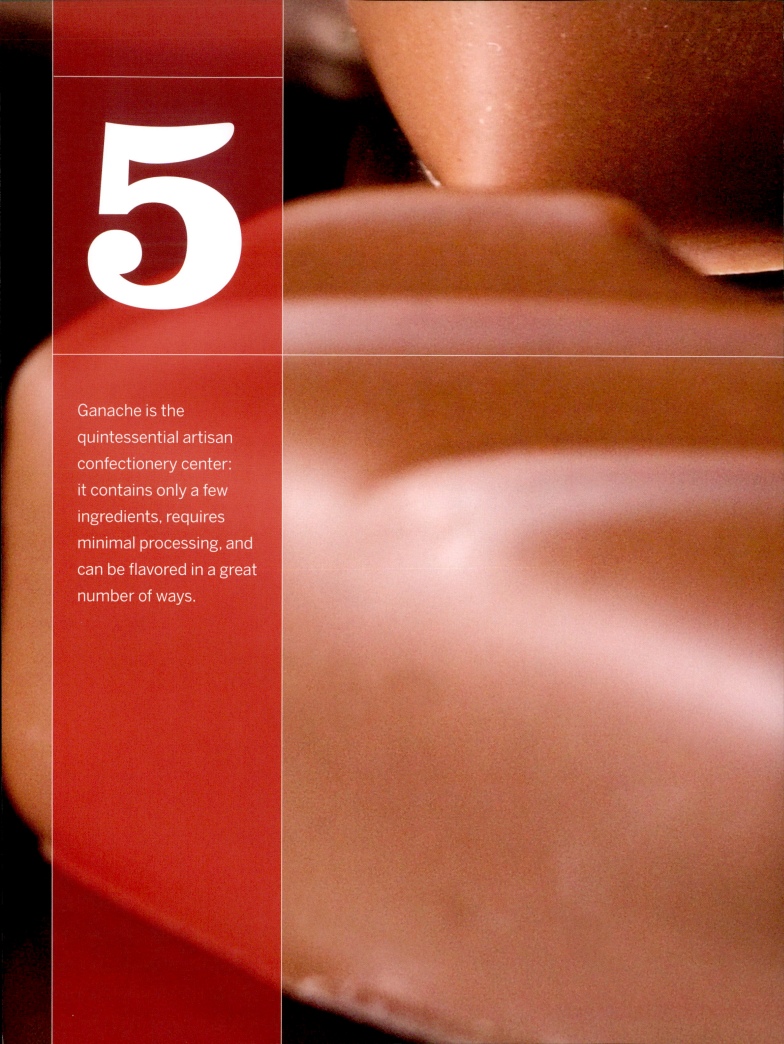

5

Ganache is the quintessential artisan confectionery center: it contains only a few ingredients, requires minimal processing, and can be flavored in a great number of ways.

CREAM GANACHE

Ganache has a creamy, smooth texture that melts readily in the mouth, and its short shelf life puts it out of reach of most large manufacturers. In the mind of the public, ganache centers—with truffles being the most prominent example—are nearly synonymous with the work of chocolatiers. The versatility of ganache contributes to its popularity; it may be piped, slabbed, or shell-molded; it may be flavored with liqueurs, purées, or infusions—or simply left as an ungilded blend of chocolate and cream. Ganache may be finished in any style that suits the confectioner, from simple truffles rolled in cocoa powder to layered slabs hand-dipped and finished with transfer sheets. Although it is widely used, ganache is a surprisingly complex system—a combination of fats, liquids, dissolved sugar, and solids that, only when handled correctly, provides exactly the flavor profile and melt-in-the-mouth texture desired.

While the term *ganache* most often applies to cream combined with chocolate, other liquid ingredients can be used to make it. Vanilla sauce combined with chocolate makes the classic confectionery center known as egg ganache. Butter combined with chocolate makes butter ganache, also a classic confectionery preparation. (See Chapter 6, pages 187–212.) Although less commonly used, water mixed with chocolate could rightfully be called water ganache. Wine, fruit juice, or other liquids mixed with chocolate could also be considered types of ganache. Still, in common usage, unless otherwise specified, *ganache* refers to the cream-and-chocolate mixture.

GANACHE AS A SYSTEM

Although ganache is ubiquitous throughout both pastry and confectionery, it is a very complex system that requires careful handling. The two aspects of ganache that require the most attention are the emulsion that comprises it and the crystallization of its polymorphic fat.

Ganache is a fat-in-water emulsion, meaning that droplets of butterfat from the cream and butter, as well as cocoa butter from the chocolate, are dispersed into a continuous liquid phase from the cream and liquid flavoring. Of course, ganache contains other components, such as cacao solids and sugar from the chocolate, milk solids and lactose from the cream, and various liquid sweeteners. Each of these ingredients plays a part in the way ganache behaves and contributes to the complexity of the system.

For the artisan confectioner, the most important thing to understand is what makes a ganache emulsion separate. There are two main reasons ganache separates: the presence of too much fat and agitation at an unstable temperature.

Excessive fat causes ganache to separate because the fat droplets are packed together so closely that they can no longer remain discrete. Once the fat droplets coalesce, they are too large to remain in suspension and will float to the surface, resulting in separation. Stirring ganache when it is at an intermediate temperature will also result in separation. When the fats

Properly mixed ganache appears smooth and silky, with a clear sheen.

are warm (i.e., above 32°C/90°F), stirring has no negative effect on a properly formulated ganache; the liquid fat droplets do not easily coalesce, so separation is avoided. Nor will ganache tend to separate if it is stirred after it has been permitted to cool to below 23°C/74°F and thus has begun to crystallize. Crystallized fats cannot form the large droplets that can lead to separation. It is when the temperature of the ganache is between 23° and 29°C/74° and 85°F and the fats are still in liquid form that the mixture is most likely to separate when stirred. Ganache that is allowed to crystallize while it is separated will always exhibit a grainy texture because the fat has not been finely dispersed. A separated ganache must be repaired prior to use.

Repairing separated ganache

1. Warm the ganache to 32° to 34°C/90° to 94°F, then stir it to re-emulsify it and melt most of the fat crystals. Finally, agitate it to disperse the fat droplets. When warming the ganache, take care not to heat it above 34°C/94°F, in order to preserve the existing Form-V cocoa butter crystals so that the ganache will set properly. (See Crystallization of Ganache, page 98.) Agitation may be accomplished by hand, with a spatula or whisk, or with a machine, such as an immersion blender or food processor. If the ganache is not excessively high in fat, warming and stirring will re-emulsify it. If this step fails to repair the ganache, it is too rich in fat and will require the addition of moisture to allow the fat to disperse.

2. Extra liquid should be added to a ganache only when step 1 fails. With the ganache between 32° and 34°C/90° and 94°F, add a minimum amount of warm liquid while stirring. Adding liquid affords space to fat droplets that are packed too closely together and so could coalesce. Several different liquids are effective in repairing ganache in this manner; these include spirits, milk, glucose syrup, and even water. Cream is not a good choice for this procedure because it contains a high percentage of fat and thus contributes to the fat phase, somewhat defeating the purpose of adding liquid. Adding water or milk will increase the ganache's water activity and limit its shelf stability, so they are not good choices for repairing ganache if shelf life is a concern. Neither spirits nor syrup contains fat, so they have a less detrimental effect on shelf stability and are the best choices for the procedure. Care must always be taken not to add excess liquid to ganache, which will soften it, making it difficult to handle. Adding the minimum amount of liquid required to re-emulsify the ganache is always the goal.

   A ganache that requires the addition of liquid to re-emulsify it is too high in fat. Its formula should therefore be adjusted for future batches. The goal of adjusting such a formula is to decrease slightly the percentage of the fat phase compared to the water phase in order to allow the dispersal of the fat droplets. This can be accomplished through a number of changes, including using a lower-fat chocolate or cream, replacing a portion of the cream with milk, reducing or eliminating butter from the formula, increasing the liquid flavoring, and reducing the amount of chocolate. In all cases, the goal is to make a ganache with a slightly lower ratio of fat to liquid. Adjustments to the formula must be made incrementally, and only experimentation will reveal when the ganache contains just enough moisture not to separate but not so much that it is too soft to handle and has a poor shelf life.

Broken ganache, characterized by separation of fats and a grainy texture, is the result of either too much fat or agitation at an unstable temperature.

EMULSIONS

Emulsions are homogeneous combinations of two ingredients that do not normally mix: fat-based liquids and water-based liquids. In an emulsion, one of the ingredients is dispersed into minute droplets—10 microns or smaller—within the other ingredient. The portion of the emulsion comprising the droplets is called the dispersed phase. The portion of the emulsion into which the droplets are dispersed is called the continuous phase. (See Figure A, page 97.) Emulsions may be either fat droplets dispersed in water (fat-in-water emulsions) or water droplets dispersed in fat (water-in-fat emulsions). Nearly any confectionery ingredient or preparation that contains both fat and water is an emulsion. Common examples include butter, which is a water-in-fat emulsion, and cream, which is a fat-in-water emulsion. Ganache is an example of a fat-in-water emulsion, while butter ganache is an example of a water-in-fat emulsion.

SEPARATION

As long as the dispersed phase of an emulsion remains in microscopic droplets and is distributed throughout the continuous phase, the emulsion remains homogeneous. When the dispersed phase coalesces into larger drops, it will no longer remain suspended within the continuous phase, resulting in separation. When an emulsion separates, it no longer appears homogeneous. The fat phase and water phase become visible independent of each other, and the viscosity of the system decreases.

Naturally, the emulsions that confectioners deal with every day are much more complex than simply water and fat. They also contain dissolved and crystalline sugars, particles of cacao, milk solids, and other ingredients. All of these ingredients interact with and affect the emulsion in various and complex ways. For the artisan confectioner, understanding the fundamentals of the fat and water phases is usually enough to diagnose and remedy difficulties encountered with emulsions.

Excessive Dispersed Phase

A very common cause of separated emulsions is an excess of the dispersed phase. (See Figure B, page 97.) When a very high percentage of the emulsion is comprised of dispersed-phase ingredients, the discrete droplets are tightly compacted, which can cause them to coalesce into larger drops, resulting in separation. There is no hard-and-fast rule regarding the percentage of the dispersed phase required in order that the mixture remain emulsified; it varies depending on many factors. In all cases, however, once the maximum percentage is exceeded, the tight packing of the droplets causes them to coalesce into larger drops, breaking the emulsion. This is commonly observed in ganache made with high-fat chocolate and high-fat cream, in fudge containing too much fat, and in marzipan without enough water present to maintain the dispersal of the oil.

Agitation

Agitation is the second most common cause of separation in the emulsions a confectioner employs. When an emulsion is agitated, the dispersed phase is put into motion, and the droplets collide. When the droplets run into one another, they can coalesce. (See Figure C, page 97.) Coalesced droplets, of course, are the definitive cause of a separated emulsion. When ganache separates as the result of stirring, it is most often because the fats are neither completely melted nor completely crystallized. (Under either of those conditions, ganache is more stable and not as prone to separation from stirring.) Marzipan, like ganache, will separate from excessive agitation, as the fat droplets combine and come out of suspension within the system.

Temperature

Temperature can almost always be a factor in emulsion separation. Different emulsions react differently to temperature. Too high a temperature will cause some emulsions to break; in other cases, too low a temperature will cause separation. The most notable example here is ganache, which is unstable when the temperature drops below about 29°C/85°F but the fat has not yet crystallized.

Other Factors Affecting Separation

Many other, more minor, factors also have a bearing on emulsions. Lower pH systems tend to stay emulsified better than less acidic mixtures; emulsifiers such as lecithin profoundly affect the stability of emulsions; the amount and type of solids within an emulsion affect how likely it is to separate; and the amount and form of sugar present also has an effect. Emulsions are complex systems that are influenced by many factors. Understanding the fundamentals of emulsions and the major causes of failed emulsions will help the artisan confectioner to be more successful with ganache and many other centers that contain emulsions.

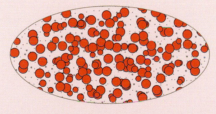

Fat-in-Water Emulsion

Figure A

An emulsion is a suspension of the dispersed phase the continuous phase.

Excessive Dispersed Phase

Figure B

An excess of the dispersed phase forces the droplets together.

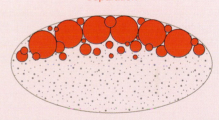

Separation

Figure C

The result is separation; the droplets are no longer discrete, but coalesce into large drops that do not remain in suspension.

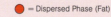 = Dispersed Phase (Fat)

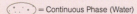 = Continuous Phase (Water)

CRYSTALLIZATION OF GANACHE

Because ganache is high in cocoa butter, it exhibits polymorphism similar to that of chocolate. (See Polymorphism of Cocoa Butter, page 55.) If ganache is not properly precrystallized with stable fat crystals, it will not set with a firm, uniform texture. This results in centers that are too soft to handle and a grainy texture produced by the development of large fat crystals during storage.

When making and handling ganache for confections, take care to create and preserve stable fat crystals that will promote a firm, uniform texture upon setting and during storage. To ensure proper crystal formation:

1. Begin with tempered chocolate.
2. Control the temperature of the ganache.
3. Agitate the ganache to temper it.
4. Control the environment.

Begin with tempered chocolate

Tempered chocolate contains stable Form-V cocoa butter crystals that seed ganache and promote proper crystallization. Making ganache with tempered chocolate helps to ensure that those crystals are present in the finished product. Whether using melted chocolate, as in the slabbing technique, or unmelted chocolate, as in the piping technique, be sure to use tempered chocolate when making a confectionery ganache.

Control the temperature of the ganache

If the temperature of ganache rises above 34°C/94°F, the stable cocoa butter crystals melt, exactly as they do in tempered chocolate. The result for the ganache is the same as it is for chocolate: it becomes untempered, resulting in a soft set with large fat crystals and a grainy texture that will only increase during storage, due to the transformation of crystals to higher forms.

Agitate the ganache to temper it

When using ganache for piping, lightly agitate it to temper it, promoting uniform crystallization and a rapid, firm set. While light agitation firms ganache, excessive agitation results in a short texture that is not as creamy or smooth as ganache should be.

Control the environment

Just like chocolate, even properly tempered ganache will form unstable crystals if it is crystallized at too low a temperature. (See Polymorphism of Cocoa Butter diagram, page 55.) Properly made and handled ganache will set perfectly at 20°C/68°F. Further, ganache should not be refrigerated. Any attempt to rush the setting process by this method will be detrimental to the result. Refrigerating ganache creates centers that are too soft to handle when they return to room temperature, and, as with chocolate, the unstable crystals the ganache contains will transform to higher forms during storage, resulting in large, grainy-feeling fat crystals. (See Refrigeration of Ganache, page 107.)

FORMULATION EXAMPLE

GANACHE FORMULATION GUIDELINES

The following example illustrates the use of the ganache formulation guidelines to create a ganache formula for piping or slabbing.

> 250 g/9 oz cream
>
> 70 g/2.5 oz glucose syrup
>
> 60 g/2 oz liqueur or other liquid flavoring
>
> 30 g/1 oz butter
>
> 620 g/22 oz dark chocolate

FORMULATION THEORY

Cream

Almost without exception, ganache contains cream. Cream is the starting point for building the rest of the formula, and the amount used is decided based purely on the desired batch size.

Glucose Syrup

Glucose syrup is commonly used in ganache to lower the water-activity level, stabilize the emulsion, and help maintain a smooth texture by preventing recrystallization of the sugar. Between 10 and 40 percent corn syrup relative to the weight of the cream is commonly added to ganache. Results vary depending on the type of chocolate, flavoring, and handling procedures used and the results desired. As a rule,

25 to 30 percent as much glucose syrup as cream provides excellent flavor, texture, and stability to the finished product.

Liqueur or Other Liquid Flavoring

The amount of liquid flavoring used depends on the type of flavoring selected and the desired flavor profile. Liquid flavoring is always counted as a liquefier in ganache formulation. The quantity of liquid flavoring added should be balanced by the addition of a corresponding amount of chocolate.

Butter

Butter is an optional ingredient but is frequently added to ganache, especially when liquid flavorings are used. The theory behind adding butter in conjunction with liquid flavoring is to replace the butterfat that would have been present had that flavoring been cream. To this end, a good guideline is to add 50 percent as much butter as liquid flavoring. For instance, if 200 grams/7 ounces of rum are used in a ganache, 100 grams/3.5 ounces of butter should also be added. Additional butter may be used to augment dairy flavor and to increase fat content when a lower-fat cream is used or to create a softer texture in a finished ganache.

Chocolate

The ratio of chocolate to liquefier is the foundation and framework of ganache formulation and a key factor in determining the consistency and shelf life of the finished product. Ratios serve more as guidelines than as ironclad rules and should take into account not only the texture and stability of the finished product but also the emulsion. When high-fat chocolates are used, the amount of liquefier may have to be increased, and ratios may have to be altered slightly for ganache that has specific requirements for a particular use. The typical ratio of chocolate to liquefier for dark chocolate is 2:1. For milk and white chocolates, which are softer, the ratio is 2.5:1 in order to make a ganache that can be handled and is shelf stable. When determining the amount of chocolate to use in a formula, remember that both the cream and the liquid flavoring are counted as liquefiers, while butter and liquid sweeteners are not.

While these guidelines provide generally good results in flavor, texture, emulsification, and shelf life, they may require fine-tuning depending on the cream, chocolate, and flavoring used. When developing a new formula, it is advisable to make small test batches until the desired results are reached.

MOISTURE CONTENT AND WATER ACTIVITY

Ganache has the highest moisture content and the highest water-activity level of all confectionery centers. To reduce the water-activity level and extend the shelf life of ganache, add invert sugar, glucose syrup, or a spirit, and use the smallest amount of liquid possible in formulation. In all cases, cream-based ganache centers stored at room temperature have a shelf life of approximately three weeks, unless a water-activity meter is employed to ensure the safety of longer storage. (See Water Activity of Confections table, page 42.) For a longer shelf life, freeze the products, following the Confectionery Freezing Technique on page 46.

FUNCTION OF INGREDIENTS IN GANACHE

Simply defined, ganache is a fat-in-water emulsion, a system of fat dispersed in water. The fat in ganache comes from cocoa butter in the chocolate and butterfat in the cream. (See Emulsions, page 96.) The water in ganache comes from the cream and from any liquid flavoring added. This fairly simple concept is complicated by the presence of sugars and cacao solids. Although confectionery ganache contains only a few ingredients, each one plays a vital role in a complex system. Understanding the functions and interactions of these ingredients allows the confectioner to manipulate formulas to obtain optimal results, create original centers, and troubleshoot his or her products.

Cream

Ganache is loosely defined as chocolate combined with cream, so cream naturally plays a significant role in ganache formulation. Cream is the major source of water in ganache. Without sufficient water, the fat cannot disperse and the ganache separates. Cream is also the major source of butterfat in ganache. When combined with cocoa butter, butterfat lowers the melting point of chocolate, both because of its lower solid fat index (SFI) relative to that of cocoa butter and because of its eutectic effect. (See Eutectics, page 411.) It is the combination of butterfat and cocoa butter that is largely responsible for the melt-in-the-mouth quality of ganache. In addition to water and fat, cream contributes milk solids, lactose, and dairy flavor.

Confectioners differ on the cream they prefer to use in ganache; some choose a very high-fat cream (40 percent butterfat), while others opt for one lower in fat (as low as approximately 32 percent butterfat). Any cream in this range can supply excellent results, as long as the confectioner understands the necessary balance of ingredients. Switching the type of cream used in a ganache will very likely necessitate changes elsewhere in the formula. (See Ganache Formulation Guidelines, page 99.) Whatever type of cream is selected, it is advisable to always work with the same type in order to ensure consistent results. Cream is always counted as a liquefier in ganache formulation.

Sweeteners

Ganache often contains an adjunct sweetener, but seldom for its flavor; most of the sweetness in ganache is provided by the chocolate. Adjunct sweeteners perform three major functions in ganache: they increase its shelf life, improve its texture, and stabilize it. The sweeteners most commonly used are glucose syrups and invert sugar, both of which work to increase shelf life in essentially the same way—by binding with water, lowering the water activity of the ganache and making it more resistant to spoilage. However, invert sugar is more effective than glucose syrup for lowering water activity and extending shelf life.

Sweeteners contribute to the smooth texture of ganache by acting as doctoring agents, preventing the recrystallization of sugar. When ganache is made, much of the sucrose in the chocolate dissolves into the liquid supplied by the cream. Over time, as the ganache is stored, this sugar can recrystallize, resulting in a grainy texture. The addition of glucose syrup or invert sugar helps to prevent sugar crystals from forming, maintaining a creamy, smooth texture.

The addition of glucose syrup also increases the viscosity of the aqueous phase of the emulsion, helping to prevent the motion and coalescence of the fat droplets, thereby preventing separation. Invert sugar has less of a stabilizing effect on the emulsion because it is not as viscous as glucose syrup. Regardless of the sweetener used, it is not counted as a liquefier in ganache formulation (even when it is a liquid such as glucose syrup), because it binds far more moisture than it contributes.

Flavorings

There are several methods for flavoring ganache, the simplest of which is to add a liquid flavoring such as a spirit, liqueur, or extract. (Note that state and federal laws govern the amount of alcohol that confectionery products may contain. Always check and adhere to regulations when using spirit.) Fruit purées or juices may also be used as liquid flavorings, but they are usually reduced first in order to remove some of the water they contain. Any of these ingredients may be used at the discretion of the confectioner, but because liquid flavoring counts as a liquefier in ganache formulation, a corresponding amount of chocolate should be added.

Adding liquid flavorings is not the only method for flavoring ganache. It is common practice to infuse ganache with an aromatic ingredient such as spices, coffee, or toasted nuts. (See Infusions, page 102.) Such infusions allow the use of flavors not easily found in liquid flavorings without adding alcohol. In addition to infusions, in which the aromatic is steeped and then removed, ground spices are often added directly to ganache. These should be added to the cream in the beginning of makeup, to facilitate the release of their flavor. Although effective for flavoring, ground spices can contribute a perceptible, sometimes undesirable, texture to ganache.

Chocolate

The chocolate in ganache provides cocoa butter for firmness in addition to cacao solids, sugar, and chocolate flavor. Since chocolate is the greatest part of ganache, it is no surprise that the chocolate used has tremendous bearing on the texture, flavor, and handling characteristics of the finished product. Using chocolate that is extremely high in fat results in a harder set and can contribute to the separation caused by excessive fat. (See Emulsions, pages 96–97.) Insufficient fat will lead to ganache that is not firm enough to handle when set. When selecting chocolate to use in a ganache formula, consider its fat content as well as its flavor profile. Once a formula has been balanced to perform well with a given chocolate, a change in chocolate is likely to require changes elsewhere in the formula, either in fats or liquids. The chocolate used in confectionery ganache must usually contain more than 32 percent cocoa butter in order to ensure proper firmness upon setting.

INFUSIONS

Anyone who has ever had a cup of coffee or tea is already familiar with infusions; both of those beverages are infusions of aromatic ingredients in water. Infusing aromatics into cream is a popular and effective method for flavoring ganache. Infusions differ from other flavorings such as extracts or purées because after the flavor is infused, the aromatic ingredient is removed, leaving only its essence behind. Often an extract is not available for a desired flavor, and even when one is, most confectioners agree that the flavor obtained by making fresh infusions is superior to that obtained with extracts. A striking example of this is vanilla beans compared to vanilla extract. Vanilla extract is a commercially prepared infusion and an expensive high-quality product. Few would argue, however, that superior vanilla flavor is obtained by steeping vanilla beans to infuse their flavor directly into a preparation.

Infusions necessarily begin with strongly flavored ingredients, referred to as aromatics. The aromatics most often used in confectionery include vanilla, coffee, tea, spices, and toasted nuts. Aromatics to be used in infusions should always be sliced, chopped, crushed, or ground in order to expose more surface area, ensuring that flavor is more efficiently released. While there are various methods for infusing flavors into substrates, including wet and dry and hot and cold methods, the fastest and most commonly used method involves liquid and heat. As the aromatic is heated in a liquid, its flavor-bearing essential oils are released into the liquid, thereby flavoring it. Infusions may be used to flavor any number of confectionery centers, and the methods may differ slightly. What follows is the procedure for flavoring a ganache with an infusion.

TO MAKE AN INFUSION-FLAVORED GANACHE:

1. Combine the aromatic ingredient and the cream. Do this while the cream is cold. Heating the cream and aromatic together helps draw the flavor out of the aromatic.

2. Heat the cream and aromatic just to the boiling point. The flavor of many aromatics, such as coffee, tea, and fresh herbs, is adversely affected by boiling. In addition, boiling the cream removes water from it, leaving excess fat, which contributes to separation.

3. Cover the mixture and allow it to steep for approximately 5 minutes. Covering holds in moisture and volatile flavor compounds. Steeping allows the flavor to infuse into the cream. Excessive steeping of some ingredients can lead to off flavors. Five minutes is generally enough time to extract sufficient flavor from the aromatic without creating poor flavor notes.

4. Strain out the aromatic. Fine-textured aromatics, such as tea and ground spices, should be strained through premoistened cheesecloth; a chinois will suffice for coarser-textured ingredients, such as whole spices.

5. Return the cream to its original weight by adding milk. Aromatics absorb moisture. While a vanilla bean will not soak up enough cream to make a difference, dry herbs, tea, and coffee all absorb liquid, which must be replaced after the aromatics have been steeped. Milk is the liquid of choice for this. Aromatics soak up more moisture than fat from cream, resulting in a cream that is very high in fat. If cream, rather than milk, were used to restore the weight, the ganache would contain too much fat and would likely separate.

6. Use the infused cream to make the ganache. The flavored cream is handled exactly the way unflavored cream is.

Butter

Butter is often added to ganache. It contributes fat to the dispersed phase of the emulsion and lowers the melting point as a result of the eutectic effect. (See Eutetics, page 411.) Whether or not to add butter depends largely on the variety of cream and chocolate chosen and whether a liquid flavoring is used. (See Ganache Formulation Guidelines, page 99.) Lower-fat creams may require the addition of butter; however, adding butter to ganache made using high-fat cream can lead to separation due to excess fat. Because butter is itself an emulsion, do not melt it before adding it to ganache, but rather soften it and stir it into the completed emulsion in order to guard against separation and to preserve the smooth mouthfeel. Butter is not counted as a liquefier in ganache formulation.

Cocoa butter

Cocoa butter is occasionally added to ganache in order to contribute to the firmness of the center. While butter softens ganache, cocoa butter results in a harder set. Adding cocoa butter firms the ganache but does not contribute to chocolate flavor, allowing other flavors to come through. Cocoa butter can be used to firm delicately flavored ganache that would be overpowered by the addition of more chocolate. It may also be added to compensate for the use of a lower-fat chocolate. Like chocolate, cocoa butter is included in ganache formulation as a stabilizer. The addition of 1 gram of cocoa butter in formulation is roughly equivalent in setting power to 2.5 to 3 grams of chocolate. Unlike chocolate, cocoa butter is pure fat, so adding it increases the fat phase of ganache more directly than adding chocolate does. When adding cocoa butter to ganache, handle it and add it with the chocolate.

Egg yolks

Egg yolks are occasionally added to ganache for their emulsifying quality and richness. Egg ganache is a traditional center for confectioners and is still used. However, due to the potential for food-borne illness when an egg ganache is mishandled, formulas for egg ganache are not included in this work.

GANACHE TECHNIQUES

There are two common techniques for using ganache: the piped and the slabbed methods. While either may be applied to a ganache formula, the steps used for each—and the results—are quite different.

technique	theory	**PIPED GANACHE**

The piped technique is used to make truffles and other ganache centers that are to be piped or possibly shaped by hand. When ganache is made using the piped technique, it sets quickly, with a relatively firm texture that allows it to hold its shape and permit handling, as when it is rolled into truffles. The defining step of the piped technique is the tabling that tempers the ganache, causing a rapid set and the firm consistency required for piping and shaping. Without this tempering, the ganache would not set with a firm, uniform consistency.

1. **CHOP TEMPERED CHOCOLATE INTO SMALL PIECES.** The chocolate used should be tempered fresh chocolate so that it contains stable Form-V cocoa butter crystals. Not all of these crystals will melt during the process of making the ganache, and the remaining crystals will seed the ganache to ensure proper setting.

2. **IF FLAVORING THE GANACHE WITH AN AROMATIC INGREDIENT, FOLLOW THE INFUSION PROCEDURE. (SEE INFUSIONS, PAGE 102.) COMBINE THE CREAM AND LIQUID SWEETENER AND BRING TO A BOIL.** The cream and sweetener—usually glucose syrup—are boiled to further sanitize the cream and to provide enough heat to melt the chocolate. The mixture should be brought only up to a boil in the smallest diameter saucepan that is practical. Boiling cream for a prolonged period of time or boiling it in too wide a saucepan results in the evaporation of water, leaving too high a percentage of fat, which contributes to separation.

3. **POUR THE HOT CREAM OVER THE CHOPPED CHOCOLATE; ALLOW IT TO SIT UNDISTURBED FOR APPROXIMATELY 1 MINUTE.** Leaving the hot cream to sit on the chocolate allows the chocolate to melt so that it will emulsify easily with the cream.

4. **USING A PADDLE, BEGIN STIRRING IN SMALL CIRCLES IN THE CENTER OF THE BOWL UNTIL THE MIXTURE RESEMBLES "CHOCOLATE MAYONNAISE."** Stirring in small circles starts the emulsion in the center of the bowl. "Chocolate mayonnaise" is an appropriate description for the ganache: not only is it an emulsion, but it is also a fat-in-water emulsion just as mayonnaise is.

5. **CONTINUE STIRRING OUTWARD IN LARGER CIRCLES UNTIL ALL OF THE CHOCOLATE HAS MELTED AND THE MIXTURE IS HOMOGENEOUS.** Once the emulsion is formed in the center of the bowl, it can be spread throughout the ganache by stirring in wider circles.

6. **IF SOME OF THE CHOCOLATE HAS NOT MELTED, PUT THE GANACHE OVER A HOT WATER BATH. BE CERTAIN, HOWEVER, NOT TO ALLOW THE TEMPERATURE OF THE GANACHE TO EXCEED 34°C/94°F.** If some of the chocolate remains unmelted by the heat in the cream, warming the ganache lightly will melt it so that the chocolate can emulsify with the cream. Overheating melts the stable cocoa butter crystals, so the ganache should not be allowed to become warmer than 34°C/94°F. This temperature ensures that stable Form-V cocoa butter crystals are left intact to seed the ganache.

7. **ADD THE BUTTER, STIRRING IT INTO THE WARM GANACHE.** The butter should be soft but not melted so that the emulsion of the butter will not separate; this will help ensure a smooth texture. The butter is added before the liquid flavoring so that there is enough heat in the ganache to allow the butter to be incorporated.

8. **ADD THE LIQUID FLAVORING, IF USING.** The temperature of the liquid flavoring should be approximately 25° to 32°C/77° to 90°F so that it neither cools nor warms the ganache excessively.

9. **POUR THE FINISHED GANACHE INTO A LARGE, FLAT PAN THAT WILL ALLOW IT TO COOL EVENLY AND EFFICIENTLY. PLACE PLASTIC WRAP DIRECTLY ON THE SURFACE OF THE GANACHE TO PREVENT IT FROM DRYING OUT.** The ganache should be pooled into a thin layer so that it cools and crystallizes quickly.

10. **ALLOW THE GANACHE TO COOL UNDISTURBED AT ROOM TEMPERATURE TO 22°C/72°F. THE GANACHE SHOULD BE ALLOWED TO REACH A FIRM BUT MALLEABLE CONSISTENCY. THIS MAY TAKE UP TO 1 HOUR DEPENDING ON AMBIENT TEMPERATURE.** Although it is possible to proceed to step 11 without allowing the ganache to cool undisturbed, better results are obtained by letting the ganache cool at room temperature to approximately 22°C/72°F and develop a

plastic consistency. Proper consistency is a more reliable indicator than temperature that the ganache is ready to work with. This step is especially crucial with milk chocolate and white chocolate, which are more prone to separation during agitation. Refrigerating the ganache at this point leads to the formation of unstable fat crystals, and the ganache will never have the proper firmness when it returns to room temperature. (See Refrigeration of Ganache, page 107.)

11. **REMOVE THE GANACHE FROM THE PAN, PLACE IT ON A MARBLE SLAB, AND TABLE IT LIGHTLY. ALTERNATIVELY, STIR IT BRIEFLY IN A BOWL.** Agitating the ganache is the defining step in the piped method. Tabling or stirring the ganache briefly helps to crystallize the fat, accelerating the setting process. Ganache that is agitated sets firmer, with a shorter texture than unagitated ganache, making it easier to pipe and handle. Properly made ganache requires very little agitation; milk chocolate ganache that has cooled to 22°C/72°F requires only a few strokes with a palette knife on a marble slab, with approximately 2 minutes between strokes. Dark chocolate ganache requires even less agitation. Minimal agitation provides the best results. Ganache that has been overagitated has an overly short texture rather than the creamy smooth texture that is desired.

12. **PIPE THE GANACHE IMMEDIATELY AND ALLOW IT TO CRYSTALLIZE AT ROOM TEMPERATURE UNTIL FIRM, ABOUT 20 MINUTES.** Once tabled, ganache sets rapidly, so it must be piped immediately before it hardens into an unusable mass.

13. **HANDLE AND DIP AS DESIRED.** After piping, allow the ganache to crystallize at room temperature, and then continue to process as desired. With tabled ganache, crystallization is rapid, taking as little as 15 minutes, but the ganache becomes firmer and easier to handle when it is allowed to crystallize longer. Leaving the piped ganache for several hours or overnight makes for ease of handling.

LEFT: *Stir the ganache in the middle of the bowl to create the emulsion, then spread out to incorporate the remaining cream and chocolate (see step 4 of the technique).* CENTER: *Tabled ganache is ready to be piped once a sharp ridge appears when a palette knife is rested on and then lifted out of the chocolate (see step 11 of the technique).* RIGHT: *Piping the prepared ganache once it has set yields consistent portions and an easy shape for later handling and finishing (see step 12 of the technique).*

GANACHE TROUBLESHOOTING

DEFECT DURING MAKEUP	CAUSE	REMEDY
SEPARATED EMULSION	Stirring at unstable temperature	Do not stir ganache while below 30°C/86°F during makeup
	Excessive fat in ganache	Reduce fat in formula (see Ganache Formulation Guidelines, page 99)
PIPED GANACHE		
TOO SOFT WHEN SET	Insufficient chocolate in ganache	Increase chocolate in formula (see Ganache Formulation Guidelines, page 99)
	Chocolate too low in cocoa butter	Use higher-fat chocolate; add cocoa butter with chocolate
	Ganache not seeded with stable crystals	Use tempered solid chocolate to make ganache; do not allow ganache to exceed 34°C/93°F during processing
	Ganache not agitated enough	Agitate ganache more before piping it
TOO FIRM WHEN SET	Too much chocolate in ganache	Reduce chocolate in formula (see Ganache Formulation Guidelines, page 99)
	Excessively high cocoa butter content in chocolate	Use lower-fat chocolate
	Insufficient butter in formula	Increase butter in formula (see Ganache Formulation Guidelines, page 99)
SEPARATED DURING AGITATION	Ganache agitated at unstable temperature	Allow ganache to cool to 22°C/72°F and to reach a plastic consistency before agitating it
	Ganache agitated excessively	Agitate less; agitate more slowly
GRAINY TEXTURE	Ganache agitated excessively	Agitate less; agitate more slowly
	Ganache allowed to crystallize while separated	Repair separated emulsion before allowing ganache to set

REFRIGERATION OF GANACHE

One of the defining qualities of confections is that they are preserved by a low water-activity level and require no refrigeration. People without a thorough understanding of the formulation and handling of ganache are accustomed to refrigerating it before forming it into centers. While it is possible to handle ganache this way, such a method is not only unnecessary but is ill advised for the professional confectioner who seeks superior texture, appearance, and shelf life. Refrigeration can have a number of adverse effects on chocolate and confectionery. The general side effects of refrigerating chocolate include the formation of sugar bloom on chocolate that has set, due to humidity and condensation, and the formation of unstable cocoa butter crystals in chocolate that has not set, resulting in poor gloss, poor snap, and the development of fat bloom during storage.

Refrigerating ganache has a detrimental effect on its consistency, making it too soft to handle at room temperature and causing the formation of large fat crystals during storage. Like chocolate, ganache is polymorphic. (See Polymorphism of Cocoa Butter, page 55.) When it is properly made using either the piped or slabbed method, it contains stable Form-V cocoa butter crystals, which seed the ganache and prompt it to set firm at room temperature. With the presence of these stable crystals, the ganache also remains stable during storage and will not change significantly during its shelf life.

When ganache is force-set at refrigerator temperatures, however, the fat crystals that form in it are unstable lower crystal forms. Such crystals will cause the ganache to be excessively soft when it is returned to room temperature, making it impossible to work with—unless it is handled and dipped while cold. Dipping cold ganache centers creates a host of problems, including condensation, resulting in thickened chocolate and sugar bloom, and an excessively thick chocolate shell and the formation of lower crystal forms, causing poor gloss and snap and a tendency to bloom during storage. Dipping cold centers also causes the shells to crack and the ganache to protrude due to expansion of the centers when they return to room temperature while the crystallizing chocolate shell is simultaneously contracting. These defects diminish shelf life by allowing moisture migration, causing the ganache to dry, and exposing the centers to oxygen, which promotes rancidity. In addition to this litany of defects, the unstable crystals initially formed during refrigeration transform to higher forms during storage, resulting in large crystals and a grainy texture.

Under certain circumstances, such as a warmer-than-ideal working environment and a rushed production schedule, briefly refrigerating properly formulated and precrystallized ganache—for no more than 3 to 4 minutes—can help to speed crystallization without adverse consequences. Beyond this minor application, refrigeration of ganache has no place in the techniques of the artisan confectioner. Superior results will always be obtained from longer crystallization at proper room temperature.

Refrigeration causes ganache centers to contract, expand, and then crack or erupt from the surface of the chocolate shell.

The slabbed technique of making and handling ganache is designed to create a center with the creamiest, smoothest texture possible. When the slabbed technique is followed, the ganache is seeded with stable cocoa butter crystals from tempered chocolate and is not agitated to alter crystallization. As a result, slabbed ganache sets softer, with a smoother texture than the same ganache made following the piped procedure. The slabbed technique requires more effort and attention to detail than some other methods for making ganache, but it consistently provides superior texture and flavor.

1. **THE CHOCOLATE USED FOR THE SLABBED TECHNIQUE SHOULD BE MELTED, TEMPERED CHOCOLATE AT ITS MAXIMUM WORKING TEMPERATURE: 32°C/90°F FOR DARK CHOCOLATE, 30°C/86°F FOR MILK AND WHITE CHOCOLATES.** Melted, tempered chocolate contains the stable Form-V cocoa butter crystals required for proper crystallization. Because it is melted, the chocolate is ready to be mixed with the liquefier to create the emulsion. In this method, the melted, tempered chocolate allows the emulsion to be formed without ever melting the stable fat crystals. When a measured amount of tempered chocolate is needed for a formula, it is most practical to temper a slightly larger quantity of chocolate than needed. The required quantity of tempered chocolate can then be scaled to allow for loss of chocolate on the marble if tabling, or gain in chocolate if seeding.

2. **IF FLAVORING THE GANACHE WITH AN AROMATIC INGREDIENT, FOLLOW THE INFUSION PROCEDURE. (SEE INFUSIONS, PAGE 102.)** Combine the cream and liquid sweetener and bring to a boil. After making an infusion if necessary, the cream and adjunct sweetener are brought to a boil in order to further sanitize the cream and incorporate the glucose syrup. The mixture should be brought only up to a boil in the smallest diameter saucepan that is practical. Boiling cream for a prolonged period of time or boiling it in too wide a saucepan results in the evaporation of water, leaving too high a percentage of fat, which contributes to separation.

3. **REMOVE THE CREAM FROM THE HEAT AND ADD THE LIQUID FLAVORING, IF USING.** Liquid flavorings are not boiled with the cream, but are added to the cream after it is removed from the heat. This prevents evaporation of volatile flavor compounds, as in the case of extracts or liqueurs, or curdling of the cream, as in the case of acidic flavorings such as fruit purées.

4. **ALLOW THE LIQUEFIERS TO COOL TO 40°C/105°F.** The slabbed method is highly temperature dependent; if the liquefiers are too warm when they are added to the chocolate, the Form-V crystals in the tempered chocolate will melt, and the ganache will not set properly, resulting in a soft ganache that cannot be handled. If the liquefiers are too cool, the ganache will not emulsify, resulting in a separated ganache. It requires practice to bring the tempered chocolate to its optimum working temperature at the same time that the cream, glucose syrup, and liquid flavoring are at 40°C/105°F. This is, however, the key to success in the slabbed technique, and it is the best way to ensure a perfect texture every time.

5. **STIR THE VERY SOFT BUTTER INTO THE TEMPERED CHOCOLATE.** The butter used in the slabbed method must be very soft, right on the cusp of melting (slightly warmer than room temperature, about 25°C/77°F so that it is incorporated into the tempered chocolate without leaving lumps. The butter should not be melted, which would separate its emulsion and prevent the ganache from having a smooth texture.

6. **POUR THE 40°C/105°F LIQUID ONTO THE CHOCOLATE ALL AT ONCE. BEGIN STIRRING IN SMALL CIRCLES IN THE CENTER OF THE BOWL, GRADUALLY EXPANDING THE CIRCLES OUTWARD UNTIL THE GANACHE IS SMOOTH.** Stirring the chocolate as the liquefiers are added is likely to cause the chocolate to seize. To avoid this, pour all of the liquefiers onto the tempered chocolate without stirring. Once the liquefiers are on the tempered chocolate, stirring in the center of the bowl forms the emulsion, and stirring outward then spreads the emulsion throughout the bowl. Stirring should be vigorous to emulsify the mixture as efficiently as possible before it loses too much of its heat. If the ganache is not handled quickly and efficiently, it will cool to an unstable temperature and will be likely to separate during stirring or when it is spread into frames.

7. **SPREAD THE FINISHED GANACHE IMMEDIATELY INTO FRAMES AND ALLOW TO CRYSTALLIZE OVERNIGHT. PLACE PLASTIC WRAP DIRECTLY ON THE SURFACE OF THE GANACHE.** When properly performed, the slabbed method produces ganache that is fully emulsified and precrystallized and requires no tabling, resulting in a

very smooth, creamy texture once crystallized. A properly made slabbed ganache always provides a much smoother texture than a ganache made using the piped technique. Slabbed ganache should be deposited into frames as quickly as possible to prevent separation due to agitation as it cools. Because it is not tabled, slabbed ganache typically requires more time for crystallization than piped ganache does. To enable it to reach its full degree of firmness, allow it to crystal-lize at room temperature overnight, covered with a sheet of plastic wrap to prevent it from drying out due to moisture migration. Allowing the ganache to crystal-lize at room temperature rather than refrigerating it prevents the formation of unstable fat crystals, which would result in an excessively soft ganache that would not remain smooth during storage. (See Refrigeration of Ganache, page 107.)

GANACHE TROUBLESHOOTING

DEFECT DURING MAKEUP	CAUSE	REMEDY
SLABBED GANACHE		
TOO SOFT WHEN SET	Insufficient chocolate in ganache	Increase chocolate in formula (see Ganache Formulation Guidelines, page 99)
	Chocolate too low in cocoa butter	Use higher-fat chocolate; add cocoa butter to chocolate
	Ganache not seeded with stable crystals	Use tempered melted chocolate to make ganache
		Do not add liquids at over 40°C/105°F
		Do not allow ganache to exceed 34°C/93°F during processing
	Ganache crystallized in refrigerator	Allow ganache to crystallize overnight at room temperature
TOO FIRM WHEN SET	Too much chocolate in ganache	Reduce chocolate in formula (see Ganache Formulation Guidelines, page 99)
	Excessively high cocoa butter content in chocolate	Use lower-fat chocolate
	Insufficient butterfat in ganache	Increase butter in formula (see Ganache Formulation Guidelines, page 99)
GRAINY TEXTURE	Ganache allowed to crystallize while separated	Repair separated emulsion before allowing ganache to set
	Ganache not seeded with stable crystals	Use tempered melted chocolate to make ganache
		Do not add liquids at over 40°C/105°F
		Do not allow ganache to exceed 34°C/93°F during processing
CHOCOLATE COVERING CRACKED AND DULL FINISH	Centers dipped while cold	Dip centers at room temperature

GANACHE

	PIPED TECHNIQUE	SLABBED TECHNIQUE
RATIO OF CHOCOLATE TO LIQUEFIERS	2:1 dark chocolate 2.5:1 milk and white chocolates	2:1 dark chocolate 2.5:1 milk and white chocolates
CONDITION OF CHOCOLATE	Unmelted, tempered chocolate at room temperature	Melted, tempered chocolate at maximum working temperature
TEMPERATURE OF LIQUEFIERS WHEN ADDED TO THE CHOCOLATE	Just below the boiling point	Boiled, cooled to 40°C/105°F
HANDLING TECHNIQUES	Make ganache by piped method; table, or agitate, prior to piping to facilitate piping and handling	Make ganache by slab method, pour immediately into frames to crystallize
RATE OF CRYSTALLIZATION	Very rapid crystallization after agitation and piping	Overnight crystallization
TEXTURE OF THE FINISHED GANACHE	Slightly firmer set, shorter texture	Smoother, softer set, creamier texture

technique | theory | HOLLOW SHELL TRUFFLES

The hollow-shell technique is a fast, efficient method for making truffles with a high degree of uniformity. Hollow shells allow for centers that are softer than could be handled for dipping and create an enjoyable textural contrast between shell and filling. The ganache used in hollow-shell truffles typically contains approximately 25 percent less chocolate than a piped or slabbed ganache.

With soft fillings, caution should be exercised regarding water activity and shelf life. As the liquid portion of the ganache is increased, the water activity rises with it, and the shelf stability is diminished. In these ganaches, extra sugars, in the form of invert sugar and glucose syrup, are added to help to lower the water-activity level.

1. **MAKE UP THE GANACHE BY THE PIPED METHOD, BUT DO NOT TABLE IT.** As with the piped technique, the chocolate used in the hollow-shell technique should be tempered solid chocolate, so that the stable cocoa butter crystals it contains will seed the ganache, resulting in a smooth, uniform texture. Ganache for hollow shells is not agitated, because it does not require as much manual handling as piped ganache, and a softer consistency is the goal. Additionally, the lower cocoa butter content makes additional tempering unnecessary.

2. **POUR THE GANACHE IN A SHALLOW LAYER IN THE BOTTOM OF A HOTEL PAN OR SHEET PAN. PLACE PLASTIC WRAP DIRECTLY ON THE SURFACE OF THE GANACHE.** Pouring a thin layer of ganache allows for rapid and efficient cooling. Covering the ganache with plastic wrap prevents the formation of a skin.

3. **ALLOW THE GANACHE TO COOL TO APPROXIMATELY 25° TO 29°C/77° TO 85°F, OR TO THICK NAPPÉ CONSISTENCY.** The ganache must be cooled enough not to soften or melt the shells when they are filled. The ganache should have a fluid consistency, however, or it will very likely trap air inside the shells, allowing for the growth of mold.

4. **FILL THE SHELLS WITH GANACHE, TAKING CARE NOT TO CREATE AIR POCKETS.** The shells should be filled to the tops, so as not to trap air (see step 3).

5. **ALLOW THE GANACHE TO CRYSTALLIZE ENOUGH TO FORM A SKIN.** If possible, the ganache should be allowed to crystallize at room temperature for several hours or overnight. This allows the ganache not only to crystallize on the surface but also to contract slightly, facilitating capping. If time is an issue, and it is not possible to allow long crystallization, the shells may be refrigerated for several minutes to allow the surface of the ganache to crystallize. However, refrigerated ganache does not contract as a ganache with a longer, more thorough crystallization process does.

6. **CAP WITH CHOCOLATE.** The truffle shells may be capped using a piping bag and tempered chocolate. If a sealing tray is employed to cap the shells, use untempered chocolate, which prevents the filled shells from adhering to the tray. The sealing tray method is particularly efficient if large quantities of truffles are being produced. When using a sealing tray, it is important that the shells be on a level surface in order for the template to seal against the shells properly.

7. **DIP OR ENROBE, AND FINISH AS DESIRED.** The filled and capped shells are like precoated truffles and must be dipped or enrobed in chocolate in order to disguise the seam and cap. Any of the usual methods for finishing truffles may be applied to these confections.

LEFT: *Ganache of any flavor can be piped into hollow shells for truffle production (see step 4 of the technique).* RIGHT: *Using a sealing tray, cap the filled shells with an even layer of tempered chocolate (see step 6 of the technique).*

FINISHING TRUFFLES

Truffles are one of the most widely made and recognized of all confections. In the United States, there is no official standard for identifying truffles, as there is in some European countries, so definitions vary. It is generally agreed, however, that truffles consist of a ganache center. And if they are to be called truffles, it is reasonable to assume that they be more or less round, like their fungi namesakes. Even within these parameters, however, truffles may be made and finished in a wide variety of ways that produce various visual styles and represent varying degrees of labor intensity.

Because of their round shape, truffles are subject to the formation of feet. To guard against this unsightly condition, regardless of the method used for finishing truffles, it is advisable to use chocolate that is seeded slightly more than usual and is therefore somewhat more viscous than chocolate used for dipping other centers.

technique | FORK-DIPPING TRUFFLES

Using a dipping fork to finish truffles creates a relatively smooth finish and a thick coating of chocolate that provides a good textural contrast to the center.

1. Precoat the truffle following the procedure on page 65.

2. Dip the precoated truffle into tempered chocolate using a round or spiral fork. Repeatedly touch the truffle to the surface of the chocolate to remove excess chocolate and prevent the formation of feet.

3. Clean the truffle on the edge of the bowl.

4. Roll the truffle off of the fork and onto a receiving tray. Move the fork over the top of the truffle to allow excess chocolate to fall on the truffle, creating a small flair on the top.

5. If desired, sprinkle a garnish on top of the truffle as the chocolate sets.

technique | HAND-DIPPING TRUFFLES

Hand-dipping is the quickest and easiest way for the artisan to finish truffles. When properly executed, this technique creates truffles that are every bit the equal of those finished by fork-dipping. Care must be taken, however, that a thick enough coating of chocolate is applied to the truffles to create the desired textural contrast to the center.

1. Precoat the truffle following the procedure on page 65.

2. Use the identical technique to apply a second coat of chocolate to each truffle. The only difference between the two coats is that the precoat should be thin, and the second coat should be thicker, to supply the crunch of tempered chocolate.

3. (Optional) After hand-dipping the truffle, roll it in any number of dry finishes to create texture, flavor, and visual effect. Frequently used finishes include sifted cocoa powder, confectioners' sugar, or a combination of the two, and toasted chopped nuts. Any type of dry finish may be used, provided it is not excessively hygroscopic, as caramelized sugar would be.

Although somewhat more labor intensive than many other finishing techniques, the poodle-curl method provides truffles with a distinctive appearance that can represent a signature item.

Decorative elements, such as these poodle curls, add textural depth and visual allure to finished truffles.

1. Spread approximately 50 grams/2 ounces of tempered chocolate in a thin band (2 mm/¹⁄₁₆ in thick) near the edge of a marble slab.

2. Using a cake comb, comb the band of chocolate, pressing hard to clear the areas where the teeth of the comb contact the stone.

3. Allow the chocolate to set to a firm but pliable consistency.

4. Use a slicing knife, cut approximately 4-millimeter/³⁄₁₆-inch sections from the band of chocolate to create curls. Each curl should be nearly a complete circle. If the chocolate is not sufficiently set, it will not curl. If it has crystallized excessively, it will crack rather than curl.

5. Place the completed curls into a shallow pan.

6. Precoat the truffle following the procedure on page 65.

7. Using a round or spiral fork, dip the precoated truffle into tempered chocolate as in the basic fork-dipping technique. (See page 112.) Then place the dipped truffle immediately into the curls. Repeat with several truffles as the chocolate on the first ones begins to thicken.

8. Work in the order in which the truffles were dipped. When the chocolate on the first one begins to thicken, use two dipping forks to roll each truffle in the poodle curls. Remove the finished truffles from the pan of curls.

LEFT: *The chocolate should be beginning to set before truffles are rolled in chocolate shavings.* RIGHT: *These Madagascar Marbles (page 120) have been rolled in chocolate shavings.*

technique | **SPIKED TRUFFLES**

1. Precoat the truffle following the procedure on page 65.

2. Using a round or spiral fork, dip the precoated truffle into tempered chocolate as in the basic fork-dipping technique. (See page 112.) Place the dipped truffle immediately on an icing screen. Repeat with 10 to 15 truffles, remembering the order in which the truffles were dipped.

3. Allow the chocolate to sit until it begins to thicken. It is ready to work with when it holds a spike when touched with a fork.

4. Work in the same order in which the truffles were dipped. Use two dipping forks to roll each truffle lightly across the screen to create spikes on its surface. The best finish is achieved by minimal rolling, to create a few well-defined spikes and leave areas of smooth chocolate.

5. Remove the truffles from the screen immediately to prevent them from sticking to it.

TOP, LEFT: *Dipped truffles are placed on an icing screen and left until the chocolate begins to set slightly.* RIGHT: *The chocolate on the outside of the truffles is ready when it holds a peak when touched.*

BOTTOM, LEFT: *The truffles are rolled lightly on the screen to create spikes.* CENTER: *The truffles are removed from the screen before the chocolate sets completely.* RIGHT: *The surface of properly spiked chocolate truffles is both smooth and spiked.*

LIQUEUR GANACHE

yield: **120 PIECES**

Heavy cream	180 g	6 oz	25%
Glucose syrup	60 g	2 oz	7%
Dark chocolate, unmelted, tempered, chopped	430 g	15 oz	60%
Butter, soft	20 g	1 oz	3%
Spirit or liqueur	30 g	1 oz	5%
BATCH SIZE	720 g	25 oz	100%
Dark chocolate, melted, tempered, for precoating	as needed		
Garnish for finishing	as needed		

1. Combine the cream and glucose syrup in a saucepan. Bring to a boil.
2. Pour the hot cream mixture over the chopped dark chocolate and let sit for 1 minute to allow the chocolate to melt.
3. Using a spoon or spatula, stir the mixture in vigorous small circles in the center of the bowl until it emulsifies.
4. Stir outward in larger circles to spread the emulsion throughout the bowl, checking to see that all of the chocolate has melted. If necessary, heat the ganache over a hot water bath to melt the chocolate. The temperature of the ganache should not exceed 34°C/94°F.
5. Stir the butter into the ganache, taking care that no lumps of butter remain.
6. Stream in the spirit or liqueur, stirring until the mixture is homogeneous.
7. Pour the ganache into a hotel pan, allowing the ganache to cover the bottom of the pan in a thin layer. Place plastic wrap directly on the surface of the ganache. Allow to rest at room temperature until slightly firm and of a plastic consistency. This may take 1 hour, depending on the ambient temperature.
8. Agitate the ganache lightly by placing it on a marble slab and working it gently to induce crystallization.
9. Pipe as desired. Allow to crystallize at room temperature until firm enough to handle, about 20 minutes.
10. Precoat the piped ganache in the tempered dark chocolate by hand-dipping.
11. Finish as desired.

    NOTE: This formula may be used to make truffles or any other type of ganache center desired. Either the piped or the slabbed method may be employed. (See pages 104–109.)

ORANGE TRUFFLES

yield: **130 TRUFFLES**

Heavy cream	130 g	5 oz	16%
Glucose syrup	40 g	1 oz	5%
White chocolate, unmelted, tempered, chopped	500 g	18 oz	62%
Cocoa butter, unmelted, tempered, chopped	30 g	1 oz	4%
Butter, soft	10 g	0.5 oz	2%
Orange liqueur	30 g	1 oz	3%
Orange confit, diced 3 mm/⅛ in	60 g	2 oz	8%
BATCH SIZE	800 g	28.5 oz	100%

White chocolate, melted, tempered,
for precoating and dipping   as needed

1. Combine the cream and glucose syrup in a saucepan. Bring to a boil.
2. Pour the hot cream mixture over the chopped white chocolate and cocoa butter and let sit for 1 minute to allow the chocolate to melt.
3. Using a spoon or spatula, stir the mixture in vigorous small circles in the center of the bowl until it emulsifies.
4. Stir outward in larger circles to spread the emulsion throughout the bowl, checking to see that all of the chocolate has melted. If necessary, heat the ganache over a hot water bath to melt the chocolate. The temperature of the ganache should not exceed 32°C/90°F.
5. Stir the butter into the ganache, taking care that no lumps of butter remain.
6. Stream in the orange liqueur, stirring until the mixture is homogeneous.
7. Stir in the diced orange confit.
8. Pour the ganache into a hotel pan, allowing the ganache to cover the bottom of the pan in a thin layer. Place plastic wrap directly on the surface of the ganache. Allow to rest at room temperature until slightly firm and of a plastic consistency. This may take 1 hour, depending on the ambient temperature.
9. Agitate the ganache lightly by placing it on a marble slab and working it gently to induce crystallization.
10. Using a pastry bag fitted with a no. 4 round tip, pipe truffles onto parchment paper. Allow to crystallize at room temperature until firm enough to handle, about 20 minutes.
11. Roll the piped truffles into balls and precoat in the tempered white chocolate by hand-dipping.
12. Using a round dipping fork, dip the precoated truffles in the tempered white chocolate and place them on an icing screen. Allow the chocolate to set until it holds a peak when touched.
13. Using two forks, roll each truffle lightly on the screen to create texture. Remove immediately and place on parchment paper.

TRUFFLE TRUFFLES

yield: **120 TRUFFLES**

Heavy cream	200 g	7 oz	28%
Glucose syrup	60 g	2 oz	9%
Dark chocolate, unmelted, tempered, chopped	410 g	15 oz	56%
Butter, soft	10 g	0.5 oz	1%
Cognac	40 g	1.5 oz	6%
White truffle oil (see Note)	about ¾ tsp	about ¾ tsp	<1%
BATCH SIZE	720 g	26 oz	100%
Dark chocolate, melted, tempered, for precoating and dipping	as needed		
Cocoa powder, sifted, for finishing	as needed		

1. Combine the cream and glucose syrup in a saucepan. Bring to a boil.
2. Pour the hot cream mixture over the chopped dark chocolate and let sit for 1 minute to allow the chocolate to melt.
3. Using a spoon or spatula, stir the mixture in vigorous small circles in the center of the bowl until it emulsifies.
4. Stir outward in larger circles to spread the emulsion throughout the bowl, checking to see that all of the chocolate has melted. If necessary, heat the ganache over a hot water bath to melt the chocolate. The temperature of the ganache should not exceed 34°C/94°F.
5. Stir the butter into the ganache, taking care that no lumps of butter remain.
6. Stream in the cognac, stirring until the mixture is homogeneous.
7. Stir in the truffle oil.
8. Pour the ganache into a hotel pan, allowing the ganache to cover the bottom of the pan in a thin layer. Place plastic wrap directly on the surface of the ganache. Allow to rest at room temperature until slightly firm and of a plastic consistency. This may take 1 hour, depending on the ambient temperature.
9. Agitate the ganache lightly by placing it on a marble slab and working it gently to induce crystallization.
10. Using a pastry bag fitted with a no. 4 round tip, pipe truffles onto parchment paper. Allow to crystallize at room temperature until firm enough to handle, about 20 minutes.
11. Roll the truffles into balls and precoat in the dark chocolate by hand-dipping.
12. Using a round dipping fork, dip the precoated truffles in the tempered dark chocolate.
13. Finish by rolling the dipped truffles in the cocoa powder immediately.

    NOTE: The amount of white truffle oil may vary widely depending on the strength of the oil and on the flavor desired.

MADAGASCAR MARBLES

yield: **190 PIECES**

WHITE CHOCOLATE GANACHE

Heavy cream	150 g	5 oz	21%
Vanilla bean, split and scraped	½ bean	½ bean	
Milk	as needed		
Glucose syrup	50 g	2 oz	8%
White chocolate, unmelted, tempered, chopped	450 g	16 oz	67%
Butter, soft	30 g	1 oz	4%
BATCH SIZE	680 g	24 oz	100%

DARK CHOCOLATE GANACHE

Heavy cream	210 g	7 oz	30%
Vanilla bean, split and scraped	½ bean	½ bean	
Milk	as needed		
Glucose syrup	60 g	2 oz	9%
Dark chocolate, unmelted, tempered, chopped	380 g	13 oz	57%
Butter, soft	30 g	1 oz	4%
BATCH SIZE	680 g	23 oz	100%
Dark chocolate, melted, tempered, for precoating and dipping	as needed		
Dark, milk, and white chocolate shavings for finishing	as needed		

TO MAKE THE WHITE CHOCOLATE GANACHE:

1. Combine the cream with the vanilla bean and its seeds in a saucepan and bring to a boil. Remove from the heat, cover, and let steep for 5 minutes.

2. Strain the infused cream through premoistened cheesecloth. Wring the vanilla bean in the cheesecloth to extract the maximum amount of flavor possible.

3. Return the cream to 150 grams by adding milk.

4. Add the glucose syrup to the flavored cream mixture. Bring to a boil.

5. Pour the hot cream mixture over the chopped white chocolate and let sit for 1 minute to allow the chocolate to melt.

6. Using a spoon or spatula, stir the mixture in vigorous small circles in the center of the bowl until it emulsifies.

7. Stir outward in larger circles to spread the emulsion throughout the bowl, checking to see that all of the chocolate has melted. If necessary, heat the ganache over a hot water bath to melt the chocolate. The temperature of the ganache should not exceed 32°C/90°F.

8. Stir the butter into the ganache, taking care that no lumps of butter remain.

9. Pour the ganache into a hotel pan, allowing the ganache to cover the bottom of the pan in a thin layer. Place plastic wrap directly on the surface of the ganache. Allow to rest at room temperature until slightly firm and of a plastic consistency. This may take 1 hour, depending on the ambient temperature.

TO MAKE THE DARK CHOCOLATE GANACHE:

1. Combine the cream with the vanilla bean and its seeds in a saucepan and bring to a boil. Remove from the heat, cover, and let steep for 5 minutes.

2. Strain the infused cream through premoistened cheesecloth. Wring the vanilla bean in the cheesecloth to extract the maximum amount of flavor possible.

3. Return the cream to 210 grams by adding milk.

4. Add the glucose syrup to the flavored cream mixture. Bring to a boil.

5. Pour the hot cream mixture over the chopped dark chocolate and let sit for 1 minute to allow the chocolate to melt.

6. Using a spoon or spatula, stir the mixture in vigorous small circles in the center of the bowl until it emulsifies.

7. Stir outward in larger circles to spread the emulsion throughout the bowl, checking to see that all of the chocolate has melted. If necessary, heat the ganache over a hot water bath to melt the chocolate. The temperature of the ganache should not exceed 34°C/94°F.

8. Stir the butter into the ganache, taking care that no lumps of butter remain.

9. Pour the ganache into a hotel pan, allowing the ganache to cover the bottom of the pan in a thin layer. Place plastic wrap directly on the surface of the ganache. Allow to rest at room temperature until slightly firm and of a plastic consistency. This may take 1 hour, depending on the ambient temperature.

TO MAKE THE MADAGASCAR MARBLES:

1. Agitate the dark chocolate ganache lightly by placing it on a marble slab and working it gently to induce crystallization. Using a pastry bag fitted with a no. 4 round tip, pipe into 4-gram balls.

2. Follow step 1 to agitate the white chocolate ganache to temper. Pipe a second 4-gram ball of white chocolate ganache on top of each dark chocolate ganache ball.

3. Allow to crystallize at room temperature until firm enough to handle, about 30 minutes.

4. Roll the truffles into balls; avoid smearing the ganaches together.

5. Precoat the truffles in the tempered dark chocolate by hand-dipping.

6. Using a round dipping fork, dip the precoated truffles in the tempered dark chocolate.

7. Finish by rolling the dipped truffles in the dark, milk, and white chocolate shavings immediately.

CHERRY KIRSCH TRUFFLES

yield: **125 TRUFFLES**

Heavy cream	220 g	8 oz	21%
Glucose syrup	70 g	2.5 oz	7%
White chocolate, unmelted, tempered, chopped	560 g	20 oz	53%
Butter, very soft	30 g	1 oz	3%
Kirschwasser	60 g	2 oz	5%
Dried cherries, finely diced	110 g	4 oz	11%
BATCH SIZE	1050 g	37.5 oz	100%
White chocolate hollow truffle shells (see page 110)	125 shells		
White chocolate, melted, untempered or tempered, for sealing	as needed		
White chocolate, melted, tempered, for dipping	as needed		

1. Combine the cream and glucose syrup in a saucepan. Bring to a boil.

2. Pour the hot cream mixture over the chopped white chocolate and let sit for 1 minute to allow the chocolate to melt.

3. Using a spoon or spatula, stir the mixture in vigorous small circles in the center of the bowl until it emulsifies.

4. Stir outward in larger circles to spread the emulsion throughout the bowl, checking to see that all of the chocolate has melted. If necessary, heat the ganache over a hot water bath to melt the chocolate. The temperature of the ganache should not exceed 32°C/90°F.

5. Stir the butter into the ganache, taking care that no lumps of butter remain.

6. Stream in the kirschwasser, stirring until the mixture is homogeneous.

7. Add the dried cherries and stir to distribute them uniformly. (If the cherries are stuck in a solid mass after chopping, they may be lightly moistened with kirschwasser to separate them.)

8. Pour the ganache into a hotel pan, allowing the ganache to cover the bottom of the pan in a thin layer. Place plastic wrap directly on the surface of the ganache.

9. Allow the ganache to rest at room temperature until it reaches 25°C/77°F, or slightly cooler, approximately 20 minutes. The cooled ganache should be of a thick but fluid consistency to properly fill the shells.

10. Agitate the ganache lightly by placing it on a marble slab and working it gently to induce crystallization. (See Note.)

11. Using a disposable pastry bag with a small opening cut in the tip, fill the truffle shells to the tops with the ganache.

12. Allow the ganache to crystallize at room temperature until the top is solid, approximately 1 hour.

13. Seal the truffles using either untempered white chocolate with a sealing tray or tempered white chocolate applied with a paper cone.

14. Using a round dipping fork, dip the truffles in the tempered white chocolate, then place them on an icing screen.

15. Allow the chocolate to begin to set so that it holds a peak when touched.

16. Roll the dipped truffles lightly on the screen to texture them. Remove immediately and place on parchment paper.

NOTE: Tabling ganache for use in hollow truffle shells is unusual, but it helps to prevent the dried cherries from settling on one side of the truffles. This step is not necessary if the ganache has crystallized sufficiently to hold the cherries in suspension.

CHAI TIGERS

yield: **120 PIECES**

Heavy cream	180 g	6 oz	25%
Chai tea blend	10 g	0.5 oz	2%
Vanilla bean, split and scraped	1 bean	1 bean	
Milk	as needed		
Glucose syrup	60 g	2 oz	8%
Milk chocolate, unmelted, tempered, chopped	460 g	16 oz	62%
Butter, very soft	20 g	1 oz	3%
BATCH SIZE	730 g	25.5 oz	100%
Milk chocolate, melted, tempered, for precoating and dipping	as needed		
Dark chocolate, tempered, for finishing	as needed		

1. Combine the cream, tea blend, and the vanilla bean and its seeds in a saucepan and bring to a boil. Remove from the heat, cover, and let steep for 5 minutes.

2. Strain the infused the cream through premoistened cheesecloth. Wring the tea solids and vanilla bean in the cheesecloth to extract the maximum amount of flavor possible.

3. Return the cream to 180 g by adding milk.

4. Add the glucose syrup to the flavored cream mixture. Bring to a boil.

5. Pour the hot cream mixture over the chopped milk chocolate and let sit for 1 minute to allow the chocolate to melt.

6. Using a spoon or spatula, stir the mixture in vigorous small circles in the center of the bowl until it emulsifies.

7. Stir outward in larger circles to spread the emulsion throughout the bowl, checking to see that all of the chocolate has melted. If necessary, heat the ganache over a hot water bath to melt the chocolate. The temperature of the ganache should not exceed 32°C/90°F.

8. Stir the butter into the ganache, taking care that no lumps of butter remain.

9. Pour the ganache into a hotel pan, allowing the ganache to cover the bottom of the pan in a thin layer. Place plastic wrap directly on the surface of the ganache. Allow to rest at room temperature until slightly firm and of a plastic consistency. This may take 1 hour, depending on the ambient temperature.

10. Agitate the ganache lightly by placing it on a marble slab and working it gently to induce crystallization.

11. Using a pastry bag fitted with a no. 4 round tip, pipe truffles onto parchment paper. Allow to crystallize at room temperature until firm enough to handle, about 20 minutes.

12. Roll the piped truffles into balls and precoat in the tempered milk chocolate by hand-dipping.

13. Using a round dipping fork, dip the precoated truffles in the tempered milk chocolate. Allow to set fully.

14. Using a paper cone, filigree each truffle with 4 stripes of the tempered dark chocolate.

AMARETTI TRUFFLES

yield: **120 TRUFFLES**

Heavy cream	150 g	5 oz	21%
Glucose syrup	50 g	2 oz	6%
Almond paste	40 g	1.5 oz	5%
Milk chocolate, unmelted, tempered, chopped	450 g	16 oz	63%
Amaretto liqueur	40 g	1.5 oz	5%
BATCH SIZE	730 g	26 oz	100%
Dark chocolate, melted, tempered, for precoating and dipping	as needed		
Pine nuts, toasted, for finishing	as needed		

1. Combine the cream, glucose syrup, and almond paste in a saucepan. Bring to a boil, stirring to break up the almond paste.

2. Pour the hot cream mixture over the chopped milk chocolate and let sit for 1 minute to allow the chocolate to melt.

3. Using a spoon or spatula, stir the mixture in vigorous small circles in the center of the bowl until it emulsifies.

4. Stir outward in larger circles to spread the emulsion throughout the bowl, checking to see that all of the chocolate has melted. If necessary, heat the ganache over a hot water bath to melt the chocolate. The temperature of the ganache should not exceed 32°C/90°F.

5. Stream in the amaretto liqueur, stirring until the mixture is homogeneous.

6. Pour the ganache into a hotel pan, allowing the ganache to cover the bottom of the pan in a thin layer. Place plastic wrap directly on the surface of the ganache. Allow to rest at room temperature until slightly firm and of a plastic consistency. This may take 1 hour, depending on the ambient temperature.

7. Agitate the ganache lightly by placing it on a marble slab and working it gently to induce crystallization.

8. Using a pastry bag fitted with a no. 4 round tip, pipe truffles onto parchment paper. Allow to crystallize at room temperature until firm enough to handle, about 20 minutes.

9. Roll the piped truffles into balls and precoat in the tempered dark chocolate by hand-dipping.

10. Using a round dipping fork, dip the precoated truffles in the tempered dark chocolate.

11. When the chocolate begins to set, place 3 pine nuts on top of each truffle.

POODLE TRUFFLES

yield: **120 TRUFFLES**

Heavy cream	180 g	6 oz	24%
Dark-roast coffee beans, coarsely ground	10 g	0.5 oz	2%
Milk	as needed		
Glucose syrup	60 g	2 oz	8%
Dark chocolate, unmelted, tempered, chopped	400 g	14 oz	54%
Butter, very soft	40 g	1.5 oz	6%
Coffee liqueur	40 g	1.5 oz	6%
BATCH SIZE	730 g	25.5 oz	100%
Dark chocolate, melted, tempered, for precoating and dipping	as needed		
Chocolate poodle curls (see page 113), for finishing	as needed		

1. Combine the cream and the ground coffee in a saucepan and bring to a boil. Remove from the heat, cover, and let steep for 5 minutes.
2. Strain the infused cream through premoistened cheesecloth. Wring the coffee grounds in the cheesecloth to extract the maximum amount of flavor possible.
3. Return the cream to 180 g by adding milk.
4. Add the glucose syrup to the flavored cream mixture. Bring to a boil.
5. Pour the hot cream mixture over the chopped dark chocolate and let sit for 1 minute to allow the chocolate to melt.
6. Using a spoon or spatula, stir the mixture in vigorous small circles in the center of the bowl until it emulsifies.
7. Stir outward in larger circles to spread the emulsion throughout the bowl, checking to see that all of the chocolate has melted. If necessary, heat the ganache over a hot water bath to melt the chocolate. The temperature of the ganache should not exceed 34°C/94°F.
8. Stir the butter into the ganache, taking care that no lumps of butter remain.
9. Stream in the coffee liqueur, stirring until the mixture is homogeneous.
10. Agitate the ganache lightly by placing it on a marble slab and working it gently to induce crystallization.
11. Using a pastry bag fitted with a no. 3 round tip, pipe truffles onto parchment paper. Allow to crystallize at room temperature until firm enough to handle, about 20 minutes.
12. Roll the piped truffles into balls and precoat in the tempered dark chocolate by hand-dipping.
13. Using a round dipping fork, dip the precoated truffles in the tempered dark chocolate and place them in the chocolate poodle curls.
14. When the chocolate begins to set, use two forks to roll the truffles in the curls to coat them completely.

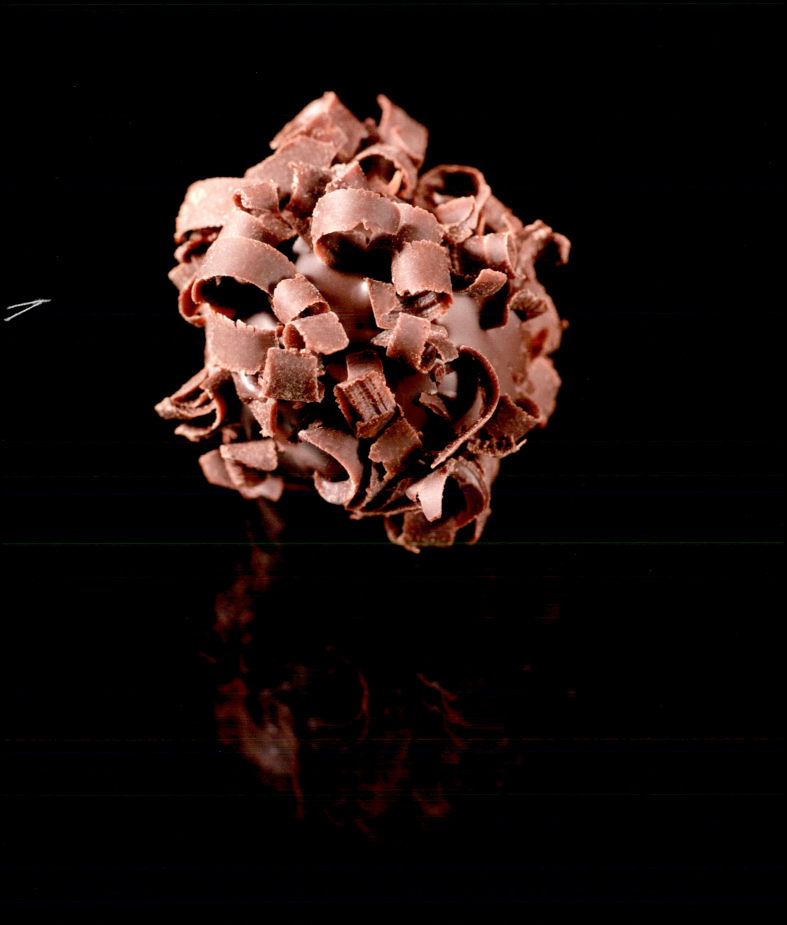

ANISE STICKS

yield: **180 PIECES**

Heavy cream	160 g	6 oz	20%
Glucose syrup	50 g	2 oz	6%
Milk chocolate, unmelted, tempered, chopped	570 g	20 oz	69%
Pernod or other anise-flavored liqueur	40 g	1.5 oz	5%
BATCH SIZE	820 g	29.5 oz	100%

Milk chocolate, melted, tempered, for precoating and dipping		as needed

1. Combine the cream and glucose syrup in a saucepan. Bring to a boil.

2. Pour the hot cream mixture over the chopped milk chocolate and let sit for 1 minute to allow the chocolate to melt.

3. Using a spoon or spatula, stir the mixture in vigorous small circles in the center of the bowl until it emulsifies.

4. Stir outward in larger circles to spread the emulsion throughout the bowl, checking to see that all of the chocolate has melted. If necessary, heat the ganache over a hot water bath to melt the chocolate. The temperature of the ganache should not exceed 32°C/90°F.

5. Stream in the anise-flavored liqueur, stirring until the mixture is homogeneous.

6. Pour the ganache into a hotel pan, allowing the ganache to cover the bottom of the pan in a thin layer. Place plastic wrap directly on the surface of the ganache. Allow to rest at room temperature until slightly firm and of a plastic consistency. This may take 1 hour, depending on the ambient temperature.

7. Agitate the ganache lightly by placing it on a marble slab and working it gently to induce crystallization.

8. Using a pastry bag fitted with a no. 3 round tip, pipe cylinders of ganache the same diameter as the tip across the width of a piece of parchment paper. Allow to crystallize at room temperature until firm enough to handle, about 20 minutes.

9. Using a small brush, precoat each cylinder of ganache with the tempered milk chocolate by brushing the top, allowing the chocolate to set, and then rolling the cyclinder over and brushing the other side.

10. Cut the cylinders into 5-cm/2-in lengths.

11. Using a 4-prong dipping fork, dip the precoated sticks in the tempered milk chocolate and place them diagonally on an icing screen. Allow the chocolate to set until it holds a peak when touched.

12. Using two forks, roll each stick lightly on the screen to create texture. Remove immediately and place on parchment paper.

BUCKWHEAT BEEHIVES

yield: **100 PIECES**

Milk chocolate discs (25-mm/1-in diameter), as bases	100 discs		
BUCKWHEAT HONEY GANACHE			
Heavy cream	180 g	6 oz	25%
Buckwheat honey	70 g	2.5 oz	9%
Milk chocolate, unmelted, tempered, chopped	450 g	16 oz	63%
Butter, softened	20 g	1 oz	3%
BATCH SIZE	720 g	25.5 oz	100%
Buckwheat honey for filling	as needed		
Coarse sugar for finishing	as needed		

TO MAKE THE MILK CHOCOLATE DISCS:

Prepare the discs using tempered milk chocolate and either a cutter or a stencil. (See page 190.) Leave the discs attached to the parchment paper to facilitate piping.

TO MAKE THE BUCKWHEAT HONEY GANACHE:

1. Combine the cream and buckwheat honey in a saucepan. Bring to a boil.

2. Pour the hot cream mixture over the chopped milk chocolate and let sit for 1 minute to allow the chocolate to melt.

3. Using a spoon or spatula, stir the mixture in vigorous small circles in the center of the bowl until it emulsifies.

4. Stir outward in larger circles to spread the emulsion throughout the bowl, checking to see that all of the chocolate has melted. If necessary, heat the ganache over a hot water bath to melt the chocolate. The temperature of the ganache should not exceed 32°C/90°F.

5. Stir the butter into the ganache, taking care that no lumps of butter remain.

6. Pour the ganache into a hotel pan, allowing the ganache to cover the bottom of the pan in a thin layer. Place plastic wrap directly on the surface of the ganache. Allow to rest at room temperature until slightly firm and of a plastic consistency. This may take 1 hour, depending on the ambient temperature.

7. Agitate the ganache lightly by placing it on a marble slab and working it gently to induce crystallization.

TO MAKE THE BUCKWHEAT BEEHIVES:

1. Using a pastry bag fitted with a no. 2 round tip, pipe a border of ganache around the edge of each disc.

2. Using a paper cone, fill the center of each disc with buckwheat honey.

3. Using a pastry bag fitted with a no. 2 round tip, pipe increasingly smaller concentric circles of ganache on top of one another, building a beehive shape on top of each disc and enclosing the pool of buckwheat honey. Allow to crystallize at room temperature until firm enough to handle, about 20 minutes.

4. Using a 3-prong dipping fork, dip each beehive in the tempered, thinned milk chocolate. Slide each piece forward on the paper immediately after dipping to avoid the formation of feet.

5. When the chocolate begins to set, place 6 to 8 crystals of coarse sugar on top of each hive.

   NOTE: See Thinning Technique and Theory, page 64.

THAI STICKS

yield: **120 PIECES**

Heavy cream	150 g	5 oz	14%
Lemongrass, sliced	60 g	2 oz	6%
Coconut milk	50 g	2 oz	5%
Ginger, peeled, sliced	10 g	0.5 oz	<1%
Thai chile	½ chile	½ chile	
Milk	as needed		
Glucose syrup	60 g	2 oz	6%
White chocolate, unmelted, tempered, chopped	650 g	23 oz	60%
Cocoa butter, melted	60 g	2 oz	6%
Lime juice	30 g	1 oz	3%
Lime zest, finely grated	2 limes	2 limes	
BATCH SIZE	1070 g	38.5 oz	100%
White chocolate, melted, tempered, for precoating and dipping	as needed		
Coarse sugar mixed with finely grated lime zest, for finishing	as needed		

1. Combine the cream, lemongrass, coconut milk, ginger, and Thai chile in a saucepan and bring nearly to a boil. Remove from the heat, cover, and let steep for 5 minutes.

2. Strain the infused mixture through premoistened cheesecloth. Wring the lemongrass, ginger, and Thai chile in the cheesecloth to extract the maximum amount of flavor possible.

3. Return the liquid to 150 g by adding milk.

4. Add the glucose syrup to the flavored cream mixture. Bring to a boil.

5. Pour the hot cream mixture over the chopped white chocolate and let sit for 1 minute to allow the chocolate to melt.

6. Using a spoon or spatula, stir the mixture in vigorous small circles in the center of the bowl until it emulsifies.

7. Stir outward in larger circles to spread the emulsion throughout the bowl, checking to see that all of the chocolate has melted. If necessary, heat the ganache over a hot water bath to melt the chocolate. The temperature of the ganache should not exceed 34°C/94°F. Stir in the melted cocoa butter.

8. Stir in the lime juice and lime zest.

9. Pour the ganache into a hotel pan, allowing the ganache to cover the bottom of the pan in a thin layer. Place plastic wrap directly on the surface of the ganache. Allow to rest at room temperature until slightly firm and of a plastic consistency. This may take 1 hour, depending on the ambient temperature.

10. Agitate the ganache lightly by placing it on a marble slab and working it gently to induce crystallization.

11. Using a pastry bag fitted with a no. 4 round tip, pipe cylinders of ganache the same diameter as the tip across the width of a piece of parchment paper. Allow to crystallize at room temperature until firm enough to handle, about 1 hour.

12. Using a small brush, precoat each cylinder of ganache with the tempered white chocolate by brushing the top, allowing the chocolate to set, and then rolling the cyclinder over and brushing the other side.

13. Cut the cylinders into 5-cm/2-in lengths.

14. Using a 4-prong dipping fork, dip the sticks into the tempered white chocolate, then place them onto parchment paper.

15. Finish with the coarse sugar mixed with lime zest.

PECAN GIANDUJA GANACHE

yield: **180 PIECES**

Pecans, toasted	380 g	13 oz	28%
Confectioners' sugar	180 g	6 oz	13%
Dark chocolate, melted	380 g	13 oz	28%
Heavy cream	310 g	11 oz	23%
Glucose syrup	100 g	4 oz	8%
BATCH SIZE	1350 g	47 oz	100%
Dark chocolate, melted, tempered, for precoating and dipping	as needed		
Pecan pieces, toasted, for finishing	180 pieces		

1. Grind the toasted pecans with a small amount of the confectioners' sugar in a food processor until liquefied.

2. Add the melted dark chocolate and the remaining confectioners' sugar and process until homogeneous.

3. Temper the gianduja by tabling, bringing it to 84°C/183°F.

4. Heat the cream and glucose syrup in a saucepan until the mixture reaches 40°C/105°F.

5. Pour the cream mixture over the tempered gianduja. Using a paddle, stir the mixture in vigorous small circles in the center of the bowl until it emulsifies.

6. Stir outward in larger circles to spread the emulsion throughout the bowl, checking to see that all of the chocolate has melted. If necessary, heat the ganache over a hot water bath to melt the chocolate. The temperature of the ganache should not exceed 34°C/94°F.

7. Pour the ganache immediately into a frame 12 × 12 × ½ in set on a heavy plastic sheet. Place plastic wrap directly on the surface of the ganache. Allow to crystallize overnight at room temperature.

8. Remove the frame from the ganache and peel the plastic sheet from the slab.

9. Precoat one side of the slab with the tempered dark chocolate.

10. Cut into rectangles, using the 15-mm and 30-mm strings on a guitar.

11. Using a 3-prong dipping fork, dip the centers in the tempered dark chocolate. When the chocolate begins to set, place a wedge of toasted pecan on each piece.

CINNAMON STACKS

yield: **120 PIECES**

Heavy cream	190 g	7 oz	26%
Glucose syrup	76 g	2 oz	9%
Cinnamon, ground	2 tsp	2 tsp	<1%
Vanilla bean, split and scraped	1 bean	1 bean	
Milk chocolate, unmelted, tempered, chopped	490 g	17 oz	66%
GANACHE BATCH SIZE	740 g	26 oz	100%
Marzipan	150 g	5 oz	
Dark chocolate, melted, tempered, thinned, for dipping (see Note)	as needed		

1. Combine the cream, glucose syrup, and ground cinnamon with the vanilla bean and its seeds in a saucepan. Bring to a boil and stir to disperse the cinnamon. Remove from the heat, cover, and let steep for 5 minutes.

2. Strain the infused the cream through premoistened cheesecloth. Wring the vanilla bean in the cheesecloth to extract the maximum amount of flavor possible.

3. Pour the hot cream mixture over the chopped milk chocolate and let sit for 1 minute to allow the chocolate to melt.

4. Using a spoon or spatula, stir the mixture in vigorous small circles in the center of the bowl until it emulsifies.

5. Stir outward in larger circles to spread the emulsion throughout the bowl, checking to see that all of the chocolate has melted. If necessary, heat the ganache over a hot water bath to melt the chocolate. The temperature of the ganache should not exceed 32°C/90°F.

6. Pour the ganache into a hotel pan, allowing the ganache to cover the bottom of the pan in a thin layer. Place plastic wrap directly on the surface of the ganache. Allow to rest at room temperature until slightly firm and of a plastic consistency. This may take 1 hour, depending on the ambient temperature.

7. While the ganache is crystallizing, roll the marzipan into a square approximately 25 × 25 cm × 1.5 mm/10 × 10 × 1/16 in. After rolling, trim the edges to make them straight.

8. Precoat one side of the marzipan with the tempered, thinned dark chocolate. Allow to set.

9. Turn the precoated marzipan over so that the chocolate-coated side is on the bottom. Cut the marzipan into 1-cm/½-in strips.

10. Agitate the ganache lightly by placing it on a marble slab and working it gently to induce crystallization.

11. Using a pastry bag fitted with a no. 3 round tip, pipe two cylinders of ganache along each marzipan strip. Top with one more cylinder resting on the bottom two to form a pyramid if seen in cross section. Allow to crystallize at room temperature until firm enough to handle, about 20 minutes.

12. Cut the strips crosswise, using the 30-mm strings on a guitar.

13. Using a 3-prong dipping fork, dip the centers into the tempered dark chocolate that has been thinned enough to allow the definition of the shapes to show through. Because the chocolate has been thinned, it may be necessary to slide each piece forward on the tray immediately after dipping to avoid the formation of feet.

NOTE: See Thinning Technique and Theory, page 64.

PEAR GANACHE

yield: **180 PIECES**

Heavy cream	140 g	5 oz	10%
Glucose syrup	90 g	3 oz	6%
Pear William liqueur	90 g	3 oz	6%
Pear purée, reduced by half	200 g	7 oz	15%
Milk chocolate, melted, tempered, at 30°C/86°F	840 g	30 oz	63%
BATCH SIZE	1360 g	48 oz	100%

Milk chocolate, melted, tempered, for precoating and dipping	as needed	

1. Combine the cream and glucose syrup in a saucepan. Bring to a boil.
2. Remove from the heat, add the Pear William liqueur and reduced pear purée, and allow the mixture to cool to 40°C/105°F.
3. Pour the cooled cream mixture over the tempered milk chocolate and let sit for 1 minute to allow the chocolate to melt.
4. Using a spoon or spatula, stir the mixture in vigorous small circles in the center of the bowl until it emulsifies.
5. Stir outward in larger circles to spread the emulsion throughout the bowl, checking to see that all of the chocolate has melted. If necessary, heat the ganache over a hot water bath to melt the chocolate. The temperature of the ganache should not exceed 32°C/90°F.
6. Pour the ganache immediately into a frame 12 × 12 × ½ in set on a heavy plastic sheet. When the ganache is firm to the touch, place plastic wrap directly on the surface of the ganache. Allow to crystallize overnight at room temperature.
7. Remove the frame from the ganache and peel the plastic sheet from the slab.
8. Precoat one side of the slab with the tempered milk chocolate.
9. Cut into rectangles, using the 15-mm and 30-mm strings on a guitar.
10. Using a 3-prong dipping fork, dip the centers in the tempered milk chocolate. Before the chocolate sets, use the fork to make a single mark diagonally from corner to corner on each piece.

EARL GREY GANACHE

yield: **180 PIECES**

Heavy cream	410 g	15 oz	30%
Earl Grey tea leaves	20 g	0.5 oz	2%
Milk	as needed		
Glucose syrup	130 g	5 oz	9%
Dark chocolate, melted, tempered, at 32°C/90°F	260 g	9 oz	19%
Milk chocolate, melted, tempered, at 30°C/86°F	440 g	16 oz	32%
Butter, soft	100 g	3 oz	8%
BATCH SIZE	1360 g	47.5 oz	100%
Milk chocolate, melted, tempered, for precoating and dipping	as needed		
Dark chocolate, tempered, for finishing	as needed		

1. Combine the cream and tea leaves in a saucepan and bring to a boil. Remove from the heat, cover, and let steep for 5 minutes.

2. Strain the infused cream through premoistened cheesecloth. Wring the tea in the cheesecloth to extract the maximum amount of flavor possible.

3. Return the cream to 350 g by adding milk.

4. Add the glucose syrup to the flavored cream mixture. Bring to a boil. Remove from the heat and allow to cool to 40°C/105°F.

5. Combine the tempered dark and milk chocolates.

6. Stir the butter into the chocolate mixture, taking care that no lumps of butter remain.

7. Pour the 40°C/105°F cream mixture over the chocolate mixture.

8. Using a spoon or spatula, stir the mixture in vigorous small circles in the center of the bowl until it emulsifies.

9. Stir outward in larger circles to spread the emulsion throughout the bowl, checking to see that all of the chocolate has melted. If necessary, heat the ganache over a hot water bath to melt the chocolate. The temperature of the ganache should not exceed 32°C/90°F.

10. Pour the ganache immediately into a frame 12 × 12 × ½ in set on a heavy plastic sheet. Place plastic wrap directly on the surface of the ganache. Allow to crystallize overnight at room temperature.

11. Remove the frame from the ganache and peel the plastic sheet from the slab.

12. Precoat one side of the slab with the tempered milk chocolate.

13. Cut into rectangles, using the 15-mm and 30-mm strings on a guitar.

14. Using a 3-prong dipping fork, dip the centers in the tempered milk chocolate. Allow to set fully. Using a paper cone, pipe a filigree of the tempered dark chocolate lengthwise on each piece.

MIMOSAS

yield: **180 PIECES**

Heavy cream	190 g	7 oz	14%
Glucose syrup	100 g	4 oz	8%
Sparkling wine	100 g	4 oz	8%
Orange juice concentrate, defrosted	40 g	1 oz	2%
White chocolate, melted, tempered, at 30°C/86°F	940 g	33 oz	66%
Cocoa butter, melted	20 g	1 oz	2%
BATCH SIZE	1390 g	50 oz	100%

Dark chocolate, melted, tempered, for precoating and dipping	as needed
Candied mimosa flowers	180 flowers

1. Combine the cream and glucose syrup in a saucepan. Bring to a boil.
2. Remove from the heat. Add the sparkling wine and orange juice concentrate and allow the mixture to cool to 40°C/105°F.
3. Combine the tempered white chocolate and the melted cocoa butter.
4. Pour the cooled cream mixture over the chocolate mixture. Using a spoon or spatula, stir the mixture in vigorous small circles in the center of the bowl until it emulsifies.
5. Stir outward in larger circles to spread the emulsion throughout the bowl, checking to see that all of the chocolate has melted. If necessary, heat the ganache over a hot water bath to melt the chocolate. The temperature of the ganache should not exceed 32°C/90°F.
6. Pour the ganache immediately into a frame 12 × 12 × ½ in set on a heavy plastic sheet. Place plastic wrap directly on the surface of the ganache. Allow to crystallize overnight at room temperature.
7. Remove the frame from the ganache and peel the plastic sheet from the slab.
8. Precoat one side of the slab with the tempered dark chocolate.
9. Cut into rectangles, using the 15-mm and 30-mm strings on a guitar.
10. Using a 3-prong dipping fork, dip the centers in the tempered dark chocolate. When the chocolate begins to set, place a candied mimosa flower on top of each piece.

DARK & STORMIES

yield: **180 PIECES**

Heavy cream	170 g	6 oz	12%
Ginger, sliced	80 g	3 oz	6%
Vanilla bean, split and scraped	½ bean	½ bean	
Milk	as needed		
Glucose syrup	40 g	1.5 oz	3%
Dark rum, Bermudan preferred	80 g	3 oz	6%
Butter, very soft	40 g	1.5 oz	3%
White chocolate, melted, tempered, at 30°C/86°F	1000 g	35 oz	70%
BATCH SIZE	1410 g	50 oz	100%

Dark chocolate, melted, tempered, for precoating and dipping	as needed

1. Combine the cream and sliced ginger with the vanilla bean and its seeds in a saucepan. Bring to a boil. Remove from the heat, cover, and let steep for 5 minutes.

2. Strain the infused the cream through premoistened cheesecloth. Wring the aromatics in the cheesecloth to extract the maximum amount of flavor possible.

3. Return the cream to 170 g by adding milk.

4. Add the glucose syrup to the flavored cream mixture. Bring to a boil.

5. Remove from the heat, add the rum, and allow to cool to 40°C/105°F.

6. Stir the butter into the tempered white chocolate, taking care that no lumps of butter remain.

7. Pour the cooled cream mixture over the chocolate mixture. Using a spoon or spatula, stir the mixture in vigorous small circles in the center of the bowl until it emulsifies.

8. Stir outward in larger circles to spread the emulsion throughout the bowl, checking to see that all of the chocolate has melted. If necessary, heat the ganache over a hot water bath to melt the chocolate. The temperature of the ganache should not exceed 32°C/90°F.

9. Pour the ganache immediately into a frame 12 × 12 × ½ in set on a heavy plastic sheet. Place plastic wrap directly on the surface of the ganache. Allow to crystallize overnight at room temperature.

10. Remove the frame from the ganache and peel the plastic sheet from the slab.

11. Precoat one side of the slab with the tempered dark chocolate.

12. Cut into rectangles, using the 15-mm and 30-mm strings on a guitar.

13. Using a 3-prong dipping fork, dip the centers in the tempered dark chocolate. Before the chocolate sets, use the fork to make a wave pattern on the surface of each piece.

LAVENDER GANACHE

yield: **180 PIECES**

Heavy cream	420 g	15 oz	31%
Dried lavender flowers	4 Tbsp	4 Tbsp	
Milk	as needed		
Glucose syrup	120 g	4 oz	9%
Butter, very soft	60 g	2 oz	5%
Dark chocolate, melted, tempered, at 32°C/90°F	750 g	27 oz	55%
BATCH SIZE	1350 g	48 oz	100%
Dark chocolate, melted, tempered, for precoating and dipping	as needed		
Dried lavender flowers, for finishing	as needed		

1. Combine the cream and dried lavender flowers in a saucepan and bring to a boil. Remove from the heat, cover, and let steep for 5 minutes.

2. Strain the infused cream through premoistened cheesecloth. Wring the lavender flowers in the cheesecloth to extract the maximum amount of flavor possible.

3. Return the cream to 420 g by adding milk.

4. Add the glucose syrup to the flavored cream mixture. Bring to a boil.

5. Remove from the heat and allow the mixture to cool to 40°C/105°F.

6. Stir the butter into the tempered dark chocolate, taking care that no lumps of butter remain.

7. Pour the cooled cream mixture over the dark chocolate mixture. Using a paddle, stir the mixture in vigorous small circles in the center of the bowl until it emulsifies.

8. Stir outward in larger circles to spread the emulsion throughout the bowl, checking to see that all of the chocolate has melted. If necessary, heat the ganache over a hot water bath to melt the chocolate. The temperature of the ganache should not exceed 34°C/94°F.

9. Pour the ganache immediately into a frame 12 × 12 × ½ in set on a heavy plastic sheet. Place plastic wrap directly on the surface of the ganache. Allow to crystallize overnight at room temperature.

10. Remove the frame from the ganache and peel the plastic sheet from the slab.

11. Precoat one side of the slab with the tempered dark chocolate.

12. Cut into rectangles, using the 15-mm and 30-mm strings on a guitar.

13. Using a 3-prong dipping fork, dip the centers in the tempered dark chocolate. When the chocolate begins to set, place 3 dried lavender flowers on top of each piece.

LEMON MINT GANACHE

yield: **180 PIECES**

Heavy cream	300 g	11 oz	22%
Glucose syrup	90 g	3 oz	7%
Lemon zest, removed with a vegetable peeler	1 lemon	1 lemon	
Mint leaves, very finely chopped	40 leaves	40 leaves	
Butter, very soft	30 g	1 oz	2%
White chocolate, melted, tempered, at 30°C/86°F	820 g	29 oz	62%
Lemon juice, at 40°C/105°F	80 g	3 oz	7%
BATCH SIZE	1360 g	87 oz	100%
Dark chocolate, melted, tempered, for precoating and dipping	as needed		
Lemon zest confit, for finishing (see Note)	as needed		

1. Combine the cream, glucose syrup, lemon zest, and chopped mint leaves in a saucepan and bring to a boil. Remove from the heat, cover, and let steep for 5 minutes.

2. Remove the lemon zest and allow the cream to cool to 40°C/105°F.

3. Stir the butter into the tempered white chocolate, taking care that no lumps of butter remain.

4. Pour the cooled cream mixture and the lemon juice over the chocolate mixture. Using a paddle, stir the mixture in vigorous small circles in the center of the bowl until it emulsifies.

5. Stir outward in larger circles to spread the emulsion throughout the bowl, checking to see that all of the chocolate has melted. If necessary, heat the ganache over a hot water bath to melt the chocolate. The temperature of the ganache should not exceed 32°C/90°F.

6. Pour the ganache immediately into a frame 12 × 12 × ½ in set on a heavy plastic sheet. Place plastic wrap directly on the surface of the ganache. Allow to crystallize overnight at room temperature.

7. Remove the frame from the ganache and peel the plastic sheet from the slab.

8. Precoat one side of the slab with the tempered dark chocolate.

9. Cut into rectangles, using the 15-mm and 30-mm strings on a guitar.

10. Using a 3-prong dipping fork, dip the centers in the tempered dark chocolate. When the chocolate begins to set, place a single piece of lemon zest confit lengthwise on each piece.

    NOTE: Prepare lemon zest confit, following Citrus Confit Technique, page 329. Remove the zest from the pith. Julienne zest 30 × 2 mm/1 ¼ × ¹⁄₁₆ in and roll in granulated sugar for ease of handling.

CARAMEL GANACHE

yield: 180 PIECES

Lemon juice	5 drops	5 drops	>1%
Sugar	80 g	3 oz	6%
Glucose syrup	80 g	3 oz	6%
Heavy cream	320 g	11 oz	24%
Brandy	30 g	1 oz	2%
Butter, very soft	30 g	1 oz	2%
Milk chocolate, melted, tempered, at 30°C/86°F	800 g	28 oz	60%
BATCH SIZE	1340 g	47 oz	100%
Milk chocolate, melted, tempered, for precoating and dipping	as needed		
Dark chocolate, melted, tempered, for finishing	as needed		

1. Rub the lemon juice into the sugar.

2. In a saucepan, caramelize the sugar mixture until amber using the dry method. (See page 222.)

3. Remove from the heat and add the glucose syrup to the caramelized sugar.

4. Bring the cream to a boil. With the caramelized sugar mixture at low heat, stream in the hot cream, making certain that the caramelized sugar mixture is entirely incorporated.

5. Remove the mixture from the heat. Add the brandy and allow to cool to 40°C/105°F.

6. Stir the butter into the tempered milk chocolate, taking care that no lumps of butter remain.

7. Pour the cooled cream mixture over the chocolate mixture. Using a paddle, stir the mixture in vigorous small circles in the center of the bowl until it emulsifies.

8. Stir outward in larger circles to spread the emulsion throughout the bowl, checking to see that all of the chocolate has melted. If necessary, heat the ganache over a hot water bath to melt the chocolate. The temperature of the ganache should not exceed 32°C/90°F.

9. Pour the ganache immediately into a frame 12 × 12 × ½ in set on a heavy plastic sheet. Place plastic wrap directly on the surface of the ganache. Allow to crystallize overnight at room temperature.

10. Remove the frame from the ganache and peel the plastic sheet from the slab.

11. Precoat one side of the slab with the tempered milk chocolate.

12. Cut into rectangles, using the 15-mm and 30-mm strings on a guitar.

13. Using a 3-prong dipping fork, dip the centers in the tempered milk chocolate. After the chocolate has set, pipe one large dot and one small dot of tempered dark chocolate at either end of the top of each piece.

CRÈME FRAÎCHE GANACHE

yield: **180 PIECES**

Crème fraîche	400 g	14 oz	29%
Glucose syrup	120 g	4 oz	9%
Milk chocolate, melted, tempered, at 30°C/86°F	830 g	29 oz	62%
BATCH SIZE	1350 g	47 oz	100%

Milk chocolate, melted, tempered, for precoating and dipping		as needed

1. Combine the crème fraîche and glucose syrup in a stainless-steel bowl. Place the mixture over a hot water bath and warm it to 40°C/105°F.

2. Pour the warm cream mixture over the tempered milk chocolate. Using a paddle, stir the mixture in vigorous small circles in the center of the bowl until it emulsifies.

3. Stir outward in larger circles to spread the emulsion throughout the bowl, checking to see that all of the chocolate has melted. If necessary, heat the ganache over a hot water bath to melt the chocolate. The temperature of the ganache should not exceed 32°C/90°F.

4. Pour the ganache immediately into a frame 12 × 12 × ½ in set on a heavy plastic sheet. Place plastic wrap directly on the surface of the ganache. Allow to crystallize overnight at room temperature.

5. Remove the frame from the ganache and peel the plastic sheet from the slab.

6. Precoat one side of the slab with the tempered milk chocolate.

7. Cut into rectangles, using the 15-mm and 30-mm strings on a guitar.

8. Using a 3-prong dipping fork, dip the centers in the tempered milk chocolate. Before the chocolate sets, use a double diagonal fork to mark each piece.

PASSION VANILLAS

yield: **180 PIECES**

VANILLA MILK CHOCOLATE GANACHE

Heavy cream	180 g	6 oz	25%
Glucose syrup	60 g	2 oz	8%
Vanilla bean, split and scraped	1 bean	1 bean	
Butter, very soft	20 g	1 oz	3%
Milk chocolate, melted, tempered, at 30°C/86°F	460 g	16 oz	64%
BATCH SIZE	720 g	25 oz	100%

PASSION FRUIT GANACHE

Heavy cream	100 g	4 oz	13%
Glucose syrup	70 g	3 oz	8%
Reduced passion fruit purée (see Note)	100 g	4 oz	13%
Butter, very soft	30 g	1 oz	3%
White chocolate, melted, tempered, at 30°C/86°F	520 g	19 oz	63%
BATCH SIZE	820 g	31 oz	100%

Dark chocolate, melted, tempered, for precoating and dipping	as needed
Basketweave transfer sheets, cut 3 × 4 cm/1 × 1½ in	180 strips

TO MAKE THE VANILLA MILK CHOCOLATE GANACHE:

1. Combine the cream, glucose syrup, and the vanilla bean and its seeds in a saucepan. Bring to a boil. Remove from the heat, cover, and let steep for 5 minutes.

2. Strain the infused cream through premoistened cheesecloth. Wring the vanilla bean in the cheesecloth to extract the maximum amount of flavor possible.

3. Allow the cream mixture to cool to 40°C/105°F.

4. Stir the butter into the tempered milk chocolate, taking care that no lumps of butter remain.

5. Pour the cooled cream mixture over the milk chocolate mixture. Using a paddle, stir the mixture in vigorous small circles in the center of the bowl until it emulsifies.

6. Stir outward in larger circles to spread the emulsion throughout the bowl, checking to see that all of the chocolate has melted. If necessary, heat the ganache over a hot water bath to melt the chocolate. The temperature of the ganache should not exceed 32°C/90°F.

7. Pour the ganache immediately into a frame 12 × 12 × ¼ in set on a heavy plastic sheet. Allow to crystallize, uncovered, at room temperature until firm, approximately 1 hour.

8. Place a second ¼-in frame on top of the frame containing the vanilla milk chocolate ganache.

TO MAKE THE PASSION FRUIT GANACHE:

1. Combine the cream and glucose syrup in a saucepan. Bring to a boil.

2. Remove from the heat and add the reduced passion fruit purée.

3. Allow the mixture to cool to 40°C/105°F.

4. Stir the butter into the tempered white chocolate, taking care that no lumps of butter remain.

5. Pour the cooled cream mixture over the white chocolate mixture. Using a paddle, stir the mixture in vigorous small circles in the center of the bowl until it emulsifies.

6. Stir outward in larger circles to spread the emulsion throughout the bowl, checking to see that all of the chocolate has melted. If necessary, heat the ganache over a hot water bath to melt the chocolate. The temperature of the ganache should not exceed 32°C/90°F.

7. Pour the mixture immediately into the second set of frames. Spread the passion fruit ganache in an even layer. Place plastic wrap directly on the surface of the passion fruit ganache. Allow to crystallize overnight at room temperature.

TO MAKE THE PASSION VANILLAS:

1. Remove the frames from the ganache and peel the plastic sheet from the slab.

2. Precoat the vanilla milk chocolate ganache side of the slab with the tempered dark chocolate.

3. Cut into rectangles, using the 15-mm and 30-mm strings on a guitar.

4. Using a 3-prong dipping fork, dip the centers in the tempered dark chocolate and place a transfer sheet on each piece.

5. For the best shine, allow the pieces to crystallize overnight before removing the transfer sheets. If that is not possible, refrigerate the finished and set pieces for 5 minutes and then remove the transfer sheets.

   NOTE: Passion fruit juice concentrate should be reduced by half. Natural-strength passion fruit purée should be reduced by three quarters.

HAZELNUT LATTES

yield: **180 PIECES**

COFFEE GANACHE

Heavy cream	180 g	6 oz	23%
Dark-roast coffee beans, coarsely ground	10 g	0.5 oz	2%
Milk	as needed		
Glucose syrup	60 g	2 oz	8%
Coffee liqueur	40 g	1.5 oz	6%
Butter, very soft	40 g	1.5 oz	6%
Dark chocolate, melted, tempered, at 32°C/90°F	400 g	14 oz	55%
BATCH SIZE	730 g	25.5 oz	100%

PRALINE GANACHE

Heavy cream	150 g	5 oz	20%
Glucose syrup	50 g	2 oz	7%
Hazelnut liqueur	30 g	1 oz	4%
Cocoa butter, melted	20 g	1 oz	3%
Praline paste	60 g	2 oz	9%
White chocolate, melted, tempered, at 30°C/86°F	420 g	15 oz	57%
BATCH SIZE	730 g	26 oz	100%

Dark chocolate, melted, tempered, for precoating and dipping	as needed
Hazelnut halves, toasted, for finishing	180 halves

TO MAKE THE COFFEE GANACHE:

1. Combine the cream and the ground coffee in a saucepan. Bring to a boil. Remove from the heat, cover, and let steep for 5 minutes.
2. Strain the infused cream through premoistened cheesecloth. Wring the coffee grounds in the cheesecloth to extract the maximum amount of flavor.
3. Return the cream to 180 g by adding milk.
4. Add the glucose syrup to the flavored cream mixture. Bring to a boil.
5. Remove from the heat, add the coffee liqueur, and allow to cool to 40°C/105°F.
6. Stir the butter into the tempered dark chocolate, taking care that no lumps remain.
7. Pour the cooled cream mixture over the chocolate mixture. Using a paddle, stir the mixture in vigorous small circles in the center of the bowl until it emulsifies.
8. Stir outward in larger circles to spread the emulsion throughout the bowl, checking to see that all of the chocolate has melted. If necessary, heat the ganache over a hot water bath to melt the chocolate. The temperature of the ganache should not exceed 34°C/94°F.

9. Pour the ganache immediately into a frame 12 × 12 × ¼ in set on a heavy plastic sheet. Allow to crystallize, uncovered, at room temperature until firm, about 1 hour.

10. Place a second ¼-in frame on top of the frame containing the coffee ganache.

TO MAKE THE PRALINE GANACHE:

1. Combine the cream and glucose syrup in a saucepan. Bring to a boil.

2. Remove from the heat and add the hazelnut liqueur. Allow to cool to 40°C/105°F.

3. Combine the cocoa butter and the praline paste. Add the mixture to the tempered white chocolate. Combine well.

4. Pour the cooled cream mixture over the white chocolate mixture. Using a paddle, stir the mixture in vigorous small circles in the center of the bowl until it emulsifies.

5. Stir outward in larger circles to spread the emulsion throughout the bowl, checking to see that all of the chocolate has melted. If necessary, heat the ganache over a hot water bath to melt the chocolate. The temperature of the ganache should not exceed 32°C/90°F.

6. Pour the praline ganache immediately into the second set of frames. Spread the praline ganache in an even layer. Place plastic wrap directly on the surface of the praline ganache. Allow to crystallize overnight at room temperature.

TO MAKE THE HAZELNUT LATTES:

1. Remove the frames from the ganache and peel the plastic sheet from the slab.

2. Precoat the coffee ganache side of the slab with the tempered dark chocolate.

3. Cut into rectangles, using the 15-mm and 30-mm strings on a guitar.

4. Using a 3-prong dipping fork, dip the centers in the tempered dark chocolate. When the chocolate begins to set, finish each piece with a toasted hazelnut half.

HABANOS

yield: **180 PIECES**

HABANERO GANACHE

Heavy cream	180 g	6 oz	24%
Habanero chile, sliced	½ chile	½ chile	
Glucose syrup	50 g	2 oz	6%
Light rum	50 g	2 oz	6%
Butter, very soft	60 g	2 oz	8%
Dark chocolate, melted, tempered, at 32°C/90°F	420 g	15 oz	56%
BATCH SIZE	760 g	27 oz	100%

MANGO GANACHE

Heavy cream	100 g	4 oz	12%
Glucose syrup	70 g	3 oz	8%
Mango purée, reduced by half	100 g	4 oz	12%
Lime juice	1 lime	1 lime	3%
Butter, very soft	30 g	1 oz	4%
White chocolate, melted, tempered, at 30°C/86°F	520 g	18 oz	61%
BATCH SIZE	820 g	29 oz	100%

Dark chocolate, melted, tempered, for precoating and dipping	as needed
Fleur de sel, for finishing	as needed

TO MAKE THE HABANERO GANACHE:

1. Combine the cream and chile in a saucepan and bring to a boil. Remove from the heat, cover, and let steep for 5 minutes. Remove the chile from the cream.

2. Add the glucose syrup to the infused cream. Bring to a boil.

3. Remove from the heat and add the rum.

4. Allow the cream mixture to cool to 40°C/105°F.

5. Stir the butter into the tempered dark chocolate, taking care that no lumps remain.

6. Pour the cooled cream mixture over the dark chocolate mixture. Using a paddle, stir the mixture in vigorous small circles in the center of the bowl until it emulsifies.

7. Stir outward in larger circles to spread the emulsion throughout the bowl, checking to see that all of the chocolate has melted. If necessary, heat the ganache over a hot water bath to melt the chocolate. The temperature of the ganache should not exceed 34°C/94°F.

8. Pour the ganache immediately into a frame 12 × 12 × ¼ in set on a heavy plastic sheet. Allow to crystallize, uncovered, at room temperature until firm, approximately 1 hour.

9. Place a second ¼-in frame on top of the frame containing the habanero ganache.

TO MAKE THE MANGO GANACHE:

1. Combine the cream and glucose syrup in a saucepan. Bring to a boil.

2. Remove from the heat and add the reduced mango purée and lime juice.

3. Allow the cream mixture to cool to 40°C/105°F.

4. Stir the butter into the tempered white chocolate, taking care that no lumps remain.

5. Pour the cooled cream mixture over the white chocolate mixture. Using a paddle, stir the mixture in vigorous small circles in the center of the bowl until it emulsifies.

6. Stir outward in larger circles to spread the emulsion throughout the bowl, checking to see that all of the chocolate has melted. If necessary, heat the ganache over a hot water bath to melt the chocolate. The temperature of the ganache should not exceed 32°C/90°F.

7. Pour the ganache immediately into the second set of frames. Spread the mango ganache in an even layer. Place plastic wrap directly on the surface of the mango ganache. Allow to crystallize overnight at room temperature.

TO MAKE THE HABANOS:

1. Remove the frames from the ganache and peel the plastic sheet from the slab.

2. Precoat the habanero ganache side of the slab with the tempered dark chocolate.

3. Cut into rectangles, using the 15-mm and 30-mm strings on a guitar.

4. Using a 3-prong dipping fork, dip the centers in the tempered dark chocolate. When the chocolate begins to set, sprinkle a few crystals of fleur de sel on each piece.

ROB ROYS

yield: **180 PIECES**

Heavy cream	260 g	9 oz	18%
Glucose syrup	120 g	4 oz	10%
Honey	130 g	5 oz	8%
Scotch whiskey	110 g	4 oz	7%
Butter, soft	50 g	3 oz	3%
Milk chocolate, melted, tempered, at 30°C/86°F	800 g	28 oz	54%
BATCH SIZE	1470 g	53 oz	100%

Milk chocolate, melted, tempered, for precoating and dipping	as needed	

1. Combine the cream and glucose syrup in a saucepan. Bring to a boil.
2. Remove from the heat, add the honey and whiskey, and allow the mixture to cool to 40°C/105°F.
3. Stir the butter into the tempered milk chocolate, taking care that no lumps remain.
4. Pour the cooled cream mixture over the milk chocolate mixture. Using a paddle, stir the mixture in vigorous small circles in the center of the bowl until it emulsifies.
5. Stir outward in larger circles to spread the emulsion throughout the bowl, checking to see that all of the chocolate has melted. If necessary, heat the ganache over a hot water bath to melt the chocolate. The temperature of the ganache should not exceed 32°C/90°F.
6. Pour the ganache immediately into a frame 12 × 12 × ½ in set on a heavy plastic sheet. Place plastic wrap directly on the surface of the ganache. Allow to crystallize overnight at room temperature.
7. Remove the frame from the ganache and peel the plastic sheet from the slab.
8. Precoat one side of the slab with the tempered milk chocolate.
9. Cut into rectangles, using the 15-mm and 30-mm strings on a guitar.
10. Using a 2-prong dipping fork, dip the centers in the tempered milk chocolate. Before the chocolate sets, use the fork to create a wave pattern on top of each piece.

LIQUEUR TRUFFLES (FOR HOLLOW SHELLS)

yield: 125 TRUFFLES

Heavy cream	280 g	10 oz	27%
Milk	90 g	3 oz	8%
Glucose syrup	100 g	3.5 oz	9%
Dark chocolate, unmelted, tempered, chopped	510 g	18 oz	49%
Liqueur or spirit	70 g	2.5 oz	7%
BATCH SIZE	1050 g	37 oz	100%
Dark chocolate hollow truffle shells (see page 110)	125 shells	125 shells	
Dark chocolate, melted, untempered or tempered, for sealing	as needed		
Dark chocolate, melted, tempered, for dipping	as needed		

1. Combine the cream, milk, and glucose syrup in a saucepan. Bring to a boil.
2. Pour the hot cream mixture over the chopped dark chocolate and let sit for 1 minute to allow the chocolate to melt.
3. Using a spoon or spatula, stir the mixture in vigorous small circles in the center of the bowl until it emulsifies.
4. Stir outward in larger circles to spread the emulsion throughout the bowl, checking to see that all of the chocolate has melted. If necessary, heat the ganache over a hot water bath to melt the chocolate. The temperature of the ganache should not exceed 34°C/94°F.
5. Stream in the liqueur or spirit, stirring the mixture until homogeneous.
6. Pour the ganache into a hotel pan, allowing the ganache to cover the bottom of the pan in a thin layer. Place plastic wrap directly on the surface of the ganache.
7. Allow to rest at room temperature until the ganache reaches 25°C/77°F, or slightly lower, approximately 20 minutes. The cooled ganache should be of a thick but fluid consistency to properly fill the shells.
8. Using a disposable pastry bag with a small opening cut in the tip, fill the truffle shells to the tops with the ganache.
9. Allow the ganache to crystallize at room temperature until the top is solid, for several hours or overnight.
10. Seal the truffles using either untempered dark chocolate with a sealing tray or tempered dark chocolate applied with a paper cone.
11. Using a round dipping fork, dip the truffles in the tempered dark chocolate.
12. Finish as desired with texture, garnish, or filigree.

ORANGE BLOSSOM TRUFFLES

yield: **160 TRUFFLES**

Heavy cream	300 g	11 oz	30%
Glucose syrup	90 g	3 oz	8%
Milk chocolate, unmelted, tempered, chopped	600 g	21 oz	56%
Butter, soft	40 g	1 oz	3%
Orange blossom water	20 g	1 oz	3%
BATCH SIZE	1050 g	37 oz	100%
Milk chocolate hollow truffle shells (see page 110)	160 shells	160 shells	
Milk chocolate, melted, untempered or tempered, for sealing	as needed		
Milk chocolate, melted, tempered, for dipping	as needed		
Red interference color, for finishing	as needed		

1. Combine the cream and glucose syrup in a saucepan. Bring to a boil.

2. Pour the hot cream mixture over the chopped milk chocolate and let sit for 1 minute to allow the chocolate to melt.

3. Using a spoon or spatula, stir the mixture in vigorous small circles in the center of the bowl until it emulsifies.

4. Stir outward in larger circles to spread the emulsion throughout the bowl, checking to see that all of the chocolate has melted. If necessary, heat the ganache over a hot water bath to melt the chocolate. The temperature of the ganache should not exceed 32°C/90°F.

5. Stir the butter into the ganache, taking care that no lumps of butter remain.

6. Stream in the orange blossom water, stirring until the mixture is homogeneous.

7. Pour the ganache into a hotel pan, allowing the ganache to cover the bottom of the pan in a thin layer. Place plastic wrap directly on the surface of the ganache.

8. Allow to rest at room temperature until the ganache reaches 25°C/77°F or slightly cooler, for approximately 20 minutes. The cooled ganache should be of a thick but fluid consistency to properly fill the shells.

9. Using a disposable pastry bag with a small opening cut in the tip, fill the truffle shells to the tops with the ganache.

10. Allow the ganache to crystallize at room temperature until the top is solid, for several hours or overnight.

11. Seal the truffles using either untempered milk chocolate with a sealing tray or tempered milk chocolate applied with a paper cone.

12. Using a round dipping fork, dip the truffles in the tempered milk chocolate.

13. After the chocolate has set, finish each piece with a brush of red interference color.

ROSE TRUFFLES

yield: **140 TRUFFLES**

Heavy cream	300 g	11 oz	32%
Glucose syrup	90 g	3 oz	9%
Dark chocolate, unmelted, tempered, chopped	500 g	18 oz	53%
Butter, soft	30 g	1 oz	3%
Rose water	15 g	1 oz	3%
BATCH SIZE	935 g	34 oz	100%
Dark chocolate hollow truffle shells (see page 110)	140 shells		
Dark chocolate, melted, untempered or tempered, for sealing	as needed		
Dark chocolate, melted, tempered, for dipping	as needed		
Crystallized rose petals, for finishing	as needed		

1. Combine the cream and glucose syrup in a saucepan. Bring to a boil. Pour the hot cream mixture over the chopped dark chocolate and let sit for 1 minute to allow the chocolate to melt.

2. Using a paddle, stir the mixture in vigorous small circles in the center of the bowl until it emulsifies.

3. Stir outward in larger circles to spread the emulsion throughout the bowl, checking to see that all of the chocolate has melted. If necessary, heat the ganache over a hot water bath to melt the chocolate. The temperature of the ganache should not exceed 34°C/94°F.

4. Stir the butter into the ganache, taking care that no lumps of butter remain. Mix in the rose water.

5. Pour the ganache into a hotel pan, allowing the ganache to cover the bottom of the pan in a thin layer. Place plastic wrap directly on the surface of the ganache.

6. Allow to rest at room temperature until the ganache reaches 25°C/77°F or slightly cooler, approximately 20 minutes. The cooled ganache should be of a thick but fluid consistency to properly fill the shells.

7. Using a disposable pastry bag with a small opening cut in the tip, fill the truffle shells to the tops with the ganache.

8. Allow the ganache to crystallize at room temperature until the top is solid, for several hours or overnight.

9. Seal the truffles using either untempered dark chocolate with a sealing tray or tempered dark chocolate applied with a paper cone.

10. Using a round dipping fork, dip the truffles in the tempered dark chocolate.

11. When the chocolate begins to set, finish each piece with a crystallized rose petal.

LAVENDER TRUFFLES: Infuse the cream with 3 Tbsp of dried lavender flowers. (See page 102.) Restore the weight of the cream using milk. Finish with a brush of blue interference color.

VIOLET TRUFFLES: Substitute ½ tsp of violet extract for the rose water. Finish with crystallized violet flower petals.

Assorted flower truffles: rose, lavender, violet, and fresh mint.

FRESH MINT TRUFFLES

yield: **165 TRUFFLES**

Mint leaves	25 leaves	25 leaves	
Sugar	30 g	1 oz	3%
Heavy cream	300 g	11 oz	30%
Glucose syrup	90 g	3 oz	8%
White chocolate, unmelted, tempered, chopped	600 g	21 oz	56%
Butter, soft	40 g	1 oz	3%
BATCH SIZE	1060 g	37 oz	100%
White chocolate hollow truffle shells (see page 110)	165 shells		
White chocolate, melted, untempered or tempered, for sealing	as needed		
White chocolate, melted, tempered, for dipping	as needed		
Crystallized mint leaves, for finishing	as needed		

1. Crush the mint leaves and sugar together using a mortar and pestle.
2. Combine the mint mixture and the cream in a saucepan and bring to a boil. Remove from the heat, cover, and let steep for 5 minutes.
3. Add the glucose syrup to the flavored cream mixture. Bring to a boil.
4. Pour the hot cream mixture over the chopped white chocolate and let sit for 1 minute to allow the chocolate to melt.
5. Using a spoon or spatula, stir the mixture in vigorous small circles in the center of the bowl until it emulsifies.
6. Stir outward in larger circles to spread the emulsion throughout the bowl, checking to see that all of the chocolate has melted. If necessary, heat the ganache over a hot water bath to melt the chocolate. The temperature of the ganache should not exceed 32°C/90°F.
7. Stir the butter into the ganache, taking care that no lumps of butter remain.
8. Pour the ganache into a hotel pan, allowing the ganache to cover the bottom of the pan in a thin layer. Place plastic wrap directly on the surface of the ganache.
9. Allow to rest at room temperature until the ganache reaches 25°C/77°F or slightly lower, approximately 20 minutes. The cooled ganache should be of a thick but fluid consistency to properly fill the shells.
10. Using a disposable pastry bag with a small opening cut in the tip, fill the truffle shells to the tops with the ganache.
11. Allow the ganache to crystallize at room temperature until the top is solid, approximately 1 hour.
12. Seal the truffles using either untempered white chocolate with a sealing tray or tempered white chocolate applied with a paper cone.
13. Using a round dipping fork, dip the truffles in the tempered white chocolate.
14. When the chocolate begins to set, place a piece of crystallized mint leaf on each truffle.

DULCE DE LECHE COFFEE TRUFFLES

yield: **170 TRUFFLES**

DULCE DE LECHE

Sweetened condensed milk, 2 unopened cans (see Note)	794 g	28 oz	
BATCH SIZE	794 g	28 oz	49%

COFFEE GANACHE

Heavy cream	260 g	10 oz	15%
Dark-roast coffee beans, coarsely ground	40 g	1.5 oz	2%
Milk	as needed		
Glucose syrup	60 g	2 oz	4%
Milk chocolate, unmelted, tempered, chopped	420 g	15 oz	26%
Irish cream liqueur	60 g	2 oz	4%
BATCH SIZE	1640 g	58.5 oz	100%
Milk chocolate hollow truffle shells (see page 110)	170 shells	170 shells	
Milk chocolate, melted, untempered or tempered, for sealing	as needed		
Milk chocolate, melted, tempered, for dipping	as needed		
Instant coffee powder, for finishing	as needed		

TO MAKE THE DULCE DE LECHE:

Immerse the two unopened cans of sweetened condensed milk in simmering water and leave them to simmer for 4 hours. Remove from the water and allow to cool to room temperature.

TO MAKE THE COFFEE GANACHE:

1. Combine the cream and ground coffee in a saucepan. Bring to a boil. Remove from the heat, cover, and let steep for 5 minutes.

2. Strain the infused cream through premoistened cheesecloth. Wring the coffee grounds in the cheesecloth to extract the maximum amount of flavor.

3. Return the cream to 260 g by adding milk.

4. Add the glucose syrup to the flavored cream mixture. Bring to a boil.

5. Pour the hot cream mixture over the chopped milk chocolate and let sit for 1 minute to melt the chocolate.

6. Using a spoon or spatula, stir the mixture in vigorous small circles in the center of the bowl until it emulsifies.

7. Stir outward in larger circles to spread the emulsion throughout the bowl, checking to see that all of the chocolate has melted. If necessary, heat the ganache over a hot water bath to melt the chocolate. The temperature of the ganache should not exceed 32°C/90°F.

8. Stream in the Irish cream liqueur, stirring the mixture until homogeneous.

9. Pour the ganache into a hotel pan, allowing the ganache to cover the bottom of the pan in a thin layer. Place plastic wrap directly on the surface of the ganache.

10. Allow to rest at room temperature until the ganache reaches 25°C/77°F, or slightly lower, approximately 20 minutes. The cooled ganache should be of a thick but fluid consistency to properly fill the shells.

TO MAKE THE DULCE DE LECHE COFFEE TRUFFLES:

1. Using a disposable pastry bag with a small opening cut in the tip, fill the truffle shells halfway to the tops with the dulce de leche.

2. Using a disposable pastry bag with a small opening cut in the tip, fill the truffle shells to the tops with the coffee ganache.

3. Allow the ganache to crystallize at room temperature until the top is solid, for several hours or overnight.

4. Seal the truffles using either untempered milk chocolate with a sealing tray or tempered milk chocolate applied with a paper cone.

5. Using a round dipping fork, dip the truffles in the tempered milk chocolate.

6. When the chocolate begins to set, drop a pinch of instant coffee powder onto the top of each truffle.

NOTE: When making the dulce de leche, be certain that the cans of sweetened condensed milk are fully immersed in the simmering water at all times to avoid the possibility of the cans bursting. The dulce de leche may be made days in advance if desired.

Dulce de Leche Coffee Truffles

HONEY HAZELNUT TRUFFLES

yield: **160 TRUFFLES**

Heavy cream	400 g	14 oz	30%
Buckwheat honey	140 g	5 oz	10%
Praline paste	400 g	14 oz	30%
Milk chocolate, unmelted, tempered, chopped	400 g	14 oz	30%
BATCH SIZE	1340 g	47 oz	100%
Dark chocolate hollow truffle shells (see page 110)	160 shells		
Toasted hazelnuts, whole	as needed		
Dark chocolate, melted, untempered or tempered, for sealing	as needed		
Dark chocolate, melted, tempered, for dipping	as needed		
Toasted hazelnuts, chopped, for finishing	as needed		

1. Combine the cream and buckwheat honey in a saucepan. Bring to a boil.

2. In a stainless-steel bowl, combine the praline paste and the chopped milk chocolate. Pour the hot cream mixture over the chocolate mixture and let sit for 1 minute to allow the chocolate to melt.

3. Using a spoon or spatula, stir the mixture in vigorous small circles in the center of the bowl until it emulsifies.

4. Stir outward in larger circles to spread the emulsion throughout the bowl, checking to see that all of the chocolate has melted. If necessary, heat the ganache over a hot water bath to melt the chocolate. The temperature of the ganache should not exceed 32°C/90°F.

5. Pour the ganache into a hotel pan, allowing the ganache to cover the bottom of the pan in a thin layer. Place plastic wrap directly on the surface of the ganache.

6. Allow to rest at room temperature until the ganache reaches 25°C/77°F, or slightly lower. The ganache should be of a thick but fluid consistency to properly fill the shells.

7. Using a disposable pastry bag with a small opening cut in the tip, fill the truffle shells halfway to the tops with the ganache.

8. Place a single whole toasted hazelnut inside each shell on top of the ganache.

9. Fill the truffles the rest of the way with ganache. Allow the ganache to crystallize at room temperature until the top is solid, approximately 1 hour.

10. Seal the truffles using either untempered dark chocolate with a sealing tray or tempered dark chocolate applied with a paper cone.

11. Using a round dipping fork, dip the truffles in the tempered dark chocolate.

12. When the chocolate begins to set, drop a pinch of chopped toasted hazelnut onto the top of each truffle.

RASPBERRY TRUFFLES

yield: **125 TRUFFLES**

Heavy cream	250 g	9 oz	23%
Glucose syrup	80 g	3 oz	7%
White chocolate, unmelted, tempered, chopped	660 g	23 oz	63%
Raspberry liqueur	80 g	3 oz	7%
BATCH SIZE	1070 g	38 oz	100%
White chocolate hollow truffle shells (see page 110)	125 shells		
Raspberry jam	as needed		
White chocolate, melted, untempered or tempered, for sealing	as needed		
White chocolate, melted, tempered, for dipping	as needed		
Dehydrated raspberry powder, for finishing	as needed		

1. Combine the cream and glucose syrup in a saucepan. Bring to a boil.

2. Pour the hot cream mixture over the chopped white chocolate and let sit for 1 minute to allow the chocolate to melt.

3. Using a spoon or spatula, stir the mixture in vigorous small circles in the center of the bowl until it emulsifies.

4. Stir outward in larger circles to spread the emulsion throughout the bowl, checking to be certain that all of the chocolate has melted. If necessary, place the ganache over a hot water bath to melt the chocolate. The temperature of the ganache should not exceed 32°C/90°F.

5. Stream in the raspberry liqueur, stirring the mixture until it is homogeneous.

6. Pour the ganache into a hotel pan, allowing the ganache to cover the bottom of the pan in a thin layer. Place plastic wrap directly on the surface of the ganache.

7. Allow to rest at room temperature until it reaches 25°C/77°F or slightly lower, approximately 20 minutes. The cooled ganache should be of a thick but fluid consistency to properly fill the shells.

8. Using a disposable pastry bag with a small opening cut in the tip, fill the truffle shells halfway to the tops with the ganache.

9. Refrigerate the filled truffle shells for 10 minutes to firm the ganache slightly.

10. Using a paper cone, pipe a small pearl of raspberry jam into the center of each shell on top of the ganache.

11. Using a disposable pastry bag with a small opening cut in the tip, fill the truffle shells the rest of the way with ganache.

12. Allow the ganache to crystallize at room temperature until the top is solid, for several hours or overnight.

13. Seal the truffles using either untempered white chocolate with a sealing tray or tempered white chocolate applied with a paper cone.

14. Using a round dipping fork, dip the truffles in the tempered white chocolate.

15. When the chocolate begins to set, sift a light dusting of dehydrated raspberry powder over the tops of the truffles.

GINGER CHARDONS

yield: **180 PIECES**

Heavy cream	300 g	11 oz	27%
Ginger, peeled, sliced	80 g	3 oz	7%
Milk	as needed		
Glucose syrup	90 g	3 oz	7%
Milk chocolate, unmelted, tempered, chopped	600 g	21 oz	52%
Butter, soft	40 g	1 oz	2%
Crystallized ginger, finely diced	60 g	2 oz	5%
BATCH SIZE	1170 g	41 oz	100%
Milk chocolate hollow truffle shells (see page 110)	180 shells	180 shells	
Milk chocolate, melted, untempered or tempered, for sealing	as needed		
Milk chocolate, melted, tempered, for dipping	as needed		

1. Combine the cream and sliced ginger in a saucepan and bring to a boil. Remove from the heat, cover, and allow to steep for 5 minutes.

2. Strain the infused cream through premoistened cheesecloth. Wring the ginger in the cheesecloth to extract the maximum amount of flavor possible.

3. Return the cream to 300 g by adding milk.

4. Add the glucose syrup to the flavored cream mixture. Bring to a boil.

5. Pour the hot cream mixture over the chopped milk chocolate and let sit for 1 minute to allow the chocolate to melt.

6. Using a paddle, stir the mixture in vigorous small circles in the center of the bowl until it emulsifies.

7. Stir outward in larger circles to spread the emulsion throughout the bowl, checking to see that all of the chocolate has melted. If necessary, heat the ganache over a hot water bath to melt the chocolate. The temperature of the ganache should not exceed 32°C/90°F.

8. Stir the butter into the ganache, taking care that no lumps of butter remain. Mix in the crystallized ginger.

9. Pour the ganache into a hotel pan, allowing the ganache to cover the bottom of the pan in a thin layer. Place plastic wrap directly on the surface of the ganache.

10. Allow to rest at room temperature until the ganache reaches 25°C/77°F or slightly lower, approximately 20 minutes. The cooled ganache should be of a thick but fluid consistency to properly fill the shells.

11. Using a disposable pastry bag with a small opening cut in the tip, fill the truffle shells to the tops with the ganache.

12. Allow the ganache to crystallize at room temperature until the top is solid, for several hours or overnight.

13. Seal the truffles using either untempered milk chocolate with a sealing tray or tempered milk chocolate applied with a paper cone.

14. Using a round dipping fork, dip the truffles in the tempered milk chocolate, then place them on an icing screen.

15. Allow the chocolate to begin to set so that it holds a peak when touched.

16. Roll the dipped truffles lightly on the screen to texture them, remove immediately, and place on parchment paper.

TOUCANS

yield: **125 PIECES**

Cocoa butter, colored yellow and red	as needed		
White chocolate, melted, tempered, for lining molds (see page 58)	as needed		
Heavy cream	80 g	2 oz	15%
Glucose syrup	20 g	1 oz	4%
Reduced passion fruit purée (see Note)	80 g	2 oz	15%
White chocolate, tempered, chopped	300 g	11 oz	15%
Butter, soft	20 g	1 oz	4%
BATCH SIZE	500 g	18 oz	100%
White chocolate, melted, untempered or tempered, for sealing	as needed		

TO PREPARE THE MOLDS:

1. Airbrush the interior of clean, polished keel-shaped molds with red cocoa butter on one end and yellow cocoa butter on the other.

2. Line the molds with the tempered white chocolate, using the shell-molding technique. (See page 77.)

To make the passion fruit ganache:

1. Combine the cream and glucose syrup in a saucepan. Bring to a boil.

2. Heat the reduced passion fruit purée in a separate saucepan to 40°C/105°F.

3. Pour the hot cream mixture and the warm reduced passion fruit purée over the chopped white chocolate and let sit for 1 minute to allow the chocolate to melt.

4. Using a spoon or spatula, stir the mixture in vigorous small circles in the center of the bowl until it emulsifies.

5. Stir outward in larger circles to spread the emulsion throughout the bowl, checking to see that all of the chocolate has melted. If necessary, heat the ganache over a hot water bath to melt the chocolate. The temperature of the ganache should not exceed 32°C/90°F.

6. Stir the butter into the ganache, taking care that no lumps of butter remain.

7. Pour the ganache into a hotel pan, allowing the ganache to cover the bottom of the pan in a thin layer. Place plastic wrap directly on the surface of the ganache.

8. Allow the ganache to rest at room temperature until it reaches 25°C/77°F or slightly lower, approximately 20 minutes. The cooled ganache should be of a thick but fluid consistency to properly fill the shells.

9. Using a disposable pastry bag with a small opening cut in the tip, fill the lined molds with the ganache to within 3 mm/⅛ in of the tops.

10. Allow the ganache to crystallize at room temperature until the top is solid, for several hours or overnight.

11. Seal the truffles using either untempered white chocolate with a sealing tray or tempered white chocolate applied with a paper cone.

12. Allow the tops to crystallize at room temperature. Then refrigerate the filled molds until the chocolate pulls away from the inside of the molds, approximately 20 minutes.

13. Place a piece of stiff cardboard over each mold and invert the mold to release the finished confections.

NOTE: Passion fruit juice concentrate should be reduced by half. Natural-strength passion fruit purée should be reduced by three quarters.

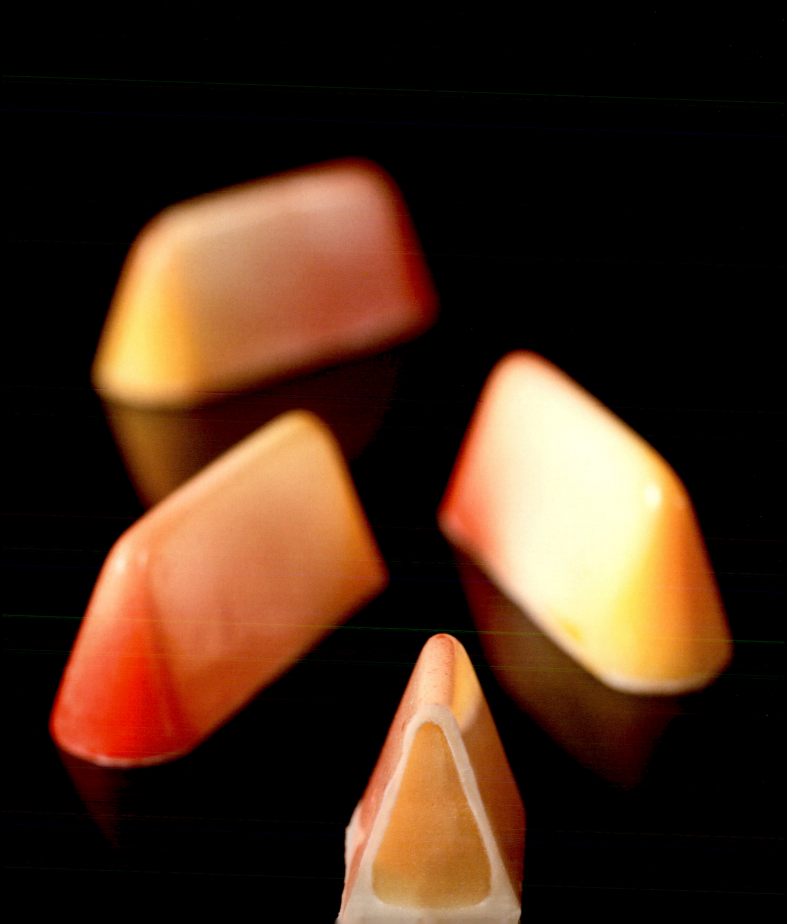

PUMPKIN CARAMEL GANACHE

yield: **125 PIECES**

GINGERBREAD SPICE MIX

Ginger, ground	50 g	2 oz	47%
Cinnamon, ground	30 g	1 oz	31%
Nutmeg, ground	10 g	0.5 oz	14%
Cloves, ground	7 g	0.25 oz	8%
BATCH SIZE	97 g	3.75 oz	100%
Cocoa butter, colored orange, yellow, and green	as needed		
Milk chocolate, melted, tempered, for lining molds (see page 58)	as needed		

PUMPKIN CARAMEL GANACHE

Lemon juice	¼ tsp	¼ tsp	<1%
Sugar	100 g	4 oz	10%
Glucose syrup	60 g	2 oz	6%
Heavy cream	200 g	7 oz	20%
Pumpkin purée	100 g	4 oz	10%
Gingerbread spice mix	1 tsp	1 tsp	21%
Milk chocolate, unmelted, tempered, chopped	500 g	18 oz	50%
Brandy	50 g	2 oz	5%
BATCH SIZE	1010 g	36 oz	100%
Dark chocolate, melted, tempered, for sealing	as needed		

TO MAKE THE GINGERBREAD SPICE MIX:

Combine ground ginger, cinnamon, nutmeg, and cloves. Blend well. Set aside.

TO PREPARE THE MOLDS:

1. Airbrush the interior of clean, polished molds with the colored cocoa butters.
2. Line the molds with the tempered milk chocolate, using the shell-molding technique. (See page 77.)

TO MAKE THE PUMPKIN CARAMEL GANACHE:

1. Rub the lemon juice into the sugar.
2. In a saucepan, caramelize the sugar mixture until amber using the dry method. (See page 222.)
3. Remove from the heat and add the glucose syrup to the caramelized sugar.
4. Bring the cream to a boil. With the caramelized sugar mixture at low heat, stream in the hot cream, making certain that the caramelized sugar mixture is entirely incorporated.
5. Add the pumpkin purée and 1 tsp of the gingerbread spice mix.
6. Return the cream mixture to a boil.

7. Pour the hot cream mixture over the chopped milk chocolate and let sit for 1 minute to allow the chocolate to melt.

8. Using a paddle, stir the mixture in vigorous small circles in the center of the bowl until it emulsifies.

9. Stir outward in larger circles to spread the emulsion throughout the bowl, checking to see that all of the chocolate has melted. If necessary, heat the ganache over a hot water bath to melt the chocolate. The temperature of the ganache should not exceed 32°C/90°F.

10. Stream in the brandy, stirring until the mixture is homogeneous.

11. Pour the ganache into a hotel pan, allowing the ganache to cover the bottom of the pan in a thin layer. Place plastic wrap directly on the surface of the ganache.

12. Allow to rest at room temperature until the ganache reaches 25°C/77°F or slightly lower. The cooled ganache should be of a thick but fluid consistency to properly fill the shells.

13. Using a disposable pastry bag with a small opening cut in the tip, fill the lined molds with the ganache to within 3 mm/⅛ in of the tops.

14. Allow the ganache to crystallize at room temperature until the top is solid, for several hours or overnight.

15. Seal the truffles using the tempered dark chocolate.

16. Allow the tops to crystallize at room temperature. Then refrigerate the filled molds until the chocolate pulls away from the inside of the molds, approximately 20 minutes.

17. Place a piece of stiff cardboard over each mold and invert the mold to release the finished confections.

VANILLA MILK CHOCOLATE TRUFFLES

yield: **125 TRUFFLES**

Heavy cream	340 g	12 oz	31%
Glucose syrup	60 g	2 oz	5%
Vanilla bean, split and scraped	1 bean	1 bean	
Milk chocolate, unmelted, tempered, chopped	670 g	24 oz	60%
Butter, soft	40 g	1.5 oz	4%
BATCH SIZE	1110 g	39.5 oz	100%
Milk chocolate hollow truffle shells (see page 110)	125 shells		
Milk chocolate, melted, untempered or tempered, for sealing	as needed		
Milk chocolate, melted, tempered, for dipping	as needed		

1. Combine the cream and glucose syrup with the vanilla bean and its seeds in a saucepan and bring to a boil. Remove from the heat, cover, and let steep for 5 minutes.

2. Strain the infused cream through premoistened cheesecloth. Wring the vanilla bean in the cheesecloth to extract the maximum amount of flavor possible.

3. Pour the hot cream mixture over the chopped milk chocolate and let sit for 1 minute to allow the milk chocolate to melt.

4. Using a paddle, stir the mixture in vigorous small circles in the center of the bowl until it emulsifies.

5. Stir outward in larger circles to spread the emulsion throughout the bowl, checking to see that all of the chocolate has melted. If necessary, heat the ganache over a hot water bath to melt the chocolate. The temperature of the ganache should not exceed 32°C/90°F.

6. Stir the butter into the ganache, taking care that no lumps of butter remain.

7. Pour the ganache into a hotel pan, allowing the ganache to cover the bottom of the pan in a thin layer. Allow to rest uncovered at room temperature until it reaches 25°C/77°F or slightly lower, approximately 20 minutes. The cooled ganache should be of a thick but fluid consistency to properly fill the shells.

8. Using a disposable pastry bag with a small opening cut in the tip, fill the hollow shells to the tops with the cooled ganache.

9. Allow the ganache to crystallize at room temperature until the top is solid, approximately 1 hour.

10. Seal the truffles using either untempered milk chocolate with a sealing tray or tempered milk chocolate applied with a paper cone.

11. Using a round dipping fork, dip the truffles in the tempered milk chocolate, then place them on an icing screen.

12. Allow the chocolate to begin to set so that it holds a peak when touched.

13. Roll the dipped truffles lightly on the screen to texture them, remove immediately, and place them on parchment paper.

GREEN FAERIES

yield: **130 PIECES**

Edible green dry luster color	as needed		
Edible green glitter	as needed		
Dark chocolate, melted, tempered, for lining molds (see page 58)	as needed		
Heavy cream	180 g	6 oz	22%
Glucose syrup	50 g	2 oz	7%
Dark chocolate, unmelted, tempered, chopped	440 g	16 oz	56%
Butter, soft	40 g	1 oz	4%
Absinthe-flavored liqueur (see Note)	90 g	3 oz	11%
BATCH SIZE	800 g	28 oz	100%
Dark chocolate, melted, tempered, for sealing	as needed		

TO PREPARE THE MOLDS:

1. Brush clean, polished molds lightly with edible green dry luster color. Sprinkle edible green glitter into each cavity of the molds.

2. Line the molds with the tempered dark chocolate, using the shell-molding technique. (See page 77.)

To make the ganache:

1. Combine the cream and glucose syrup in a saucepan. Bring to a boil.

2. Pour the hot cream mixture over the chopped dark chocolate and let sit for 1 minute to allow the chocolate to melt.

3. Using a paddle, stir the mixture in vigorous small circles in the center of the bowl until it emulsifies.

4. Stir outward in larger circles to spread the emulsion throughout the bowl, checking to see that all of the chocolate has melted. If necessary, heat the ganache over a hot water bath to melt the chocolate. The temperature of the ganache should not exceed 34°C/94°F.

5. Stir the butter into the ganache, taking care that no lumps of butter remain.

6. Stream in the absinthe-flavored liqueur and stir until the mixture is homogeneous.

7. Pour the ganache into a hotel pan, allowing the ganache to cover the bottom of the pan in a thin layer. Place plastic wrap directly on the surface of the ganache.

8. Allow to rest at room temperature until the ganache reaches 25°C/77°F or slightly lower, approximately 20 minutes. The cooled ganache should be of a thick but fluid consistency to properly fill the molds.

9. Using a disposable pastry bag with a small opening cut in the tip, fill the lined molds with the ganache to within 3 mm/⅛ in of the tops.

10. Allow the ganache to crystallize at room temperature until the top is solid, for several hours or overnight.

11. Seal the truffles using the tempered dark chocolate.

12. Allow the tops to crystallize at room temperature. Then refrigerate the filled molds until the chocolate pulls away from the inside of the molds, approximately 20 minutes.

13. Place a piece of stiff cardboard over each mold and invert the mold to release the finished confections.

NOTE: Authentic absinthe is not legal for sale in the United States, so an absinthe-flavored liqueur should be substituted for this confection.

6

Butter ganache is a confectionery center of European provenance that is not widely used in America. Introducing butter ganache centers into the confectioner's product line can provide the savvy confectioner with flavors and textures that are not easily found elsewhere.

BUTTER GANACHE

Butter ganache shares several traits with the more commonly used cream ganache: both may be used as either a pastry glaze or a confectionery center; the guideline for the ratio of chocolate to liquefiers is identical for each; and, like cream ganache, butter ganache is an emulsion. However, each of these similarities comes with a qualification: even when used as a glaze for pastries, butter ganache, unlike cream ganache, must be tempered in order to prevent the formation of bloom and to ensure a smooth texture; the ingredients considered liquefiers in butter ganache are different from those considered liquefiers in cream ganache; and the emulsion in butter ganache is a water-in-fat emulsion rather than a fat-in-water emulsion like cream ganache. Butter ganache may be used either by piping or slabbing; like cream ganache, there is a difference in makeup technique, depending on how the product is to be used. In addition, butter ganache always sets firmer than cream ganache due to its higher fat and lower water content. It is this lower water content—and accompanying lower water-activity level—that gives butter ganache a longer shelf life than cream ganache. An enrobed butter ganache center can be stored at room temperature for six to eight weeks. Butter ganache is quickly made up and crystallizes rapidly after depositing. It can usually be dipped in chocolate within thirty minutes of piping or slabbing. Because butter ganache sets up quickly, preparation is particularly important. Before beginning, be sure to have ready all depositing and portioning equipment, such as pastry bags, chocolate discs, frames, and spreading tools.

technique | theory | BUTTER GANACHE

Like cream ganache, butter ganache may be piped or spread into a slab. The method for making up the ganache differs slightly—especially in the temperature of the butter and the amount of mixing—depending on which of these two methods is used.

1. **MIX SOFT BUTTER WITH SWEETENER.** The butter for a piped butter ganache should not be softened as much as the butter for a slabbed butter ganache. When piping, it is best to warm the butter to approximately 20°C/68°F; for slabbing, the temperature should be nearly 30°C/86°F. Depending on the intended use of the butter ganache, the butter and sweetener are also mixed differently. If a butter ganache is to be piped, the two ingredients should be creamed together well in order to aerate the mixture. This is usually accomplished using a mixer, with a paddle or whip attachment run at medium speed. The light texture this method creates helps the piped pieces to hold their shape and provides a light mouthfeel to the finished confection. If the butter ganache is to be slabbed, it is preferable to mix the butter and sweetener together gently, just combining them but not aerating the mixture. This is best accomplished by hand, unless the batch is very large and hand mixing is impractical. A slabbed butter ganache does not require a light texture to maintain its shape as it sets, so aeration is unnecessary. If aerated, a slabbed ganache will not cut cleanly, resulting in irregular shapes, lack of uniformity, corners that are not square, and sides that crumble when they are cut.

Using chocolate discs as bases, pipe butter ganache confections, such as these Rainiers (page 211), to a decorative peak, then finish as desired (see step 4 of the technique).

2. **ADD MELTED, TEMPERED CHOCOLATE TO THE BUTTER-SWEETENER BLEND.** The chocolate used to make butter ganache must be tempered and near its optimal working temperature before being added to the butter-sweetener mixture. Just as when using chocolate alone, using tempered chocolate ensures that the butter ganache will set quickly, without the formation of bloom and, most important, with a smooth, firm, homogeneous texture. Using untempered chocolate in butter ganache results in a product that takes a long time to set, is insufficiently firm upon setting, and develops large fat crystals over time, resulting in a grainy mouthfeel in the finished product. The chocolate must be near its optimal working temperature for two reasons: so that it does not solidify as soon as it is combined with the butter and so that the butter ganache remains at a workable consistency for a period of time after mixing so that it can be piped or spread. Even when making a moderately large batch, it is advisable to add the chocolate into the butter by hand; a mixer paddle throws chocolate around the inside of the bowl, creating chocolate chips in the ganache. A mixer should be used for only very large batches of butter ganache, and even then, the chocolate must be added carefully and the bowl scraped well to ensure good distribution of the chocolate.

3. **MIX IN LIQUID FLAVORINGS.** Liquid flavoring is part of the dispersed phase of the butter ganache emulsion and therefore should be added in a steady stream while the mixture is stirred. This ensures that the liquid is properly dispersed throughout the continuous fat phase. The added liquid should be neither too cold nor too hot, but at around room temperature (20°C/68°F), so as not to crystallize the fat—which it would do if too cold—or soften the fat and perhaps remove the temper—which it would do if too hot.

4. **PIPE OR SLAB AS DESIRED.** Once mixed, the butter ganache may be piped or slabbed as desired. If slabbing, simply spread the ganache into a frame, allow it to crystallize, bottom-coat it, cut it, and then dip the pieces. When piping individual pieces of butter ganache, pipe directly onto chocolate discs, which serve as bases when the piped pieces are dipped. Piping onto bases effectively seals the bottom of each piece to prevent exposure to oxygen, to block moisture migration, and to make the pieces easier to handle with a dipping fork. Such bases serve the same function as precoating but eliminate the need to bottom-coat each piece prior to dipping. As a rule, tabling butter ganache is not necessary because the chocolate used to make it is tempered and therefore contains stable fat crystals. However, if a butter ganache is too soft to pipe after mixing, tabling to prompt crystallization quickly brings it to piping consistency. This step is optional, and it is only used when the butter ganache is excessively soft after makeup.

BUTTER GANACHE RATIOS

The basic ratio for butter ganache is two parts chocolate to one part liquefier by weight: a basic dark chocolate butter ganache uses twice as much chocolate as butter and liquid flavoring combined. This ratio is not nearly as critical as it is with cream ganache. Butter ganache has a lower water content than cream ganache, so rapid spoilage due to excessive moisture is seldom a concern. The water in butter ganache is the dispersed phase of the emulsion, and because the moisture content is relatively low, there is less likelihood that the emulsion will separate. Also, due to its high fat content, it is unlikely that butter ganache will become too soft to handle. For all of these reasons, the ratios for butter ganache are far more flexible than those for cream ganache. The higher the percentage of butter used, the softer and lighter the finished center will be. Common formulations range from as little as 1:1 for a soft center, to as high as 2:1 for a firm dark chocolate center. No set amount of liquid flavoring must be used; the amount depends on the flavoring selected and the desired results. In general, it is acceptable to use as much liquid favoring as butter without creating a high probability that the emulsion will separate.

Liquid flavoring—in whatever quantity—must be counted as a liquefier in the formulation, so a corresponding amount of additional chocolate should also be added. When using milk chocolate or white chocolate, the amount of chocolate in the basic ratio is increased by approximately 25 percent. A basic milk or white chocolate butter ganache must contain approximately 2.5 parts chocolate to 1 part liquefier in order to create a similar texture to a 2:1 dark chocolate butter ganache.

FUNCTION OF INGREDIENTS IN BUTTER GANACHE

Butter

The butter used in butter ganache must be fresh unsalted butter of the highest quality. Before using it, warm it to 20° to 30°C/68° to 86°F, the temperature depending on whether the ganache is to be piped or slabbed. Softening the butter is essential to incorporating the melted tempered chocolate without forming chips and for emulsifying the liquid ingredients into the butter. Butter is one of the ingredients counted as a liquefier in the ratio for butter ganache formulation.

Sweeteners

The sweeteners used in butter ganache should be nongranular sweeteners—that is, products that do not feel grainy in the mouth. Nongranular sweeteners are used because there is not enough liquid in butter ganache to dissolve granulated sugar. The sweeteners commonly used in butter ganache include glucose syrups and fondant as well as honey and jam, which act as both flavoring and sweetener. Despite the fact that it contains crystalline sugar, fondant qualifies as nongranular because its crystals are so small as to be undetectable on the palate. Confectioners' sugar is not acceptable because the particles in it are larger than the crystals in fondant and can be felt in the mouth. Also, American confectioners' sugar contains 3 percent cornstarch, further diminishing that sugar's usefulness in butter ganache. Even when they are liquid, sweeteners are not considered liquefiers in butter ganache. They bind far more moisture than they contribute to the system.

Chocolate

When mixing butter ganache, use liquid tempered chocolate at or near its maximum working temperature. (See Tempering Chocolate, Temperature, page 56.) It is necessary to temper the chocolate that goes into butter ganache, for all the same reasons that it is necessary to temper chocolate in general: due to the presence of cocoa butter, butter ganache exhibits the same polymorphic qualities that chocolate does. (See Polymorphism of Cocoa Butter, page 55.) If the chocolate in butter ganache is not precrystallized, the butter ganache will not set quickly and firmly and will not have a smooth, homogeneous texture. Butter ganache made with untempered chocolate not only will be unacceptably soft but it will not retain a smooth texture and will slowly develop large fat crystals in the hours and days after it sets.

Liquid flavorings

Liqueurs and spirits are the liquid flavorings most commonly used in butter ganache, although concentrated fruit purées may also be used successfully. It is not advisable to use natural-strength fruit purées due to their high water content, which can contribute to a diminished shelf life for the finished ganache. The liquid flavoring should be at room temperature (20°C/68°F) when added to the ganache. Dry flavorings such as spices may also be used, although they will detract from the smooth texture of the center. Liquid flavorings are counted as liquefiers in the ratios for butter ganache formulation.

BUTTER GANACHE TROUBLESHOOTING

DEFECT	CAUSE	REMEDY
DURING MAKEUP		
SEPARATED EMULSION	Too much liquid in formula	Use more chocolate and/or butter in formula
	Ingredients too cold	Use ingredients at proper temperatures (20° to 30°C/68° to 86°F)
	Liquid added too quickly	Stream in liquid flavorings while stirring
PIPED GANACHE		
TOO SOFT TO PIPE; WON'T HOLD SHAPE WHEN PIPED	Ingredients too warm	Use ingredients at proper temperatures (20° to 25°C/68° to 77°F)
	Too much liquid in formula	Use higher ratio of chocolate to liquefiers
	Needs more time to crystallize	Allow ganache to sit at room temperature for several minutes, to firm
		Table ganache to expedite crystallization
SETS VERY SLOWLY	Chocolate not tempered	Use tempered chocolate
		Use liquid flavoring at proper temperatures (20° to 25°C/68° to 77°F)
DEVELOPS GRAINY TEXTURE AFTER STORAGE	Chocolate not tempered	Use tempered chocolate
	Ingredients too warm	Use ingredients at proper temperatures (20° to 30°C/68° to 86°F)
BUTTER CHUNKS IN FINISHED GANACHE	Butter too cold	Use ingredients at proper temperatures (20° to 30°C/68° to 86°F)
	Insufficient mixing	Mix butter well with other ingredients
CHIPS OF CHOCOLATE IN FINISHED GANACHE	Ingredients too cold	Use ingredients at proper temperatures (20° to 30°C/68° to 86°F)
	Insufficient mixing while adding chocolate	Mix well when adding chocolate; scrape bowl
SLABBED GANACHE		
CRUMBLED CORNERS AND SIDES AFTER CUTTING	Excessive aeration	Do not aerate butter and sweetener when mixing
	Too much chocolate in ratio	Reduce chocolate in ratio
	Too cold	Cut ganache when at proper temperature (above 20°C/68°F)

MAKING CHOCOLATE DISCS FOR BASES

When piping individual centers, such as butter ganache for Rainiers (page 211) or cream ganache for Buckwheat Beehives (page 132), it is worthwhile to pipe them onto chocolate bases that in effect serve as the precoat for the finished pieces. The chocolate discs perform the two vital functions of a precoat: making the centers easier to handle for dipping and ensuring that the centers are entirely sealed with chocolate, thereby preventing loss of quality due to moisture migration and exposure to oxygen. If chocolate bases are not used, the artisan confectioner who is not using an enrober is faced with precoating each piece individually—clearly not an efficient technique. Two methods can be employed for making the chocolate bases. Either one works well, and it is up to the confectioner to decide which is more practical for a particular operation.

USING A STENCIL

Using a stencil is an efficient technique for making chocolate bases, but it requires stencils of the correct size, shape, and thickness for each application. Stencils may be made of a variety of plastics or rubber materials that are approved for food use. Silicone stencils are excellent, but other food-safe plastics may be used as well because stencils used for chocolate are not exposed to high temperatures.

1. Select a stencil of the desired size, shape, and thickness for the pieces being made. Generally, a thickness of 2 to 3 mm/$\frac{1}{16}$ to $\frac{1}{8}$ in is appropriate.

2. Place the stencil on parchment paper on a flat work surface. Working directly on a table is preferable to working on a sheet pan. Sheet pans are almost never completely flat, and discs stenciled on them will have varying thicknesses and will likely have edges that are poorly defined.

3. Spread a 2-mm/$\frac{1}{16}$-in layer of tempered chocolate of the same variety in which the centers will be dipped over the entire stencil. Do not scrape down to the stencil during this initial spreading. If the excess chocolate is cleaned from the top of the stencil at this point, the disc will not have clean, sharp edges.

4. Allow the chocolate to set until it reaches a plastic state, approximately 5 minutes.

Proceeding to the next step too soon will result in discs with irregular edges. Waiting too long to remove the excess chocolate will make the chocolate too brittle to work with.

5. Use a scraper to remove the excess chocolate from the top of the stencil, leaving only the cutout filled with the chocolate. The chocolate should scrape off easily and smoothly when it has set to the correct point.

6. Peel the stencil from the parchment paper immediately, leaving the bases adhered to the paper. If the stencil is not removed immediately after the chocolate reaches a plastic state, the bases will come away with the stencil rather than adhering to the parchment paper. Should the discs come loose from the paper, reattach them using a dot of untempered chocolate before piping on them.

USING A CUTTER

Using a cutter is a slightly less efficient technique for making bases than using a stencil, but it offers more flexibility in choice of sizes and shapes.

1. Using the same type of chocolate in which the center is to be dipped, spread a layer of tempered chocolate approximately 2 mm/$\frac{1}{16}$ in thick onto parchment paper. Vibrate the paper lightly to remove irregularities in the chocolate.

2. Allow the chocolate to set until it has lost its gloss and is no longer tacky. The chocolate should be very nearly fully set before proceeding to the next step.

3. Using a round cutter of the desired size, make cuts in the sheet of freshly set chocolate. The discs should remain attached to the parchment paper. It is critical to make the cuts before the chocolate has set completely in order to prevent the cutouts from coming away with the cutter blade. Cutting the chocolate too soon, however, will produce uneven edges and discs that will not easily release from the surrounding chocolate.

4. As the chocolate continues to harden, remove most of the material from around the cutouts. It is important to leave the cutouts attached to the paper. A chocolate disc not affixed to paper will move freely with the force of the bag, making piping very difficult. Removing the chocolate from between the discs prevents the chocolate from curling due to contraction as it sets on the parchment.

5. Pipe the centers onto the cutouts as desired, and finish as required.

GINGERBREAD SQUARES

yield: **150 SQUARES**

Butter, soft	140 g	5 oz	20%
Gingergread Spice (recipe follows)	1 tsp	1 tsp	< 1%
Molasses	110 g	4 oz	16%
Milk chocolate, melted, tempered, at 30°C/86°F	400 g	14 oz	57%
Anise liqueur	50 g	2 oz	7%
BATCH SIZE	700 g	25 oz	100%
Dark chocolate, melted, tempered, for precoating and dipping	as needed		
Turbinado sugar, for finishing	as needed		

1. By hand, mix together the butter, spice, and molasses until well combined.
2. Stream the tempered milk chocolate into the butter mixture while stirring, taking care not to allow chunks of chocolate to form in the butter mixture.
3. Stream in the anise liqueur, stirring until the mixture is homogeneous.
4. Spread the ganache immediately into a frame 12 × 12 × ¼ in set on parchment paper. Allow to crystallize until firm enough to handle, about 20 minutes.
5. Remove the frame from the butter ganache slab.
6. Precoat one side of the slab with the tempered dark chocolate.
7. Allow the precoat to crystallize. Then cut the slab into squares, using the 22.5-mm strings on a guitar.
8. Dip the squares in the tempered dark chocolate.
9. As the chocolate begins to set, use a 3-prong dipping fork to make a diagonal mark on the top of each piece and finish with several crystals of the turbinado sugar.

GINGERBREAD SPICE

yield: **97 G/13.75 OZ**

Cinnamon, ground	30 g	1 oz	31%
Ginger, ground	50 g	2 oz	47%
Nutmeg, ground	10 g	0.5 oz	14%
Cloves, ground	7 g	0.25 oz	8%
BATCH SIZE	97 g	3.75 oz	100%

Combine the ground ginger, cinnamon, nutmeg, and cloves. Blend well. Set aside.

ORANGE BUTTER GANACHE

yield: **150 PIECES**

Butter, very soft (30°C/86°F)	110 g	4 oz	15%
Fondant (page 290)	40 g	1.5 oz	5%
Milk chocolate, melted, tempered, at 30°C/86°F	480 g	17 oz	69%
Orange juice concentrate	50 g	2 oz	8%
Orange liqueur	20 g	1 oz	3%
BATCH SIZE	700 g	25.5 oz	100%
Dark chocolate, melted, tempered, for precoating and dipping	as needed		
Orange zest confit, for finishing (see Note)	as needed		

1. By hand, mix together the butter and fondant until well combined.

2. Stream the tempered milk chocolate into the butter mixture while stirring, taking care not to allow chunks of chocolate to form.

3. Stream in the orange juice concentrate and orange liqueur, stirring until the mixture is homogeneous.

4. Spread the ganache into a frame 12 × 12 × ¼ in set on parchment paper. Allow to crystallize until firm enough to handle, about 20 minutes.

5. Remove the frame from the slab.

6. Precoat one side of the slab with the tempered dark chocolate.

7. Allow the precoat to crystallize. Then cut the slab into squares, using the 22.5-mm strings on a guitar.

8. Dip the squares in the tempered dark chocolate.

9. When the chocolate begins to set, place a piece of the candied orange zest diagonally across the top of each piece.

    NOTE: To prepare the orange zest confit, follow the Citrus Confit Technique, page 329. Remove the zest from the pith. Cut strips of the zest 25 mm/1 in wide. Cut the strips in thin julienne (1 mm) and coat lightly with granulated sugar for ease of handling.

MADRAS SQUARES

yield: **150 PIECES**

Butter, very soft (30°C/86°F)	160 g	6 oz	23%
Madras-style curry powder	1 Tbsp	1 Tbsp	<1%
White chocolate, melted, tempered, at 30°C/86°F	350 g	12 oz	50%
Cream of coconut (such as Coco Lopez)	190 g	7 oz	27%
BATCH SIZE	700 g	25 oz	100%
Dark chocolate, melted, tempered, for precoating and dipping	as needed		
Madras-style curry powder, for finishing	as needed		
Sweetened coconut shreds, for finishing	as needed		

1. By hand, mix together the butter and curry powder until well combined.
2. Stream the tempered white chocolate into the butter mixture while stirring, taking care not to allow chunks of chocolate to form.
3. Stream in the cream of coconut, stirring until the mixture is homogeneous.
4. Spread the ganache into a frame 12 × 12 × ¼ in set on parchment paper. Allow to crystallize until firm enough to handle, about 20 minutes.
5. Remove the frame from the slab.
6. Precoat one side of the slab with the tempered dark chocolate.
7. Allow the precoat to crystallize. Then cut the slab into squares, using the 22.5-mm strings on a guitar.
8. Dip the squares in the tempered dark chocolate.
9. Before the chocolate sets, use a 3-prong fork to make a diagonal wave pattern on the top of each piece. Finish with a small pinch of the curry powder and a piece of shredded coconut.

APRICOT BUTTER GANACHE

yield: **150 PIECES**

Butter, very soft (30°C/86°F)	160 g	6 oz	22%
Apricot jam	80 g	3 oz	11%
Milk chocolate, melted, tempered, at 30°C/86°F	430 g	15 oz	61%
Apricot brandy	40 g	1.5 oz	6%
BATCH SIZE	710 g	25.5 oz	100%
Milk chocolate, melted, tempered, for precoating	as needed		
Apricot jam, for finishing	as needed		
Milk chocolate, melted, tempered, thinned, for dipping (see Note)	as needed		
Coarse sugar, for finishing	as needed		

1. By hand, mix together the butter and jam until well combined.
2. Stream the tempered milk chocolate into the butter mixture while stirring, taking care not to allow chunks of chocolate to form.
3. Stream in the brandy, stirring until the mixture is homogeneous.
4. Spread the ganache into a frame 12 × 12 × ¼ in set on parchment paper. Allow to crystallize until firm enough to handle, about 20 minutes.
5. Remove the frame from the slab.
6. Precoat one side of the slab with the tempered milk chocolate.
7. Allow the precoat to crystallize. Then cut the slab into squares, using the 22.5-mm strings on a guitar.
8. Pipe a small bulb of jam onto the center of each square.
9. Dip the squares in the thinned milk chocolate. Slide each piece forward on the paper immediately after dipping to avoid the formation of feet.
10. When the chocolate begins to set, place several crystals of the coarse sugar on top of each piece.

    NOTE: See Thinning Technique and Theory, page 64.

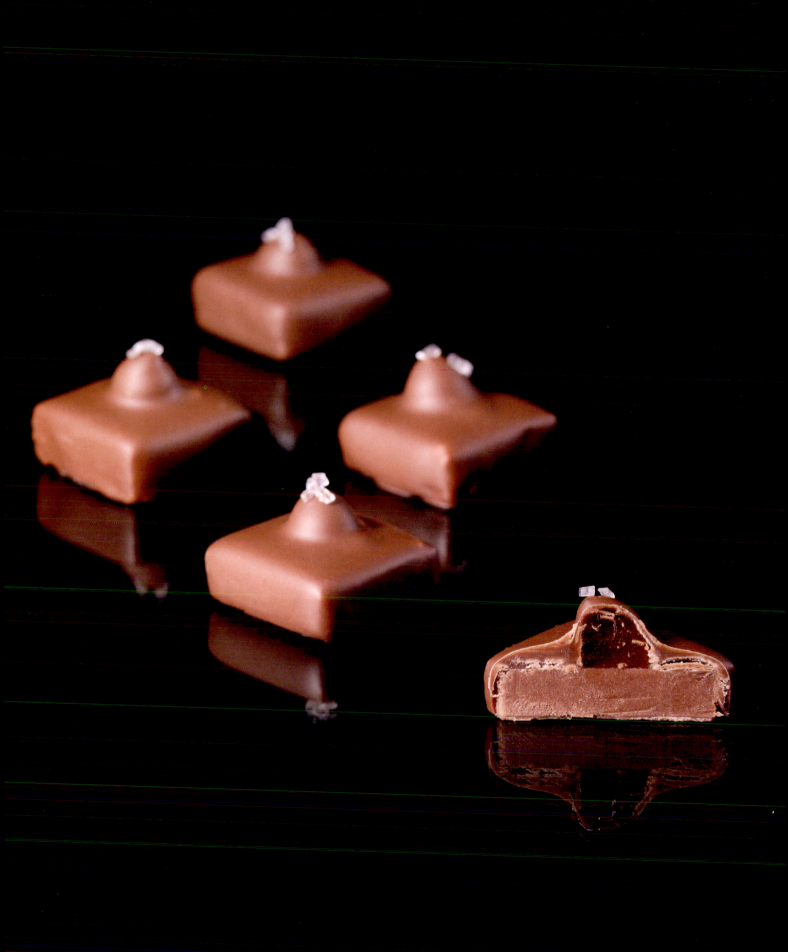

TRUFFLE HONEY SQUARES

yield: **150 PIECES**

Butter, very soft (30°C/86°F)	160 g	6 oz	22%
Truffle honey	80 g	3 oz	12%
Milk chocolate, melted, tempered, at 30°C/86°F	440 g	16 oz	62%
Cognac	20 g	1 oz	4%
BATCH SIZE	700 g	26 oz	100%
Dark chocolate, melted, tempered, for precoating and dipping	as needed		
Coarse sugar, for finishing	as needed		

1. By hand, mix together the butter and truffle honey until well combined.
2. Stream the tempered milk chocolate into the butter mixture while stirring, taking care not to allow chunks of chocolate to form.
3. Stream in the cognac, stirring until the mixture is homogeneous.
4. Spread the ganache into a frame 12 × 12 × ¼ in set on parchment paper. Allow to crystallize until firm enough to handle, about 20 minutes.
5. Remove the frame from the slab.
6. Precoat one side of the slab with the tempered dark chocolate.
7. Allow the precoat to crystallize. Then cut the slab into squares, using the 22.5-mm strings on a guitar.
8. Dip the squares in the tempered dark chocolate.
9. Invert the dipped squares onto textured plastic sheets. When the chocolate has set, remove the pieces from the plastic and display upright.

RASPBERRY BITES

yield: **150 PIECES**

Butter, very soft (30°C/86°F)	160 g	6 oz	23%
Raspberry jam	220 g	8 oz	31%
Milk chocolate, melted, tempered, at 30°C/86°F	160 g	6 oz	23%
Dark chocolate, melted, tempered, at 32°C/90°F	130 g	5 oz	18%
Framboise eau-de-vie	30 g	1 oz	5%
BATCH SIZE	700 g	26 oz	100%
Dark chocolate, melted, tempered, for precoating and dipping	as needed		
Dehydrated raspberry powder, for finishing	as needed		

1. By hand, mix together the butter and jam until well combined.
2. Stream the tempered milk and dark chocolates into the butter mixture while stirring, taking care not to allow chunks of chocolate to form.
3. Stream in the framboise, stirring until the mixture is homogenous.
4. Spread the ganache into a frame 12 × 12 × ¼ in set on parchment paper. Allow to crystallize until firm enough to handle, about 20 minutes.
5. Remove the frame from the slab.
6. Precoat one side of the slab with the tempered dark chocolate.
7. Allow the precoat to crystallize. Then cut the slab into squares, using the 22.5-mm strings on a guitar.
8. Dip the squares in the tempered dark chocolate.
9. When the chocolate begins to set, sift a light dusting of dehydrated raspberry powder over the top of each piece.

PASSION FRUIT HONEY BUTTER GANACHE

yield: **150 PIECES**

Butter, very soft (30°C/86°F)	100 g	3.5 oz	15%
Honey	80 g	3 oz	12%
Milk chocolate, melted, tempered, at 30°C/86°F	450 g	16 oz	64%
Passion fruit juice concentrate, reduced by half	60 g	2 oz	9%
BATCH SIZE	690 g	24.5 oz	100%
Dark chocolate, melted, tempered, for precoating and dipping	as needed		
Star transfer sheets, cut 3 × 3 cm/1 × 1 in, creased diagonally	150 squares	150 squares	

1. By hand, mix together the butter and honey until well combined.

2. Stream the tempered milk chocolate into the butter mixture while stirring, taking care not to allow chunks of chocolate to form.

3. Stream in the reduced passion fruit juice concentrate, stirring until the mixture is homogeneous.

4. Spread the ganache into a frame 12 × 12 × ¼ in set on parchment paper. Allow to crystallize until firm enough to handle, about 20 minutes.

5. Remove the frame from the slab.

6. Precoat one side of the slab with the tempered dark chocolate.

7. Allow the precoat to crystallize. Then cut the slab into squares, using the 22.5-mm strings on a guitar.

8. Dip the squares in the tempered dark chocolate.

9. Before the chocolate sets, place a creased transfer sheet diagonally from corner to corner on each piece, to leave both the image on the transfer sheet and to create an indentation in the surface of the chocolate.

10. For the best shine, allow the pieces to crystallize overnight before removing the transfer sheets. If that is not possible, refrigerate the chocolates for 5 minutes and then remove the transfer sheets.

STRAWBERRY BALSAMIC BUTTER GANACHE

yield: **150 PIECES**

Butter, very soft (30°C/86°F)	150 g	5 oz	21%
Strawberry jam	150 g	5 oz	21%
White chocolate, melted, tempered, at 30°C/86°F	360 g	13 oz	52%
Balsamic vinegar (see Note)	40 g	1.5 oz	6%
BATCH SIZE	700 g	24.5 oz	100%
Dark chocolate, melted, tempered, for dipping	as needed		
White chocolate, melted, tempered, for precoating and finishing	as needed		
Dehydrated strawberry powder, for finishing	as needed		

1. By hand, mix together the butter and jam until well combined.
2. Stream the tempered white chocolate into the butter mixture, taking care not to allow chunks of chocolate to form.
3. Stream in the balsamic vinegar, stirring until the mixture is homogeneous.
4. Spread the ganache into a frame 12 × 12 × ¼ in set on parchment paper. Allow to crystallize until firm enough to handle, about 20 minutes.
5. Remove the frame from the slab.
6. Precoat one side of the slab with the tempered white chocolate.
7. Allow the precoat to crystallize. Then cut the slab into squares, using the 22.5-mm strings on a guitar.
8. Dip the squares in the tempered dark chocolate.
9. After the chocolate sets, pipe a spot of tempered white chocolate on top of each piece. Dust lightly with dehydrated strawberry powder before the white chocolate sets.

   NOTE: It is imperative to use a very high-quality aged balsamic vinegar that exhibits sweet dried-fruit flavors.

ESSENCE OF AGAVE

yield: **150 PIECES**

Butter, very soft (30°C/86°F)	100 g	3.5 oz	14%
Agave syrup	80 g	3 oz	12%
Lime zest, finely grated	1 lime	1 lime	
Milk chocolate, melted, tempered, at 30°C/86°F	450 g	16 oz	65%
Tequila	40 g	1.5 oz	6%
Lime juice	20 g	1 oz	3%
BATCH SIZE	690 g	25 oz	100%
Dark chocolate, melted, tempered, for precoating and dipping	as needed		
Fleur de sel, for finishing	as needed		

1. By hand, mix together the butter, agave syrup, and lime zest until well combined.
2. Stream the melted tempered milk chocolate into the butter mixture while stirring, taking care not to allow chunks of chocolate to form.
3. Stream in the tequila and lime juice, stirring until the mixture is homogeneous.
4. Spread the ganache into a frame 12 x 12 x ¼ in set on parchment paper. Allow to crystallize until firm enough to handle, about 20 minutes.
5. Remove the frame from the slab.
6. Precoat one side of the slab with the tempered dark chocolate.
7. Allow the precoat to crystallize. Then cut the slab into squares, using the 22.5-mm strings on a guitar.
8. Dip the squares in the tempered dark chocolate.
9. Use a 3-prong fork to make a diagonal wave. As the chocolate thickens, place a few crystals of fleur de sel on top of each piece.

LEMON LOGS

yield: **125 PIECES**

Butter, soft (25°C/77°F)	130 g	5 oz	17%
Fondant (page 290)	100 g	4 oz	13%
Lemon zest, finely chopped and frozen	10 g	0.5 oz	1%
White chocolate, melted, tempered, at 30°C/86°F	510 g	18 oz	64%
Lemon juice	40 g	1.5 oz	5%
BATCH SIZE	790 g	29 oz	100%
Dark chocolate, melted, tempered, for precoating and dipping	as needed		
Lemon sugar, for finishing (see Note)	as needed		

1. Using a 5-qt planetary mixer, cream together the butter, fondant, and frozen lemon zest until well aerated.

2. By hand, stream the tempered white chocolate into the butter mixture, taking care not to allow chunks of chocolate to form.

3. Slowly stream in the lemon juice, stirring until the mixture is homogeneous.

4. Using a pastry bag fitted with a no. 6 round tip, pipe cylinders of the ganache the same diameter as the tip across the width of a piece of parchment paper. (If the ganache is too soft to pipe, allow it to sit for several minutes at room temperature, turning it occasionally until it firms to the proper piping consistency, or speed the process by tabling the ganache to expedite crystallization.)

5. Allow the piped ganache to crystallize until firm enough to handle, about 20 minutes.

6. Release the logs from the parchment paper and roll them over so that the bottoms face up. Using a small brush, precoat the bottoms of the logs with the tempered dark chocolate.

7. Allow the precoat to crystallize. Then cut the logs into 30-mm/1¼-in lengths using a guitar.

8. Dip the precoated logs in the tempered dark chocolate. When the chocolate begins to set, sprinkle a small amount of lemon sugar on each piece.

   NOTE: To make lemon sugar, mix 60 g/2 oz of coarse sanding sugar with the finely chopped zest of 1 lemon. For ease of handling, dry the flavored sugar on a sheet pan in a low oven prior to use.

SPIKED EGGNOGS

yield: **130 PIECES**

Dark chocolate discs (25-mm/1-in diameter), as bases	130 discs	130 discs	
EGGNOG GANACHE			
Butter, soft (25°C/77°F)	170 g	6 oz	23%
Glucose syrup	40 g	1.5 oz	5%
Nutmeg, ground	1 tsp	1 tsp	<1%
Vanilla bean, split and scraped	1 bean	1 bean	
White chocolate, melted, tempered, at 30°C/86°F	500 g	18 oz	67%
Dark rum	40 g	1.5 oz	5%
BATCH SIZE	750 g	27 oz	100%
Dark chocolate, melted, tempered, thinned, for dipping (see Note)	as needed		

TO MAKE THE DARK CHOCOLATE DISCS:

Prepare the discs using the tempered dark chocolate and either a cutter or a stencil. (See page 190.) Leave the discs attached to the parchment paper to facilitate piping.

TO MAKE THE EGGNOG GANACHE:

1. Using a 5-qt planetary mixer, cream together the butter, glucose syrup, nutmeg, and vanilla bean seeds until well aerated.

2. By hand, stream the tempered white chocolate into the butter mixture, taking care not to allow chunks of chocolate to form.

3. Stream in the dark rum, stirring until the mixture is homogeneous.

4. Using a pastry bag fitted with no. 4 French star tip, pipe pointed stars 3 cm/1 in high on top of the chocolate discs. (If the ganache is too soft to pipe, allow it to sit for several minutes at room temperature, turning it occasionally until it firms to the proper piping consistency, or speed the process by tabling the ganache to expedite crystallization.)

5. Allow the piped ganache to crystallize until firm enough to handle, about 20 minutes.

6. Release the pieces from the parchment paper and dip them in the thinned dark chocolate. The chocolate should be thinned enough so that the ridges created by the star tip show prominently through the chocolate coating. Slide each piece forward on the paper immediately after dipping to avoid the formation of feet.

NOTE: See Thinning Technique and Theory, page 64.

RAINIERS

yield: **120 PIECES**

Dark chocolate discs (25-mm/1-in diameter), as bases	120 discs	120 discs	
WHITE CHOCOLATE GANACHE			
Brandied cherry halves	120 halves	120 halves	
Butter, soft (25°C/77°F)	120 g	4 oz	15%
Cherry jam (see Note)	120 g	4 oz	15%
White chocolate, melted, tempered, at 30°C/86°F	510 g	18 oz	64%
Kirschwasser	50 g	2 oz	6%
BATCH SIZE	800 g	28 oz	100%
Dark chocolate, melted, tempered, for dipping	as needed		
White chocolate, melted, tempered, for finishing	as needed		

TO MAKE THE DARK CHOCOLATE DISCS:

Prepare the discs using the tempered dark chocolate and either a cutter or a stencil. (See page 190.) Leave the discs attached to the parchment paper to facilitate piping.

TO MAKE THE WHITE CHOCOLATE GANACHE:

1. Place a cherry half in the center of each disc. Be certain that a border of the chocolate disc is exposed all around the cherry.

2. Using a 5-qt planetary mixer, cream together the butter and jam until well aerated.

3. By hand, stream the tempered white chocolate into the butter mixture, taking care not to allow chunks of chocolate to form.

4. Stream in the kirschwasser, stirring the mixture until homogeneous.

5. Using a pastry bag fitted with a no. 5 round tip, pipe pointed cones of the ganache on each cherry half, taking care that the ganache makes contact with the chocolate disc around the perimeter of the fruit. (If the ganache is too soft to pipe, allow it to sit for several minutes at room temperature, turning it occasionally until it firms to the proper piping consistency, or speed the process by tabling the ganache to expedite crystallization.)

6. Allow the ganache to crystallize until firm enough to handle, about 20 minutes.

7. Release the pieces from the parchment paper and dip them in the tempered dark chocolate.

8. After the chocolate has set, use a paper cone to pipe a small snowcap of white chocolate on top of each piece.

NOTE: If the cherry jam is very moist, reduce it over low heat prior to use.

MACADAMIAS

yield: **90 PIECES**

Dark chocolate discs (25-mm/1-in diameter), as bases	90 discs	90 discs	
MILK CHOCOLATE GANACHE			
Butter, very soft (30°C/86°F)	120 g	4 oz	18%
Fondant (page 290)	30 g	1 oz	5%
Milk chocolate, melted, tempered, at 30°C/86°F	400 g	14 oz	64%
Dark rum	60 g	2 oz	8%
Orange juice concentrate	20 g	1 oz	5%
Macadamias, toasted	90 nuts	90 nuts	
BATCH SIZE	630 g	22 oz	100%
Dark chocolate, melted, tempered, thinned for dipping (see Note)	as needed	as needed	

TO MAKE THE DARK CHOCOLATE DISCS:

Prepare the discs using the tempered dark chocolate and either a cutter or a stencil. (See page 190.) Leave the discs attached to the parchment paper to facilitate piping.

TO MAKE THE MILK CHOCOLATE GANACHE:

1. Using a 5-qt planetary mixer, cream together the butter and fondant until well aerated.

2. By hand, stream the tempered milk chocolate into the butter mixture, taking care not to allow chunks of chocolate to form.

3. Stream in the dark rum and orange juice concentrate, stirring until the mixture is homogeneous.

4. Using a pastry bag fitted with a no. 6 round tip, pipe a bulb of the ganache on each chocolate disc. Be certain that the ganache reaches the edge of the disc. (If the ganache is too soft to pipe, allow it to sit for several minutes at room temperature, turning it occasionally until it firms to the proper piping consistency, or speed the process by tabling the ganache to facilitate crystallization.)

5. Before the ganache sets, place a toasted macadamia on top of each bulb of ganache.

6. Allow the ganache to crystallize until it is firm enough to handle, about 20 minutes.

7. Release the pieces from the parchment paper and dip them in the thinned dark chocolate. Slide each piece forward on the paper immediately after dipping to avoid the formation of feet.

NOTE: See Thinning Technique and Theory, page 64.

7

Noncrystalline confections include hard candy, toffee, brittle, soft caramels, and taffy. Each of these confections differs in the ingredients it contains and the amount of water in the finished product.

NONCRYSTALLINE CONFECTIONS

It is the interaction of those ingredients that makes each of these confections unique. Hard candies are purely a solution of sugars in a minute quantity of water. Brittles are virtually identical, but they contain nuts for flavor and browning. Toffee is a similar system, but it has the addition of dairy products to promote browning. And soft caramels most nearly resemble toffee but have a higher water content, resulting in a soft texture. All of these confections share not only common ingredients but common methodologies as well. In all cases, sugars—mainly sucrose—make up the bulk of the confection, and the sugars present are in an amorphous, glass, or noncrystalline state. Almost without exception, noncrystalline confections contain other sugars, such as glucose syrup, that prevent the recrystallization of the sucrose. Noncrystalline sugars are brittle and hard when the water content is low and elastic and chewy when the water content is higher. Amorphous sugar is sugar that is dissolved in liquid, and it is the opposite of the highly ordered crystalline form of sugar that constitutes the granulated sugar we commonly use.

To make noncrystalline candies, the sugar is first dissolved in liquid and then cooked to remove the desired amount of water. The temperature to which the solution is cooked, and therefore the amount of water remaining, plays a key role in determining the consistency of the finished product: the higher the temperature, the more water is removed, and the harder the resulting product will be.

INVERSION

Inversion is the name given to the hydrolysis of sucrose into fructose and dextrose. To put it simply, when it is exposed to acid, heat, and water, sucrose, a disaccharide, breaks into the two monosaccharides that make it up. This reaction is ongoing as long as the sugar and acid are in a fluid state; the longer the acid is exposed to the sugar, the more the sugar is inverted. This reaction may also occur from exposure to the enzyme invertase, as when making cordials. The word *inversion* refers to the direction that polarized light rotates passing through the sugars, and may be a descriptive term for chemists, but is virtually meaningless to con-

fectioners. The important points to remember about inversion are the qualities of invert sugar (the resulting mixture of fructose and dextrose) as compared with sucrose. Invert sugar is:

- Sweeter than sugar. Sugar is rated as 100 in sweetness; invert sugar is 130.

- More hygroscopic than sugar. Products high in invert sugar are stickier than those without it.

- Comprised of reducing sugars. Unlike sucrose, both fructose and dextrose contribute to Maillard browning, therefore invert sugar is more likely to brown during cooking. (See Maillard Reaction, page 231.)

- Used primarily to inhibit the recrystallization of sucrose.

Inversion

Sucrose (Disaccharide) — Acid, Water, Heat (in cooking) / Invertase (in centers) → Fructose + Dextrose (Monosaccharides)

SUGAR COOKING

Stages of sugar cooking

The stages of sugar cooking are named for the appearance the syrup has when a small sample of it is removed and dropped into cold water. Confectioners use their fingers for this test, dipping them first into ice water, grabbing a little boiling syrup, then returning the syrup quickly to the ice water. The cooled syrup is then examined to determine the stage to which it has been cooked. The higher the temperature the syrup has reached, the less water remains in the sugar, and the firmer the resulting sample of sugar is. The following table describes a few of the stages of sugar cooking commonly used. Some confectioners break the stages down further, but for greater accuracy it is better to simply use a thermometer.

STAGES OF SUGAR COOKING

STAGE	APPEARANCE	TEMPERATURE	APPROXIMATE SUGAR CONTENT	COMMON USES
THREAD	Cooled syrup forms a thread between fingers when separated	106° to 112°C/223° to 234°F	80%	Dragées
SOFT BALL	Cooled syrup forms a soft, malleable ball	113° to 115°C/235° to 239°F	85%	Fudge, pralines, patisserie fondant, caramels
MEDIUM BALL	Cooled syrup forms a ball that will flatten with resistance	118° to 121°C/245° to 250°F	87%	Confectionery fondant
FIRM BALL	Cooled syrup forms a ball that will not flatten between fingers	121° to 129°C/250° to 265°F	92%	Marshmallow, gummies, soft nougat
SOFT CRACK	Cooled syrup forms a flexible but firm sheet between fingers	132° to 143°C/270° to 289°F	95%	Firm nougat
HARD CRACK	Cooled syrup forms a brittle sheet between fingers; cooled syrup has a clean break when bitten	148° to 156°C/298° to 313°F	99%	Hard candy, hard nougat, brittle, toffee
CARAMEL	Sugar turns brown, is extremely brittle, has characteristic caramel flavor and aroma that increases with temperature	170°C/338°F and up	100%	Used to contribute flavor to ganache, fondant, fudge, and other products where caramel flavor is desired

SATURATION AND SUPERSATURATION

The presence of glucose impedes crystallization.

Saturation and supersaturation are vital concepts for the confectioner to understand, as they are directly linked to crystallization. Sugar readily dissolves in water, but water can dissolve only a finite quantity of sugar at a given temperature. Once that quantity is reached, any additional sugar added to the water will not dissolve but instead will simply settle out of the solution. At room temperature, approximately 67 percent sucrose is the upper limit of the amount of sugar that can be dissolved in water. The warmer the water is, the more sugar can be dissolved in it. When the water holds as much sugar as will dissolve at a given temperature, it is called a saturated solution, and it is not possible to dissolve more sugar into it without heating to a higher temperature.

Supersaturated solutions are created by dissolving sugar in water, boiling the solution to evaporate a portion of the water, and then cooling the concentrated syrup without agitation. Once cooled, the solution holds a greater percentage of sugar than could have been dissolved at that temperature without heating: it is now a supersaturated solution. All noncrystalline sugar confections are examples of supersaturated solutions. Even hard candy and brittles, which are glasslike, are solutions, although they contain very little water. Supersaturated solutions are unstable systems. Sugar molecules are attracted to one another, and with so many of them in such a small amount of liquid, they are quite likely to join together, leading to the formation of crystals. The higher the degree of supersatura-

tion, the more likely the solution is to crystallize. Crystallization may be initiated by a number of causes, including agitation, impurities in the sugar, and uneven cooling of the syrup. Regardless of how crystallization begins, once crystals begin to form, the crystals themselves become nuclei (seeds) for the formation of more crystals, and the reaction proceeds until it has finished. When supersaturated solutions crystallize, they separate into two components: sugar crystals, which precipitate out; and the remaining syrup, which is no longer supersaturated due to the precipitation of the excess sugar, but is now merely saturated. It is the nature of supersaturated solutions to crystallize, and if that is not the desired outcome, steps must be taken to prevent crystallization.

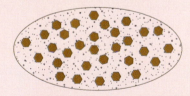

Supersaturated sugar solution

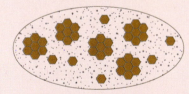

Formation of sugar crystals

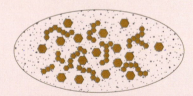

The presence of glucose impedes crystallization.

Preventing crystallization (wet method)

Much of the art of confectionery is based on the science of crystallization. In the case of hard candy, toffee, brittle, and caramels, the object is to prevent crystallization in order to create the organic "glass" that is the defining quality of these products. Table sugar (sucrose) is crystalline in nature, and, unless steps are taken to prevent it, sucrose reverts to a crystalline state. Understanding and controlling crystallization is the basis of the entire field of confectionery. Therefore, it is important for the professional to have a basic comprehension of the crystallization process and how to control it. Fortunately, no advanced degree in physics or chemistry is required in order to grasp the fundamentals of sugar crystallization. Once a professional understands the key concepts, he or she can manipulate the formulas and procedures to get precisely the desired results. The following sugar-cooking procedure illustrates the principles involved. Each of the steps is designed to help prevent crystallization.

technique | theory | STANDARD WET-SUGAR COOKING

Knowing the simple procedures of the standard wet-sugar cooking method—and having an understanding of the basic theory behind each of those procedures—is invaluable to the confectioner and will help him or her succeed consistently in sugar confectionery. Two simple goals are at the heart of sugar cooking: the sugar must first be dissolved, and then the desired amount of water must be removed. Each of the following steps helps to prevent recrystallization of the sugar.

1. **IN A POT OR CANDY KETTLE, COMBINE SUGAR WITH 20 PERCENT OR MORE WATER TO MAKE THE SUGAR THE TEXTURE OF WET SAND.** The water in this procedure is the solvent: it is the substance into which the sugar dissolves. Without the water, the sugar could not go from a crystalline state to an amorphous, or noncrystalline, state. The precise amount of water used is not critical, provided it is sufficient to dissolve the sugar fully. Twenty percent is a satisfactory amount. At the boiling point, sugar solutions can dissolve approxim-ately 80 percent sugar. So, when the 20 percent solution is heated to boiling, it is certain that all of the sugar will dissolve. Using more water will not generally be harmful to the finished product, but, since the goal of sugar cooking is to remove the desired amount of water, the cooking time will be increased by using a greater percentage of water. (See Sugar Cooking, page 217.)

2. **PLACE THE POT ON THE HIGHEST POSSIBLE HEAT WITHOUT THE FLAME COMING UP THE SIDES.** Sugar should always be cooked on the highest possible heat. There are two primary reasons for this: to minimize unwanted browning and to prevent crystallization. Sugar cooked to a high temperature, as when making hard candy, browns more when it is cooked slowly than when it is cooked quickly. The browning not only affects the candy's color but also brings with it caramel flavor notes that are often not welcome. The more quickly the sugar reaches the terminal temperature,

the less browning occurs. Cooking a sugar solution rapidly helps to prevent crystallization by putting more energy into the system, making the sugar solution less likely to revert to a crystalline state. These two factors are the reasons why, in confectionery shops, syrups are cooked in copper kettles on powerful candy stoves. The copper conducts heat extremely well, and the rounded bottom of the kettle provides a large surface area for heating, resulting in a fast cook. The stoves in confectionery shops are fitted to accept the kettles for the most efficient transfer of heat into the syrup.

3. **STIR CONSTANTLY WITH A WOODEN SPOON UNTIL THE SOLUTION COMES TO A BOIL.** Stirring a syrup as it comes to a boil helps to ensure that the sugar crystals circulate throughout the syrup, dissolving quickly and completely. Any undissolved sugar crystals remaining in the solution act as seeds, or nuclei, forming more sugar crystals, which themselves then initiate further crystallization. Confectioners traditionally use wooden paddles or spoons for stirring, as metal conducts heat away from the solution, resulting in cool spots in the syrup that are more prone to crystallization.

4. **WHEN THE SOLUTION REACHES A BOIL, STOP STIRRING.** Stirring—as beneficial as it is to the syrup during heating—becomes detrimental once the solution begins to boil. Stirring, or any other agitation, of a supersaturated solution can initiate crystallization by causing the

sugar molecules to collide and bond together to form crystals. (See sugar crystallization diagrams, page 218.) The exception to this rule applies when the solution contains a dairy product or another type of ingredient that will burn if not stirred during cooking. In formulas containing such ingredients, allowances are made for this excess agitation in the form of extra doctoring agents.

5. **REMOVE IMPURITIES FROM THE TOP OF THE SOLUTION.** When syrup first reaches a boil, gray foam often coalesces on the surface of the sugar. This foam can be caused by traces of mineral salts left in the sugar from the refining process or by any other impurities that may be present in the syrup. These impurities should be removed in order to improve the appearance of the finished product and to prevent the impurities from becoming seeds on which sugar crystals can form. The quantity of impurities in the sugar depends on the refining and storage of that sugar and may range from being virtually nonexistent to covering the entire top of the syrup.

6. **ADD A DOCTORING AGENT TO THE SOLUTION.** In confectionery, doctoring agents—also called "doctors"—are ingredients added to help prevent or control the crystallization of sugar. Three categories of doctoring agents are typically used in candy making: glucose syrups, acids, and invert sugar. While all of them help to control crystallization, each has its own characteristic effects on the final product.

   • **GLUCOSE SYRUPS.** Glucose syrup is ubiquitous as a doctoring agent throughout confectionery. Glucose syrups with different dextrose equivalents (DEs) affect the finished product slightly differently with regard to texture, flavor release, and hygroscopicity. When using glucose syrup as a doctoring agent, add it after the solution reaches a boil, as it is easier for the sugar to fully dissolve in the water without the presence of the syrup. Low-DE syrups contribute to a chewy texture and less sweetness. Higher-DE syrups result in a shorter texture and greater levels of sweetness. (See Characteristics of Glucose Syrups, page 4.)

   • **ORGANIC ACIDS.** Tartaric acid, cream of tartar, lemon juice, and vinegar are also commonly used as doctoring agents in sugar cooking. These ingredients work by inverting a portion of the sugar in the syrup. (See Inversion, page 216.) In addition to preventing crystallization, inversion makes the finished product softer, sweeter, shorter textured, more hygroscopic, and more prone to browning. Inversion is an ongoing process; as long as the sugar and acid are together in a fluid state, inversion will continue, resulting in a softer, stickier, and potentially browner finished product. In most cases these are qualities to be avoided. This is the reason some candy formulas specify the temperature at which to add the acid used as a doctoring agent.

   • **INVERT SUGAR.** Invert sugar may be added to syrups directly. By adding invert sugar directly, rather than relying on acids to invert a portion of the sugar, the confectioner can get more consistent results that are not affected by variables such as the output of the stove, the strength of acids, or the hardness and pH of water. Regardless of whether invert sugar is a discrete ingredient or is created by inversion during cooking, it has the same tendency to increase sweetness, provide rapid flavor release, increase hygroscopicity, and contribute to potential Maillard browning. (See Maillard Reaction, page 231.)

7. **USING A MOISTENED PASTRY BRUSH, WASH DOWN THE SIDES OF THE SUGAR POT TO REMOVE ANY SUGAR RESIDUE.** Repeat this step as often as necessary to keep the sides of the pot clean, but do not clean more often than necessary. Brushing the sides of the sugar pot with a wet brush removes the sugar crystals that are likely to form there and returns them to the solution. If such crystals are allowed to remain undissolved on the sides of the pot, they are likely to make their way back into the mixture after cooking, seeding it and initiating crystallization. Unless these crystals become part of the solution, they quickly become part of the problem! Remember that the goal when cooking sugar is to remove water from the syrup. Therefore it is counterproductive to wash the sides of the pot excessively, as this simply introduces more water that must again be removed. Clean the side of the pot only when there is sugar present on it.

8. **INSERT A THERMOMETER INTO THE SOLUTION AND COOK TO THE DESIRED TEMPERATURE.** Alternatively, use a refractometer or a finger test to measure the concentration of sugar in the solution. Various methods exist for determining the percentage of water and sugar present in a cooking solution. The most common method is to use a thermometer and to cook the syrup to a predetermined temperature. At standard atmospheric conditions, sugar cooked to a given temperature will always contain the same percentage of dissolved solids. The following graph indicates the relationship between the temperature to which the sugar is cooked and the resulting dissolved-solids content.

The thermometer is the most accessible, reliable method for determining the sugar density of a cooking mixture. Another highly accurate method is the use of a refractometer. Available in a variety of ranges, a refractometer quickly and accurately measures the density of a syrup without the fluctuations due to atmospheric pressure, altitude, and relative humidity that are inherent with a thermometer. Another time-honored method is to test the mixture using a bowl of ice water and one's fingers. (See Stages of Sugar Cooking, page 217.) The finger test, while adequate for some purposes, and having enjoyed many years of use by confectioners, is subjective and dependent on the experience and skill of the confectioner. More consistent, accurate results are obtained by using either a thermometer or refractometer.

theory

BOILING POINT OF COOKING SYRUP

It is a common occurrence that the temperature of the boiling syrup remain at or below approximately 106°C/223°F for quite some time before it begins to steadily rise. Why does the temperature of cooking syrup climb so slowly at first and then much more rapidly? When the syrup reaches 106°C/223°F, the solution becomes saturated, and the temperature rises more rapidly, actually accelerating as it cooks. If 1 kilogram/2.2 pounds of sugar were combined with 200 grams/7 ounces of water and cooked, it would quickly reach 106°C/223°F (saturation) and would continue cooking relatively quickly beyond that temperature. If the same kilogram of sugar were combined with a kilogram of water, the syrup would take much longer to become saturated. Once it reached 106°C/223°F, however, that sugar would cook just as quickly as the batch that began with less water. All the extra cooking time for the batch of sugar with the kilogram of water would have been spent removing water to reach the point of saturation. Once saturation is reached, the syrups would cook at the same rate. This is the reason the confectioner uses a minimum of water to dissolve sugar for cooking, so as not to waste time waiting for a syrup to reach saturation and for the temperature to rise.

The higher the sugar content of a syrup, the higher its boiling temperature is. Pure water boils at 100°C/212°F; an 80-percent sugar solution boils at 110°C/230°F. When the solution reaches 98 percent sugar, the boiling point is raised to 155°C/311°F. Early in cooking, a large amount of water is present in the syrup; much of this water must be removed in order to noticeably increase the percentage of sugar and therefore raise the boiling point. It takes time to remove this water. Later in cooking, a smaller amount of water remains in the syrup; as a result, removing less water brings about a larger corresponding increase in the percentage of sugar and in the boiling point. Therefore, the boiling point rises quickly. The less water that remains in the syrup, the more quickly the sugar percentage increases, and the faster the temperature rises.

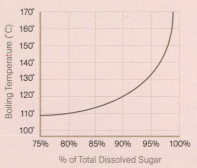

Boiling Point of Cooking Syrup

The important difference between the standard wet-sugar cooking technique and the dry technique is that the dry technique is used only for making caramel, while the wet technique can be used to make a variety of syrups, from thread stage to hard crack or caramel. The key reason for this difference is the use of water as a solvent. When cooking sugar by the wet method, the sugar is dissolved in water, then a portion of the water is removed. In the dry method, the sugar is not dissolved, but rather is melted. Because no water is added, the only possible outcome of the dry method is melted, caramelized sugar.

1. **PRIOR TO CARAMELIZING, WORK A SMALL AMOUNT OF LEMON JUICE OR OTHER DOCTORING AGENT INTO THE SUGAR.** As always when cooking sugar, the addition of acid inverts some of the sugar, preventing crystallization and softening the finished product. In the dry method the acid also helps to prevent the formation of agglomerates of sugar as the sugar melts. Again, many formulas provide specific information as to the amount and type of acid to use. Excessive acid softens the finished product. As a rule, only a few drops per pound of sugar are required to help prevent crystallization and to prevent lumps from forming.

2. **PLACE THE SUGAR IN A HEAVY-BOTTOMED SUGAR POT OR SAUCEPAN.** Place the pot on high heat, stirring the sugar constantly with a wooden spoon to ensure that the sugar heats evenly. The sugar may either be placed in the pot all at once or added in stages, with the confectioner allowing each addition of sugar to melt fully before adding the next. Each of these methods has its merits. When the amount of sugar being caramelized is small, it is easiest to put all of the sugar in the pot, place the pot on direct heat, and caramelize the sugar. If the amount of sugar is larger, it is more efficient to add the sugar in stages, which eliminates the need to stir the entire quantity of sugar as it heats. Both variations on the method proceed more quickly if the pot is preheated. Regardless of which technique is employed, constant stirring is required in order to heat and melt the sugar evenly without forming lumps. This amount of stirring is contraindicated for the wet method, in which stirring initiates crystallization of the dissolved sugar. There the sugar is dissolved in water, and the desired result is to maintain the sugar's amorphous form while removing water. In the dry method, however, the sugar is already in crystalline form, and the desired outcome is to melt the crystals. When making caramel by either method, a wooden spoon is the preferred implement for stirring because it conducts little heat.

3. **CONTINUE STIRRING THE SUGAR OVER HIGH HEAT UNTIL IT IS COMPLETELY MELTED AND CARAMELIZED TO THE DESIRED DEGREE.** The dry method is used exclusively to caramelize sugar. It is not possible with the dry method to reach intermediate stages of sugar cookery such as thread, soft ball, and so on because there is no water present. The degree of caramelization desired depends on the product being made; deeper caramel color and flavor are more desirable for some products than for others. The darker the color of the caramel, the more bitter the caramel flavor carried into the finished product will be. This may or may not be desirable, depending on the intended use of the caramel and the flavor sought.

HARD CANDY

Hard candy is one of the oldest types of confections, consisting of little more than sugar boiled with water until virtually all of the water is removed, leaving a glassy, supersaturated, noncrystalline solution.

technique	theory	BASIC HARD CANDY

The confectioner's objective when cooking hard candy is to heat the syrup as quickly as possible to the highest possible temperature, removing nearly all of the water without allowing the syrup to brown. After it is cooked to the desired temperature, the syrup may be poured onto a lightly oiled marble slab in order to cool quickly. It is repeatedly folded so that it cools evenly to a malleable, plastic state, after which it can be pulled to aerate it and to make it opaque. Pulled sugar can be used to make ribbon candy, lollipops, canes or sticks, or individual candies.

1. **COMBINE THE SUGAR, WATER, AND GLUCOSE SYRUP AND COOK TO THE DESIRED TEMPERATURE.** See Standard Wet-Sugar Cooking Technique and Theory, page 219.

2. **POUR THE HOT SYRUP ONTO AN OILED STONE TABLE TO COOL.** Fold the sugar to ensure even cooling. A thick stone surface, like marble, or another type of cooling table quickly draws heat from the sugar. The hot sugar must be turned at regular intervals to prevent any of it from reaching a glassy state, which would render it unusable and could promote crystallization of the entire batch.

3. **AS THE SUGAR COOLS, CUT THE BATCH INTO AS MANY PIECES AS REQUIRED FOR COLORING.** A single batch can be colored with several colors, increasing the efficiency of the operation. This permits making multicolored stripes on candy canes and other hard candies without requiring the confectioner to cook multiple batches.

4. **ADD THE REQUIRED COLORS, ACID (IF USING), AND FLAVORINGS TO THE COOLING BATCH.** Most flavorings used for hard candy are not heat stable. Flavorings must be added as the sugar cools to prevent the flashing off of volatile compounds, which would result in loss of flavor. Acid is added as the sugar cools rather than during cooking to prevent excessive inversion, which would make the sugar soft and overly hygroscopic.

5. **COOL EACH PORTION EVENLY TO A PLASTIC CONSISTENCY WHILE FOLDING IT TO MIX IN COLORS AND FLAVORINGS.** The acid, flavoring, and color must be incorporated evenly into the sugar. If the batch is to be pulled, these ingredients are mixed in during that process. If the batch is to be left unpulled, it is vital to distribute these ingredients evenly by folding them in during the cooling process.

6. **PULL THE PIECES TO AERATE AS DESIRED FOR THE PRODUCT BEING MADE.** Pulling aerates the sugar, makes it more opaque and lighter in color, increases its volume, and gives it a more delicate bite. Lighter colors should be pulled fully, while darker colors should be pulled minimally—or not at all—in order to maintain the color contrast they provide.

7. **PLACE THE PIECES UNDER A WARMER TO MAINTAIN MALLEABILITY.** Some type of warming apparatus is required for hard-candy work. This may range from a simple heat lamp, to food warmers, to special blocking tables with rows of gas burners at the back. In all cases, the idea is to maintain the sugar in a plastic, malleable state.

8. **ASSEMBLE AS DESIRED.** The prepared portions of the batch may now be assembled as desired. The most common method for assembling a batch of hard candy is to form the majority of the sugar into a cylinder (which has been pulled) and to jacket that cylinder with stripes of the remaining sugar in contrasting colors. This is the technique used to create the stripes commonly seen on candy canes.

9. **PULL A ROPE OF A DESIRED DIAMETER FROM THE BATCH. CUT AND SHAPE AS DESIRED.** Once jacketed, the log of sugar may be pulled out into a long rope and cut into the desired portions for shaping into canes, lollipops, and so on.

TOP, LEFT: *Once it has been poured onto marble to facilitate even cooling, hard candy can be flavored or colored as desired (see step 2 of the technique).* RIGHT: *Once the sugar has cooled to a plastic state, it is pulled to incorporate air, which slightly softens its texture (see step 6 of the technique).*

BOTTOM, LEFT: *Decorative effects, such as striping, can be added to hard candy by jacketing one sheet of pulled sugar around another, then twisting and pulling the sugar to create the desired effect (see step 8 of the technique).* RIGHT: *While the hard candy is still in a plastic state, the confectioner uses scissors to give it the desired shape and size (see step 9 of the technique).*

Coloring hard candy

Color may be added to the candy during cooking. This has the advantage of distributing the color evenly and removing any moisture from it. The disadvantage of adding color during the cooking phase is that the entire batch will be a single color. It is more common to color a single batch of syrup with multiple colors. This can be done by pouring several separate pools of the cooked syrup onto the marble and coloring each pool independently. The colorings used for hard-candy production should not contain acid, which is sometimes used as a preservative. Acid will invert some of the sugar in the solution, resulting in softer, more hygroscopic candy and a reduced shelf life. If the coloring to be used does contain acid, the confectioner can minimize the amount of inversion created by adding the coloring agent after the sugar has been poured onto the cooling table or as close to the end of the cooking phase as possible.

Flavoring hard candy

The flavoring used to make hard candy must be extremely concentrated in order for it to flavor the candy without adding too much moisture. For this reason, fruit purées and juices cannot be used. Extracts, oils, and manufactured flavors can all be used successfully in hard-candy production. Because they are usually not heat stable and will dissipate or be significantly altered if they are exposed to the high temperatures of cooking, these flavorings are added after the cooking process is complete, once the mass of syrup has begun to cool. Manufacturers of flavorings stipulate the recommended amount to be used, usually stated as a percentage of the finished batch. Due to their potency, flavorings must be measured and handled with care to ensure consistent results. When a fruit flavoring is used in candies, it is usually accompanied by the addition of a dry acid to provide some of the tart flavor notes found in fruit. The acids most commonly used are citric, malic, and tartaric acids. These should be added only after the sugar has begun to cool on the marble so as not to cause excessive inversion, which would result in undue stickiness and hygroscopicity.

After the mass of sugar is cooked, colored, flavored, and cooled to a plastic state, the confectioner pulls it to aerate it, keeps it warm and jackets or stripes it if desired, then cuts and packages it. Regardless of how the candy is formed, it must always be protected from humidity, as amorphous sugar is hygroscopic. If the candy is exposed to humidity, it will absorb moisture, which will migrate through the confection, leaving it crystallized throughout. Immediately after production, hard candy must always be wrapped or otherwise protected from exposure to humid air.

The moisture content of hard candy must be only 1 to 2 percent in order for the candy to reach the proper hardness and maintain a viable shelf life. Sucrose alone is not well suited to hard-candy production, due to its tendency to recrystallize at high concentrations; to suppress that crystallization, it is necessary to add doctoring agents. In the past, hard candy was frequently made using cream of tartar as a doctoring agent. While this is still possible, the results with cream of tartar are inconsistent due to disparities in the speed of cooking, the hardness of water, and the potency of the acid, all of which result in differing amounts of inversion from batch to batch. In addition to these inconsistencies, hard candy made using acid as the only doctoring agent is extremely hygroscopic, which creates handling and storage difficulties and a shortened shelf life. Today, in order to help prevent crystallization and facilitate handling, glucose syrup is added to the formula. In commercial applications, there is as much as 50 percent glucose syrup in hard candy. In those automated operations, the higher percentage of glucose syrup is required to prevent the sugar from crystallizing as the result of the sheer force applied by the mass-production machinery. For smaller-scale handwork applications, a ratio of 70 percent sucrose to 30 percent glucose syrup is commonly used;

the smaller quantity of glucose syrup results in better flavor release. In open-kettle cookery, hard candy is usually cooked to between 150° and 160°C/300° and 320°F, which results in the requisite low moisture content that provides hardness and shelf life.

technique | theory | MOLDED HARD CANDY

Another technique for handling hard candy is that of molding. Hard candy may be molded in the simplest possible method—by merely pouring it out onto a flat, oiled surface to create a thin round disc—or it may be poured into any shape mold that can tolerate the heat of the sugar. Metal has historically been the material of choice and remains a viable option. Silicone molds are becoming commonplace for sugarwork as well, and although the material is costly, silicone offers the advantage of flexibility, which allows the confectioner to mold more elaborate shapes. In addition, while sugar can adhere to metal molds if they are not handled well, there is no danger of sugar sticking to silicone.

1. **PREPARE THE MOLDS.** Metal molds that are to be used for sugar must first be oiled. Food-grade mineral oil is the lubricant of choice, as repeated use of vegetable oils causes a sticky residue to build up on the molds, rendering them ineffective for use. A very thin film of mineral oil applied repeatedly conditions metal molds, ensuring that the sugar releases cleanly each time the mold is used.

2. **COOK THE SUGAR.** Hard candy to be molded is cooked to the same temperature, and using the same technique, as any other hard candy. The same formula can also be used. Or, if desired, the percentage of glucose syrup may be reduced because the sugar will not undergo the agitation of pulling. When making one color of molded sugar, it is beneficial to add the color during cooking so that it is dispersed evenly and fully, otherwise colors may be gently stirred into the sugar after cooking. A sugar pot specifically designed for this task—one made with a spout to facilitate accurate pouring—is beneficial.

3. **COOL THE SUGAR.** Cooked sugar to be molded should be cooled somewhat before it is poured into molds. This step prevents the formation of bubbles in the finished pieces. As soon as the cooked sugar is removed from the heat, the sugar pot should be immersed briefly in cold water to immediately stop carryover cooking that will otherwise caramelize and darken the sugar. After the cooked sugar is shocked by cold water, the pot should be left undisturbed to cool for several minutes, the exact time varying with the size of the batch. The objective is to allow the sugar to cool until all bubbles have subsided and it achieves a honeylike consistency, which will facilitate the pouring into the molds.

4. **FLAVOR THE SUGAR.** The flavorings for molded hard candy should be added only after the sugar has cooled somewhat to prevent volatile flavor components from flashing off due to heat. When fruit flavorings are used, the addition of a small amount of acid, such as citric acid, provides a more interesting and realistic flavor in the finished product. When an acid is used, it too should be added after cooking to prevent excessive inversion of the sugar and subsequent softening of the finished product. Flavorings and acid should be stirred gently into the batch to prevent the incorporation of air bubbles.

5. **POUR THE SUGAR INTO THE MOLDS.** When the viscosity of the cooked sugar is correct for pouring, it can easily be poured from the spout of the sugar pot in a thin stream into the molds. A butter knife or spoon can be used to accurately cut off the stream of sugar when the mold is full and to prevent drips. If lollipops are being made, sticks should be inserted into the sugar after it has been poured.

6. **ALLOW THE MOLDED SUGAR TO COOL.** Molded sugar must be cooled nearly to room temperature before it is unmolded. It is best to allow the sugar to cool at room temperature rather than under refrigeration. Candy molded in metal always cools faster than that molded in silicone, as metal conducts heat much more efficiently. When elaborate shapes are being molded, removing the sugar while it is still slightly warm (approximately 50°C/120°F) allows the safe release of the candy. If such shapes cool completely, the candy can become too friable to remove from the mold without breaking.

7. **UNMOLD THE FINISHED PIECES.** Metal sugar molds are often made in two pieces. When the sugar within has cooled sufficiently to release from the mold, a light tapping with a metal object will free the sugar and facilitate release. The halves of the mold may then be split, releasing the sugar within. Silicone molds are usually of one piece, and the sugar is removed simply by flexing the mold and pulling the hardened candy from the opening.

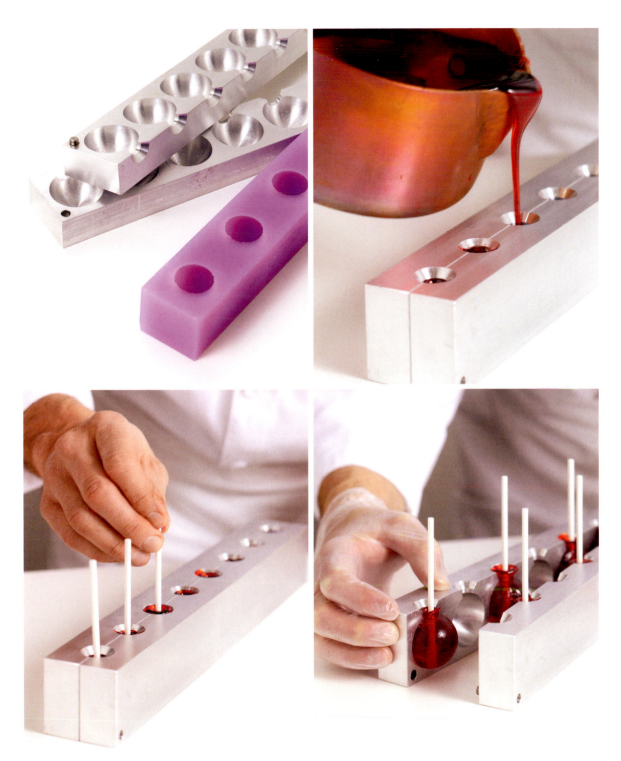

TOP, LEFT: *Hard candy molds.* RIGHT: *Cooked sugar should be the consistency of honey when poured into molds.*

BOTTOM, LEFT: *Sticks are placed into the sugar as it begins to set to make lollipops.* RIGHT: *When the sugar has cooled, the candies are removed by splitting the two-piece mold.*

FILLED HARD CANDY

Types of fillings

Hard candy may be filled with centers that remain soft after the candy has hardened. This provides a contrast between texture and flavor. Such fillings are either fat based or water based. When water-based fillings are used, the water content of the filling is of paramount importance, as an excess of water will attack the hard candy from the inside out, causing crystallization. For all water-based fillings, the total water content must not exceed 15 to 18 percent. These fillings typically consist of low-moisture jams, glucose syrup, or invert sugar; they may also contain fats.

Fat-based fillings are not usually problematic in terms of water content and are therefore more commonly used, as they typically contain very little moisture. These fillings may be made from chocolate or various nut pastes or nuts, such as peanut butter, almonds, and hazelnuts. In lower-quality confections, as a cost-saving measure, these fillings may be based on fats other than those found in the nut. Such fillings are not addressed in this book. Whether water-based fillings or those made from fat systems are used, it is imperative that the consistency and temperature of the filling be nearly identical to those of the warm hard candy when the two are combined.

Incorporating fillings

Fillings may be incorporated into handmade hard candy by several methods. The filling may simply be wrapped in a blanket of the hard-candy mixture while it is in a plastic state, to make a single filled log. The log may then be jacketed and stretched into a rope of the desired

LEFT: *A peanut butter filling is blanketed in sugar to create a filled hard candy.* CENTER: *Stretching the sugar for filled hard candy aerates and tenderizes the finished product.* RIGHT: *Finished Peanut Butter Honeycombs (page 252) are tubes of peanut butter filling covered with delightfully crunchy hard candy.*

diameter, leaving a single tube of filling within the candy exterior. The rope may then be cut into sticks or pillows. Alternatively, the filling may be wrapped, as in the first method, and then the log repeatedly pulled and folded in half a number of times. In this way, a honeycomb of filling is created within the candy, resulting in a more delicate texture.

Yet another method for incorporating the filling is similar to that for filling puff pastry. The candy mass is laid out in a rectangle while in a plastic state. The filling is then placed in a layer over half of the candy, and the candy is folded over to envelop the filling. With the filling inside, the candy is repeatedly rolled into a rectangle using a rolling pin and then folded over itself— while kept in a plastic state by intermittent heating. After several folds, distinct layers of hard candy alternating with layers of filling are created. The result is a delicate layered confection. After the final fold, the candy may be cut while still warm. It must then be enrobed in chocolate for protection from humidity. While this method is practical for the hand-working confectioner, it has its disadvantages. When a nut filling is used, the oil from the nuts can be exposed to the chocolate used for enrobing, with which it is not compatible. The nut oil then migrates through the chocolate, softening it and causing bloom over time. (See Fat Migration, page 410.) Milk chocolate is slightly more resistant than dark chocolate to fat migration and is most often used for this type of confection.

| technique | theory | **LAMINATED CANDY** |

Laminated hard candy is a specific and somewhat labor-intensive type of filled candy. While it is traditionally made with caramel and ground nut fillings, the use of flavored hard candy with chocolate filling opens up a world of flavor and color potential. Although making these products well requires some practice, the result is well worth the effort; the uniquely flaky texture is unforgettable.

1. **MAKE THE FILLING AND KEEP IT WARM.** Fillings for laminated hard candy must be extremely low in moisture. In most cases, the filling is made by increasing the viscosity of a fat system, by using a nut paste or chocolate, or by adding confectioners' sugar, glucose syrup, or both. The filling must have a stiff, doughlike consistency when it is hot or it will not laminate properly with the candy. The filling must remain hot so that it does not cool and harden the candy during lamination.

2. **COOK THE HARD CANDY.** It is traditional to use caramelized sugar to make laminated confections like Leaf Croquant (page 244). However, cooked hard candy also works well for this application and has the added advantage of allowing myriad flavors and colors to be used. When hard candy for laminating is formulated, a higher percentage of glucose syrup than usual is added to prevent crystallization through the agitation the candy receives during the repeated rolling and folding.

3. **COOL AND PULL THE CANDY.** With laminated confections like Leaf Croquant, the caramel is not pulled but is simply poured into a rectangle and allowed to firm slightly before applying the filling. Hard candy, if it is used, is lightly pulled to help to accentuate the color

and to facilitate more even rolling during lamination. In either case, the sugar should be at a firm but plastic consistency when the filling is folded into it. The filling and the sugar should both be hot and of a similarly malleable consistency.

4. **LOCK IN THE FILLING.** Stretch the sugar into a rectangle approximately 6 mm/¼ in thick. Place the hot filling over half the sugar, leaving a 25-mm/1-in border at the three edges. Fold the sugar over, and seal the three remaining edges around the filling. Sealing the sugar helps to keep the filling enclosed in the candy. If the sugar becomes too firm, place the entire piece in a warm oven until the sugar has softened but not liquefied.

5. **ROLL AND FOLD THE LAMINATED CANDY REPEATEDLY, APPLYING A TOTAL OF SIX 3-FOLDS.** Just as a laminated dough like puff pastry contains many layers of butter and dough, laminated hard candy and its filling are formed into many alternating layers using 3-folds. The temperature of the candy, and therefore the viscosity of the sugar during the folding process, is crucial. Sugar that is too hard will squeeze the filling out the ends during rolling, while sugar that is too soft will tear. The

candy must be rewarmed repeatedly during the process, and this is best accomplished while the candy is rolled out and thin, so that it warms quickly and evenly.

6. **CUT THE CANDY WHILE IT IS WARM.** Temperature remains crucial during cutting. If the candy is cut while it is too hot, it will exhibit rounded edges rather than square straight corners. If the candy is too cold when it is cut, the pieces will break apart along the layers of lamination. A sharp knife and the correct temperature ensure clean, even cuts.

TOP, LEFT: *Prepared chocolate filling is locked into the sugar (see step 4 of the technique).* RIGHT: *The candy is rolled out and folded several times to create layers (see step 5 of the technique).*

BOTTOM, LEFT: *Laminated hard candies must be cut while slightly warm (see step 6 of the technique).* RIGHT: *Many thin layers create a delicate, flaky texture.*

MAILLARD REACTION

The term *Maillard reaction* is used to describe not a single event but a wide range of complex nonenzymatic browning reactions. Maillard browning plays a key role in flavor development in many types of foods, including confections. While the entire series of Maillard reactions are many and complex, the basic fundamentals are easy enough to understand.

When exposed to heat, the amino acids found in proteins combine with various sugars to create compounds with brown colors and with flavors that may be described as "roasted" or as tasting like caramel. The Maillard reaction is responsible for the flavors in many familiar and favorite foods: chocolate flavor is created during cacao roasting via the Maillard reaction. Coffee flavor is likewise a result of Maillard browning. Amber and brown beer or ales owe their color and much of their flavor to the Maillard reaction. A well-browned crust of bread and the seared outside of a piece of roasted meat are also examples of Maillard browning. Clearly no single flavor is developed by these reactions; rather individual flavors that occur vary depending on the amino acids and the reducing sugars present, on the temperature at which the reaction occurs, and on many other factors, including pH and time.

It is not necessary for a confectioner to understand all the complexities of these reactions, but a basic knowledge of the components involved and of the conditions conducive to Maillard browning help a candy maker control the process and thus obtain the amount of browning desired. In general, the more protein—often from dairy products—a mixture contains, the more browning occurs. Higher temperatures likewise result in more browning. Just as important as temperature is the time that the mixture is held at a given temperature. Longer times spent cooking lead to more browning than would have developed during very rapid cooking at the same temperature. This is a major reason why hard candy and other products in which browning is not desired should be cooked as rapidly as possible, while soft caramels and brittles should be cooked more slowly.

Reducing sugars are required for Maillard browning. The term *reducing sugar* refers to a complex test that is performed in chemistry and is beyond the scope of the confectioner. What is helpful to know is that these sugars include lactose, found in dairy products; dextrose and fructose, found in invert sugar; and some of the sugars found in glucose syrup. All of these sugars play roles in Maillard reactions. Sucrose is not a reducing sugar and will not itself contribute to Maillard browning unless it is broken down into its component monosaccharides. (See Inversion, page 216.)

Maillard Reaction

Amino Acids + Reducing —Heat→ Various Brown-Colored,
(From Proteins)   Sugars   Caramel-Flavored Compounds

BRITTLES

Peanut brittle is an example of a traditional American candy whose popularity seems never to wane. Brittles are similar to hard candy in that they consist of sugar and glucose syrup boiled to a high temperature to remove most of the water. Brittles also contain nuts or seeds, which contain protein and, therefore, contribute to Maillard browning during the cooking process. This reaction is responsible for the characteristic color and flavor of brittles. Brittles may also contain butter for flavor and richness and baking soda to aerate the product. When baking soda is added to a brittle, it is done after cooking. The baking soda reacts with the slightly acidic pH of the cooked sugar-nut mixture, creating a fine foam of carbon dioxide gas that aerates the caramel. As the brittle cools and hardens, it retains this gas, which gives the brittle a lightened texture and delicate bite. Because of its aeration, brittle may be left in relatively thick pieces and still be palatable to bite. Alternatively, brittle may be left unaerated and, when it reaches a plastic consistency, pulled and stretched thin to create a lacy matrix of caramel between the nuts. This method requires more labor and skill on the part of the confectioner, but the result is a very delicate confection.

| technique | theory | BASIC BRITTLE |

Brittles are simple confections to cook, requiring no special knowledge or tools beyond those used in the fundamental sugar-cooking technique. Brittles, like hard candies, are high-boiled sweets; that is, they are cooked using water to dissolve the sugar, but the water is essentially all evaporated during cooking due to the high temperature to which they are cooked. The two key steps to cooking brittles are to stir constantly once the nuts are added in order to prevent scorching and to cook to the desired temperature to develop sufficient caramel color and flavor—without overcooking and promoting bitter flavor notes.

1. **COMBINE SUGAR AND WATER. BRING TO A BOIL WHILE STIRRING.** In all sugar cooking water acts as a solvent to dissolve the sugar. Sugar dissolves more readily in water if the glucose syrup is not added until after the sugar has fully dissolved. Stirring helps to ensure that all of the sugar crystals dissolve in the water. (See Standard Wet-Sugar Cooking Technique and Theory, page 219.)

2. **ADD GLUCOSE SYRUP AND CONTINUE COOKING TO APPROXIMATELY 110°C/230°F.** Once the syrup reaches a boil and the sugar has dissolved, the glucose syrup can be added; the mixture is then cooked to remove water. Stirring at this step is not recommended because of the potential for crystallizing the sugar.

3. **ADD THE NUTS AND CONTINUE COOKING, STIRRING CONSTANTLY.** Nuts to be used in brittles should be untoasted. They will toast in the syrup as it cooks and reaches the high end of its temperature range. The nuts are not added until this point so that they do not soak up excessive water from the cooking syrup. Once the nuts are added, the batch must be stirred constantly to prevent the nuts from scorching. Because

stirring during cooking is mandatory, most brittle formulas contain a relatively high percentage of glucose syrup to prevent crystallization from this agitation. The nuts provide the amino acids that are required for Maillard browning, and these react with reducing sugars found in the glucose syrup to provide the characteristic roasted flavor and color.

4. **AT APPROXIMATELY 155°C/311°F, REMOVE THE BRITTLE FROM THE FIRE.** Although 155°C/311°F is below the temperature at which sucrose caramelizes, the brittle should be golden brown at this temperature due to ongoing Maillard reactions. The optimum temperature may vary somewhat depending on the variety of nut used, the DE of the glucose syrup, and the speed with which the brittle is cooked. A skilled confectioner watches the color of the batch as well as the thermometer.

5. **ADD BUTTER, VANILLA EXTRACT, SALT, AND BAKING SODA.** Butter is added for flavor and shortness of texture. Vanilla extract should be added at the end of cooking so that the volatile flavor compounds do not flash off during cooking. Salt is added for flavor, always

at the end of cooking to prevent excessive inversion of the sugar in the batch, which would result in a sticky, somewhat soft brittle. Baking soda aerates the brittle, giving it a delicate bite. If the brittle is to be pulled, baking soda may be omitted, although baking soda also raises the pH of the batch and promotes specific Maillard browning reactions that give brittle its golden hue and flavor profile. This browning is easily observable when the baking soda is added and may be due to inversion of sugar by the baking soda, resulting in many more reducing sugars (dextrose and fructose) in the batch to react with the amino acids.

6. **POUR THE MIXTURE ONTO A MARBLE COOLING SLAB AND SPREAD IT OUT. PULL THE BRITTLE TO MAKE IT THIN, IF DESIRED.** Brittle is usually left to cool in sheets that are about 6 to 8 mm/¼ to ³/₁₆ in thick. After cooling, the brittle is broken into pieces for packaging or consumption. For a more delicate confection, the brittle may be allowed to cool until it reaches a plastic consistency and then pulled into very thin lacy sheets as it continues cooling. Pulling brittle requires not only more labor but also the skill to handle the batch at the right moment, when it is neither too hot and soft nor too cool and brittle.

Stretching brittle before it sets creates a thinner product with a more delicate texture (see step 6 of the technique).

TOFFEE AND CARAMELS

The difference between toffee and caramels is a gray area that depends largely on the authority consulted. For the purposes of this book, *toffee* refers to hard caramels that contain dairy products, and *caramels* refer to chewy caramel-flavored confections—and should not be confused with *caramel*, which is sugar heated until it melts and turns brown. The similarities between toffee and caramels are greater than their differences. Each contains sugar, glucose syrup, a dairy product, and fat, although the exact percentages of each vary somewhat between the two; other flavorings are optional. Both caramels and toffee derive their flavor from Maillard browning of the protein in the dairy product and from the reducing sugars found in the glucose syrup and the dairy product. The major difference between toffee and caramels is water content, which is determined by the temperature to which the confection is cooked. Since toffee is cooked to a significantly higher temperature, it contains less water, browns more, and has a much harder texture. The reverse is true for caramels; they are cooked to a lower temperature and therefore contain more water and have a softer texture. They also exhibit less Maillard browning due to their lower cooking temperature.

technique | theory | TOFFEE AND CARAMELS

Toffee and caramels are simple but time-consuming confections to produce. The dairy products contained in both require constant stirring as they cook to prevent scorching. They have a tendency to foam in the early stages of cooking, requiring a low heat to prevent boiling over, and the best flavors and color are developed when they are cooked slowly, not quickly like hard candy. The time required to cook them while stirring constantly is the reason most operations that produce caramels have a fire mixer, which automatically stirs the batch as it cooks, reducing labor costs.

1. **COMBINE THE LIQUIDS WITH THE SUGAR AND BRING TO BOIL WHILE STIRRING.** The sugar alone is added to the liquid in order to ensure that it fully dissolves. Stirring the mixture prevents scorching of the dairy product.

2. **ADD THE GLUCOSE SYRUP AND CONTINUE COOKING OVER MODERATE HEAT, STIRRING CONSTANTLY.** Once the mixture reaches a boil, the glucose syrup is added and the heat moderated. Cooking the mixture on a moderate heat not only prevents scorching of the milk solids but also develops better flavor in caramels than rapid cooking does.

3. **COOK TO THE DESIRED TEMPERATURE, CHECKING THE CONSISTENCY MANUALLY IF NECESSARY.** As with all sugar confectionery, the temperature to which the mixture is cooked determines the final water content and therefore the firmness of the confection. Toffee is usually cooked to approximately 145°C/293°F; caramels are cooked to approximately 115°C/239°F. When cooking caramels, it is always advisable to test the texture of the mixture manually rather than relying solely on temperature.

4. **ADD SALT AND FLAVORING IF DESIRED.** Salt is usually added at the end of cooking because of its tendency to invert sugar if it is added earlier in the process. Excessive inversion causes stickiness and hygroscopicity in the finished product. Flavorings such as vanilla extract are added at the end of cooking to prevent the evaporation of volatile flavor compounds and the loss of flavor due to the high heat of cooking.

5. **POUR THE MIXTURE INTO FRAMES OR SPREAD AS DESIRED.**

6. **TOFFEE DROPS ARE CUT USING A CARAMEL CUTTER AS THE SLAB COOLS TO A PLASTIC CONSISTENCY.** Because they are not coated in chocolate, toffee drops must be wrapped or packaged immediately.

7. **FOR BUTTERCRUNCH, CHOCOLATE PROTECTS MOISTURE AS WELL AS PROVIDES FLAVOR.**

LEFT: *Using a rolling cutter facilitates consistent and equal portioning of finished toffee (see step 6 of technique).* RIGHT: *Precoating finished toffee with tempered chocolate eases handling and later enrobing and finishing (see step 7 of technique).*

FUNCTION OF INGREDIENTS IN BRITTLES, TOFFEE, AND CARAMELS

Toffee and caramels may be made in a variety of styles, but they all contain the same essential ingredients. Brittle also contains most of these same ingredients, except that it lacks dairy products.

Sugar

Sugar gives toffee its sweetness and contributes to its hardness. Sucrose itself does not contribute to Maillard browning, and toffee never reaches a temperature sufficient to caramelize sucrose, so other than a small quantity that may be inverted during cooking, sugar does not significantly add to the caramelized flavor of toffee.

Glucose syrup is a key ingredient in toffee production. As usual, glucose syrup acts as a doctoring agent, helping prevent crystallization of the supersaturated sugar solution. Without the addition of glucose syrup, toffee and caramels would recrystallize rapidly, resulting in a greatly shortened shelf life. Glucose syrup also provides a source of the reducing sugars necessary for Maillard browning. All the caramel flavor found in caramels is a result of Maillard browning. In fact, the candies might more accurately be called "Maillards." Glucose syrup also contributes greatly to the chewy texture of caramels. Insufficient use of glucose syrup or the use of a high-conversion glucose syrup results in caramels with a short texture instead of the characteristic chew.

Milk

Perhaps the defining ingredient in toffee and caramels is the dairy product; it is the milk solids that elevate these confections from simply cooked sugar to rich, brown, flavorful candies. Milk provides browning, texture, and emulsification to these confections. The milk solids provide both the protein and the reducing sugar required for Maillard browning. Without milk solids, these candies would not brown significantly. Another role milk proteins play in toffee and caramels is that of emulsifier. As both toffee and caramels contain fat and water, they are therefore emulsions, specifically, fat-in-water emulsions. (See Emulsions, page 96.) The milk solids help to keep the fat dispersed in the aqueous phase, preventing coalescence and separation. Insufficient milk in toffee and caramels would lead to an oily mouthfeel from fat that was not well emulsified.

Another vital role of milk solids in caramels is their contribution to the confection's "stand-up" quality, or resistance to cold flow. Sugar and glucose alone cooked to a moisture content similar to that of caramels would ooze and flow at room temperature. It is the presence of the proteins in the milk solids that prevent flow and allow caramels to hold their shape when cut.

Many different types of dairy products are suitable for use in toffee and caramels, each with its own unique advantages and disadvantages. Processed dairy products such as sweetened condensed milk and evaporated milk are often used in caramel production. Sweetened condensed milk is the form of dairy most commonly used for these confections. It offers a low water and high milk-solids content, which results in a greatly reduced cooking time. Sweetened condensed milk is also less prone to curdling during cooking than is evaporated milk. The main advantage of using fresh dairy products to make toffee or caramels is the flavor they provide; the disadvantage is the increased boiling time required to remove the moisture, which makes the proteins more prone to curdling. Additional expense and storage requirements are also considerations in the choice of fresh dairy products.

Nuts

Brittles always contain some form of nuts or seeds as an integral part of the formula. Toffee and caramels may also contain these ingredients. Aside from flavor and texture, nuts contribute the proteins that are required for Maillard browning, resulting in the development of caramelized flavors. When nuts are added late in cooking, or after the completion of cooking, they do not contribute to browning and are added solely for flavor and texture. Nuts are high in fat, and so they also contribute to richness.

Fat

Fat is another important part of toffee and caramels formulation. Fat contributes to mouthfeel, provides flavor (when the right fat is used), and ensures ease of cutting and handling. Fat also contributes to these confections' shorter texture, and, if the fat used is a hard fat such as cocoa butter, aids in the candy's setting, or stand-up. The fat content of toffee makes a profound difference in the texture of the product. Toffee with a high fat content has a short, tender break in the mouth. Such toffees are usually referred to as "crunches." Toffee with a lower fat content has a hard texture more like that of hard candy. As with other confections that contain added fat, toffee and caramels may be made with less expensive fats, such as hydrogenated vegetable oil, that add no flavor of their own but are used to produce candies of lesser quality at lower cost. The only fats considered in this book for the production of toffee and caramels are butter and cocoa butter. Butter adds flavor, provides additional milk solids, and melts below body temperature, ensuring that no waxy film is left behind after the candy is chewed. Cocoa butter adds little flavor but melts below body temperature and provides firmness to the cooled product. Butterfat is added through the milk or cream in the formula or through the direct addition of butter during cooking. Cocoa butter may be added as a discrete ingredient, or it may be present in the chocolate used to make chocolate caramels. In toffee and caramels fat added early in cooking is emulsified into the sugar solution and held in a dispersed state by the milk solids. It is common practice to add a small quantity of butter near the end of cooking caramels. Fat added late in cooking is not locked up in the emulsion and is therefore free to release its flavor and rich mouthfeel much more quickly than fat that is thoroughly emulsified. Fat added later in cooking is also available to lubricate the cutters or knives used to cut the finished caramels. An excess of unemulsified fat, however, results in an oily exterior and a greasy mouthfeel.

TAFFY

Saltwater taffy became popular in the late nineteenth century. Molasses taffy was its predecessor and is known to have been made in colonial America. As the name implies, molasses taffy is a chewy pulled candy made and flavored with molasses, a form of flavorful sweetener available long before the flavorings used to make saltwater taffy. Molasses taffy is typically cooked to a higher temperature, resulting in a firmer candy than the softer, chewy saltwater taffy.

The name *saltwater taffy* is not a reference to ingredients—most taffy contains little or no salt—but is the result of an offhand remark that changed the name of the candy forever. As the story is often told, one David Bradley, a shop owner in Atlantic City in the late 1800s, was enjoying success selling taffy to tourists. When his shop was flooded by a storm, and ocean water damaged most of the store's inventory, a young girl came in and asked if Bradley had any taffy for sale. Bradley is reputed to have replied sarcastically that he had only "saltwater taffy." The name stuck. Whether or not the story is true, the confection is still a popular seashore treat.

Taffy is a confection that is better defined by its characteristics than by its ingredients, which may vary greatly among formulas. Taffy is a chewy candy that is pulled to aerate it and may contain frappe to make it even lighter. The technique for cooking taffy is similar to that used to produce soft caramels; taffy is then pulled using a technique similar to the one used to aerate hard candy. Taffy must be wrapped immediately after pulling and cutting, because it exhibits pronounced cold flow, and the pieces will lose their shapes and re-agglomerate if they are not wrapped. While there are several varieties of taffy, the most famous variety—saltwater taffy—is the type sold in seashore resort areas.

1. **COMBINE THE SUGARS AND LIQUIDS AND COOK TO THE DESIRED TEMPERATURE, STIRRING IF DAIRY PRODUCTS ARE IN THE BATCH.** As always when cooking sugar, the object is to dissolve the sugar and to remove the desired amount of water in order to control the firmness of the finished product. (See Standard Wet-Sugar Cooking Technique and Theory, page 219.) Most taffy contains some dairy products, so stirring during cooking is generally required.

2. **ADD OPTIONAL INGREDIENTS LIKE SALT AND FRAPPE.** Salt is added at the end of cooking to prevent excessive inversion of the sugar during cooking, which would result in a very soft, sticky candy. If the salt is added after the batch is on the marble, however, it may not dissolve, leaving discernible salt crystals in the finished batch. Frappe, if added, is also added after cooking in order to preserve its aerating qualities.

3. **POUR THE MIXTURE ONTO A COOLING TABLE. FOLD IT PERIODICALLY WHILE IT IS COOLING.** The batch is poured onto a stone slab in order to draw the heat out of it quickly. Unlike hard candy, taffy must be cooled to nearly room temperature before pulling, as it is far too soft while warm to effectively incorporate air while being pulled. The taffy should be turned periodically while on the stone to promote even cooling so that the batch remains homogeneous.

4. **ADD FLAVORINGS AND COLORS IF DESIRED.** The flavorings for saltwater taffy are usually manufactured ones that are not heat stable. They should not be added until the taffy has cooled on the marble to prevent the flashing off of volatile flavor compounds. A single batch of taffy may easily be given multiple colors by simply dividing the batch and coloring parts of it separately. Coloring the batch with several colors allows the confectioner to create unique looks by striping, jacketing, or otherwise combining the different colors in a single confection.

5. **PULL THE TAFFY TO LIGHTEN IT.** Pulling the taffy gives it its characteristic light texture. It should be well pulled to make it light and airy.

6. **TWIST THE TAFFY INTO ROPES OR CUT AS DESIRED.** The different colors of taffy may be combined in any configuration desired to create stripes, bull's-eyes, or other visual effects. Taffy is most commonly cut into individual portions, but it may be formed into sticks, sheets, or other shapes.

7. **WRAP THE CUT TAFFY IMMEDIATELY.** Taffy must be wrapped immediately in order to prevent it from flowing back into one large multicolored mass. Wax paper is commonly used for wrapping.

Having been aerated and striped, this colored taffy is easily portioned using scissors (see step 6 of the technique).

Taffy ingredients and procedure

Saltwater taffy always contains sugar, glucose syrup, fat, and flavoring. In addition to these core ingredients, taffy may also contain milk products, cornstarch, gelatin, and/or frappe. Regardless of the ingredients, the basic principles and techniques are the same: Cook the sugar mixture to approximately 116°C/240°F, then pour it onto a slab to cool. If adding flavoring that is not heat stable, add it now. Once cooled to a consistency that can be handled, pull the plastic mass, either on a hook or by hand, to thoroughly aerate it. Taffies of different colors may be twisted, rolled, or formed together to create colorful stripes or other patterns. The taffy is then stretched into a rope with a diameter of about 25 mm/1 in and cut using oiled scissors. It is necessary to wrap each piece of taffy immediately after cutting, as taffy exhibits considerable cold flow and will lose its shape and absorb moisture if left unwrapped.

DEFECTS IN NONCRYSTALLINE CONFECTIONS

DEFECT	CAUSE	REMEDY
HARD CANDY		
CANDY CRYSTALLIZES DURING WORK	Insufficient doctoring agent	Increase doctoring agent in formula
	Excessive agitation	Pull the sugar less
	Poor sugar-cooking technique	Follow good sugar-cooking technique (see page 217)
	Contaminated work area	Keep work area clear of sugar granules or other foreign matter
CANDY IS STICKY, SOFT	Excessive acid or invert sugar	Reduce acid or invert sugar in formula
	Temperature reached during cooking too low	Cook candy to higher temperature to remove more water
	Moisture absorbed from air	Protect product from moisture
CANDY HAS CARAMELIZED FLAVOR AND COLOR	Temperature reached during cooking too high	Cook candy to lower temperature
	Candy cooked too slowly	Cook candy as quickly as possible
	Excessive acid or invert sugar	Reduce acid or invert sugar in formula
CANDY CRYSTALLIZES DURING STORAGE	Excessive water in product	Cook candy to higher temperature
	Moisture absorbed from air	Protect product from moisture
FILLED HARD CANDY		
ENROBED CANDY HAS FAT ON ITS SURFACE	Fat migration from fat-based filling	Keep filling contained in sugar
CANDY CRYSTALLIZES DURING STORAGE	Excessive moisture in filling	Use lower-moisture filling
CANDY IS STICKY, SOFT	Excessive moisture in filling	Use lower-moisture filling
FILLING IS UNEVENLY DISTRIBUTED IN CANDY	Unequal consistency of filling and sugar	Ensure that filling and sugar are the same consistency when combining

DEFECTS IN NONCRYSTALLINE CONFECTIONS

DEFECT	CAUSE	REMEDY
CARAMELS, BRITTLE, AND TOFFEE		
CANDY IS INSUFFICIENTLY BROWNED	Temperature reached during cooking too low	Cook to higher temperature
	Candy cooked too quickly	Cook more slowly to allow more Maillard browning
	Insufficient reducing sugars	Increase glucose, invert sugar, or lactose in formula
	Insufficient protein	Increase milk solids in formula
CANDY IS EXCESSIVELY BROWNED	Temperature reached during cooking too low	Cook to lower temperature
	Candy cooked too slowly	Cook on higher heat
	Scorching	Stir to keep bottom of pot clean
CANDY IS STICKY, SOFT	Excessive acid or invert sugar	Reduce acid or invert sugar in formula
	Temperature reached during cooking too low	Cook to higher temperature
	Moisture absorbed from atmosphere	Protect product from exposure to moisture
CANDY CRYSTALLIZES DURING WORK	Excessive agitation	Do not agitate while cooling
	Insufficient doctoring agent	Increase doctoring agent in formula
CANDY CRYSTALLIZES DURING STORAGE	Insufficient doctoring agent	Increase doctoring agent in formula
	Moisture absorbed from atmosphere	Increase doctoring agent in formula
CANDY LACKS STAND-UP; EXHIBITS COLD FLOW (CARAMELS)	Insufficient milk solids	Increase milk solids in formula
	Temperature reached during cooking too low	Cook to higher temperature
TAFFY		
CANDY IS TOO SOFT	Temperature reached during cooking too low	Cook to higher temperature
CANDY IS TOO FIRM	Temperature reached during cooking too high	Cook to lower temperature
CANDY CRYSTALLIZES DURING WORK	Insufficient doctoring agent	Increase doctoring in formula
	Excessive manipulation	Pull taffy less
CANDY CRYSTALLIZES DURING STORAGE	Insufficient doctoring agent	Increase doctoring agent in formula
	Moisture absorbed from atmosphere	Protect product from exposure to moisture

CHOCOLATE TAFFY

yield: **300 PIECES**

Glucose syrup	830 g	29 oz	41%
Sugar	500 g	18 oz	25%
Water	170 g	6 oz	8%
Sweetened condensed milk	170 g	6 oz	8%
Salt	15 g	0.5 oz	1%
Chocolate liquor	330 g	12 oz	17%
BATCH SIZE	2015 g	71.5 oz	100%

1. Combine the glucose syrup, sugar, water, and sweetened condensed milk in a heavy saucepan.

2. Cook to 116°C/240°F while stirring constantly.

3. Remove from the heat, add the salt, and stir to dissolve. Add the chocolate liquor and stir to incorporate.

4. Pour the mixture onto an oiled marble slab. Turn occasionally as the batch cools to a plastic consistency. Pull generously to aerate.

5. Pull into a rope 1 cm/½ in in diameter. Cut the rope into 25-mm/1-in pieces.

6. Wrap immediately to maintain shape and to protect from humidity.

   NOTE: Unlike hard candies, taffy must cool to nearly room temperature before it reaches a firm enough state to be effectively pulled.

MOLASSES TAFFY

yield: **200 PIECES**

Glucose syrup	570 g	20 oz	42%
Molasses	340 g	12 oz	25%
Sugar	230 g	8 oz	17%
Invert sugar	110 g	4 oz	8%
Coconut fat	50 g	2 oz	4%
Butter	40 g	1 oz	3%
Salt	1 tsp	1 tsp	<1%
Vanilla extract	10 g	0.5 oz	1%
BATCH SIZE	1350 g	47.5 oz	100%

1. Combine the glucose syrup, molasses, sugar, invert sugar, coconut fat, and butter in a heavy saucepan.
2. Cook to 122°C/252°F while stirring constantly.
3. Remove from the heat, add the salt, and stir to dissolve.
4. Pour the mixture onto an oiled marble slab. Pour the vanilla extract onto the batch.
5. Turn occasionally as the batch cools to a plastic consistency. Pull generously to aerate.
6. Pull into a rope 1 cm/½ in in diameter. Cut the rope into 25-mm/1-in pieces.
7. Wrap immediately to maintain shape and to protect from humidity.

NOTES: A temperature of 122°C/252°F will produce taffy of a relatively firm consistency. For a softer taffy, cook the batch several degrees lower.

Unlike hard candies, taffy must cool to nearly room temperature before it reaches a firm enough state to be effectively pulled.

Hard candies

HARD CANDY

yield: **APPROXIMATELY 250 PIECES**

Sugar	1150 g	41 oz	64%
Water	290 g	10 oz	16%
Glucose syrup	360 g	13 oz	20%
Cream of tartar (optional)	½ tsp	½ tsp	<1%
BATCH SIZE	1800 g	64 oz	100%
Coloring	as needed		
Citric acid	as needed		
Flavoring	as needed		

TO COOK THE BATCH:

1. Combine the sugar and water in a heavy saucepan. Bring to a boil while stirring.

2. Add the glucose syrup and cream of tartar, if using. Cook to 156°C/313°F without stirring.

3. Pour the mixture onto an oiled marble slab. Add the coloring and citric acid, if using.

4. Turn occasionally as the batch cools to a plastic consistency. Add the flavoring and pull as desired.

5. Jacket, form, and cut as desired.

To stripe the candy:

1. Pour two pools of sugar onto an oiled marble slab: one 80 percent of the batch, the other 20 percent.

2. Pull the larger pool until it is white.

3. Add a strong dark red color to the smaller pool and pull very little, so as not to lighten the color.

4. Keep both sugars warm under a warmer.

5. Cut the white sugar into two pieces, one twice as big as the other. The larger piece will be the center of the candy; the smaller piece will be the white part of the jacket.

6. Roll the center into a stump 20 cm/8 in long.

7. Flatten the white jacket sugar into a ribbon 8 cm/3 in wide and 20 cm/8 in long.

8. Fashion the red sugar into a narrow ribbon 25 mm/1 in wide and 20 cm/8 in long.

9. Attach the red and white ribbons side by side.

10. Pull the ribbon to double its length and cut it in half crosswise.

11. Reattach the ribbon with alternating colors adjacent.

12. Pull again to double its length and again cut it in half.

13. Reattach the ribbon, joining the red to the red.

14. Pull again to double its length and cut it in half once more.

15. Reattach once again, white against white.

16. Place the center onto the ribbon and wrap it to jacket. Seal the jacket tightly around the center.

17. Pull the jacketed log into a rope of the desired diameter. Cut and shape it as desired to make canes, sticks, pillows, or lollipops.

NOTES: This formula may also be used for casting lollipops or clear toys; slabbed and cut during cooling; or used for coating candy apples.

The procedure for the classic candy striping is shown on page 224.

Cream of tartar makes the candy easier to work with but increases its hygroscopicity.

The procedure for molding hard candy is discussed on page 226.

LEAF CROQUANT

yield: **100 PIECES**

FILLING

Almonds, lightly toasted	450 g	16 oz	43%
Confectioners' sugar	60 g	2 oz	6%
Glucose syrup	30 g	1 oz	3%

CARAMEL

Lemon juice	¼ tsp	¼ tsp	<1%
Sugar	450 g	16 oz	43%
Glucose syrup	60 g	2 oz	5%
BATCH SIZE	1050 g	37 oz	100%

Dark chocolate, melted, tempered, for dipping	as needed	

TO MAKE THE FILLING:

1. In a food processor, grind the almonds with the confectioners' sugar to a very smooth, soft consistency. (This is easier to accomplish if the nuts are warm.)

2. Remove the nut mixture from the processor, add the glucose syrup, and work into a malleable dough.

3. Form the nut mixture into a square approximately 25 × 25 cm/10 × 10 in on parchment paper. Keep warm

TO MAKE THE CARAMEL:

1. Rub the lemon juice into the sugar. Place in a heavy-bottomed saucepan and caramelize using the dry method. (See page 222.) Be certain that all the sugar crystals have melted and that the sugar has reached a medium-amber color for proper flavor development.

2. Remove from the heat and add the glucose syrup.

3. Pour the caramel into a rectangle approximately 30 × 56 cm/12 × 22 in on a silicone baking mat. Allow to cool slightly to a plastic consistency.

TO MAKE THE CENTERS:

1. Place the square of filling onto one end of the caramel, leaving a border approximately 25 mm/1 in wide on each side and at the end of the rectangle of caramel.

2. Fold the silicone baking mat and the caramel over the filling to enclose it. Peel the mat off the caramel and lightly seal the edges of the caramel to envelop the filling.

3. Warm the filled slab to keep the caramel malleable. Roll the slab into a rectangle approximately 20 × 51 cm/8 × 20 in and then fold into 3-folds, as with puff pastry.

4. Alternately warm and fold the slab, to make a total of five 3-folds.

5. After the fifth 3-fold, roll out the slab to 1 cm/½ in thick. Use a sharp chef's knife to cut the caramel into pieces 1 × 4 cm/½ × 1½ in. (The candy must be kept moderately warm for cutting.)

6. Allow to cool completely. Dip the pieces in the tempered dark chocolate. Before the chocolate sets, use a 3-prong dipping fork to make a diagonal wave pattern on the top surface of each piece.

PEANUT BUTTER FILLING: Use 400 g/14 oz of melted peanut butter combined with 100 g/4 oz of glucose syrup in place of the almond dough.

BIRDFOOD

yield: **1740 G/61 OZ**

Almonds, slivered, toasted	200 g	7 oz	10%
Cashews, toasted	100 g	4 oz	5%
Pecans, toasted	100 g	4 oz	5%
Sunflower seeds	80 g	3 oz	4%
Sesame seeds	50 g	2 oz	3%
Popcorn, popped, unsalted	150 g	5 oz	8%
Sugar	530 g	19 oz	27%
Glucose syrup	250 g	9 oz	13%
Brown sugar	180 g	6 oz	9%
Water	180 g	6 oz	9%
Butter	50 g	2 oz	3%
Baking soda, sifted	10 g	1¾ tsp	<1%
Salt	2 tsp	2 tsp	<1%
Butter, clarified	50 g	2 oz	3%
BATCH SIZE	1930 g	69 oz	100 %

1. Combine the almonds, cashews, pecans, sunflower seeds, and sesame seeds in a stainless steel bowl. Place in a 121°C/250°F oven to keep warm.

2. Place the popcorn in a separate bowl and keep it warm in a 121°C/250°F oven.

3. Combine the sugar, glucose syrup, brown sugar, and water in a large kettle or pot. Cook to 116°C/240°F while stirring constantly.

4. Add the butter and cook to 150°C/300°F while stirring.

5. Remove from the heat, add the baking soda, and stir to dissolve. Stir in the salt.

6. Pour in the nuts and seeds and return to moderate heat.

7. Stir over heat until all of the ingredients are coated with a thin, even layer of caramel.

8. Add the warm popcorn and stir over moderate heat until the popcorn is coated with the caramel.

9. Pour the clarified butter onto the mixture and mix lightly. Do not overmix so that the butter stays on the surface rather than mixing into the caramel.

10. Pour the mixture onto an oiled marble slab. Separate into individual pieces and allow to cool. Wrap immediately to protect from humidity.

PEPPERMINT FLAKE

yield: **150 PIECES**

FILLING

Confectioners' sugar	410 g	15 oz	49%
Chocolate liquor, melted	400 g	14 oz	45%
Cocoa butter, melted	50 g	2 oz	6%
BATCH SIZE	860 g	31 oz	100%

HARD CANDY BASE

Sugar	750 g	27 oz	56%
Water	220 g	8 oz	17%
Glucose syrup	375 g	13 oz	27%
Cream of tartar	1 tsp	1 tsp	< 1%
Red gel food color	as needed		
Peppermint extract	10 g	0.5 oz	<1%
BATCH SIZE	1355 g	48.5 oz	100%

Dark chocolate, melted, tempered, for dipping	as needed

TO MAKE THE FILLING:

1. Mix the confectioners' sugar, chocolate liquor, and cocoa butter in a 5-qt planetary mixer. The dough should be stiff; if necessary, adjust the consistency with additional confectioners' sugar or cocoa butter.

2. Form the filling into a 20-cm/8-in square on parchment paper. Keep it warm in a 93°C/200°F oven.

TO MAKE THE HARD CANDY:

1. Combine the sugar and water in a heavy saucepan. Bring to a boil while stirring.

2. Add the glucose syrup and cream of tartar and cook to 156°C/313°F without stirring.

3. Pour the mixture onto an oiled marble slab and add the coloring and peppermint extract.

4. Turn occasionally as the batch cools to a plastic consistency.

5. Pull the candy lightly to aerate.

6. Stretch the candy into a rectangle 30 × 51 cm/ 12 × 20 in.

TO FINISH:

1. Place the filling on one end of the hard candy, leaving a border approximately 25 mm/1 in wide on each side and at the end of the rectangle of hard candy.

2. Fold the hard candy over to envelop the filling. Seal the edges with a rolling pin.

3. Roll into a rectangle approximately 30 × 51 cm/12 × 20 in. If the sugar becomes brittle, warm it in a 163°C/325°F oven to return it to a plastic, malleable consistency.

4. Fold into 3-folds, as with puff pastry.

5. Turn the batch 90 degrees and roll back to a rectangle approximately 30 × 51 cm/12 × 20 in.

6. Rewarm the batch in the oven to a plastic consistency. Fold again into a 3-fold. Repeat this process for a total of five 3-folds, reheating the batch as needed.

7. Roll out to 9 mm/⅜ in thick. Use a chef's knife to cut into pieces 1 × 4 cm/½ × 1½ in. (The candy must be kept moderately warm for cutting.)

8. Allow to cool completely. Dip the pieces in the tempered dark chocolate. Before the chocolate sets, use a 3-prong dipping fork to make a diagonal wave pattern on the top surface of each piece.

NOTE: It is best to rewarm the batch while it is rolled out thin so that it warms quickly and evenly.

SKIPPING STONES

yield: **APPROXIMATELY 100 PIECES**

Sugar	400 g	14 oz	40%
Glucose syrup	200 g	7 oz	19%
Water	200 g	7 oz	19%
Molasses	200 g	7 oz	19%
Salt	½ tsp	½ tsp	<1%
Butter	30 g	1 oz	3%
Baking soda, sifted	10 g	1½ tsp	<1%
BATCH SIZE	1040 g	36 oz	100%

Dark chocolate, melted, tempered, for dipping	as needed

1. Combine the sugar, glucose syrup, and water in a heavy saucepan. Cook to 155°C/311°F, keeping the sides of the saucepan clean.

2. Add the molasses and cook to 145°C/293°F while stirring constantly.

3. Add the salt while the mixture is still boiling.

4. Remove from the heat, add the butter, and stir well until fully incorporated.

5. Stir in the baking soda, stirring just until incorporated and the mixture is well aerated.

6. Pour the mixture onto oiled parchment paper and use an offset palette knife to spread very lightly to 6 mm/¼ in thick. Allow to cool undisturbed.

7. When cooled completely, break into irregular pieces of desired size.

8. Dip the pieces in the tempered dark chocolate. Before the chocolate sets, use a 3-prong dipping fork to make a diagonal wave pattern on the top surface of each piece.

CLOCKWISE, FROM UPPER LEFT: *Cocoa Nib Brittle, Peanut Brittle, Sesame Brittle*

PEANUT BRITTLE

yield: **2 THIN SHEETS (APPROXIMATELY 41 × 61 CM/16 × 24 IN)**

Sugar	790 g	28 oz	29%
Water	340 g	12 oz	13%
Glucose syrup	570 g	20 oz	21%
Raw peanuts	910 g	32 oz	34%
Butter	60 g	2 oz	2%
Vanilla extract	15 g	0.5 oz	1%
Salt	2 tsp	2 tsp	<1%
Baking soda, sifted	10 g	1¾ tsp	<1%
BATCH SIZE	2695 g	95 oz	100%

1. Combine the sugar and water in a heavy saucepan. Bring to a boil while stirring.
2. Add the glucose syrup and continue cooking to 115°C/239°F without stirring.
3. Add the peanuts and cook to 155°C/311°F over moderate heat, stirring constantly.
4. Remove from the heat and add the butter, vanilla extract, and salt and mix well. Add the baking soda and stir well to incorporate.
5. Pour the mixture onto an oiled marble slab and spread to approximately 6 mm/ ¼ in thick with an offset palette knife.
6. If desired, when the brittle cools to a plastic consistency, pull into thin sheets to make a more delicate candy.
7. When cooled completely, break into pieces and store protected from humidity.

COCOA NIB BRITTLE: Replace the peanuts with 200 g/7 oz of cocoa nibs.

PECAN CHIPOTLE BRITTLE: Replace the peanuts with 700 g/25 oz of chopped pecans. Add 1 tsp of chipotle powder before adding the baking soda. Use more chipotle powder for smokier flavor and more heat if desired.

SESAME BRITTLE: Replace the peanuts with 500 g/18 oz of sesame seeds.

PEANUT BUTTER HONEYCOMB

yield: **250 PIECES**

FILLING			
Peanut butter	240 g	9 oz	11%
Glucose syrup	60 g	2 oz	3%
HARD CANDY BASE			
Sugar	1180 g	42 oz	56%
Water	240 g	8 oz	11%
Glucose syrup	300 g	11 oz	14%
Molasses	80 g	3 oz	4%
Salt	1 tsp	1 tsp	<1%
Baking soda, sifted	10 g	1¾ tsp	1%
BATCH SIZE	2110 g	75.5 oz	100%
Desiccated coconut, for finishing	as needed		

TO MAKE THE FILLING:

In a saucepan, heat the peanut butter to 100°C/212°F. Remove from the heat and stir in the glucose syrup. Keep the mixture warm.

TO MAKE THE HARD CANDY BASE:

1. Combine the sugar and water in a heavy saucepan and bring to a boil. Add the glucose syrup and cook to 130°C/266°F.

2. Add the molasses and salt and cook to 155°C/311°F.

3. Remove from the heat and stir in the baking soda.

4. Pour onto an oiled marble slab and turn occasionally until cooled to a plastic consistency. Pull until well aerated.

5. Divide the pulled sugar into two portions: one 60 percent of the batch, the other 40 percent. Keep each portion warm under a warmer or in a low oven.

6. Stretch the larger piece of sugar into a rectangle approximately 18 × 25 cm/7 × 10 in. Place the peanut butter filling in the center and roll the sugar over the filling to make a cylinder. Seal the ends to encase the filling.

7. Stretch the filled cylinder to 61 cm/24 in, then fold it back in half. Repeat this eight times. Return to a cylindrical shape. Fold again if necessary to make a stubby log approximately 18 cm/7 in long.

8. Stretch the smaller piece of sugar into a ribbon 10 cm/4 in wide. Pull to 61 cm/24 in long. Cut and attach the two halves side by side. Repeat a total of four times to make a thin, even layer that is approximately 23 × 30 cm/9 × 12 in. This is the jacket for the candy.

9. Wrap the jacket around the filled cylinder.

10. Cut off the ends of the cylinder, which contain no filling. Discard them or rework them into the next batch.

11. Pull into a rope 6 mm/¼ in in diameter and cut into 5-cm/2-in segments. Drop segments into desiccated coconut immediately.

12. Bag or wrap immediately to protect from humidity.

PEANUT BUTTER TAFFY

yield: **300 PIECES**

Glucose syrup	680 g	24 oz	34%
Sugar	340 g	12 oz	16%
Molasses	270 g	10 oz	14%
Sweetened condensed milk	270 g	10 oz	14%
Salt	2 tsp	2 tsp	1%
Peanut butter	410 g	14 oz	21%
BATCH SIZE	1980 g	70 oz	100%

1. Combine the glucose syrup, sugar, molasses, and sweetened condensed milk in a heavy saucepan. Cook to 118°C/245°F while stirring constantly.

2. Remove from the heat, add the salt, and stir to dissolve. Add the peanut butter and stir well to incorporate.

3. Pour the mixture onto an oiled marble slab. Turn occasionally as the batch cools to a plastic consistency.

4. Pull the taffy until light in color and texture.

5. Pull into a rope 1 cm/½ in in diameter. Cut the rope into 25-mm/1-in pieces.

6. Wrap immediately to maintain shape and protect from humidity.

   NOTES: A temperature of 118°C/245°F will produce taffy of a relatively firm consistency. For a softer taffy, cook the batch several degrees lower.

   Unlike hard candies, taffy must cool to nearly room temperature before it reaches a firm enough state to be effectively pulled.

PECAN BUTTERCRUNCH

yield: **1700 G/60 OZ**

Butter, melted	450 g	16 oz	45%
Sugar	450 g	16 oz	45%
Water	90 g	3 oz	8%
Salt	1 tsp	1 tsp	<1%
Vanilla extract	15 g	0.5 oz	2%
BATCH SIZE	1005 g	35.5 oz	100%
Dark chocolate, melted, tempered, for coating	680 g	24 oz	32%
Pecans, toasted, chopped, salted, for finishing	450 g	16 oz	21%

1. Combine the melted butter, sugar, water, and salt in a heavy saucepan. Bring to a boil, stirring constantly.
2. Cook over moderate heat to 146°C/295°F while stirring constantly.
3. Remove from the heat and add the vanilla extract. Stir in well.
4. Pour the mixture onto a silicone baking mat. Spread quickly to the edges before the toffee sets.
5. Allow to cool completely. Blot the toffee with a towel to remove any excess oil from the surface.
6. Coat one side of the toffee with half of the tempered dark chocolate and sprinkle with half of the toasted salted nuts immediately.
7. When the chocolate sets, turn the toffee over and coat the other side.
8. Break into pieces of the desired size.
9. Store protected from heat and humidity.

MACADAMIA COFFEE TOFFEE: Add 15 g/0.5 oz of coffee extract at 140°C/284°F. Coat toffee with melted, tempered milk chocolate and use toasted salted macadamias in place of the pecans.

CLOCKWISE FROM TOP: *Chocolate-Dipped Soft Caramels.*
Soft Caramel, Chocolate Soft Caramel

SOFT CARAMELS (USING EVAPORATED MILK)

yield: **182 PIECES**

Sugar	680 g	24 oz	30%
Evaporated milk	680 g	24 oz	30%
Heavy cream	280 g	10 oz	13%
Vanilla bean, split and scraped	1 bean	1 bean	
Glucose syrup	570 g	20 oz	25%
Butter	40 g	1.5 oz	2%
Salt	1 tsp	1 tsp	<1%
BATCH SIZE	2250 g	79.5 oz	100%

Dark chocolate, melted, tempered, for precoating and dipping	as needed

1. Combine the sugar, evaporated milk, cream, and vanilla bean and its seeds in a heavy sauce-pan. Bring to a boil while stirring constantly.

2. Add the glucose syrup and continue cooking over medium heat, while stirring, until the mixture reaches 110°C/230°F. Add the butter. Cook while stirring until the mixture reaches 115°C/239°F. Add the salt and remove from the heat.

3. Remove the vanilla bean, and pour the mixture into a frame 12 × 12 × ½ in set on oiled parchment paper. Allow to cool to room temperature.

4. Remove the frame, and precoat one side of the slab with the tempered dark chocolate. Mark with a 20-mm/⅞-in caramel cutter, then cut, using a sharp, oiled chef's knife.

5. Dip the caramels in the tempered dark chocolate. Before the chocolate sets, use a 3-prong dipping fork to make a diagonal wave pattern on the top surface of each piece.

   NOTE: The temperature given for fully cooked caramel, 115°C/239°F, is a very good estimate, but results may vary depending on the ingredients used. Always check caramels for consistency by hand during cooking.

   The variations below may be applied to any of the three formulas for soft caramels. (See pages 258–261.)

ANISE SOFT CARAMELS: Make a slurry of 10 g/0.5 oz of ground anise seed and enough water to moisten it well. Add at the beginning of cooking. Dip the finished caramels in tempered dark chocolate and place several whole toasted anise seeds on top of each piece as the chocolate sets.

CHOCOLATE SOFT CARAMELS: Add 250 g/9 oz of dark chocolate at the beginning of cooking. Dip the finished caramels in tempered dark chocolate and finish with two piped diagonal parallel lines of tempered dark chocolate.

CINNAMON SOFT CARAMELS: Make a slurry of 10 g/0.5 oz of ground cinnamon and water. Add at the beginning of cooking. Dip the finished caramels in tempered dark chocolate and sift a smattering of ground cinnamon on top of each piece as the chocolate begins to set.

COFFEE SOFT CARAMELS: Infuse the evaporated milk with 30 g/1 oz of ground coffee prior to making the caramels. Strain the coffee out before adding the other ingredients. Dip the finished caramels in tempered milk chocolate and finish with two piped diagonal parallel lines of tempered dark chocolate.

RAINFOREST SOFT CARAMELS: Stir in 400 g/14 oz of toasted cashews and 250 g/9 oz of toasted macadamias mixed with 2 tsp of salt at the end of cooking. Spread into a frame 12 × 16 × ½ in set on oiled parchment paper. Dip in chocolate or wrap.

RASPBERRY SOFT CARAMELS: Add 340 g/12 oz of hot raspberry purée when the temperature of the mixture reaches 112°C/234°F. Dip in tempered dark chocolate and finish with two piped diagonal parallel lines of tempered white chocolate.

CARAMEL CREAMS

yield: **APPROXIMATELY 150 PIECES, DEPENDING ON THE MOLDS USED**

Foil cups lined with dark chocolate (see page 87)	150 cups	150 cups	
CARAMEL CREAM FILLING			
Lemon juice	¼ tsp	¼ tsp	
Sugar	570 g	20 oz	57%
Heavy cream, heated	290 g	10 oz	29%
Butter	140 g	5 oz	14%
Spirit or liqueur (optional)	as needed		
BATCH SIZE	1000 g	35 oz	100%
Dark chocolate, melted, tempered, for capping	as needed		
Milk chocolate, melted, tempered, for finishing	as needed		

1. Rub the lemon juice into the sugar.
2. In a heavy saucepan, caramelize the sugar mixture until amber using the dry method. (See page 222.)
3. Add the hot cream slowly while stirring over low heat.
4. Stir in the butter until melted and combined.
5. Mix in the spirit or liqueur, if using.
6. Allow to cool to room temperature. (When cooled, the consistency should be that of a very thick fluid. If too much moisture is removed from the cream while cooking, the caramel will be stiff. Add syrup, cream, or spirit to restore the proper consistency.)
7. Fill the chocolate-lined foil cups to within 3 mm/⅛ in of the tops with the caramel.
8. Cap the filled cups using tempered dark chocolate and a paper piping cone, and pipe three dots of tempered milk chocolate on each finished confection.

SOFT CARAMELS (USING FRESH DAIRY PRODUCTS)

yield: **182 PIECES**

Milk	1360 g	48 oz	47%
Sugar	680 g	24 oz	23%
Heavy cream	280 g	10 oz	10%
Vanilla bean, split and scraped	1 bean	1 bean	
Glucose syrup	570 g	20 oz	19%
Butter	40 g	1.5 oz	1%
Salt	1 tsp	1 tsp	<1%
BATCH SIZE	2930 g	103.5 oz	100%

Dark chocolate, melted, tempered, for precoating and dipping   as needed

1. Combine the milk, sugar, cream, and vanilla bean and its seeds in a heavy saucepan. Bring to a boil while stirring constantly.

2. Add the glucose syrup and continue cooking over moderate heat while stirring constantly.

3. When the mixture reaches 110°C/230°F, add the butter and continue cooking while stirring.

4. When the mixture reaches 117°C/243°F, add the salt, remove from the heat, and remove the vanilla bean.

5. Pour the mixture into a frame 12 × 12 × ½ in set on oiled parchment paper. Allow to cool to room temperature.

6. Precoat the slab with the tempered dark chocolate. Mark with a 20-mm/⅞-in caramel cutter, then cut, using a sharp, oiled chef's knife.

    NOTES: The temperature given for fully cooked caramel, 117°C/243°F, is a very good estimate, but results may vary depending on the ingredients used. Always check caramels for consistency by hand during cooking.

    See Soft Caramels (Using Evaporated Milk), page 257, for finishing details and variations.

SOFT CARAMELS (USING SWEETENED CONDENSED MILK)

yield: **182 PIECES**

Sugar	500 g	18 oz	30%
Sweetened condensed milk	360 g	13 oz	21%
Water	200 g	7 oz	12%
Vanilla bean, split and scraped	1 bean	1 bean	
Glucose syrup	430 g	15 oz	25%
Butter	200 g	7 oz	12%
Salt	1 tsp	1 tsp	<1%
BATCH SIZE	1690 g	60 oz	100%

Dark chocolate, melted, tempered, for precoating and dipping	as needed

1. Combine the sugar, sweetened condensed milk, water, and vanilla bean and its seeds in a heavy saucepan. Bring to a boil while stirring constantly.

2. Add the glucose syrup and continue cooking over medium heat while stirring constantly.

3. When mixture reaches 110°C/230°F, add the butter and continue cooking while stirring.

4. When mixture reaches 117°C/243°F, add the salt, remove from the heat, and remove the vanilla bean.

5. Pour the mixture into a frame 12 × 12 × ½ in set on oiled parchment paper. Allow to cool to room temperature.

6. Precoat the slab with the tempered dark chocolate. Mark with a 20-mm/⅞-in caramel cutter, then cut, using a sharp, oiled chef's knife.

7. Dip the caramels in the tempered dark chocolate. Before the chocolate sets, use a 3-prong dipping fork to make a diagonal wave pattern on the top surface of each piece.

NOTES: The temperature given for fully cooked caramel, 117°C/243°F, is a very good estimate, but results may vary depending on the ingredients used. Always check caramels for consistency by hand during cooking.

See Soft Caramels (Using Evaporated Milk), page 257, for finishing details and variations.

SALTWATER TAFFY

yield: **300 PIECES**

Glucose syrup	1070 g	38 oz	54%
Sugar	570 g	20 oz	29%
Sweetened condensed milk	160 g	6 oz	8%
Water	120 g	4 oz	6%
Salt	1 tsp	1 tsp	<1%
Frappe (page 389)	70 g	2.5 oz	3%
BATCH SIZE	1990 g	70.5 oz	100%
Flavoring	as needed		
Coloring	as needed		

1. Combine the glucose syrup, sugar, sweetened condensed milk, and water in a heavy saucepan.

2. Cook to 116°C/240°F while stirring constantly.

3. Remove from the heat, add the salt, and stir to dissolve.

4. Pour the mixture onto an oiled marble slab. Turn occasionally to cool evenly.

5. Add the frappe and fold to incorporate.

6. Divide as desired for mixing flavors and colors.

7. Add flavoring and coloring as desired.

8. Pull generously to aerate until very light.

9. Combine the different-colored pieces as desired. Form a rope 1 cm/½ in in diameter. Cut the rope into 25-mm/1-in pieces.

10. Wrap immediately to maintain shape and to protect from humidity.

    NOTES: If the frappe has been stored for a period of time, it is helpful to warm it prior to using.

    Unlike hard candies, taffy must cool to nearly room temperature before it reaches a firm enough state to be effectively pulled.

BRAZIL NUT ENGLISH TOFFEE

yield: **1 SHEET (41 × 61 CM × 6 MM/16 × 24 × ¼ IN)**

Sugar	1200 g	42 oz	36%
Butter	500 g	18 oz	15%
Brown sugar	300 g	11 oz	9%
Glucose syrup	300 g	11 oz	9%
Sweetened condensed milk	300 g	11 oz	9%
Salt	30 g	1 oz	1%
Vanilla extract	30 g	1 oz	1%
Brazil nuts, toasted, coarsely chopped, salted	700 g	25 oz	21%
BATCH SIZE	3360 g	120 oz	100%

1. Combine the sugar, butter, brown sugar, glucose syrup, sweetened condensed milk, and salt in a heavy saucepan. Cook to 150°C/302°F while stirring constantly.
2. Remove from the heat and stir in the vanilla extract.
3. Pour the mixture into a frame 16 × 24 × ¼ in set on oiled parchment paper.
4. Press the toasted Brazil nuts into the toffee and allow to cool.
5. Break into pieces of the desired size. Store protected from humidity.

TOFFEE DROPS

yield: **182 PIECES**

Sugar	750 g	27 oz	50%
Milk	250 g	9 oz	16%
Heavy cream	250 g	9 oz	16%
Glucose syrup	250 g	9 oz	16%
Salt	10 g	2 tsp	1%
Vanilla extract	10 g	0.5 oz	1%
BATCH SIZE	1520 g	54.5 oz	100%

Chocolate, melted, tempered, for dipping (optional)	as needed	

1. Combine the sugar, milk, and cream in a heavy saucepan. Bring to a boil while stirring constantly.
2. Add the glucose syrup and continue to cook over moderate heat to 140°C/284°F while stirring.
3. Add the salt and continue cooking to 145°C/293°F.
4. Remove from the heat and stir in the vanilla extract.
5. Pour the mixture into a frame 12 × 12 × ¼ in set on oiled parchment paper.
6. Allow to cool to a plastic consistency. Roll repeatedly with a 20-mm/⅞-in caramel cutter to deeply mark pillow-shaped squares.
7. When cooled completely, break into pieces along the marks. Wrap immediately to protect from humidity.
8. The toffee drops may be dipped halfway in tempered chocolate, if desired.

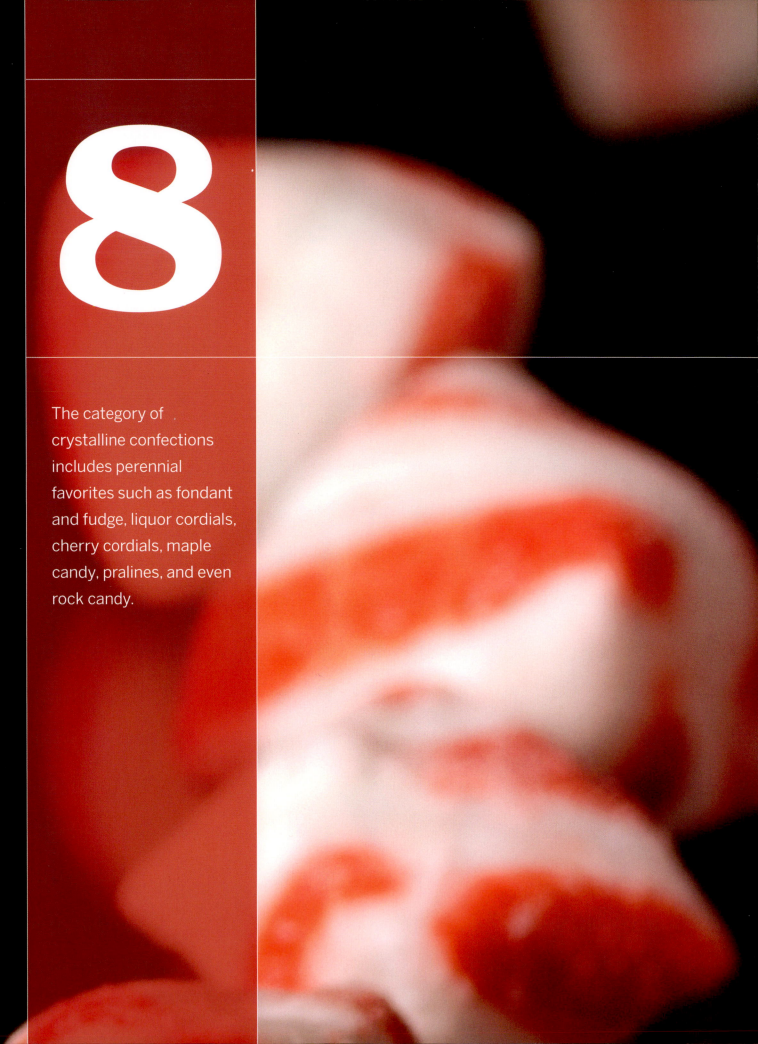

8

The category of crystalline confections includes perennial favorites such as fondant and fudge, liquor cordials, cherry cordials, maple candy, pralines, and even rock candy.

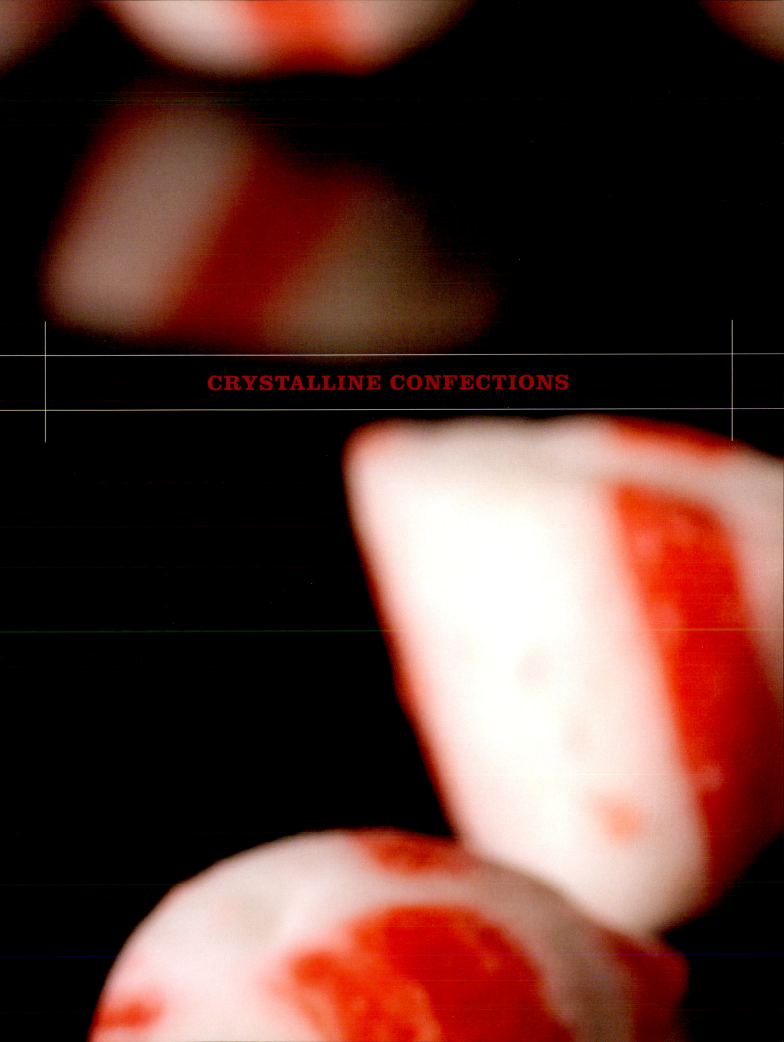

CRYSTALLINE CONFECTIONS

The two crystalline confections that are the most similar are fondant and fudge. Fondant is a system of minute sugar crystals surrounded by a saturated sugar solution; fudge is simply fondant with the addition of milk, fat, and flavoring—often chocolate. All crystalline confections are based on creating a supersaturated sugar solution and then promoting crystallization of that solution using varying degrees of agitation. In almost all cases, the desired result is a smooth texture achieved by agitating the syrup vigorously, promoting the immediate formation of many very small sugar crystals. Only in the case of rock candy is the desired result large sugar crystals, and here, the larger the better. To form these large sugar crystals, the syrup is left undisturbed without any agitation for days as the crystals slowly form. While the smoothness of fondant and fudge is determined by the size of the sugar crystals, its relative firmness is determined by the moisture content. As in all sugar confectionery, the moisture content is controlled by the temperature to which the syrup is cooked, and therefore the concentration of sugar in the syrup. It is interesting to note that crystalline confections, most notably fudge and pralines, are often thought of as "homemade" products. In spite of the fact that these candies are often made by nonprofessionals, achieving the proper crystal size and moisture content, and therefore a smooth creamy texture, is not a simple feat. A basic understanding of the principles of crystallization will be beneficial to the artisan confectioner in making crystalline confections with the correct texture every time.

FONDANT AND FUDGE

Fondant consists of minute sugar crystals surrounded by saturated sugar syrup. Fudge is nearly identical, the difference being that in addition to the sugar crystals and syrup, it contains flavoring, fat, and a dairy product. Although both of these confections contain crystalline sugar, when they are properly made, neither should feel the least bit grainy in the mouth. The smooth texture is a result of the formation of extremely small sugar crystals—under 25 microns—that cannot be detected on the tongue.

Fondant

While it is rare that a pastry chef makes his or her own fondant from scratch, it is somewhat more commonplace for a confectioner to do so, primarily to control the texture of the finished product. Many manufactured fondants made for pastry use are too soft and too resistant to recrystallization for use in confectionery. The fondant formula used in this book is for confectionery fondant that has a firmer texture than most pastry fondants in order to allow subsequent flavoring and handling, including dipping in chocolate.

Either commercial fondant or fondant made by the confectioner can be used, with various techniques, to create confections. One of the more common methods is to heat the fondant to a high temperature, usually 60° to 70°C/140°F to 158°F, flavor it, then deposit it in either rigid molds or starch molds or on parchment paper placed on a flat surface. Heating the fondant to a high temperature causes it to set firm upon cooling. Examples of commercial confections made using this method are mint fondants such as Peppermint Patties. Other types of flavorings can be used with this technique, including herbs and spices, liqueurs and spirits, extracts and infusions, and manufactured natural or artificial flavors. Regardless of the type of flavoring used, care must be taken to avoid acidic preparations that prevent the fondant from recrystallizing. When acidic flavors, such as fruit purées, are used, they must be added only after the fondant is heated, and immediately prior to its being deposited, so that no excessive inversion that prevents setting takes place. Likewise, an excess of any liquid flavoring prevents the fondant from setting firmly enough for handling. Fondants made using this technique are usually dipped in chocolate, but because crystalline sugar is not extremely hygroscopic, they also may be left undipped without suffering damage from humidity.

Fudge

Like fondant, fudge is a system of sugar crystals surrounded by saturated syrup. Fudge is made more complex by the addition of fat, dairy products, and flavoring ingredients. Each of the ingredients in a fudge formula plays a vital role in determining the final texture, flavor, appearance, and shelf life of the product. Fudge formulations are a delicate balance of all the components, and relatively small variations in the quantities of the ingredients tend to cause profoundly different results. Due to its crystalline nature, fudge is not a hygroscopic product. On the contrary, with its relatively high equilibrium relative humidity (ERH), fudge left exposed to air has a tendency to dry out. It is therefore necessary to take steps to prevent moisture loss. After it is cut, fudge should be wrapped, packaged, or enrobed as soon as possible. While it can produce excellent confections and is highly effective in preventing moisture migration, dipping or enrobing fudge in chocolate is not common, in part because of fudge's inherent sweetness and its origins as a simple, unadorned American confection. Still, enrobing fudge in chocolate can create textural and flavor contrast and unique pieces.

The general procedure for making these confections is identical. Paying close attention to the following two crucial steps will help to ensure proper texture and mouthfeel in the finished product.

- Let the cooked mixture cool undisturbed before beginning agitation.
- Agitate the cooled mixture constantly until it is well crystallized.

Cooled syrups, when agitated, form many more, and much smaller sugar crystals than would form if the syrup were warm. The result is a smoother mouthfeel. It is therefore important to allow the syrup to cool to approximately 50°C/120°F before starting agitation. Equally important is constant agitation. If the syrup is not agitated constantly as it crystallizes, it will form fewer, larger crystals, which results in a coarse texture. Failure to follow either of these two crucial steps results in a fondant or fudge that has a grainy, sugary texture.

---

technique | theory | **FONDANT AND FUDGE**

1. **COMBINE SUGARS WITH LIQUIDS. COOK TO THE DESIRED TEMPERATURE.** The sugars in fondant or fudge may include sucrose, glucose syrup, and invert sugar, and other sugars, such as maple syrup, used for lending unusual flavor notes. After the syrup comes to a boil, the glucose syrup is added. (Standard practice when cooking sugar mixtures is to bring the mixture to a boil without the addition of glucose syrup. This helps ensure the dissolution of the sugar.) The liquids may be water alone, as with fondant, or various dairy products, as with fudge. As with all sugar confectionery, the sugar is cooked in order to first dissolve it and then to increase the percentage of dissolved solids by removing water. When cooking fudge, the syrup should be stirred continuously to prevent scorching of the ingredients. When cooking fondant, stirring is not required,

and is in fact ill advised, as the agitation of stirring may promote premature crystallization of the sugar. When making crystalline confections, sufficient water must be removed to ensure that the solution will be supersaturated upon cooling, and will therefore crystallize. As with virtually all confections, water content is a prime determinant of the relative firmness of the finished product. As always when cooking sugar, the temperature to which the mixture is cooked controls the water content: cooking to a higher temperature removes more water, resulting in a firmer product. When a fondant or fudge formula yields a product that is too soft, raising the cooking temperature will result in a firmer texture for the next batch. Conversely, if the batch is too firm and brittle, cooking the next batch several degrees lower will soften the resulting product.

2. **STIR IN SALT AT THE END OF COOKING.** Salt should be added at the end of cooking. Cooking a batch with salt contributes to inversion, making the batch softer and more hygroscopic; it may even hinder the crystallization of the sugar. If the salt is added after the batch begins to cool, however, it tends not to dissolve, leaving discernible crystals of salt in the candy. The salt should be added immediately after cooking so as to prevent excessive inversion, but while the batch is hot enough that the salt will dissolve.

3. **POUR THE SYRUP ONTO A MARBLE SLAB AND ALLOW IT TO COOL TO APPROXIMATELY 50°C/120°F.** Allowing the syrup to cool prior to agitation is one of the most crucial steps in the fondant/fudge technique to create a smooth texture in the finished product. Leaving the cooked syrup undisturbed on the marble slab cools it quickly so agitation can begin. If the syrup is agitated while it is still hot, the result will be the formation of fewer, larger crystals. Large crystals give the confection a sugary, grainy mouthfeel that is not desirable. Cooling the syrup to approximately 50°C/120°F causes the formation of many small crystals during agitation, which provides the desired smooth mouthfeel.

4. **PLACE THE REQUIRED FLAVORINGS, SEEDING MATERIALS, AND INCLUSIONS ON TOP OF THE SYRUP.** Flavorings such as chocolate, peanut butter, or extracts, and inclusions such as nuts are placed on top of the syrup as it cools. Cooking acidic flavorings, such as fruit purées, with the syrup will cause inversion of some of the

sugar, resulting in a soft, sticky candy that will be difficult to crystallize as required. If exposed to the high heat of cooking, other types of flavors, such as extracts or manufactured flavors, can flash off, leaving little flavor in the finished mixture. For this reason it is preferable to pour them onto the syrup as it cools. Often a small amount of previously made fondant can be added as the syrup cools to seed it and promote the formation of small sugar crystals. Seeding the syrup in this way considerably reduces the amount of agitation required and encourages the formation of the desirable small sugar crystals.

5. **AGITATE THE MIXTURE BY TABLING UNTIL CRYSTALLIZED.** Once cooled to approximately 50°C/120°F, the syrup is ready to be agitated to induce crystallization. Proper agitation on the marble is another crucial step to creating a smooth texture in the finished product. Once begun, agitation should be constant in order to create the proper smooth texture. Intermittent agitation induces the formation of fewer, larger crystals that cause a sugary, grainy texture. Constant agitation yields the desired result by creating many small crystals that are smooth on the palate. In the case of fudge, knowing when to stop agitation can require some experience. It should be agitated until the syrup begins to turn creamy and slightly opaque, and until the texture shortens slightly. Typically, this may require five to ten minutes of manual agitation with a relatively small batch. If fudge is overagitated, it can crystallize on the marble, which makes it impossible to spread into the

LEFT: *Like fondant, fudge is agitated while cooling, to create a system of small sugar crystals.* RIGHT: *Once cooled, fudge is spread into a frame to create a slab of uniform thickness for subsequent cutting (see step 6 of the technique).*

LEFT: *A marble slab cools fondant syrup quickly and evenly, preventing premature crystallization as the syrup cools (see step 3 of the technique).* CENTER: *Agitating the cooled fondant syrup promotes even formation of small crystals, which give the product a smooth mouthfeel.* RIGHT: *The fondant's cooled crystalline structure traps air when agitated, yielding a soft and creamy product (see step 5 of the technique).*

frame. If it is underagitated, it is likely to form large sugar crystals and exhibit undesirable graininess. Fondant, on the other hand, is agitated until it fully crystallizes on the table. There is little doubt when this happens: the syrup changes from a thick, sticky, elastic substance to a short-textured, rather hard mass.

6. **DEPOSIT FUDGE IN A FRAME AND ALLOW IT TO CRYSTALLIZE UNTIL SET. STORE FONDANT OVERNIGHT IN A SEALED CONTAINER.** Fudge is usually spread into a frame or pan, where it is allowed to complete crystallization, after which it can be cut. This usually takes less than an hour, but sometimes it is best to allow it to crystallize overnight before cutting. This is particularly so with fudges that include a frappe. When fondant is freshly made it is very firm and short textured. Usually it is stored in an airtight container overnight, a process known as ripening. During this time, fondant's system of sugar crystals surrounded by syrup reaches equilibrium. As a result, the fondant has a softer, more malleable texture. Although not imperative for confectionery applications, allowing fondant to ripen before use makes it easier to handle.

FUNCTION OF INGREDIENTS IN FONDANT AND FUDGE

While fondant and fudge are produced by the same method, fondant contains only sugar, while any ingredient list for fudge includes dairy products, fats, and paste or solid flavorings and garnish.

Sugar

Fondant and fudge consist largely of sucrose. The high sugar content is necessary to permit the crystallization that defines these confections. Sucrose is not well suited to act as the only sugar in these confections, however. Unless doctoring agents are added, sucrose will crystallize very rapidly, giving the confections a grainy texture.

Glucose syrup

Almost every formula for fudge and fondant contains glucose syrup as a doctoring agent. Glucose syrup slows the formation of sugar crystals and helps create a smooth texture. Insufficient glucose syrup can permit large sugar crystals to form, resulting in a grainy texture. Excessive glucose syrup gives fudge an elastic, gummy texture, rather than the short texture that is desired. Because the glucose syrups most commonly used are much less sweet than sucrose, the addition of glucose syrup also helps reduce the sweetness of fudge. Too much glucose syrup, however, can prevent the requisite crystallization and results in a bland flavor in the finished confections.

Invert sugar

Invert sugar is frequently used in fudge, in conjunction with glucose syrup, to control crystallization and help create the small sugar crystals that result in a smooth texture. In addition to its doctoring properties, invert sugar acts as a humectant, helping to retain moisture in the finished product and prevent the fudge from drying out, which it is prone to do. Invert sugar also has preservative effects due to its high degree of solubility, which lowers the water-activity level, resulting in a longer shelf life for the finished product. Used in excess, invert sugar gives fudge an excessively soft, pliable texture that is undesirable, and its extreme sweetness leads to an overly sweet confection.

Dairy

Milk products are used in fudge to contribute to flavor, hold fat in the emulsion, and provide body. Various types of milk products may be used in fudge, ranging from evaporated or condensed milk to whole milk or heavy cream. Because evaporated and condensed milk have had much of their water removed during processing, they require a shorter cooking time. Fresh dairy products are valued for their superior flavor. Each dairy product has its own unique advantages. (For specific information on dairy products, see page 8.)

Fats

Fats in fudge formulas, which may come from milk or cream, added butter, chocolate, or other flavoring ingredients such as nut pastes, contribute to fudge's short texture, rich mouthfeel, ease of handling, and—if butter or cocoa butter is used—its flavor. Lower-cost, lesser-quality fudge may contain other hard fats that do not contribute flavor but are added purely to affect texture. Because the noncrystalline portion of fudge is a fat-in-water emulsion, excessive fat content leads to an oily appearance and mouthfeel due to separation. Most often the fat separates as the sugar begins to crystallize during agitation. Insufficient fat produces fudge that lacks richness and does not exhibit a good melting characteristic in the mouth.

Flavorings

Fudge may be flavored with any number of ingredients, including chocolate, maple syrup, brown sugar, peanut butter, and praline paste. The flavoring ingredient used will affect the formulation due to its own characteristics, such as sugar type and content, fat type and content, acidity, and moisture content. Because of this, it is not practical to provide a master formula for fudge that will only then be flavored in various ways; each formula must represent an interaction between all of the ingredients in the formula. Inclusions such as nuts, dried fruit, and marshmallows may be added as desired—typically after cooking and before agitation, in order to keep them discrete from the fudge. Inclusions provide an opportunity for the confectioner to create unique signature products using basic formulas.

Frappe

An optional ingredient in fudge is a frappe. Frappe is used as an aerator in confections, much the way meringue is used to lighten baked goods. The aerators in the frappe itself may be albumen, usually dried and not from fresh egg white, gelatin, or, in large production or manufacturing, soy protein. In all cases, to make the frappe, the aerator is combined with cooked sugar and whipped to incorporate air. The frappe can be made in quantity ahead of time and stored until use. The desired amount is scaled out as needed and is added after the mixture is cooked and before agitation has begun. The addition of a frappe makes for a lighter-textured candy. In addition to lightening the fudge, frappes tend to help control crystallization, acting as a doctoring agent and resulting in a smoother, softer product. Because air is incorporated when it is whipped, fudge made with a frappe dries out more readily than fudge made with no frappe. For that reason, extra care must be taken to wrap or store the product in a way that will protect it from moisture loss.

Premade fondant

Another optional ingredient that is often incorporated into fudge and fondant formulations is premade fondant. Because fondant is a system containing very small sugar crystals, it acts as a seed when added to fudge, causing the fudge to crystallize more readily and with the minute crystals necessary for smooth texture. When using fondant to seed fudge, add it only after the fudge mixture has been cooked and has begun to cool on the marble. This timing ensures that the fondant crystals do not dissolve—which would defeat the purpose of using the premade fondant. A small percentage of fondant is sufficient to seed fudge and initiate crystallization.

CHERRY CORDIALS

Cherry cordials can be made by a variety of techniques, including starch molding, shell molding, panning, and simple dipping. Regardless of the method, the concepts are identical: a preserved cherry is covered with heated fondant to which invertase has been added. The fondant-covered cherry is then enclosed in a chocolate coating. Over a period of days, the sugar in the fondant is broken down by the invertase and combines with the moisture in the cherry, resulting in a liquid center and a cherry inside a chocolate shell. Cherries used for cordials must be preserved, either with spirits, as in brandied cherries, or with sugar and preservatives, as in maraschino cherries. Fresh cherries may not be used; they could not have a satisfactory shelf life. In the production of cherry cordials, it is important to allow time for the fondant to liquefy before selling or serving them. This may take from five days to three weeks, depending on the amount of invertase used, the temperature at which the cordials are stored, and the liquid content of the fondant and the cherry. When dipping by hand, it is important to put each fondant-coated cherry onto a chocolate disc prior to dipping, in order to prevent the syrup from leaking through the bottom as the fondant liquefies.

INVERTASE

When fondant is used as a center, the enzyme invertase can be added to it in order to cause it to soften or liquefy after the fondant has been dipped in chocolate. When a formulation includes invertase, centers can be made up that are firm enough to handle easily, but that after dipping in chocolate, soften to create a creamier texture. A naturally occurring enzyme derived from yeast, invertase inverts sucrose, creating dextrose and fructose. (See Inversion, page 216.) Due to the high solubility of invert sugar, the fondant then softens or liquefies as the inverted sugar dissolves in the moisture present in the center.

To use invertase with fondant centers, heat the fondant to 70°C/158°F, or slightly higher, then add flavoring. The invertase is then added to the flavored fondant, provided the temperature of the fondant is not significantly above 70°C/158°F. Heating invertase above 71°C/160°F damages it, hindering its activity. Heating it above 82°C/180°F destroys it, so it is important to control the temperature of the enzyme. Invertase is effective in very small quantities. In retail confectionery, 45 to 140 grams/2 to 5 ounces of invertase are used to soften 45 kilograms/100 pounds of fondant, or 0.1 to 0.3 percent invertase to the weight of the fondant. In small batches, 0.75 to 1.50 grams/¼ to ½ teaspoon is sufficient to work on 1 kilogram/2 pounds of fondant. Adding more invertase speeds up the reaction but does not change the final result. The speed of the reaction is also affected by the temperature at which the centers are stored. Like most reactions, inversion occurs more rapidly at warm temperatures than at cooler ones. Invertase-treated confections should be stored at warm room temperature in order to allow the centers to soften efficiently.

Centers treated with invertase must be dipped the same day they are made, as the inversion begins immediately, and the centers may become too soft to handle. In confections with higher-liquid centers, such as cherry cordials, the fondant combines with the moisture in the cherry and liquefies completely over several days. In confections with lower-moisture centers, such as mint fondants, the fondant will become soft and creamy, but will not completely liquefy.

LIQUOR CORDIALS

Several methods are used for making liquor cordials, including filling lined chocolate molds and capping them; filling hollow chocolate shells and allowing the syrup to form a skin of crystallization before completing the chocolate coating; and employing the classic technique of starch molding. (See Starch-Molding Technique and Theory, page 90.) Starch-molded liquor cordials are classic confections in which a thin eggshell of crystalline sugar surrounds syrup that is generously flavored with a spirit or liqueur; the piece is then enrobed in chocolate. When bitten, the chocolate and sugar shell give way to release the liquid center. Eating the finished confection is a singular experience.

Various liqueurs or spirits can be used with this technique, although it may be necessary to adjust the temperature to which the sugar is cooked: when using unsweetened spirits that are 80 proof or above, cook the sugar to a slightly higher temperature than you would if using a liqueur that contains sugar and is lower proof, like Grand Marnier or anisette. When using sweetened liqueurs, cook the sugar to a lower temperature in order to prevent the formation of a thick skin of crystallization. As a general rule, if the crystallized skin is too thick, cook the next batch to a slightly lower temperature; if the skin is too thin, cook the next batch to a slightly higher temperature. A difference of 2 or 3 degrees centigrade/36 or 37 degrees Fahrenheit results in a noticeable difference in the finished product. When cooking the syrup, take care to apply good sugar-cooking procedures: clean the sides of the sugar pot, skim impurities from the surface of the sugar, avoid excessive agitation, and carefully monitor the final temperature of the syrup.

LIQUOR CORDIALS (USING HOLLOW TRUFFLE SHELLS)

Using hollow truffle shells to produce liquor chocolates relies on ready-made truffle shells. Use of these convenient products eliminates the need for starch molding. However, the size and shape of the finished product is dependent on the size and shape of the shells available. When using truffle shells for liquor chocolate production, boil a concentrated syrup exactly as you would for starch molding. After the syrup is boiled to the desired degree, remove it from the heat and add a measured amount of spirit or liqueur. Then leave the flavored syrup to cool without agitation, covering it with a clean, damp cloth to prevent moisture loss that could cause crystals to form. Once the syrup is cooled to 26°C/78°F, deposit it in the shells, and leave the filled shells undisturbed overnight. The syrup exposed to the air forms a thin skin of sugar crystals, which seal the syrup in the shell. The filled, sealed shells are then ready to be capped with chocolate, dipped in chocolate, and decorated as desired. As a shortcut— or remedy, if the sugar fails to crystallize—float a thin layer of melted tempered cocoa butter on top of the syrup in the shells and allow it to set in order to seal the opening. Shells sealed in this manner may be dipped and decorated as usual once the cocoa butter sets.

LEFT: *Prepared syrup, flavored generously with a liquor or cordial, is piped into hollow truffle shells and allowed to set overnight.* RIGHT: *Having been left to crystallize, the candies form a thin sugar skin, which prepares them for capping with tempered chocolate.*

LIQUOR CORDIALS

To make starch-molded liquor cordials:

1. **PREPARE STARCH MOLDS IN THE DESIRED SHAPES. (SEE STARCH-MOLDING TECHNIQUE AND THEORY, PAGE 90.)** Any shape imprinter desired may be used to make liquor cordials. Because of the centers' liquid state and relatively high alcohol content, however, excessively large shapes should be avoided, as they are difficult to eat in the requisite one bite. Any time starch is used for molding, it should be well dried prior to use. It is especially imperative that the starch be dried when making liquor cordials. Properly dried starch repels moisture, thus holding the syrup in the prepared cavities. Starch that is not adequately dried attracts moisture, absorbing the syrup before the syrup can form a skin of crystallization.

2. **COMBINE THE SUGAR AND WATER, AND BOIL THE SYRUP TO A SUPERSATURATED STATE WITHOUT ADDING A DOCTORING AGENT.** Any type of doctoring agent prevents the crystallization on which these confections depend. The temperature to which the syrup is cooked, as well as sugar-cooking technique, is particularly critical for making cordials. An accurate thermometer is a must, as are cleaning the sides of the saucepan and skimming impurities from the syrup as it cooks. Syrup that is overcooked is prone to excessive crystallization, resulting in thick shells or fully crystallized pieces. Conversely, syrup that is undercooked will not form the skin of crystallization that makes these confections possible to handle. Impurities or sugar crystals can induce excessive crystallization of the sugar, causing crystallization of the finished pieces.

3. **ADD A MEASURED QUANTITY OF WARM SPIRIT OR LIQUEUR TO THE SYRUP, WITH MINIMAL AGITATION AND WITHOUT ALLOWING THE SYRUP TO COOL SIGNIFICANTLY.** Excessive agitation while cooling can promote crystallization of the syrup, resulting in fully crystallized centers rather than liquid-filled ones. The liquor brings the syrup just above the point of saturation at room temperature—72° Brix on a refractometer—which allows just a skin of crystallization to form, containing the saturated-syrup center.

4. **DEPOSIT THE FLAVORED SYRUP IN THE PREPARED STARCH MOLDS AND COVER IT BY SIFTING A LAYER OF THE DRY STARCH OVER THE FILLED MOLDS. THE MOLDS SHOULD BE FULLY BURIED IN THE DRY STARCH.** The dry starch surrounding the syrup performs two vital functions: it acts as a mold, holding the syrup in the desired shape, and the starch granules act as nuclei onto which the sugar will crystallize to form the skin of the centers. It is important to sift the dry starch over the deposited syrup so that the syrup will form crystals on all its surfaces, including the top.

5. **AFTER FOUR TO FIVE HOURS, TURN THE SHELLS OVER IN THE STARCH TO ENSURE EVEN CRYSTALLIZATION.** Turning the cordials is an optional step, but without it the side that is up in the starch will form a relatively thin shell of sugar crystals and will be more delicate to handle and dip in chocolate. Turning the cordials too early results in excessive breakage of the centers, but waiting too long to turn them defeats the purpose of doing so. The centers should be turned as soon as they can be very gently handled without breaking.

6. **TWENTY-FOUR HOURS AFTER DEPOSITING THE SYRUP, REMOVE THE FINISHED CENTERS AND BRUSH OFF THE EXCESS STARCH WITH A SOFT, DRY PASTRY BRUSH.** The cordials are ready to be dipped in chocolate and decorated as desired, but they must always be handled gently to prevent breaking the thin shell of crystallization.

PRALINES

The word *praline* has various meanings, depending on the culture using it. Many Europeans use the word *praliné* in the way that Americans refer to chocolates—to mean a center dipped or enrobed in chocolate. Praline paste is a paste made of ground hazelnuts and caramel. *Praline,* pronounced PRAH-leen in some areas of the southern United States, particularly New Orleans, refers specifically to a confection consisting of pecans and a crystallized brown sugar mixture. Pralines are made by cooking the brown sugar mixture with pecans, cooling it slightly, and then stirring

Pralines, being portioned here with a scoop, set with a slightly coarser crystalline structure than fudge or fondant.

it to induce crystallization. As the mixture begins to crystallize, the pralines are deposited by spoon or scoop on parchment paper and allowed to continue crystallizing. Because of the method of crystallization, pralines tend to have a more crystalline texture than fudge or fondant and are best when consumed while fresh. Pralines are of Creole origin and have come to be synonymous with the hospitality of New Orleans.

OTHER CRYSTALLINE CONFECTIONS

Two other old-fashioned and well-known, if somewhat specialized, crystalline confections are rock candy and maple candy. While the confectioner may not find it economically practical to make either, each is a superb example of the effect of agitation on the crystallization of sugar.

Rock candy

To make rock candy, a supersaturated sugar solution is boiled without the addition of a doctoring agent and is then carefully poured into a meticulously cleaned vessel. Strings or sticks that have been seeded with granulated sugar are suspended in the syrup, and the whole assembly is covered and left undisturbed for a period of two to three weeks. During that time, large sugar crystals form on the seeds, resulting in the characteristic rock-candy appearance. The strings or sticks with the crystals on them are then removed from the syrup, rinsed briefly in cold water, and allowed to dry. Rock candy is an example of the formation of large crystals due to little or no agitation. Larger crystals and a reduced processing time can be achieved by keeping the syrup warm during crystallization.

Pillow mints

Pillow mints are those delightful little melt-in-your-mouth mints that are seen in such disparate places as the cash register at a diner, or as wedding favors. They are crystalline sugar confections, and it seems probable that they, like their cousin fudge, were first made purely

LEFT: *Cooked sugar must be cooled nearly to room temperature before pulling.* CENTER: *Fully pulled sugar is opaque and light in texture.* RIGHT: *After they are cut, the candies are dropped into confectioners' sugar to crystallize.*

by accident. Pillow mints almost certainly resulted from hard candy that was formulated, cooked, and handled incorrectly, resulting in crystallization of the sugar, and the short, quickly dissolving texture that is the hallmark of these confections.

Pillow mints are formulated very much like hard candy, but they contain no glucose syrup. Instead, they are doctored only with cream of tartar, which inverts a small percentage of the sugar during cooking; this practice was not uncommon in nineteenth-century candy making. While invert sugar helps to prevent crystallization of the sucrose, it is not nearly as effective a doctoring agent as are most glucose syrups, so the formulation left the candies vulnerable to crystallization.

The mints are cooked to a lower temperature than hard candies. By cooking to a lower temperature, more water remains in the candy. When the water content of hard candies is high, they are far more likely to crystallize, so, by undercooking the candies, the stage was further set for crystallization.

The final straw that promotes crystallization in pillow mints is the agitation that is inflicted on the sugar during pulling. Pillow mints are pulled vigorously in order not only to incorporate air and create a light texture, but also to agitate the sugar, promoting crystallization.

When formulated, cooked, and handled properly, pillow mints will remain amorphous throughout the makeup process, and will crystallize into tender, light mints after resting for a day or two.

After being reheated to 63°C/145°F, maple fondant is deposited in molds and allowed to crystallize.

Maple candy

In earlier times, maple candy was one of the few confections available. The classic method for making it is to boil maple syrup in order to concentrate the sugar, which is primarily sucrose. After boiling, the syrup is cooled somewhat, then stirred to induce crystallization. It is then poured into molds to crystallize the rest of the way. When making maple candies by this method, timing is critical: the syrup must be poured after seeding has begun but before the crystallization process is complete. Pouring the syrup into the molds before adequate seeding has taken place produces candies with a very sugary texture. Waiting too long to pour the syrup into the molds results in a pot full of crystallized sugar. Allowing the syrup to cool prior to agitation helps create smaller sugar crystals than would be created if the syrup were stirred while it is very hot. Because maple candy contains no doctoring agents, the texture is usually somewhat coarse compared to that of fondant or fudge.

An alternative, and slightly more fail-safe method of making maple candy is to boil the syrup, concentrating its sugar, and then to agitate it on a marble slab, creating maple fondant. After the fondant has been made, it can be heated to 63°C/145°F over a water bath and then deposited in the molds. This method has the advantage of promoting the formation of smaller sugar crystals, giving the finished product a smoother texture. (See Maple Candies, page 300.)

DEFECTS IN CRYSTALLINE CONFECTIONS

DEFECT	CAUSE	REMEDY
FUDGE		
GRAINY TEXTURE	Sugar crystals too large	Allow syrup to cool to 50°C/120°F before starting agitation
		Agitate constantly until crystallization is well under way
		Clean sides of pot well to eliminate sugar crystals that could seed the mixture
		Increase doctoring agents in formula
ELASTIC, GUMMY TEXTURE	Excessive glucose syrup in formula	Decrease glucose syrup in formula
	Fudge not adequately crystallized	Agitate more on marble slab before depositing
FINISHED FUDGE TOO SOFT	Excessive moisture in fudge	Cook mixture to a higher temperature
	Too much invert sugar in formula	Reduce invert sugar in formula
	Insufficient crystallization	Use a lower percentage of doctoring agents; agitate more on marble slab before depositing
FINISHED FUDGE TOO FIRM	Too little moisture in fudge	Cook mixture to a lower temperature
	Excessive crystallization	Use a higher percentage of doctoring agents
OIL SEEPING FROM FUDGE	Too much fat in formula	Reduce fat by reducing butter, replacing some cream with milk, using lower-fat flavoring, and so on
	Too little moisture in fudge	Cook syrup to a lower temperature
FINISHED FUDGE DRIES OUT RAPIDLY	Fudge not protected from exposure to air	Wrap fudge immediately after cutting
	Insufficient humectant	Use more invert sugar or other humectant in formula
FINISHED FUDGE MOLDS IN STORAGE	Poor sanitation practices employed with finished product	Follow good food-handling practices to reduce contamination
	Water-activity level too high	Reduce water activity by using more invert sugar and/or glucose syrup

DEFECTS IN CRYSTALLINE CONFECTIONS

DEFECT	CAUSE	REMEDY
FONDANT		
GRAINY TEXTURE	Sugar crystals too large	Allow syrup to cool to 50°C/120°F before starting agitation
		Clean sides of pot well to eliminate sugar crystals that could seed the mixture
		Agitate constantly until crystallization is well under way
	Fondant deficient in doctoring agents	Increase doctoring agents in formula
FINISHED FONDANT TOO SOFT	Fondant not heated to a high enough temperature	Heat fondant to at least 60°C/140°F
	Too much doctoring agent in formula	Use fondant with fewer doctoring agents
	Flavorings used in fondant are acidic	Use flavorings with less acid; add flavorings only after heating and immediately before depositing
	Too much invertase in formula	Use less invertase in formula
FINISHED FONDANT MOLDS IN STORAGE	Insufficient dissolved-solids content	Increase percentage of glucose or invert sugar in formula
WHITE SPOTS ON FONDANT	Fondant overheated	Heat fondant only to 71°C/160°F
FONDANT WITH INVERTASE ADDED SETS, BUT SOFTENS TOO QUICKLY	Too much invertase in formula	Use less invertase in formula
FONDANT WITH INVERTASE ADDED DOES NOT SOFTEN	Insufficient invertase in formula	Use more invertase in formula
	Invertase was overheated	Do not heat invertase above 71°C/160°F
LIQUOR CORDIALS		
LIQUOR CORDIALS DO NOT SET	Syrup not cooked to a high enough temperature	Cook syrup to a higher temperature
	Too much liquor added	Add prescribed amount of liquor to bring finished product to 72° Brix
	Acidic flavorings used	Do not use acidic flavorings
LIQUOR CORDIALS OVERCRYSTALLIZED	Syrup cooked to too high a temperature	Cook syrup to a lower temperature, so that when liquor is added it brings it to 72° Brix
	Poor sugar-cooking procedure	Clean sides of pot well; skim impurities
	Mixture overagitated	Do not stir syrup after it reaches a boil; mix liquor with syrup by gently pouring, not by whisking
STARCH-MOLDED LIQUOR CORDIALS SINK INTO STARCH BED	Starch bed contains too much moisture	Dry starch beds in low-temperature oven for several hours

MINT FONDANTS

yield: **160 PIECES**

Mint leaves	40 leaves	40 leaves	<1%
Fondant (page 290)	1000 g	35 oz	100%
Brandy, crème de menthe, or water, for thinning	as needed		
Mint oil or extract	as needed		
Invertase (optional)	½ tsp	½ tsp	<1%
BATCH SIZE	1000 g	35 oz	100%
Dark chocolate, melted, tempered, for enrobing (optional)	as needed		

1. Using a food processor, grind the mint leaves with approximately one quarter of the fondant.

2. Combine the mint fondant with the remaining fondant. Heat over a water bath to 70°C/160°F.

3. Adjust the consistency, if necessary, using the brandy, crème de menthe, or water, and add the mint oil or extract if desired. The fondant should be thin enough to flow through a funnel without setting but not so thin that it will not set in the molds.

4. Add invertase if softened centers are desired.

5. Pour the fondant into a warm funnel. Deposit in oval molds 20 × 30 mm/ ⅞ × 1¼ in and allow to set, approximately 15 minutes. If necessary, the funnel may be rewarmed in hot water during depositing.

6. Remove the fondant from the molds and enrobe in the tempered dark chocolate, if desired.

   NOTE: When using invertase, enrobe the fondants immediately after setting.

FRUIT FONDANTS: Fruit purées or concentrates may be added to the fondant, but only after it has been heated. Because these flavors are acidic, they must not be heated with the fondant. If they are, the fondant will not crystallize properly after it cools.

LEMON FONDANTS: After heating the fondant, add 15 g/0.5 oz of lemon extract, 10 g/0.5 oz of frozen lemon zest, and 10 g/0.5 oz of lemon juice.

MINT JULEPS: Thin the fondant using bourbon whiskey. After dipping, finish the molded fondant with granulated sugar mixed with very finely chopped mint leaves.

POKER CHIPS

yield: **200 PIECES**

Premade fondant	1000 g	35 oz	100%
Flavoring (see Variations)	as needed		
Coloring, if desired	as needed		
BATCH SIZE	1000 g	35 oz	100%
Dark or milk chocolate, melted, tempered, for dipping, if desired	as needed		
Cocoa butter spray (optional; see Note)	as needed		

1. Heat the fondant over a water bath to 70°C/160°F. Remove from the heat.
2. Add the flavoring and mix to combine.
3. Deposit in silicone mats with 25-mm/1-in round holes or drop directly onto parchment paper using a fondant funnel.
4. Allow to crystallize until firm, about 10 minutes.
5. Dip partially or completely in tempered chocolate if desired.

   NOTE: For a longer shelf life, seal the finished pieces with cocoa butter spray after they have crystallized.

COFFEE POKER CHIPS: After fondant is heated, add 30 g/1 oz of coffee-flavored liqueur and 30 g/1 oz of coffee extract.

LEMON-THYME POKER CHIPS: After fondant is heated, add 30 g/1 oz of lemon juice, 1 Tbsp of chopped fresh thyme leaves, and 2 tsp of lemon zest.

PASSION FRUIT POKER CHIPS: After fondant is heated, add 60 g/2 oz of passion fruit purée, reduced by half.

RASPBERRY POKER CHIPS: After fondant is heated, add 60 g/2 oz of raspberry purée, reduced by half.

UFOS

yield: **160 PIECES**

FONDANT DISCS

Fondant (page 290)	1000 g	35 oz	98%
Coffee liqueur	15 g	0.5 oz	1%
Coffee extract	15 g	0.5 oz	1%
BATCH SIZE	1030 g	36 oz	100%

GANACHE

Heavy cream	125 g	4 oz	22%
Glucose syrup	30 g	1 oz	6%
Dark chocolate, unmelted, tempered, chopped	310 g	11 oz	60%
Cognac	30 g	1 oz	6%
Butter, soft	15 g	1 oz	6%
BATCH SIZE	510 g	18 oz	100%

Dark chocolate, melted, tempered, thinned with cocoa butter, for dipping (see Note)	as needed

TO MAKE THE FONDANT DISCS:

1. Heat the fondant over a water bath to 71°C/160°F. Remove from the heat and add the coffee liqueur and coffee extract.

2. Deposit in oval silicone molds 23 × 34 × 3 mm/ ⅞ × 1⅜ × ⅛ in. Allow to crystallize until set, about 20 minutes. Remove from the molds.

TO MAKE THE GANACHE:

1. Combine the cream and glucose syrup in a saucepan. Bring to a boil.

2. Pour the hot cream mixture over the chopped dark chocolate and let sit for 1 minute to allow the chocolate to melt.

3. Using a spoon or spatula, stir the mixture in vigorous small circles in the center of the bowl until it emulsifies.

4. Stir outward in larger circles to spread the emulsion throughout the bowl, checking to see that all of the chocolate has melted. If neces-sary, heat the ganache over a hot water bath to melt the chocolate. The temperature of the ganache should not exceed 34°C/93°F.

5. Stream in the cognac, stirring until the mixture is homogeneous.

6. Stir in the butter, taking care that no lumps of butter remain.

7. Agitate the ganache lightly by placing it on a marble slab and working it gently to induce crystallization.

TO MAKE THE UFOS:

1. Using a pastry bag fitted with a no. 3 round tip, pipe domes of ganache onto the fondant discs. Allow to set completely.

2. Dip each piece in tempered dark chocolate that has been slightly thinned with cocoa butter.

NOTE: See Thinning Technique and Theory, page 64.

ORANGE PINWHEELS

yield: **250 PIECES**

Fondant (page 290)	1000 g	35 oz	95%
Orange juice concentrate	50 g	2 oz	5%
Orange extract or flavoring	as needed		
Orange coloring	as needed		
Orange liqueur or water, for thinning	as needed		
BATCH SIZE	1050 g	37 oz	100%
Cocoa butter spray	as needed		
Dark chocolate, melted, tempered, for dipping	as needed		

1. Prepare starch molds using a pinwheel imprinter. (See Starch-Molding Technique and Theory, page 90.)

2. Heat the fondant over a water bath to 71°C/160°F. Blend in the orange juice concentrate, orange extract, and coloring to achieve the desired flavor and color.

3. Adjust the consistency, if necessary, using the orange liqueur or water. The fondant should be thin enough to flow through a funnel without setting but not so thin that it will not set in the molds.

4. Pour the fondant into a warm funnel. Deposit in the molds and allow to set. If necessary, the funnel may be rewarmed in hot water during depositing.

5. Remove the crystallized fondants from the molds and brush the excess starch off of each piece using a soft, dry pastry brush. Seal the tops of the molded fondant with cocoa butter spray.

6. Dip the pieces up to the top edges in the tempered dark chocolate.

FONDANT

yield: **APPROXIMATELY 1300 G/46 OZ**

Sugar	1000 g	35 oz	67%
Glucose syrup	200 g	7 oz	13%
Water	200 g	7 oz	13%
Premade fondant (optional)	100 g	4 oz	7%
BATCH SIZE	1500 g	53 oz	100%

1. Combine the sugar, glucose syrup, and water in a saucepan. Bring to a boil, stirring constantly.

2. Stop stirring. Cook to 117°C/243°F.

3. Pour the hot mixture onto a marble slab that has been lightly splashed with cold water.

4. Sprinkle cold water lightly on top of the syrup. Allow to cool to 50°C/120°F.

5. If using premade fondant to seed the syrup, place it on top of the syrup.

6. Using a scraper, agitate the mixture until the fondant crystallizes completely, turning it until it is a short-textured mass. This will take about 8 minutes with the added premade fondant and about 20 minutes without it.

7. Store the fondant in an airtight container overnight to ripen.

   NOTE: Cooking the mixture to 117°C/243°F creates a medium-texture fondant for confectionery use. If a harder fondant is desired, the temperature may be increased up to 125°C/257°F. For a softer fondant, cook to a lower temperature—as low as 113°C/235°F.

CHERRY CORDIALS, SHELL-MOLDED

yield: **125 PIECES**

Cocoa butter, colored red, melted (at 30°C/85°F), for lining molds (see page 83)	as needed		
Dark chocolate, melted, tempered, for lining molds (see page 58)	as needed		
Premade fondant	1000 g	35 oz	100%
Invertase	½ tsp	½ tsp	<1%
BATCH SIZE	1000 g	35 oz	100%
Brandy, for thinning	as needed		
Brandied cherries	125 cherries	125 cherries	

1. Rub the red cocoa butter into cherry cordial molds, covering only portions of the mold.

2. Line the molds with the tempered dark chocolate, using the shell-molding technique, page 77.

3. Warm the fondant to 28°C/82°F. Add the invertase, mixing thoroughly. Thin the fondant with the brandy, if necessary, to make it somewhat fluid.

4. Place a brandied cherry in each lined mold.

5. Pipe the fondant into the molds to within 3 mm/⅛ in of the top.

6. Seal the molds with the chocolate, using the shell-molding technique, page 77.

7. Follow the shell-molding technique, page 77, to allow the chocolate to set and to remove the finished pieces from the molds.

8. Store at room temperature for 7 to 12 days prior to use to allow the fondant to liquefy from the action of the invertase.

CHERRY CORDIALS, HAND-DIPPED

yield: **125 PIECES**

Fondant (purchased, or see page 290)	1000 g	35 oz	100%
Brandy, for thinning	as needed		
Invertase	½ tsp	½ tsp	<1%
BATCH SIZE	1000 g	35 oz	100%
Brandied cherries with stems	125 cherries	125 cherries	
Confectioners' sugar, sifted	as needed		
Dark chocolate discs made with a no. 8 round tip (see page 190)	125 discs	125 discs	
Dark chocolate, melted, tempered, for securing bases and for dipping	as needed		

1. Heat the fondant over a water bath to 70°C/160°F.

2. If necessary, thin the fondant with the brandy until is of a viscosity into which the cherries can be dipped.

3. Add the invertase, mixing thoroughly.

4. Holding the brandied cherries by their stems, dip into the hot fondant. Place each piece on parchment paper covered lightly with confectioners' sugar. The fondant may be kept over a hot water bath to keep it warm during this step.

5. When the fondant sets, affix the cherries to the chocolate discs either with a dot of melted chocolate or simply with the sticky fondant coating.

6. Holding the cherries by the stems, with the chocolate discs attached, dip each in the tempered dark chocolate.

7. Store at room temperature for 7 to 12 days prior to use to allow the fondant to liquefy from the action of the invertase.

CHERRY CORDIALS, STARCH-MOLDED

yield: **125 PIECES**

Dark chocolate discs, as bases	125 discs	125 discs	
FONDANT FILLING			
Premade fondant (purchased, or see page 290)	1000 g	35 oz	100%
Brandy, for thinning	as needed		
Invertase	½ tsp	½ tsp	<1%
BATCH SIZE	1000 g	35 oz	100%
Brandied cherries	125 cherries	125 cherries	
Dark chocolate discs (see page 190)	125 discs	125 discs	
Dark chocolate, melted, tempered, for securing bases and for dipping and finishing	as needed		

TO PREPARE THE MOLDS AND MAKE THE DARK CHOCOLATE DISCS:

1. Prepare starch molds using a dome imprinter. (See Starch-Molding Technique and Theory, page 90.)

2. Prepare the discs using the tempered dark chocolate and either a cutter or a stencil. The discs should be the same diameter as the starch molds.

TO MAKE THE FONDANT FILLING:

1. Heat the fondant over a water bath to 70°C/160°F.

2. Adjust the consistency, if necessary, using the brandy. The fondant should be thin enough to flow through a funnel without setting but not so thin that it will not set in the molds.

3. Add the invertase, mixing thoroughly.

4. Pour the fondant into a warm funnel. Deposit in the starch molds, filling them one-third full. It is important that the fondant be kept hot during depositing. If necessary, the funnel may be rewarmed in hot water during depositing.

5. Place a brandied cherry on top of the hot fondant in each mold.

6. Fill the molds the rest of the way with the hot fondant. Allow to crystallize until set, approximately 30 minutes.

7. Remove the crystallized fondants from the molds and brush the excess starch off of each piece using a soft, dry pastry brush.

8. Place each dome on a dark chocolate disc. Secure each dome with a small dot of tempered dark chocolate.

9. Using a dipping fork, dip each cordial in the tempered dark chocolate. After the chocolate has set, pipe a whirl of tempered dark chocolate on each piece.

10. Store at room temperature for 7 to 12 days prior to use to allow the fondant to liquefy from the action of the invertase.

LIQUOR CORDIALS, STARCH-MOLDED

yield: **150 PIECES**

Sugar	740 g	26 oz	57%
Water	260 g	9 oz	20%
Liqueur or spirit, warm (see Note)	300 g	10.5 oz	23%
BATCH SIZE	1300 g	45.5 oz	100%
Dark chocolate, melted, tempered, for dipping	as needed		
White chocolate, melted, tempered, for finishing	as needed		

1. Prepare starch molds using a bottle imprinter. (See Starch-Molding Technique and Theory, page 90.)

2. Combine the sugar and water in a saucepan and cook to 119°C/246°F. Clean the sides of the saucepan well while cooking, using a pastry brush and water. Remove any impurities from the surface of the syrup.

3. Remove the syrup from the heat. Gently blend in the liqueur or spirit. Take care that it is well incorporated, but do not overagitate.

4. Funnel the warm syrup into the prepared starch molds. Sift a layer of dry starch over the molds, completely covering them.

5. Allow to set undisturbed for 4 to 5 hours. Turn the pieces over to ensure even crystallization. (This step is optional, but recommended.)

6. Leave the cordials overnight to crystallize in the starch.

7. Remove the crystallized cordials from the molds and brush the excess starch off of each piece using a soft, dry pastry brush.

8. Dip the bottle-shaped cordials in the tempered dark chocolate. Using a paper cone, pipe two diagonal stripes of the tempered white chocolate across the necks of the bottles.

   NOTE: Unsweetened spirits should be warmed to 119°C/246°F. Sweetened spirits should be warmed to 117°C/243°F.

LIQUOR CORDIALS (USING HOLLOW TRUFFLE SHELLS): Cover the saucepan of hot flavored syrup with a damp towel. Allow to cool to 26°C/79°F. Fill hollow truffle shells with the syrup. Leave to crystallize overnight. Cap with chocolate and dip in tempered chocolate, as for truffles. (See Hollow-Shell Technique and Theory, page 110.)

ICED ROSETTES

yield: **160 PIECES**

GANACHE

Heavy cream	250 g	9 oz	25%
Glucose syrup	75 g	3 oz	8%
Dark chocolate, unmelted, tempered, chopped	600 g	21 oz	58%
Grand Marnier	50 g	2 oz	6%
Butter, soft	25 g	1 oz	3%
BATCH SIZE	1000 g	36 oz	100%

SYRUP

Sugar	7000 g	247 oz	70%
Water	300 g	106 oz	30%
BATCH SIZE	7300 g	353 oz	100%

TO MAKE THE GANACHE:

1. Combine the cream and glucose syrup in a saucepan. Bring to a boil.

2. Pour the hot cream mixture over the chopped dark chocolate and let sit for 1 minute to allow the chocolate to melt.

3. Using a paddle, stir the mixture in vigorous small circles in the center of the bowl until it emulsifies.

4. Stir outward in larger circles to spread the emulsion throughout the bowl, checking to see that all of the chocolate has melted. If necessary, heat the ganache over a hot water bath to melt the chocolate. The temperature of the ganache should not exceed 34°C/93°F.

5. Stream in the orange liqueur until the mixture is homogeneous.

6. Stir the butter into the ganache, taking care that no lumps of butter remain.

7. Place the ganache on marble and agitate lightly to induce crystallization.

8. Using a pastry bag fitted with a no. 3 star tip, pipe the ganache into rosettes on a sheet pan lined with parchment paper.

9. Allow the rosettes to crystallize for 30 minutes until firm, then place them in a crystallizing pan.

TO MAKE THE SYRUP:

1. Boil the sugar and water together, cleaning the sides of the pot well using a pastry brush and water. Adjust the density to 72° Brix, adding more sugar or water as necessary.

2. Cover the syrup mixture with a moist towel and allow to cool, undisturbed, until it reaches 23°C/74°F.

3. When the syrup has cooled, gently pour it into the crystallizing pan to cover the ganache rosettes. Leave undisturbed for 1 to 3 days, depending on the desired result.

4. Remove the rosettes from the syrup, and allow to dry on an icing screen overnight.

NOTE: For more information on crystallization, see page 68.

MAPLE CANDIES

yield: **250 PIECES**

Maple syrup	1970 g	70 oz	99%
Butter, to prevent foaming	30 g	1 oz	1%
BATCH SIZE	2000 g	71 oz	100%

TRADITIONAL METHOD:

1. Boil the syrup and butter in a saucepan to 115°C/240°F.
2. Remove the pan from the heat and allow to cool to 90°C/195°F.
3. Stir with a wooden spoon until creamy.
4. Reheat stirring constantly until fluid.
5. Pour into rubber maple candy molds and allow to crystallize before unmolding.
6. Wrap the candies to protect them from moisture loss.

METHOD VARIATION 1 ("BOB SYRUP"):

1. Boil the syrup and butter in a saucepan to 115°C/240°F.
2. Remove the pan from the heat and pour approximately 10% of the syrup onto marble.
3. Agitate the syrup on the marble until it is creamy.
4. When the syrup in the pan reaches 50°C/120°F, stir in the syrup from the marble.
5. Pour into rubber maple candy molds and allow to crystallize before unmolding.
6. Wrap the candies to protect them from moisture loss.

METHOD VARIATION 2 (MAPLE FONDANT):

1. Cook the maple syrup and butter in a saucepan over high heat to 112°C/234°F.
2. Pour the hot syrup onto a marble slab. Allow to cool to 50°C/120°F.
3. Agitate by tabling vigorously with a scraper until creamy, about 7 minutes.
4. Allow the syrup to crystallize undisturbed on the marble slab until hard, about 10 minutes.
5. (Optional) Seal the maple fondant in an airtight plastic container and allow to ripen overnight.
6. Heat the maple fondant over a water bath to 70°C/160°F.
7. Pour the fondant into a warm funnel. Deposit in maple candy molds and allow to set. If necessary, the funnel may be rewarmed in hot water during depositing.
8. Allow the candies to crystallize for 30 minutes, or until firm, before unmolding.
9. Wrap the candies to protect them from moisture loss.

CHOCOLATE FUDGE

yield: **132 PIECES**

Sugar	830 g	29 oz	41%
Milk	260 g	9 oz	13%
Glucose syrup	190 g	7 oz	10%
Invert sugar	120 g	4 oz	6%
Heavy cream	120 g	4 oz	6%
Premade fondant	300 g	11 oz	14%
Chocolate liquor, melted	180 g	6 oz	9%
Vanilla extract	10 g	0.5 oz	1%
BATCH SIZE	2010 g	70.5 oz	100%

1. Combine the sugar, milk, glucose syrup, invert sugar, and cream in a saucepan. Cook to 115°C/239°F, stirring constantly.

2. Pour the hot mixture onto a marble slab. Place the fondant, chocolate liquor, and vanilla extract on top of the syrup.

3. Allow the mixture to cool to 50°C/120°F. Using a scraper, agitate until the mixture turns creamy and opaque, about 8 minutes.

4. Deposit into a frame 12 × 12 × ½ in set on lightly oiled parchment paper.

5. Place another piece of lightly oiled parchment paper on top of the fudge. Using a rolling pin, flatten the top. Allow the fudge to crystallize before removing the parchment paper. Or, if desired, leave rippled for a more natural appearance. Crystallization will take about 30 minutes.

6. Cut into 25-mm/1-in squares. Wrap to prevent drying.

PENUCHE

yield: **132 PIECES**

Sugar	470 g	17 oz	23%
Light brown sugar	470 g	17 oz	23%
Heavy cream	310 g	11 oz	15%
Invert sugar	190 g	7 oz	10%
Milk	160 g	6 oz	8%
Glucose syrup	100 g	4 oz	5%
Salt	1 tsp	1 tsp	<1%
Pecans, toasted, chopped	190 g	7 oz	10%
Premade fondant	120 g	4 oz	6%
Vanilla extract	10 g	0.5 oz	<1%
BATCH SIZE	2020 g	73.5 oz	100%

1. Combine the sugar, light brown sugar, cream, invert sugar, milk, and glucose syrup in saucepan. Cook to 118°C/245°F, stirring constantly. Stir in the salt.

2. Pour the cooked batch onto a marble slab. Place the pecans, fondant, and vanilla extract on top of the syrup.

3. Allow the mixture to cool to 50°C/120°F. Using a scraper, agitate until the mixture turns creamy and opaque, about 8 minutes.

4. Deposit into a frame 12 × 12 × ½ in set on lightly oiled parchment paper.

5. Place another piece of lightly oiled parchment paper on top of the fudge. Using a rolling pin, flatten the top. Allow the fudge to crystallize before removing the parchment paper. Or, if desired, leave rippled for a more natural appearance. Crystallization will take about 30 minutes.

6. Cut into 25-mm/1-in squares. Wrap to prevent drying.

VANILLA FUDGE: Replace the light brown sugar with granulated sugar. Cook the batch with the seeds and pod from a split and scraped vanilla bean. Remove the pod after cooking.

MAPLE FUDGE

yield: **132 PIECES**

Maple syrup	1390 g	49 oz	56%
Heavy cream	350 g	12 oz	14%
Invert sugar	170 g	6 oz	7%
Glucose syrup	130 g	5 oz	5%
Walnuts, toasted, chopped	260 g	9 oz	10%
Premade fondant	170 g	6 oz	7%
Vanilla extract	20 g	1 oz	1%
BATCH SIZE	2490 g	88 oz	100%

1. Combine the maple syrup, cream, invert sugar, and glucose syrup in a saucepan. Cook to 118°C/245°F, stirring constantly.

2. Pour the cooked batch onto a marble slab. Place the walnuts, fondant, and vanilla extract on top of the syrup.

3. Allow the mixture to cool to 50°C/120°F. Using a scraper, agitate until the mixture turns creamy and opaque, about 8 minutes.

4. Deposit into a frame 12 × 12 × ½ in set on lightly oiled parchment paper.

5. Place another piece of lightly oiled parchment paper on top of the fudge. Using a rolling pin, flatten the top. Allow the fudge to crystallize before removing the parchment paper. Or, if desired, leave rippled for a more natural appearance. Crystallization will take about 30 minutes.

6. Cut into 25-mm/1-in squares. Wrap to prevent drying.

PEANUT BUTTER FUDGE

yield: **132 PIECES**

Sugar	790 g	28 oz	38%
Evaporated milk	280 g	10 oz	14%
Invert sugar	250 g	9 oz	12%
Heavy cream	100 g	4 oz	5%
Molasses	100 g	4 oz	5%
Glucose syrup	60 g	2 oz	3%
Salt	1 tsp	1 tsp	<1%
Peanut butter	360 g	13 oz	17%
Premade fondant	140 g	5 oz	6%
BATCH SIZE	1980 g	71 oz	100%

1. Combine the sugar, evaporated milk, invert sugar, cream, molasses, and glucose syrup in a saucepan. Cook to 117°C/243°F, stirring constantly.

2. Mix in the salt.

3. Pour the cooked batch onto a marble slab. Place the peanut butter and fondant on top of the syrup.

4. Allow the mixture to cool to 50°C/120°F. Using a scraper, agitate until the mixture turns creamy and opaque, about 8 minutes.

5. Deposit into a frame 12 × 12 × ½ in set on lightly oiled parchment paper.

6. Place another piece of lightly oiled parchment paper on top of the fudge. Using a rolling pin, flatten the top. Allow the fudge to crystallize before removing the parchment paper. Or, if desired, leave rippled for a more natural appearance. Crystallization will take about 30 minutes.

7. Cut into 25-mm/1-in squares. Wrap to prevent drying.

CHOCOLATE FUDGE WITH FRAPPE

yield: **132 PIECES**

Chocolate liquor	210 g	7 oz	17%
Dark chocolate, unmelted, tempered, chopped	110 g	4 oz	8%
Butter	20 g	1 oz	2%
Sugar	650 g	23 oz	47%
Milk	190 g	7 oz	14%
Invert sugar	40 g	1 oz	3%
Glucose syrup	40 g	1 oz	3%
Salt	1 tsp	1 tsp	<1%
Frappe (page 389)	110 g	4 oz	4%
Premade fondant	50 g	2 oz	2%
BATCH SIZE	1420 g	50 oz	100%

OPTIONAL INCLUSIONS

Walnuts, toasted, chopped, *and*	250 g	9 oz
Dried cherries, chopped, *or*	150 g	5 oz
Hazelnuts, toasted, chopped, *and*	250 g	9 oz
Dried apricots, chopped, *or*	150 g	5 oz
Macadamias, chopped, *and*	250 g	9 oz
Shredded coconut, toasted	75 g	3 oz

1. Combine the chocolate liquor, dark chocolate, and butter and melt over a water bath. Set aside.

2. Combine the sugar, milk, invert sugar, and glucose syrup in a saucepan. Cook to 112°C/234°F, stirring constantly. Remove from the heat and stir in the salt.

3. Pour the cooked sugar mixture into a large bowl. Allow to cool, undisturbed, to 90°C/194°F.

4. Add the frappe to the mixture, stirring to incorporate.

5. Add the melted chocolate mixture, stirring until it is incorporated.

6. Add the fondant and stir until the mixture cools to 70°C/160°F.

7. Add optional inclusions, if desired. (See Note.)

8. Deposit into a frame 12 × 12 × ½ in set on lightly oiled parchment paper.

9. Place another piece of lightly oiled parchment paper on top of the fudge. Using a rolling pin, flatten the top. Allow the fudge to crystallize overnight before removing the parchment paper. Or, if desired, leave rippled for a more natural appearance.

10. Cut into 25-mm/1-in squares. Wrap to prevent drying.

   NOTE: This fudge is very smooth and sweet. It benefits from inclusions.

PECAN PRALINES

yield: **45 PIECES**

Sugar	350 g	12 oz	25%
Light brown sugar	350 g	12 oz	25%
Heavy cream	180 g	6 oz	12%
Milk	100 g	3 oz	7%
Butter	90 g	3 oz	6%
Pecans, toasted, chopped	350 g	12 oz	25%
Salt	1 tsp	1 tsp	<1%
Vanilla extract	5 g	0.25 oz	<1%
BATCH SIZE	1425 g	48.25 oz	100%

1. Combine the sugar, light brown sugar, cream, milk, and butter in a saucepan and cook to 110°C/230°F while stirring constantly.

2. Add the pecans and salt and cook to 114°C/237°F while continuing to stir constantly.

3. Remove from the heat and add the vanilla extract. Allow to cool, undisturbed, to 100°C/212°F.

4. Using a wooden spoon, stir vigorously until the mixture begins to look creamy, about 45 seconds.

5. Using a no. 50 scoop, deposit the pralines on parchment paper. (If the mixture crystallizes too much in the pan, becoming too thick, warm briefly on direct heat while stirring to restore proper viscosity.)

6. Use as soon as possible after making. Pralines lose quality quickly in storage.

CHOCOLATE PEANUT PRALINES: Omit the butter and instead add 50 g/2 oz of cocoa powder and 60 g/2 oz of peanut butter to the mixture. Replace the toasted pecans with toasted chopped peanuts.

YANKEE PRALINES

yield: **45 PIECES**

Maple syrup	500 g	8 oz	17%
Sugar	350 g	12 oz	25%
Heavy cream	180 g	6 oz	13%
Milk	100 g	4 oz	9%
Butter	90 g	3 oz	6%
Walnuts, toasted, chopped	250 g	9 oz	19%
Dried cranberries, coarsely chopped	150 g	5 oz	11%
Salt	1 tsp	1 tsp	< 1%
Vanilla extract	5 g	0.25 oz	< 1%
BATCH SIZE	1625 g	47.25 oz	100%

1. Combine the maple syrup, sugar, cream, milk, and butter in a saucepan and cook to 110°C/230°F while stirring constantly.

2. Add the walnuts, cranberries, and salt, and continue to cook, stirring constantly, to 114°C/237°F.

3. Remove from the heat and add the vanilla extract. Allow to cool, undisturbed, to 100°C/212°F.

4. Using a wooden spoon, stir vigorously until the mixture begins to look creamy, about 45 seconds.

5. Using a no. 50 scoop, deposit the pralines on parchment paper. (If the mixture crystallizes too much in the pan, becoming too thick, warm briefly on direct heat while stirring to restore proper viscosity.)

6. Use as soon as possible after making. Pralines lose quality quickly in storage.

PILLOW MINTS

yield: **250 PIECES**

Sugar	2000 g	71 oz	83%
Water	400 g	14 oz	17%
Cream of tartar	1 tsp	1 tsp	< 1%
Red gel food coloring	as needed		
Peppermint extract	10 g	0.5 oz	<1%
BATCH SIZE	2410 g	85.5 oz	100%
Confectioners' sugar, for storing	as needed		

1. Combine the sugar and water in a saucepan.
2. Bring to a boil while stirring. When the sugar reaches a boil, add the cream of tartar.
3. Continue to cook without stirring to 132°C/270°F.
4. Pour onto a marble slab in two pools, one small and one large. Allow the sugar to cool for several minutes, until approximately 50°C/120°F, without disturbing.
5. Begin to work the sugar to ensure even cooling by turning it occasionally.
6. Add the red coloring to the small pool of sugar.
7. Add the peppermint extract to both pools.
8. When the sugar has cooled to approximately 40°C/100°F, pull the uncolored sugar until it is very light and white.
9. Pull the red sugar until it is slightly lightened.
10. Form the white sugar into a log, and make 4 stripes on the outside of the log using red sugar.
11. Pull into a rope about 1 cm/½ in in diameter. Cut the rope into 1-cm/½-in pieces using scissors. (See page 224.)
12. Store overnight or for several days if needed, in confectioners' sugar until the mints fully crystallize and become tender.
13. When the candy is completely crystallized, use a soft, dry pastry brush to brush off the excess confectioners' sugar. Package as desired.

9

The confectionery category of jellies includes commercial varieties such as jelly beans, gumdrops, pectin jellies, jujubes, Turkish delight, and gummies.

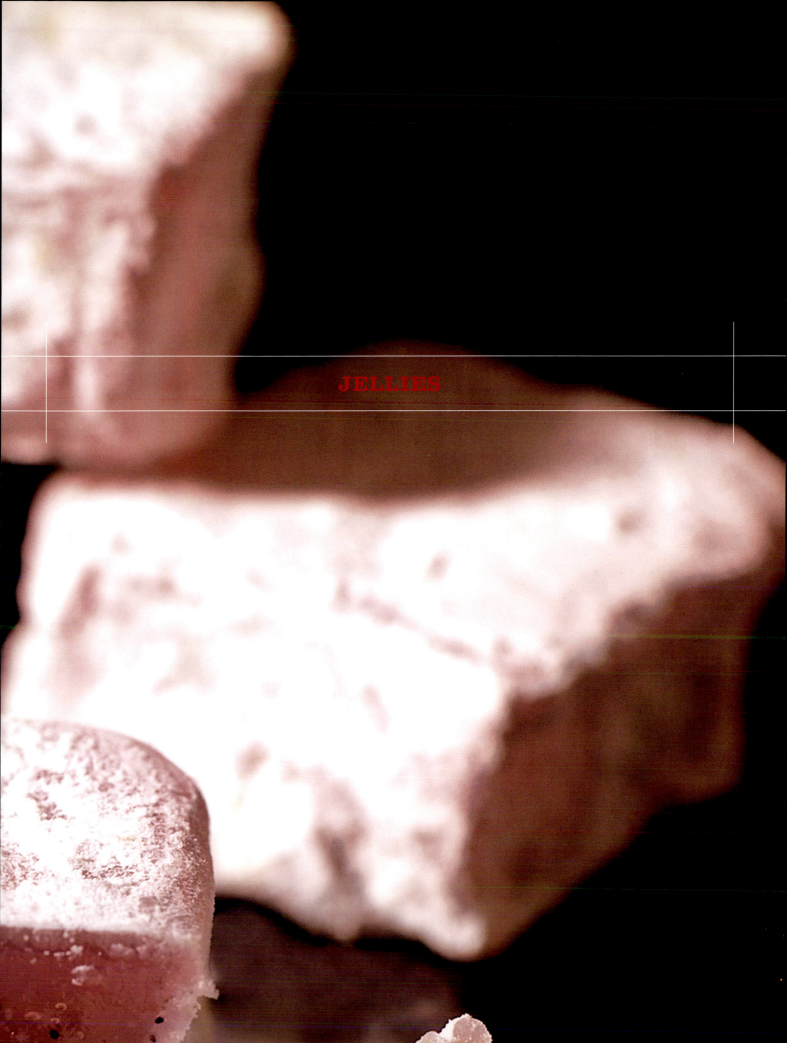

JELLIES

While there are noticeable differences among varieties of jellies, all of them share some common characteristics:

All jellies are supersaturated solutions bound into a stable gel. To ensure a good shelf life, all jellies must have sugar content above the normal saturation level of sucrose. A saturated sucrose solution at room temperature is only around 67 percent dissolved solids. At this level of saturation, the products would ferment and be prone to molding. Stability is not achieved until the solids increase to above 75 percent.

All jellies are flavored—or there would be little joy in eating them. A large range of flavors is used in jellies, from manufactured flavors to concentrated fruit juices or fresh purées and natural extracts. Acids are added as part of the flavor profile, as well as to aid in setting in pectin jellies. (For more information on the function of acids in jellies, see page 325.) The color of jellies may come from natural ingredients such as purées or juices or it may be added in the form of food-safe dyes.

All jellies require a binding agent that will form a gel, allowing the jellies to be molded, cut, and otherwise handled. Four primary binding agents are used in confectionery: pectin, gelatin, agar, and modified starch. Each has its own unique requirements, methods for handling, and texture, so each is best suited to particular uses and methods of production. In commercial manufacturing, a few other binders are used for jelly production. These are mostly gums, such as gum arabic, but they are of extremely limited interest to the artisan confectioner.

GELATIN JELLIES, OR GUMMIES

Gelatin is the binding agent of choice in making the ubiquitous gummy products, such as gummy bears. It is uniquely suited to this application due to the chewy, elastic texture it creates. (See Comparison of Various Binding Agents table, page 324.) Gelatin creates a thermoreversible gel that has an elastic texture and melts below body temperature; so gelatin jellies are chewy, but they melt in the mouth and release their flavor easily. In processing, gelatin is degraded by exposure to excessive heat; extended temperatures over 80°C/176°F will gradually denature the proteins in gelatin and reduce its ability to form a gel. The higher the temperature, the more rapidly the gelatin will degrade. Brief exposure to temperatures up to 100°C/212°F may at times be mandatory in production and will not significantly affect the gelatin, but prolonged exposure to high temperatures should be avoided.

Gelatin is also adversely affected by exposure to acidity, especially in conjunction with heat. If acid is added to gelatin jellies for flavor, it must be added as close as possible to the time of depositing. The other factor to avoid when using gelatin as a binding agent is exposure to protease enzymes, which are commonly found in tropical fruit such as pineapple and papaya. If fresh fruit juices or purées are to be used with gelatin, they should first be boiled in order to deactivate these enzymes. Once set, gelatin jellies can be remelted and will gel again upon cooling. This is a decided advantage in processing—and in making use of rework—as it permits a batch to be rewarmed and deposited without loss of quality. Gummy candies typically contain 4.5 to 7.5 percent gelatin, based on the weight of the finished product, depending on the bloom strength of the gelatin and the desired strength of the gel. Gelatin gummies are not likely to be an economically viable product for most artisan confectioners, but they can provide an opportunity to create unique signature shapes for a niche market.

The technique for using gelatin to make jellies utilizes the familiar technique for cooking sugar syrup to remove water, thus controlling the firmness of the finished product. The syrup is then cooled somewhat; gelatin, flavors, and color are added; and the confection is deposited in starch molds. The syrup contains glucose syrup in addition to the sucrose and water in order to prevent crystallization. Steps must be taken to protect the gelatin from exposure to excessive heat and to acid because it is damaged by exposure to these conditions. Flavorings for gelatin jellies must be low-moisture flavors in order not to soften the candies excessively. Starch molds are the only practical method of molding gelatin jellies because of their extremely sticky nature.

1. **HYDRATE THE GELATIN IN COLD WATER.** Gelatin must be hydrated before use in order to fully melt when heated. Gelatin that is not hydrated will not melt properly and will leave hard granules of gelatin in the finished product. Gelatin used for confectionery applications is usually hydrated in a minimum amount of water so as not to add too much moisture to the finished product, which would soften it and reduce its shelf life. While gelatin for pastry use is commonly hydrated in 8 parts water to 1 part gelatin, the ratio for confectionery use is on the order of 4 or 5 parts water to 1 part gelatin. In order to be certain that all of the gelatin is hydrated in the small amount of water, the water should be stirred as the gelatin is added so that the gelatin is evenly distributed. The water should be cold so that the gelatin absorbs it uniformly rather than being only softened and partially melted by it.

2. **COOK THE SUGARS TO THE DESIRED TEMPERATURE USING THE STANDARD SUGAR-COOKING TECHNIQUE. (SEE PAGE 219.)** The temperature to which the sugars are cooked is most crucial to the texture of the finished product. Any time sugar is cooked, the object is to dissolve it, then to remove some of the water, leaving behind the desired concentration of sugar. The higher the temperature to which the sugar is cooked, the more water is removed and the firmer the finished product will be. The firmness of the finished candy is substantially influenced by a temperature difference of only one or two degrees in the sugar. Gummy candies are typically cooked to a temperature of 120° to 135°C/248°F to 275°F in order to yield a dissolved-solids content of approximately 75 percent or higher upon depositing.

3. **REMOVE THE SYRUP FROM HEAT AND ALLOW TO COOL, UNDISTURBED, TO BELOW 100°C/212°F.** Allowing the syrup to cool to below 100°C/212°F before adding the gelatin prevents excessive denaturation of the proteins and ensures that the candy has the desired texture when it sets. If the syrup is cooled too much, however, it thickens excessively, making it difficult to mix in the gelatin and deposit the jellies in the molds.

4. **MELT THE GELATIN OVER A WATER BATH.** When it is added to the sugar, the gelatin should already be melted. This ensures that it fully melts in the water and doesn't leave hard granules in the finished candy and that it doesn't rob too much heat from the syrup, which would make depositing the jellies difficult. Gelatin should always be melted over a water bath to avoid scorching or damage from high heat. Do not stir the gelatin with a whip while melting, but stir gently with a rubber spatula. Stirring with a whip incorporates air bubbles into the gelatin, which remain in the finished jellies, diminishing their clarity.

5. **ADD THE MELTED GELATIN TO COOLED SYRUP.** The melted gelatin is stirred into the syrup to distribute it well. Again, this should be accomplished taking care not to incorporate air bubbles into the jelly.

6. **ADD FLAVORING, ACID, AND COLOR TO THE MIXTURE.** Flavors for gummies are usually highly concentrated artificial or "natural" varieties. (For information on manufactured flavors, see page 9.) These flavors are not heat stable. If they are added to very hot syrup, volatile compounds in the flavors will flash off, so it is important to add them after the syrup has cooled somewhat. In fruit-flavored gelatin jellies, acid is added to provide a contrast of flavor that is more authentic and interesting than a purely sweet confection. Citric acid is the most commonly used acid, although malic and tartaric acids may also be used. Color may be added either during cooking or along with the flavor and acid. Although it is not necessary to add the color late in processing, as it is for flavor, it is easier to accurately evaluate the color of the jelly once the requisite water has been removed by cooking.

7. **DEPOSIT THE GELATIN MIXTURE IMMEDIATELY INTO STARCH MOLDS.** Starch molds are the only efficient method for producing gelatin gummies, as gummies are too adhesive to pull away cleanly from other molds. (See Starch-Molding Technique and Theory, page 90.) Starch molds have the additional advantage of providing an economical way to produce a variety of shapes.

It is not necessary to buy all new molds to make a new shape, only to create a new imprinter to use in the existing starch. The mixture will become viscous as it cools, causing tailing during depositing. To keep the mixture fluid, dip the funnel into a boiling water bath and stir the gelatin mixture to maintain a workable viscosity.

8. **ALLOW THE GELATIN TO CURE OVERNIGHT BEFORE REMOVING IT FROM THE MOLDS.** The gelatin must fully set while the gummies are held in the starch molds. This is often done in a warm drying room, but it can also be accomplished at room temperature. The gelling strength of gelatin plateaus after around twenty hours, so allowing the gummies to remain in the starch overnight ensures that they will not lose their shape during subsequent handling.

9. **REMOVE EXCESS STARCH.** The cured gummies are taken from the starch, and the excess starch is removed. This can be accomplished through airflow, but care must be taken to avoid creating excess airborne starch, which can cause an explosion when exposed to an open flame. (See page 90.)

10. **APPLY A LIGHT COATING OF OIL, OR SAND THE GELATIN WITH SUGAR.** Most gummy products are coated with a light film of oil, which prevents adhesion, slows moisture migration, and provides gloss. Like all jellies, gummies may also be sanded with a layer of granulated sugar or sour sugar. Gummies to be sanded are generally lightly steamed first, to moisten their exterior, allowing for better adhesion of the sugar.

---

theory | **BLOOM STRENGTH**

Bloom strength is the measurement that is used to describe how firm a gel will be formed by a standard quantity of gelatin dissolved in a standard quantity of water. The term "Bloom" pays respect to the American scientist Oscar T. Bloom, who in 1925 patented a machine called a Bloom Gelometer that measures the strength of gelatin gels. Modern variations of this original machine are still in use today. Typical Bloom ratings run from 50 to 300 Bloom; the higher the Bloom rating, the firmer the gel will be that is formed. Higher Bloom gelatins not only require a smaller amount of gelatin in the formulation, they typically have a shorter texture, higher melting points, more neutral odor and flavor, and gel more quickly than lower Bloom gelatins, and so are desirable for most confectionery applications. The commonly available granulated gelatin in America is 250 Bloom, and is the standard used for gelatin in all formulas in this book.

PECTIN JELLIES

Pectin (see Comparison of Various Binding Agents table, page 324) produces a tender, relatively short-textured gel with a very pleasant mouthfeel. Pectin is the most demanding of the hydrocolloids used in jelly production, but it produces a superior product with an excellent texture and good flavor release. Pectin is used in making both high-quality jelly bean centers and the jellies that many artisan confectioners call by their French name, *pâtes de fruit*. The pectin of choice for confectionery use is high-methoxyl (HM), slow-setting (low-DM) pectin. Low-methoxyl (LM) pectins are chemically modified products that do not require a high sugar content to set, but do require the presence of calcium. This variety of pectin is used in low-sugar confectionery and will therefore not be considered in this book. The use of any pectin other than the slow-setting variety can cause production difficulties, as the pectin begins to gel very rapidly. LM pectin forms a gel that is not thermoreversible; the results for the confectioner can be many unfilled molds and a large container of set pectin jelly that cannot be used in rework. To form a proper gel, HM pectin requires a dissolved-solids content of 60 percent or higher, and a pH of approximately 3.0 to 3.6. Both of these conditions are easily achieved in confectionery; the dissolved solids of all confections must be above 75 percent to be shelf stable, and acidity not only permits the pectin to gel but adds flavor contrast as well. Pectin is degraded by extended cooking; it should therefore be cooked to the desired temperature as quickly as possible. Pectin is used at a rate of approximately 1 to 1.5 percent of the weight of the finished product. Pectin jellies may be made using manufactured flavors, but most artisan confectioners use fruit purées as a basis for these candies.

---

technique | theory | **PECTIN**

The technique for making pectin jelly, like that for producing other jellies, involves cooking sugar syrup to remove water and concentrate the sugar content to the required level. Unlike other hydrocolloids used in jelly making, pectin is cooked together with both the syrup and—when a purée or juice is used—the flavoring. Pectin is somewhat more fickle than other binding agents, and it will not bind if the sugar content and the pH are not correct. Even so, pectin has been used by generations of home cooks to make jellies, jams, and preserves from fresh fruit, usually without the benefit of a refractometer or even a thermometer. The steps to make these spreads are nearly identical to the technique below that is used to make confectionery jellies.

1. **MIX THE POWDERED PECTIN WITH FIVE TIMES ITS WEIGHT IN GRANULATED SUGAR.** Combining the powdered pectin with the granulated sugar helps to prevent the pectin from forming agglomerates when it is added to the liquid ingredients, which would result in hard lumps in the cooked jelly.

2. **WHISK THE PECTIN/SUGAR MIXTURE INTO THE LIQUIDS.** The pectin-sugar mixture must be whisked into the liquids to prevent lumps from forming.

3. **BRING THE MIXTURE TO A BOIL, STIRRING CONSTANTLY.** The mixture is brought to a boil to dissolve the pectin; stirring is essential to prevent scorching.

4. **ADD THE REMAINING SUGAR.** The remaining sugar in the formula is added while the mixture is on the heat; the mixture is stirred continuously to ensure that the sugar dissolves fully.

5. **CONTINUING TO STIR, COOK TO THE DESIRED TEMPERATURE OR DISSOLVED-SOLIDS CONTENT.** See step 2 in Gelatin Technique and Theory, page 317. In pectin jelly production, the dissolved solids may be determined either by measuring the temperature with a thermometer or by measuring the dissolved solids using a refractometer. The latter method is always more accurate. Because pectin is degraded cooking it for longer than thirty minutes, it is important to cook batches relatively quickly. This becomes more of a challenge when cooking large batches that necessarily take longer to cook.

6. **ADD ACID TO THE MIXTURE.** After the mixture reaches the required dissolved-solids content, acid is added to encourage formation of a gel. Lemon juice, citric acid, and malic acid are commonly used for this. If the acid were added earlier in the process, the pectin might gel prematurely, making depositing difficult. Pectin gels are not thermoreversible, and there is little recourse if the gel forms prematurely.

7. **DEPOSIT IMMEDIATELY INTO MOLDS OR FRAME.** Pectin jellies may be starch molded, produced in flexible molds, or poured into frames for slabbing and cutting.

8. **ALLOW TO SET.** When used in starch molding, pectin jellies—unlike gelatin jellies—may be removed from the starch as soon as they set. Similarly, slabbed pectin jellies may be cut immediately upon setting, and jellies poured into starchless molds may also be turned out as soon as they are set.

9. **FINISH AS DESIRED.** Pectin jellies may be sanded with sugar or coated with a light film of oil.

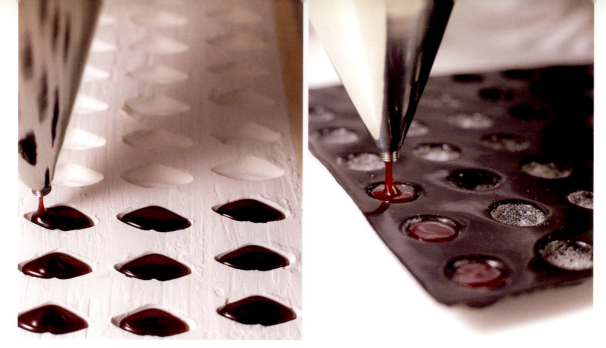

LEFT: *A starch mold is filled with prepared pectin syrup. It will be left undisturbed overnight to allow the candies to set (see step 7 of the technique).* RIGHT: *Pectin jelly syrup must be formed as soon as it is ready. Here, a syrup is funneled into fleximolds lined with a thin layer of sugar, for easy removal and cosmetic appeal (see step 7 of the technique).*

AGAR JELLIES

Agar (see Comparison of Various Binding Agents table, page 324) is a simple-to-use hydrocolloid that produces a thermoreversible clear gel with a very short texture. Agar gel does not melt at, or anywhere near, body temperature. Once gelled, agar jellies do not melt until they are heated to approximately 65° to 72°C/150° to 160°F. Agar's characteristic hysteresis—setting at 30° to 40°C/86° to 105°F and melting at a much higher temperature—makes it an easy gelling agent to use in confectionery, as there is little likelihood of a gel forming prematurely. The high melting point and short texture of agar jellies are not always popular with American consumers. However, the shortness can be moderated by using a fairly high percentage of 42-DE glucose syrup in formulation, to provide more body to the finished confection. Agar does not require acid or high dissolved solids to set, as pectin does, and is not adversely affected by protease enzymes, as gelatin is. It is, however, hydrolyzed by exposure to acid at high temperatures. Acidic flavorings such as fruit purées must be added after cooking is completed, or the agar will be degraded and will not gel properly. Agar is a powerful binding agent; it is used at a rate of approximately 0.5 to 1.5 percent of the finished confection. The strength of the gel that agar produces varies depending on the place of origin of the agar, and there is no specification for its strength, as there is for gelatin and pectin. Once the formulations for agar jellies have been perfected using agar from one source, it is advisable to continue to use agar from the same source.

technique	theory	AGAR

Because agar is derived from sea vegetables, it is suitable for use in vegetarian or vegan products. It cuts cleanly, making it ideal for citrus slices, and it reliably binds regardless of sugar content. Agar jellies are simple to make, and because the fruit purée is not cooked with the batch, but is added after cooking, the flavor is fresh and bright. The only drawbacks of agar are its melting point, which is high above body temperature, and its short texture, which some people find off-putting. Agar is a polysaccharide, similar to starch. The agar jelly technique involves cooking water and sugars together with the agar in order to remove water and to gelatinize the agar, exactly as must be done when cooking with starch. The major caveat regarding the use of agar is that it must never be boiled with acidic ingredients, as they will hydrolyze the agar, preventing it from binding.

1. **SOAK THE AGAR IN COLD WATER.** Agar is available in several forms: flakes, strips, and powder. If using any form other than powder, it is necessary to soak the agar for several hours in cold water to ensure that it will dissolve during cooking. If using powdered agar, this step may be omitted, but the dry powdered agar should be mixed with about ten times its weight in granulated sugar to ensure its even dispersion in the water.

2. **COMBINE THE SOAKED AGAR WITH THE SUGARS AND WATER IN SAUCEPAN.** When making agar jellies, it is necessary to begin with a large amount of water in order to dissolve the agar. Agar is not easily soluble in water; it requires in the range of fifty parts water for each part of agar in a formula to dissolve fully. Most of this water will be removed during cooking after the agar has dissolved.

3. **BRING THE MIXTURE SLOWLY TO BOIL, STIRRING.** Because agar does not dissolve easily in water, it is advantageous to heat it slowly, while stirring, allowing it time to dissolve fully. This step is especially crucial if the agar used is in strip or flake form. With these forms of agar, it may be necessary to strain the mixture, in order to remove any pieces of undissolved agar.

4. **STIR CONSTANTLY WHILE COOKING TO THE DESIRED TEMPERATURE OR DESIRED DISSOLVED-SOLIDS CONTENT.** See step 2 in Gelatin Technique and Theory, page 317, for a discussion of dissolved solids. It is necessary to stir the agar jelly constantly as it cooks, to prevent severe scorching.

5. **REMOVE FROM THE HEAT AND ALLOW TO COOL TO 70°C/158°F.** Once the agar has dissolved and the mixture has been cooked to the dissolved-solids content desired, it is necessary to allow the jelly to cool slightly before adding any acidic flavorings. Acids like those in fruit purées could hydrolyze the agar, which would reduce its capacity to form a gel.

6. **ADD FLAVORS AND AN ACID OR FRUIT PURÉE.** Once the mixture has cooled to 70°C/158°F, acidic flavorings—either fruit purées or flavoring with a separate addition of acid—can be added without hindering the agar's gelling capacity. If fruit purées are used, they should be warmed slightly so as not to cool the mixture suddenly and cause it to set prematurely.

7. **DEPOSIT IMMEDIATELY INTO FRAME, MOLDS, OR STARCH MOLDS.** Agar is suited to use with starch molding, molding in flexible plastic, or slabbing. Agar jellies begin to set at around 40°C/105°F, so it is important to deposit them while they are still well above this temperature. Because the gel formed by agar is thermo-reversible, it is possible to rewarm the jelly should it begin to congeal during depositing. However, care should be taken not to heat it excessively with the acid in it, which can degrade its gelling ability.

8. **ALLOW TO SET.** Agar-based gels set rapidly and can be cut and finished immediately upon setting. Or the agar jelly can be left in uncut slabs overnight if desired.

9. **FINISH AS DESIRED.** Agar jellies are most often finished with a sanding of sugar.

Agar jelly syrup is deposited into a mold or frame and allowed to set.

TOP, LEFT: *Agar jelly can be used to create confections with multiple layers. Here a thin sheet of jelly with frappe added is fitted into a mold to make citrus slices.* RIGHT: *A flavored and colored syrup is poured into the mold fitted with the first sheet of jelly.*

BOTTOM, LEFT: *The compound agar confection is removed and finished as desired. In this case, the outside is painted with orange food coloring to replicate the rind of a citrus fruit.* RIGHT: *Using a guitar ensures clean cutting and even portioning of finished jellies.*

STARCH JELLIES

Modified starches are very commonly used in the large-scale manufacture of jellies, but they are not as frequently employed by artisan confectioners. The main advantage of starch in manufacturing is cost: starch is inexpensive, and is typically used to make less expensive candies. It is possible, however, for artisan confectioners to make high-quality starch jellies. Turkish delight is one example. It is made with open-kettle cooking, poured into a slab, and cut without requiring a special drying room, as do starch-molded jellies. The use of superior flavors, layering techniques, and unique inclusions can raise the quality of starch-based jellies from the ordinary to the superior, the level sought by artisan confectioners.

While modified starches are commonly used in confectionery, owing to their relative ease of handling and the clear gels that they create, starches that have not been modified, called "native starches," can also be used if they are handled properly. Native cornstarch is traditional for making Turkish delight, and it is cooked with an acid to essentially modify the starch during the cooking process. The result is a starch jelly that remains relatively fluid during cooking and creates a clear gel.

Starches for confectionery use—known as thin boiling starches—are characterized by a fluidity number: 40, 50, 60, and so on. The number indicates how viscous the mixture will be during processing, with higher numbers indicating lower viscosity and easier flow for cooking and depositing. For most handwork, starch with a fluidity of about 60 is the best choice; the starch content of finished jellies made with this starch is approximately 10 to 12 percent.

| technique | theory | **STARCH** |

There are two primary methods for cooking starch jellies; the method used influences the texture of the gel that forms. To create a softer gel, bring the sugars to a boil with the water. Then make a slurry of the starch separately, and stream it into the cooking sugar without breaking the boil. This method is commonly used for casting jellies in starch molds. Starch jellies cast in starch molds require one to two days of drying time in a warm environment, and therefore are not practical or economical for most artisan confectioners. The following method—the time-honored technique for producing Turkish delight—produces a slightly firmer, shorter-textured jelly that is less likely to suffer from sweating during storage. Jellies made using this method can be slabbed, cut, and finished as desired.

1. **USING COLD WATER, MAKE A SLURRY OF THE STARCH.** Starch requires water for the starch to dissipate and gelatinize properly. Dispersing the starch is vital for ensuring full gelatinization and even distribution of the starch in the finished product.

2. **HEAT THE STARCH SLURRY TO A GENTLE SIMMER, STIRRING. SIMMER FOR 5 MINUTES WHILE STIRRING.** Simmering the starch fully gelatinizes it without the presence of sugars, which can inhibit that process. Starch that is not fully gelatinized leads to overly soft jellies that sweat during storage.

3. **ADD THE SUGARS TO THE BATCH, AND COOK, STIRRING CONSTANTLY, UNTIL THE BATCH REACHES APPROXIMATELY 78 PERCENT SOLIDS.** Due to the viscosity of gelatinized starch, care must be taken throughout cooking to stir the batch to prevent scorching. A dissolved-solids content of 78 percent ensures shelf stability and proper gel strength. Confectioners who make starch jellies regularly can evaluate the solids content of a batch by looking at the viscosity of the cooking jelly as it falls off of a spatula. While this method is effective in the hands of an experienced candy maker, the most accurate and consistent method for measuring the solids is to use a refractometer. This tool removes any question of dissolved-solids content and permits greater uniformity from batch to batch.

4. **REMOVE FROM THE HEAT. MIX IN THE COLORING, FLAVORING, ACID, AND INCLUSIONS, IF BEING USED.** Flavoring, acid, and inclusions are all added after cooking so as not to damage either the components or the starch. Flavorings contain volatile organic compounds that will flash off or be significantly changed by exposure to high heat, so they should never be cooked with the starch. If the jelly is cooked with the acid, the starch will hydrolyze, preventing proper setting. Inclusions should not be cooked with the jelly so that they don't absorb moisture, which would make them soggy.

5. **POUR THE MIXTURE INTO A FRAME. LET SIT OVERNIGHT AT ROOM TEMPERATURE BEFORE CUTTING AND FINISHING.** A minimum of six to eight hours of setting time is required for the starch to form a gel.

FUNCTION OF INGREDIENTS IN JELLIES

Binding agents

All of the binding agents used in jellies are hydrocolloids. These are large molecules that disperse in water and, under the right conditions, bind together to form a gel consisting of a continuous three-dimensional network that traps water and particles. The binding agent in jellies performs two major functions: it increases the viscosity of the system to a point that allows it to be molded, cut, and otherwise handled; and it helps to prevent crystallization of the sugar in the jelly by locking sugar molecules in place, preventing aggregation and crystallization.

A Gel Has Not Formed

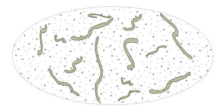

Unbound hydrocolloids in
a continuous phase of water

A Gel Has Formed

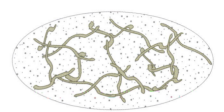

A gel is formed when hydrocolloids bind
to form a three-dimensional network that
traps water, preventing motion.

COMPARISON OF VARIOUS BINDING AGENTS

	GELATIN	AGAR	PECTIN	STARCH
SOURCE OF BINDER	Hydrolyzed collagen from animal sources	Red algae from Japan, New Zealand, Australia, Spain, and other areas	Extracted from fruit; commercial sources are apples and citrus skins	Cornstarch that is modified by hydrolyzing with acid
PERCENTAGE OF BINDER IN FINISHED PRODUCT	4.5% to 9%; bloom strengths vary	0.5% to 1.5%; gelling strength varies with source	1% to 1.5%	10% to 12%
TEXTURAL PROPERTIES OF JELLIES	Chewy, elastic; melt below body temperature	Short, clean breaking; do not melt below body temperature	Relatively short; dissolve readily in mouth	Smooth, firm, not as chewy as gelatin
UNIQUE REQUIREMENTS OF BINDER	Cannot be boiled; cannot tolerate excessive acid or tropical fruit enzymes	Cannot be boiled with acidic ingredients	Commonly used HM pectins require high solids and pH of 3.0 to 3.6; LM pectins require presence of calcium	Requires boiling to gelatinize; cannot be boiled with acidic ingredients
THERMO-REVERSIBILITY	Thermoreversible; gel sets and melts at approximately 30°C/86°F	Thermoreversible; gel requires 85° to 90°C/185° to 194°F to remelt	Nonreversible gel	Nonreversible gel
SETTING TIME/ CONDITIONS	Should remain in starch molds overnight at warm room temperature	Gels quickly, once cooled to below 40°C/105°F; once set, can be cut and finished immediately	Gels quickly, with variations, depending on type of pectin used; once set, can be cut and finished immediately	Sets in 6 to 8 hours at room temperature; is often dried for 48 hours or more before cutting

Sweeteners

SUCROSE

Sucrose (see page 2) is usually the majority sweetener in jellies, providing all the qualities it does in other applications: sweetness, bulk, tenderness, and good flavor release. As in other areas of confectionery, sucrose is often supplemented with other sweeteners to prevent crystallization and to alter the flavor profile. While it is common to add glucose syrup or other doctoring agents to jellies, it is not absolutely essential, due to the doctoring function already played by the binding agent used to make these confections.

GLUCOSE SYRUP

Glucose syrup (see page 4) is usually the second most prevalent sweetener in a jelly formula. It acts as a doctoring agent, contributes body, reduces sweetness, and retains moisture in the jelly. An excessive level of glucose syrup causes toughness, so glucose syrup should be limited to less than 60 percent of the total sweetener.

INVERT SUGAR

Invert sugar (see page 4) is a tenderizer, doctoring agent, and humectant. It may either be added directly to jelly formulas or created during cooking by the addition of acid. Cream of tartar is most commonly used for the latter purpose. Excessive invert sugar will lead to soft, overly sweet products.

Flavorings

The flavors in jellies may be produced by fresh or concentrated fruit juices or purées, extracts, or manufactured flavorings. (See page 9.) Higher-quality confections are usually created by using purées, extracts, or juices, but this is not always practical or possible. Starch jellies in particular are better suited to small amounts of concentrated flavorings than to the addition of fresh purées, due to the water content and acidity of purées. Where practical, it is appropriate for the artisan confectioner to use naturally occurring flavors such as purées or extracts rather than those created in a factory.

Acids

A variety of acids (see page 9) may be used in the production of jellies, ranging from cream of tartar, which is used as a doctoring agent in some starch jelly formulations, to citric, tartaric, and malic acids, which are added either to aid in creating a gel (in pectin jellies) or purely for flavor enhancement (in agar, starch, and gelatin jellies). When using acids for flavoring, it is critical to remember that acid hydrolyzes both sugar and starch when cooked along with them. Therefore, when using strong acids, add them after cooking is completed.

Coloring agents

As with flavors, artisan confectioners are best advised to use coloring (see page 9) from naturally occurring ingredients such as purées, rather than from manufactured products. There are times, however, when artificial color may be needed to augment an existing product, such as kiwi purée, which is discolored by exposure to heat, or to provide all of the color, as when synthetic flavorings are used. Most food dyes are not affected by the heat that develops in cooking jellies, so they can be added at any point during the process. Still, it is common practice to add them at the end of cooking, after the requisite water has been removed, in order to more accurately judge the amount of color required.

CANDIED FRUIT

Candied fruit is made by replacing the water in the cells of fruit with a supersaturated sugar solution. The syrup's low water-activity level prevents microbial activity and spoilage. Fruit preserved with sugar has been made since ancient times; originally honey or concentrated grape juice was used, and later refined sugar was employed. Candied fruit began as a method to preserve a harvest when there were few other options for preservation. Historically, candied fruit was used both as a confectionery treat by itself and for baked goods made for special occasions, such as Christmas pudding and wedding cakes. Today candying is not necessary to preserve fruit; better techniques for preserving produce abound, and much of the candied fruit on the market is of poor quality and artificially colored, offering little in the way of flavor. Like most crafts, however, there is a world of difference between mediocre mass-produced candied fruit and that created by skilled artisans. Candying fruit is not a technically demanding procedure, but it requires time, patience, and attention to detail. The process itself may take from ten days to several weeks, depending on the fruit used and how it is prepared. The possibilities are nearly endless for the type of fruit to candy, the adjunct flavoring ingredients to use, and the ways to present and use the finished product. As with any other branch of confectionery, there is both a science and an art to producing beautiful candied fruit.

Candying fruit requires not only an understanding of the process, but also flexibility. Candying is not a purely by-the-numbers procedure; the confectioner must evaluate the product and adjust the process accordingly. While small pieces of fruit may be successfully candied in just a few days, large pieces must be processed much more slowly in order to allow the sugar to fully penetrate the fruit. In general, a better result is always obtained from proceeding more slowly than from rapidly increasing the syrup's density. When in doubt, slow down, increasing the density less, or skipping a day of increase by simply boiling the syrup but not removing a significant amount of water.

When fruit is properly candied, it is uniformly translucent. Opaque spots on candied fruit indicate places that have not been penetrated by the syrup; fruit with such spots will spoil during storage. If such spots are observed during the process, bring the fruit to a boil with

LEFT: *Tomatoes, spaghetti squash, and cherries halfway through the candying process*

RIGHT: *Completely candied fruits and vegetables.* BACK ROW, LEFT TO RIGHT: *Pear, spaghetti squash, clementines, pineapple ring, and prickly pear.* FRONT ROW, LEFT TO RIGHT: *Papaya, Bing cherries, kumquats, and lotus root*

the syrup, but do not increase the density that day. If the spots are gone the next day, resume increasing the density; if they are still evident, boil again without removing water.

Seasonings may be added during the candying process. Whole spices such as vanilla beans, cinnamon, nutmeg, cloves, and coriander are best suited to this use. The spices can simply be added to the syrup on the first day and be kept with the fruit throughout the entire process. If too much spice flavor becomes evident, remove the spices from the syrup.

| technique | theory | **FRUIT CANDYING** |

The technique for candying fruit is a simple matter of macerating the fruit in syrup and boiling the syrup regularly to increase its sugar concentration. This is repeated until the syrup reaches 75° Brix, at which point the fruit is shelf stable due to the water-binding capacity of the sugar. The main areas of concern in the technique are that the syrup fully penetrate the fruit, thus preserving it, and that the syrup doesn't crystallize. The former is guarded against by increasing the density of the syrup slowly over time, and the latter is prevented by the addition of glucose syrup during the candying process.

1. **PEEL AND CUT THE FRUIT AS DESIRED.** The best fruit for candying is firm, slightly underripe, and free from blemishes and bruises, which can cause spoilage during processing. Very soft fruits, like strawberries, would disintegrate during candying and are therefore not used. Tropical fruits, such as pineapple, mango, and papaya, are especially good candidates for candying, as are pears and cherries. Fruit to be candied is usually peeled to facilitate the diffusion of syrup into the fruit. The fruit or vegetable is usually cut into slices or wedges, which provides more surface area for the syrup to penetrate. These are not hard-and-fast rules, however. Some items are better candied with the peel attached, to provide strength during the candying process; spaghetti squash is one such example. While it is more expedient to slice the fruit for candying, dramatic results can be obtained from candying whole fruit or vegetables like pears, pumpkins, pineapples, and kumquats.

2. **BLANCH THE FRUIT IN BOILING WATER.** Fruit to be candied should almost always be blanched to soften the cell walls to allow the exchange of syrup and water within the fruit. Blanching also helps to deactivate the enzymes that are responsible for browning and can contribute to spoilage. With softer fruit, such as melon, pineapple, and papaya, blanching is best accomplished by immersing the fruit in water that is already at a rapid boil, and boiling it for one to three minutes. Very firm fruits or vegetables, such as carrots, beets, and sweet potatoes, are better blanched by placing them in cold water and bringing both to a boil together. Soft fruits or vegetables that are prone to falling apart—such as spaghetti squash, rhubarb, and very ripe melon—are better left unblanched so as not to further soften them.

3. **PREPARE A 40° BRIX SYRUP.** Syrup for candying always starts at a low density, to allow the exchange of syrup and water to occur. If a heavier syrup is used in the beginning, the water comes out of the fruits' cells more rapidly than the syrup can go in, resulting in tough, shriveled fruit. A density of 40° Brix is a good starting point for the syrup.

4. **POUR THE HOT SYRUP OVER THE BLANCHED FRUIT.** The syrup is always hot when combined with the fruit. This lowers its viscosity and aids it in penetrating the fruit.

5. **PLACE THE FRUIT AND SYRUP IN A NONREACTIVE CONTAINER, AND PUT A WEIGHT SUCH AS A DINNER PLATE ON THE SURFACE OF THE SYRUP TO KEEP THE FRUIT IMMERSED.** The vessels used for candying must be made of nonreactive material such as stainless steel or ceramic. Other metals may impart an unpleasant metallic flavor to the fruit. It is necessary to weigh down the fruit to keep it immersed in order to prevent oxidation and spoilage. The container and weight used may be as simple as a water bath with a dinner plate or may be a specially designed candying tray with fitted screens to contain the fruit.

6. **STORE THE FRUIT AT WARM ROOM TEMPERATURE OVERNIGHT.** During candying, fruit is best kept at a warm room temperature of 25° to 35°C/77° to 95°F. Warmth reduces the viscosity of the syrup and allows it to penetrate the fruit more quickly. Because of the temperatures involved, sanitation practices are of the utmost concern throughout the process. If the syrup is below 60° Brix and will not be boiled for two or three days, it should be refrigerated during that time to prevent fermentation.

7. **DRAIN THE SYRUP FROM THE FRUIT. MEASURE THE DENSITY OF THE SYRUP USING A REFRACTOMETER.** Experienced confectioners candy fruit without the use of a refractometer, and it is possible to do an excellent job without using this instrument. For accuracy, however, a refractometer is the best way to ensure consistent results from batch to batch.

8. **INCREASE THE DENSITY OF THE SYRUP BY 5° BRIX EITHER BY BOILING IT OR BY ADDING SUGAR AND HEATING THE SYRUP TO DISSOLVE THE SUGAR.** The density of the syrup must be increased gradually, in order to allow it to penetrate the fruit fully and preserve it. The density of the syrup should be measured each day before boiling, and the density increased by 5° Brix every day. This is because, as water is released from the fruit, the density of the syrup falls. If the syrup is put away at 40° Brix, and the next day it measures at 35° Brix, it should be increased from the current 35° Brix to the new density of 40° Brix.

    There are two options for increasing sugar concentration: boiling to remove water, or dissolving more sugar in the syrup. Neither technique has an advantage over the other. If removing water, bring the syrup to a boil and skim as necessary, checking periodically with a refractometer until the desired density is reached. If adding sugar, heat the syrup to a boil, skimming as required, and then add sugar, making sure it dissolves, until the correct density is achieved.

9. **COVER THE FRUIT AND STORE AT WARM ROOM TEMPERATURE OVERNIGHT.** See step 6.

10. **REPEAT STEPS 8 AND 9 EACH DAY, BRINGING THE FRUIT TO A BOIL WITH THE SYRUP APPROXIMATELY EVERY THREE DAYS.** The gradual increase of sugar concentration continues each day. It is advisable to bring the fruit up to the boiling point in the syrup every few days to deter bacterial growth.

11. **WHEN THE SYRUP REACHES 50° BRIX, ADD GLUCOSE AT THE RATE OF 15 PERCENT OF THE WEIGHT OF THE SYRUP.** As the syrup approaches the point of saturation, it is important to add glucose syrup to prevent crystallization of the sugar. It is best not to add glucose syrup prematurely, however; glucose syrup is more resistant to penetrating the fruit than sucrose due to its larger molecular size. Approximately 15 percent glucose to the total weight of the syrup is sufficient to prevent crystallization. Used in excess, glucose syrup can result in a gummy texture in the finished fruit. Glucose syrup should be added only once, unless more sugar is added to the syrup later. In that case it is advisable to add more glucose syrup in approximately the same proportion.

12. **CONTINUE TO INCREASE THE SYRUP'S DENSITY BY 5° BRIX EACH DAY UNTIL IT REACHES 75° BRIX.** When the dissolved solids reach 75° Brix, the syrup and fruit are shelf stable, provided the syrup has fully permeated the fruit.

13. **ALLOW THE FRUIT TO REMAIN IN THE SYRUP AT WARM ROOM TEMPERATURE FOR SEVERAL MORE DAYS.** Continuing to soak the fruit in the syrup helps to ensure that it has been fully penetrated by the syrup. This is especially important with large pieces of fruit or those with skins that resist penetration. During this final soaking period, the density of the syrup should be checked daily to verify that it has not fallen, which would indicate that the fruit is still releasing water. If the density falls, the syrup should again be boiled to increase the sugar content.

14. **BRING THE SYRUP AND FRUIT TO A BOIL BRIEFLY. REMOVE THE FRUIT FROM THE SYRUP AND DRY IT ON A SCREEN IN A WARM ROOM FOR A DAY OR LONGER.** Heating the syrup lowers its viscosity and facilitates draining after the fruit is placed on a screen. Leave the fruit on the screen to drain for one to three days, preferably in a warm room-temperature environment.

15. **THE FRUIT MAY BE STORED FOR LATER USE, COATED WITH A SYRUP GLAZE, OR COATED WITH A CRYSTALLINE SKIN AS DESIRED.** At this point the fruit should be completely shelf stable and can be stored for use in baking or confectionery. It is also possible to glaze the fruit with fresh syrup containing a high proportion of glucose syrup to create a glazed effect. Another method of finishing is to boil sugar syrup containing no doctoring agent to the thread stage and to seed it either by tabling a small quantity until it begins to crystallize or by adding a little fondant. After seeding the syrup, dip the fruit in it and allow it to dry. During drying, the syrup forms crystals on the outside of the fruit, protecting it and providing a stylish finish. Candied fruit may also be immersed in a supersaturated sugar solution free of a doctoring agent. This method causes large sugar crystals to form over the entire exterior of the fruit for a unique finish. This technique is particularly striking with large pieces, such as pumpkins and pineapples.

CITRUS CONFIT

The term *confit*, from the French word for "preserved," is applied to various types of preserved foods. In European parlance, the term *fruit confit* refers to the fully candied fruit discussed previously. In this case, the term *citrus confit* refers to citrus skins that have been blanched and then simmered in heavy syrup. The result is what could well be called "half-candied" citrus skins; they are saturated with syrup and have an extended shelf life, but they are not as shelf stable as fully candied fruits are. Citrus skins are uniquely suited to this quick version of candying because they have a relatively low moisture content to begin with and do not spoil easily. These skins are often used for baking and pastry applications, and also find use in confectionery centers such as orange ganache. When partially dried and dipped in chocolate, citrus confit makes a fine confectionery center on its own.

Quartered citrus skins, having been simmered in a heavy syrup to create citrus confit, find many uses in baking and pastry or can stand on their own as a confectionery center.

---

technique | theory | **CITRUS CONFIT**

Making citrus confit is a simple, quick method of sweetening and preserving citrus skins for baking, pastry, or confectionery use. Unlike candied fruit, which requires at least ten days to make, citrus confit can be made in just a couple of hours. It is an excellent method of utilizing a product that otherwise might go to waste. There are essentially two simple steps to making citrus confit: blanching and simmering. The skins are blanched multiple times in fresh water to remove their bitterness, after which they are simmered in a heavy syrup to sweeten them and improve their shelf life. While any citrus skins may be used to make confit, oranges and lemons provide the most consistent results.

1. **QUARTER THE CITRUS AND REMOVE THE SKINS.** Any type of citrus is suited to making confit, although oranges and lemons are most commonly used. Juicing oranges such as Valencia are preferable to navel oranges because of their thinner skin and superior flavor. The citrus is quartered to make it easier to remove the skins in uniform pieces.

2. **BLANCH THE SKINS IN FRESH WATER THREE TIMES.** There are two reasons to blanch the skins: to remove some of the bitterness from the pith and to soften the cell walls of the citrus in order to allow the syrup to penetrate. Putting the skins in fresh cold water and bringing them to a boil three times removes the bitter oils from the skins. This is particularly important with thick skins such as those on grapefruit and navel oranges. Blanching softens the cell walls and allows water and sugar to move in and out of the cells just as the technique for candying fruit does.

3. **COVER THE SKINS WITH A 65° BRIX SYRUP OF SUGAR AND GLUCOSE.** A 65° Brix solution containing sweeteners of approximately 70 percent sugar and 30 percent glucose syrup is boiled, and then the skins are added. The glucose syrup prevents crystallization during storage—particularly important at refrigeration temperatures, at which time the syrup becomes supersaturated. Glucose syrup also moderates sweetness, as the glucose syrup commonly used is only about 40 percent as sweet as sugar.

4. **BRING TO A SIMMER, KEEPING THE SKINS IMMERSED, AND CONTINUE SIMMERING FOR SIXTY TO NINETY MINUTES, UNTIL THE SKINS ARE TRANSLUCENT.** Simmering is intended to allow the syrup to penetrate the citrus skins, which is the ultimate goal of the confit procedure. The temperature should not exceed a low simmer; an active boil would toughen and shrivel the outside of the skins. Keeping the skins immersed is crucial to ensuring that the syrup penetrates them evenly. A weight such as a dinner plate placed directly on top of the skins helps to keep them immersed in the syrup.

5. **REMOVE FROM THE HEAT. ALLOW THE SKINS TO COOL IN THE SYRUP.** The skins will be stored in the syrup. Prior to refrigeration, they should be allowed to cool together to room temperature. During this time care should be taken to keep the container covered to prevent mold spores from falling on the syrup, causing spoilage during storage.

6. **STORE THE CITRUS CONFIT, REFRIGERATED, IN THE SYRUP.** Citrus confit is not very fermentable, due to its high dissolved-solids content—which is not sufficient, however, to make citrus confit truly shelf stable. Osmophilic molds can grow on the surface if the confit is not refrigerated. Covered and refrigerated, citrus confit will keep for weeks.

DEFECTS IN JELLIES

DEFECT	CAUSE	REMEDY
GELATIN JELLIES (GUMMIES)		
TOUGH GUMMIES	Overcooked	Cook to lower temperature
	Excessive gelatin in formula	Decrease gelatin in formula
	High-bloom-strength gelatin	Use lower-bloom-strength gelatin
	Excessive glucose syrup in formula	Reduce glucose syrup in formula
SOFT GUMMIES	Undercooked	Cook to higher temperature
	Insufficient gelatin	Increase gelatin in formula
	Low-bloom-strength gelatin	Use higher-bloom-strength gelatin
DIFFICULTY DEPOSITING	Too cool while depositing	Keep warm while depositing
AGAR JELLIES		
TOUGH TEXTURE	Too much agar in formula	Decrease agar in formula
	Excessive glucose syrup in formula	Reduce glucose syrup in formula
	Change in variety of agar	Use agar from the same origin
	Cooked to too high a temperature	Cook to lower temperature
SWEATING	Undercooked	Cook to higher temperature
UNDISSOLVED AGAR	Cooked too rapidly	Begin cooking slowly to ensure dissolution of agar
	Insufficient soaking	Soak strips or flakes overnight before use
	Unstrained after dissolving	Strain after dissolving strips or flakes
SCORCHING	Insufficient stirring during cooking	Stir constantly, scraping sides during cooking
	Excessive heat during cooking	Moderate the heat to maintain low boil during cooking
STARCH JELLIES		
SWEATING	Insufficient gelatinization of the starch	Gelatinize starch with water before adding the sugars
		Use 8 parts water to 1 part starch to gelatinize fully
	Undercooked	Cook to higher temperature
SOFT JELLIES	Insufficient starch in formula	Increase starch in formula
	Acid added too soon	Add acid after cooking
	Undercooked	Cook to higher temperature
TOUGH TEXTURE	Overcooked	Cook to lower temperature
	Excessive starch in formula	Reduce starch in formula
	Excessive glucose syrup in formula	Reduce glucose syrup in formula
SCORCHING	Insufficient stirring during cooking	Stir and clean sides while cooking
	Excessive heat during cooking	Moderate heat during cooking

DEFECTS IN JELLIES

DEFECT	CAUSE	REMEDY
PECTIN JELLIES		
SOFT JELLIES	Undercooked	Cook to higher temperature
	Undissolved pectin	Disperse pectin in sugar; stir into liquid ingredients while cold
TOUGH TEXTURE	Excessive pectin in formula	Reduce pectin in formula
	Overcooked	Cook to lower temperature
	Excessive glucose syrup in formula	Reduce glucose syrup in formula
SWEATING	Excessive acid in formula	Reduce acid in formula
	Undercooked	Cook to higher temperature
FAILURE TO GEL	Insufficient pectin in formula	Increase pectin in formula
	Insufficient acidity	Increase acid in formula
	Undercooked	Cook to higher temperature
CANDIED FRUIT		
CRYSTALLIZATION	Insufficient doctoring agent	Add more glucose syrup
		Reboil already crystallized fruit with a small amount of water to dissolve crystals, then add more glucose to prevent recrystallization
FERMENTED DURING PROCESS	Microbial activity	Boil syrup each day
		Bring fruit to temperature with syrup every few days
		Cover during storage
TOUGH TEXTURE	Density increased too quickly	Increase density only 5 percent or less each day
DISINTEGRATING FRUIT	Overripe fruit	Use fruit that is slightly underripe
	Soft fruit	Use firm fruit for candying
	Overblanched fruit	Blanch the fruit minimally
POOR SHELF LIFE	Insufficient solids content	Syrup must reach 75 percent solids
	Fruit not fully permeated	Increase density slowly; leave fruit in syrup several days after 75 percent solids level is achieved
FRUIT NOT ENTIRELY TRANSLUCENT	Areas of the fruit not permeated by syrup	Heat fruit with syrup to assist with permeation

DEFECTS IN JELLIES

DEFECT	CAUSE	REMEDY
CITRUS CONFIT		
TOUGH SKINS	Cooked too rapidly	Cook in syrup at a low simmer
BITTER SKINS	Insufficient blanching	Blanch at least three times, in fresh water each time, to remove bitterness
	Very thick skins	Use skins with less pith
CRYSTALLIZATION	Insufficient doctoring agent	Increase amount of glucose syrup in formula
SPOILAGE DURING STORAGE	Insufficient solids content	Use syrup of 65 percent solids or more
	Poor storage conditions	Store covered in refrigerator

GELATIN GUMMIES

yield: **300 PIECES**

Gelatin	100 g	3.5 oz	6%
Water, cold	260 g	9 oz	17%
Sugar	520 g	18 oz	35%
Glucose syrup	430 g	15 oz	29%
Water	190 g	7 oz	13%
Flavoring	as needed		
Citric acid	as needed		
Coloring	as needed		
BATCH SIZE	1500 g	52.5 oz	100%
Vegetable oil, for coating	as needed		

1. Prepare starch molds with desired imprints. (See Notes; see Starch-Molding Technique and Theory, page 90.)

2. Hydrate the gelatin by stirring it into the cold water.

3. Combine the sugar, glucose syrup, and 190 g of water in a saucepan. Cook to 135°C/275°F. Remove from the heat and allow to cool to 120°C/250°F.

4. Melt the gelatin over a water bath, then add to the syrup. Add the flavoring, citric acid, and coloring as desired.

5. Using a preheated funnel, deposit the mixture in the starch molds. (See Starch-Molding Technique and Theory, page 90.)

6. Dust starch over the tops of the filled molds and store them at room temperature overnight.

7. Remove the gummies from the molds. Use a soft, dry pastry brush to remove the excess starch. Toss the gummies with a small amount of vegetable oil to seal them and add shine.

NOTES: If bear-shaped molds are desired, affix purchased store-bought gummy bears to a stick to make imprints.

It is vital to keep the batch hot while depositing. Keep a pot of water boiling and immerse the filled funnel in order to reheat the mixture when necessary.

Peach Melba Jellies

PECTIN JELLIES

yield: **180 PIECES**

Fruit purée	350 g	12 oz	20%
Apple compote (see Notes)	200 g	7 oz	11%
Glucose syrup	160 g	6 oz	9%
Sugar	80 g	3 oz	4%
Pectin	20 g	1 oz	1%
Sugar	660 g	23 oz	37%
Glucose syrup	310 g	11 oz	17%
Lemon juice	20 g	1 oz	1%
BATCH SIZE	1800 g	64 oz	100%
Sugar, for finishing		as needed	

1. Combine the fruit purée, apple compote, and 160 g of glucose syrup in a saucepan.
2. Mix together the 80 g of sugar and the pectin. Whisk the mixture into the purée-syrup mixture.
3. Bring to a boil, stirring constantly.
4. Add the 660 g of sugar and return to a boil while stirring.
5. Add the 310 g of glucose syrup and continue cooking over low heat, stirring, until the batch reaches 106°C/223°F, or 75° Brix. This takes approximately 8 minutes of gentle boiling.
6. Add the lemon juice and pour the mixture into a frame 12 × 12 × ½ in set on oiled parchment paper. Sprinkle sugar on top of the jelly before it sets.
7. Allow to set until firm, at least 1 hour; overnight if desired.
8. Cut into rectangles, using the 15-mm and 30-mm strings on a guitar.
9. Roll the rectangles in granulated sugar immediately.

NOTES: Apple compote is available commercially under such trade names as Superpomme. If you wish to make the apple compote, peel, core, and slice apples. Cook with a little sugar and minimum water to make applesauce. Spread the sauce in a hotel pan and place it in a low oven to continue removing water, until the mixture is the consistency of thick applesauce. Purée prior to use.

Any flavor of purée or juice will work to produce a variety of jellies. Different flavors and colors may be layered to create unique pieces. Jellies may be starch molded to make different pieces. After molding and extracting the jellies from the starch, remove the excess starch with a soft, dry pastry brush. Toss the jellies with a little vegetable oil to seal the pieces and add shine. Jellies may also be deposited into fleximolds that have been oiled and sugared to facilitate release.

PEACH MELBA JELLIES: Starch molds are imprinted with channels, then filled first halfway with peach pectin jelly, and then the rest of the way with raspberry pectin jelly. After the jellies set, they are removed from the starch, moistened lightly, rolled in sugar, and cut into pieces using the 15-mm strings on a guitar. Each piece is then rolled in granulated sugar.

PECTIN CITRUS SLICES

yield: **150 PIECES**

CITRUS "SKINS"

Orange juice concentrate	170 g	6 oz	16%
Apple compote (see Note)	100 g	4 oz	9%
Glucose syrup	80 g	3 oz	8%
Sugar	40 g	2 oz	4%
Pectin	20 g	1 oz	2%
Sugar	330 g	12 oz	31%
Glucose syrup	160 g	6 oz	15%
Lemon juice	10 g	0.5 oz	1%
Frappe (page 389)	150 g	5 oz	14%
BATCH SIZE	1060 g	39.5 oz	100%

INTERIORS

Orange juice concentrate	220 g	8 oz	19%
Apple compote (see Note)	120 g	4 oz	10%
Glucose syrup	100 g	4 oz	9%
Sugar	50 g	2 oz	4%
Pectin	20 g	1 oz	2%
Sugar	420 g	15 oz	37%
Glucose syrup	200 g	7 oz	17%
Lemon juice	30 g	1 oz	2%
BATCH SIZE	1160g	42 oz	100%
Orange color diluted with spirit	as needed		
Sugar mixed with citric acid	as needed		

TO MAKE THE CITRUS "SKINS":

1. Combine the orange juice concentrate, apple compote, and the 80 g of glucose syrup in a saucepan.

2. Mix the 40 g of sugar with the pectin. Whisk into the fruit mixture.

3. Bring to a boil, stirring constantly.

4. Add the 330 g of sugar and return to a boil while stirring.

5. Add the 160 g of glucose syrup and continue cooking over low heat, stirring, until the batch reaches 106°C/223°F, or 78° Brix. This takes approximately 6 minutes of gentle boiling.

6. Add the lemon juice.

7. Whip the frappe into the hot jelly until homogeneous. (If the frappe has been stored for some time, warm it prior to adding.)

8. Pour the mixture into a frame 12 × 16 × ¼ in set on heavy plastic. Allow to set until firm, about 30 minutes.

9. Cut the set jelly and the plastic sheet attached to it lengthwise into 3 strips 10 × 15 cm/4 × 6 in.

10. Place the strips in 3 half-pipe molds 41 cm × 43 × 34 mm/16 × 1¾ × 1⅜ in with the plastic-lined side down.

TO MAKE THE INTERIORS:

1. Combine the orange juice concentrate, apple compote, and the 100 g of glucose syrup in a saucepan.

2. Mix the 50 g of sugar with the pectin. Whisk into the fruit mixture.

3. Bring to a boil, stirring constantly.

4. Add the 420 g of sugar and return to a boil while stirring.

5. Add the 200 g of glucose syrup and continue cooking over low heat, stirring, until the batch reaches 106°C/223°F, or 78° Brix. This takes approximately 9 minutes of gentle boiling.

6. Add the lemon juice.

7. Pour the mixture onto the "skins" in the 3 half-pipe molds, dividing the mixture equally among the molds. Note that the jelly will not come completely to the tops of the "skins" in the molds.

8. Allow to set at room temperature overnight.

TO MAKE THE PECTIN CITRUS SLICES:

1. Remove the filled skins from the molds and place flat side down on granulated sugar. Peel the plastic sheet from each piece.

2. Trim the excess "skin" from the sides of each piece.

3. Paint the "skins" with orange coloring diluted with spirit.

4. Sprinkle sugar over the pieces to facilitate handling.

5. Cut, using the 15-mm strings on a guitar. Remove from the cutter, lift the strings, and repeat, cutting the cut pieces in half. The pieces should resemble slices of citrus fruit with the skins intact.

6. Sand each piece with the sugar–citric acid mixture.

   NOTE: Apple compote is available commercially under such trade names as Superpomme. If you wish to make the apple compote, peel, core, and slice apples. Cook with a little sugar and minimum water to make applesauce. Spread the sauce in a hotel pan and place it in a low oven to continue removing water, until the mixture is the consistency of thick applesauce. Purée prior to use.

VARIATIONS: Lemon, lime, blood orange, and grapefruit slices may all be made by substituting frozen lemonade, limeade, or grapefruit juice concentrate for the orange juice concentrate. Use a few drops of the appropriate color in the jelly mixtures and on the "skins."

PBJs

yield: **156 PIECES**

JELLY

Raspberry purée	180 g	6 oz	19%
Apple compote (see Note)	100 g	4 oz	12%
Glucose syrup	80 g	3 oz	9%
Sugar	40 g	1.5 oz	4%
Pectin	10 g	0.5 oz	1%
Sugar	330 g	12 oz	36%
Glucose syrup	160 g	6 oz	17%
Lemon juice	20 g	1 oz	2%
BATCH SIZE	920 g	34 oz	100%

PEANUT BUTTER GIANDUJA

Milk chocolate, melted, tempered, at 30°C/86°F	450 g	16 oz	64%
Peanut butter	250 g	9 oz	36%
BATCH SIZE	700 g	25 oz	100%

Dark chocolate, melted, tempered, for precoating and dipping	as needed		
Peanuts, toasted, chopped, for finishing	as needed		

TO MAKE THE JELLY:

1. Combine the raspberry purée, apple compote, and the 80 g of glucose syrup in a saucepan.

2. Mix the 40 g of sugar with the pectin. Whisk into the purée mixture.

3. Bring to a boil, stirring constantly.

4. Add the 330 g of sugar and return to a boil, stirring.

5. Add the 160 g of glucose syrup and continue cooking over low heat, stirring, until the batch reaches 106°C/223°F, or 75° Brix. This takes approximately 6 minutes of gentle boiling.

6. Add the lemon juice.

7. Pour the mixture into a frame 12 × 12 × ¼ in set on oiled parchment paper. Allow to set.

TO MAKE THE PEANUT BUTTER GIANDUJA:

1. Combine the tempered milk chocolate and peanut butter in a stainless-steel bowl.

2. Table on stone until cooled to room temperature but still fluid, about 3 minutes.

3. Place a second frame 12 × 12 × ¼ in on top of the one containing the jelly. Spread the gianduja on top of the jelly. Allow to crystallize until set, about 30 minutes.

TO MAKE THE PBJS:

1. Precoat the gianduja side of the slab with the tempered dark chocolate.

2. Cut into squares, using the 22.5-mm strings on a guitar.

3. Dip each square in the tempered dark chocolate. When the chocolate begins to set, use a 3-prong dipping fork to mark the top of each piece diagonally, and finish with a few toasted chopped peanuts.

NOTE: Apple compote is available commercially under such trade names as Superpomme. If you wish to make the apple compote, peel, core, and slice apples. Cook with a little sugar and minimum water to make applesauce. Spread the sauce in a hotel pan and place it in a low oven to continue removing water, until the mixture is the consistency of thick applesauce. Purée prior to use.

TROPICAL FLOWERS

yield: **180 PIECES**

HIBISCUS INFUSION

Water	250 g	9 oz	77%
Dried hibiscus flowers	50 g	2 oz	15%
Sugar	30 g	1 oz	8%
BATCH SIZE	330 g	12 oz	100%

HIBISCUS JELLY

Hibiscus infusion	180 g	6 oz	19%
Apple compote (see Note)	100 g	4 oz	12%
Glucose syrup	80 g	3 oz	9%
Sugar	40 g	1.5 oz	4%
Pectin	20 g	1 oz	1%
Sugar	330 g	12 oz	36%
Glucose syrup	160 g	6 oz	17%
Lemon juice	20 g	1 oz	2%
BATCH SIZE	920 g	34 oz	100%

VANILLA MILK CHOCOLATE GANACHE

Heavy cream	180 g	6 oz	25%
Glucose syrup	60 g	2 oz	8%
Vanilla bean, split and scraped	1 bean	1 bean	
Butter, very soft	20 g	1 oz	3%
Milk chocolate, melted, tempered, at 30°C/86°	460 g	16 oz	64%
BATCH SIZE	720 g	25 oz	100%

Dark chocolate, melted, tempered, for precoating and dipping	as needed
White chocolate, melted, tempered, for finishing	as needed

TO MAKE THE HIBISCUS INFUSION:

1. Combine the water, dried hibiscus flowers, and sugar in a saucepan. Bring just to a boil. Cover and remove from the heat. Allow to steep for 5 minutes. Strain the hibiscus infusion through premoistened cheesecloth. Wring the flowers in the cheesecloth to extract the maximum amount of flavor possible.

2. The liquid should be very close to the required quantity. If more liquid is needed, pour water through the flowers to get the necessary amount. If less is needed, scale and use the required amount.

TO MAKE THE HIBISCUS JELLY:

1. Combine the hibiscus infusion, apple compote, and the 80 g of glucose syrup in a saucepan.
2. Combine the 40 g of sugar with the pectin. Whisk into the purée mixture.
3. Bring to a boil, stirring constantly.
4. Add the 330 g of sugar and return to a boil while stirring.
5. Add the 160 g of glucose syrup. Continue cooking over low heat, stirring, until the batch reaches 106°C/223°F, or 75° Brix. This takes approximately 6 minutes of gentle boiling.
6. Add the lemon juice.
7. Pour into a frame 12 × 12 × ¼ in set on oiled parchment paper. Allow to set until cooled to room temperature and gelled, approximately 1 hour.

TO MAKE THE VANILLA MILK CHOCOLATE GANACHE:

1. Combine the cream and glucose syrup with the vanilla bean and its seeds in a saucepan. Bring to a boil.
2. Remove the vanilla bean from the flavored cream. Allow the mixture to cool to 40°C/105°F.
3. Stir the butter into the tempered milk chocolate, taking care that no lumps remain.
4. Pour the cooled cream mixture over the milk chocolate mixture. Using a spoon or spatula, stir the mixture in vigorous small circles in the center of the bowl until it emulsifies.
5. Stir outward in larger circles to spread the emulsion throughout the bowl, checking to see that all of the chocolate has melted. If necessary, heat the ganache over a hot water bath to melt the chocolate. The temperature of the ganache should not exceed 34°C/94°F.
6. Place a second frame 12 × 12 × ¼ in on top of the one containing the hibiscus jelly. Spread the milk chocolate ganache over the jelly. Allow to crystallize, covered, overnight.

TO MAKE THE TROPICAL FLOWERS:

1. Precoat the milk chocolate ganache side of the slab with the tempered dark chocolate.
2. Cut into rectangles, using the 15-mm and 30-mm strings on a guitar.
3. Dip each piece in the tempered dark chocolate. After the chocolate sets, finish with 3 dots of white chocolate on top of each piece.

NOTE: Apple compote is available commercially under such trade names as Superpomme. If you wish to make the apple compote, peel, core, and slice apples. Cook with a little sugar and minimum water to make applesauce. Spread the sauce in a hotel pan and place it in a low oven to continue removing water, until the mixture is the consistency of thick applesauce. Purée prior to use.

AGAR JELLIES

yield: **180 PIECES**

Sugar	510 g	18 oz	28%
Powdered agar	20 g	0.75 oz	1%
Water, cold	410 g	15 oz	23%
Glucose syrup	440 g	16 oz	25%
Fruit juice or purée	410 g	15 oz	23%
BATCH SIZE	1790 g	64.75 oz	100%
Sugar, for finishing	as needed		

1. Mix the sugar with the powdered agar. Whisk into the cold water.

2. Add the glucose syrup. Cook over moderate heat, stirring, until the batch reaches 106°C/223°F, or 78° Brix. This takes approximately 8 minutes of gentle boiling.

3. Remove from heat and allow to cool to 90°C/194°F. Add the fruit juice or purée and pour into a frame 12 × 12 × ½ in set on oiled parchment paper.

4. Allow to set until firm, about 1 hour. Cut into rectangles, using the 15-mm and 30-mm strings on a guitar.

5. Dredge the rectangles in granulated sugar.

6. Store overnight on an icing screen to allow the outside to dry before further storage.

   NOTE: Agar jellies may be layered, starch molded, or molded in fleximolds to create unique products.

AGAR CITRUS SLICES

yield: 150 PIECES

CITRUS "SKINS"

Sugar	230 g	8 oz	24%
Powdered agar	10 g	0.5 oz	1%
Water, cold	190 g	7 oz	21%
Glucose syrup	170 g	6 oz	18%
Orange juice concentrate	190 g	7 oz	20%
Frappe (page 389)	150 g	5 oz	16%
BATCH SIZE	940 g	33.5 oz	100%

INTERIORS

Sugar	320 g	11 oz	29%
Powdered agar	10 g	0.5 oz	1%
Water, cold	260 g	9 oz	24%
Glucose syrup	240 g	9 oz	22%
Orange juice concentrate	260 g	9 oz	24%
BATCH SIZE	1090 g	38.5 oz	100%
Coloring, diluted with spirit	as needed		
Sugar mixed with citric acid, for finishing	as needed		

TO MAKE THE CITRUS "SKINS":

1. Mix the 230 g of sugar with the powdered agar. Whisk into the 190 g of cold water.
2. Add the 170 g of glucose syrup and bring to a boil while stirring. Cook over moderate heat, stirring, until the batch reaches 106°C/223°F, or 78° Brix. This takes approximately 5 minutes of gentle boiling.
3. Remove from the heat. Add the 190 g of orange juice concentrate and the frappe. (If the frappe has been stored for some time, warm it prior to adding.)
4. Spread the mixture into a frame 12 × 16 × ¼ in set on a heavy plastic sheet. Allow the jelly to set, about 15 minutes.
5. Cut the set jelly and the plastic sheet attached to it lengthwise into 3 strips 10 × 41 cm/4 × 16 in.
6. Place the strips in 3 half-pipe molds 41 cm × 43 × 34 mm/16 × 1¾ × 1⅜ in, with the plastic-lined side down.

TO MAKE THE INTERIORS:

1. Mix the 320 g of sugar with the powdered agar. Whisk into the 260 g of cold water.
2. Add the 240 g of glucose syrup and bring to a boil while stirring. Cook over moderate heat, stirring, until the batch reaches 106°C/223°F, or 78° Brix. This takes approximately 8 minutes of gentle boiling.

3. Remove from the heat and allow to cool to 90°C/194°F. Add the 260 g of orange juice concentrate and pour into the three molds containing the citrus "skins." Note that the jelly will not fill the molds to the tops of the "skins."

4. Allow to set at room temperature for 2 hours.

TO MAKE THE AGAR CITRUS SLICES:

1. Remove the 3 gelled strips from the molds and place flat side down on granulated sugar. Peel the plastic sheet from each piece.

2. Trim the excess "skin" from the sides of each piece.

3. Paint the "skins" with the orange coloring diluted with spirit.

4. Sprinkle sugar over each piece.

5. Cut the molded jelly using the 15-mm strings of a guitar. Remove from the cutter, lift the strings, and repeat, cutting the cut pieces in half. The pieces should resemble slices of citrus fruit with the skins intact.

6. Sand each piece with the sugar–citric acid mixture. Store overnight on an icing screen to allow drying before further storage.

NOTE: It is best to cut the slices and dry on an icing screen the same day they are made. See page 322 for step-by-step photography of this method.

VARIATIONS: Lemon, lime, blood orange, and grapefruit slices may all be made by substituting frozen lemonade, limeade, or grapefruit juice concentrate for the orange juice concentrate. Use a few drops of the appropriate color in the jelly mixture and on the "skins."

CITRUS CONFIT

yield: **100 CITRUS SKIN QUARTERS**

Lemon or orange skins, quartered	25 skins	25 skins	
Sugar	1500 g	53 oz	50%
Water	1130 g	40 oz	38%
Glucose syrup	380 g	14 oz	12%
BATCH SIZE	3010 g	107 oz	100%

1. Blanch the citrus skins 3 times, in fresh water each time.
2. Combine the sugar, water, and glucose syrup in a saucepan and bring to a boil.
3. Immerse the blanched skins in the syrup and bring to a simmer. (It may be necessary to weight the skins with a dinner plate to keep them immersed in the syrup.)
4. Simmer over very low heat for 60 to 90 minutes, until translucent.
5. Cool to room temperature, covered.
6. Store the skins refrigerated in the syrup.

TURKISH DELIGHT (USING NATIVE STARCH)

yield: **160 PIECES**

SYRUP

Sugar	1360 g	48 oz	80%
Water	340 g	12 oz	20%
Cream of tartar	1½ tsp	1½ tsp	< 1%
BATCH SIZE	1700 g	60 oz	100%

TURKISH DELIGHT

Water	1020 g	36 oz	60%
Cornstarch	170 g	6 oz	10%
Cream of tartar	1½ tsp	1½ tsp	< 1%
Rose water	15 g	0.5 oz	< 1%
Pink coloring	as needed		
Pistachios	510 g	18 oz	30%
BATCH SIZE	1715 g	60.5 oz	100%

Mixture of 2 parts confectioners' sugar and 1 part cornstarch, sifted, for dusting	as needed

TO MAKE THE SYRUP:

1. Cook the sugar, the 340 g of water, and the cream of tartar to 126°C/259°F, using the standard wet-sugar cooking technique. (See pages 219–221.)
2. Set aside and leave undisturbed.

TO MAKE THE TURKISH DELIGHT:

1. Combine the 1020 g of water, the cornstarch, and the cream of tartar in a saucepan. Cook the mixture, stirring constantly, until it boils. The mixture will be very thick. Continue boiling, stirring constantly, for 3 minutes.
2. Stream the hot syrup into the starch mixture, whisking constantly, over low heat.
3. Bring to a gentle boil over low heat, continuing to whisk constantly. Cook until the mixture is smooth and clear, about 20 to 25 minutes.
4. Remove from the heat and stir in the rose water, coloring, and pistachios.
5. Pour into a frame 12 × 12 × ¾ in set on an oiled plastic sheet. Spread the jelly evenly in the frame.
6. Place a second oiled plastic sheet onto the top of the jelly and allow to set undisturbed overnight.
7. Remove the plastic sheets from the jelly and dust generously with the sifted confectioners' sugar–cornstarch mixture.
8. Cut into rectangles 1 × 4 cm, using a sharp, oiled chef's knife. Roll the individual pieces in the confectioners' sugar–cornstarch mixture.

TURKISH DELIGHT

yield: **140 PIECES**

Water	1130 g	40 oz	40%
Thin boiling starch (60° fluidity)	140 g	5 oz	5%
Sugar	910 g	32 oz	32%
Glucose syrup	230 g	8 oz	8%
Vanilla bean, split and scraped	1 bean	1 bean	
Rose water	1 tsp	1 tsp	<1%
Citric acid	½ tsp	½ tsp	<1%
Pink coloring	as needed		
Pistachios	400 g	14 oz	15%
BATCH SIZE	2810 g	99 oz	100%

Mixture of 2 parts confectioners' sugar and 1 part cornstarch, sifted, for dusting	as needed

1. Combine the water and starch in a saucepan, mix thoroughly, and simmer for 5 minutes, stirring constantly.

2. While maintaining the liquid at a simmer, mix together the sugar and glucose syrup and add to the simmering liquid, along with the vanilla bean and its seeds.

3. Continue cooking over moderate heat, stirring, until the batch reaches 106°C/223°F, or 78° Brix.

4. Remove from the heat and remove the vanilla bean. Stir in the rose water, citric acid, and pink coloring. Add the pistachios.

5. Pour into a frame 12 × 12 × ¾ in set on an oiled plastic sheet. Spread the hot mixture evenly in the frame.

6. Place a second oiled plastic sheet onto the top of the jelly and allow to set, undisturbed, overnight.

7. Remove the plastic sheets from the jelly and dust generously with the sifted confectioners' sugar–cornstarch mixture.

8. Cut into 25-mm/1-in squares using a sharp, oiled chef's knife. Roll the individual pieces in the confectioners' sugar–cornstarch mixture.

CARDAMOM CASHEW TURKISH DELIGHT: Add 2 tsp ground cardamom along with the sugar. Omit the rose water and coloring. Replace the pistachios with toasted cashews.

SAFFRON TURKISH DELIGHT WITH PISTACHIOS: Add ¾ tsp saffron threads to the batch along with the sugar. Omit the rose water and coloring.

VARIOUS FLAVORS: Manufactured flavors and citric acid may be used in the recommended quantities as desired. Omit the rose water and pistachios. Use appropriate coloring for the flavor chosen.

10

Aerated confections are to the confectioner what mousses and soufflés are to the pastry chef: sweetened foams that may or may not contain inclusions.

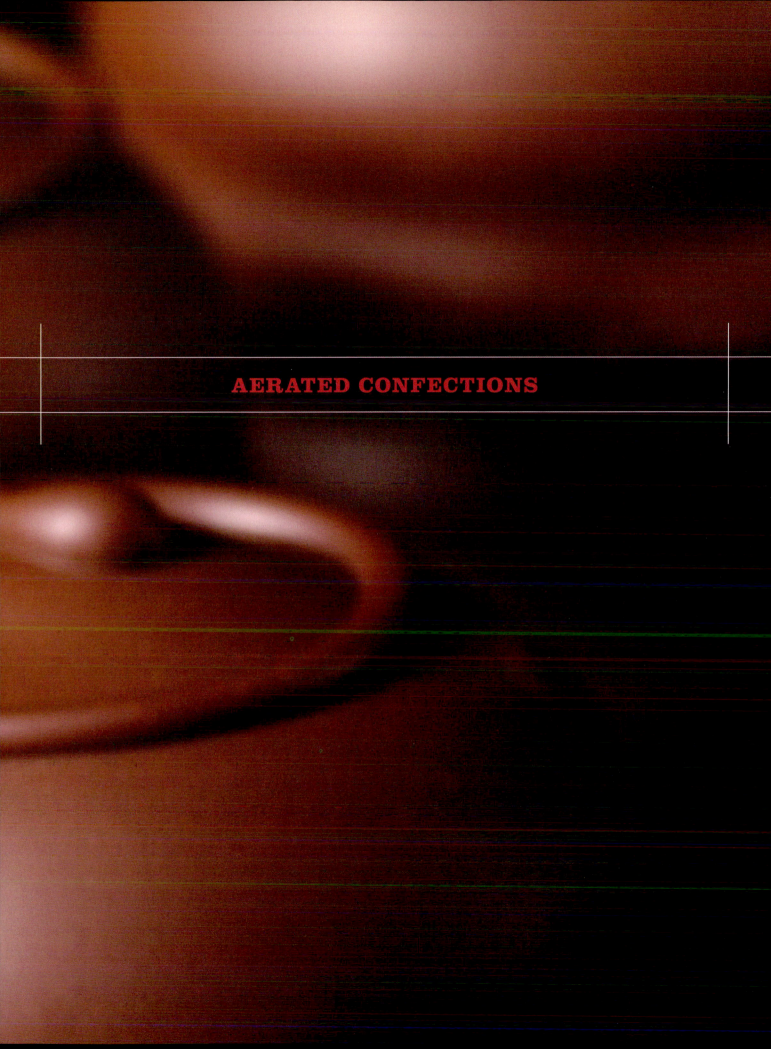

AERATED CONFECTIONS

In confections and desserts, the more effectively aerated a mixture is, the lighter the finished product will be—and the happier the consumer. Both aerated confections and mousses use some of the same ingredients for aeration, and the aeration of both is usually achieved by mechanical means. Aerated confections contain much less moisture than aerated desserts, however, and have a higher dissolved-solids content, with a corresponding low water-activity level, which provides the requisite shelf life. Among the most popular aerated confections are marshmallow, divinity, and nougat, all of which are mechanically leavened by whipping cooked sugars that are combined with an ingredient that acts as an aerator. Whipping is by far the most common method for aerating confections, but other methods are also used. Sponge candy is an example of an aerated confection that is chemically leavened using baking soda. And confectioners use pressurized gas to create the light texture of some confections such as milk chocolate soufflés. In all cases, the object is to incorporate gas bubbles into the mixture and trap them there to create a light product.

WHIPPED AERATED CONFECTIONS

Marshmallow

Marshmallow has a long history. Most food historians place its origin in ancient Egypt, where the mucilaginous sap from the root of the marshmallow plant was mixed with honey to create this confection. Marshmallow made in this period was reserved for royalty, for use as a salubrious dietary supplement or as a respiratory curative. Today's marshmallow is a far cry from this early concoction. Modern marshmallow is made using sugar, glucose syrup, gelatin, and flavoring. Some marshmallow products are made using albumen as the sole aerator, and some are made using both albumen and gelatin. As opposed to the extruded cylindrical mass-produced marshmallows, artisan marshmallows are spread into a slab, allowed to set, and cut with either a wire cutter or a knife. Marshmallows formed in slabs may be either enrobed in chocolate or lightly dredged in starch and consumed without enrobing. The most common marshmallows are uncrystallized, but grained, or crystallized, marshmallows are also made. These confections contain less glucose syrup, and after they are aerated they are seeded with confectioners' sugar to induce crystallization. Grained marshmallows have a shorter texture than those that are ungrained.

Divinity

Like fudge, divinity is a genuinely American confection; its roots go back to early twentieth-century America. Divinity is best described as a hybrid of nougat and marshmallow, with some of the characteristics of each. Like marshmallow, divinity is softer and lighter than nougat, containing both more moisture and more air than typical nougat. Like nougat, divinity is aerated using albumen. It contains less moisture than marshmallow and no gelatin. As a result, divinity is shorter textured but slightly firmer than marshmallow, and is lighter and softer than most nougat. Divinity is sometimes called seafoam or divinity fudge, the latter name being accurate when the divinity is crystallized through the introduction of fondant or another type of seed after whipping, as is commonly done. Divinity frequently contains pecans or walnuts and is often spooned into quenelles or kisses, but it may be spread into a slab and cut. It is seldom enrobed; it is usually consumed unadorned.

Nougat

The word *nougat* is derived from the Latin word *nux*, meaning "walnut." There is evidence that, in ancient times, precursors of today's nougat were made using egg whites, honey, and nuts. Given the derivation of the word, it stands to reason that nougat often contains nuts, but this is no longer its defining quality. Nougat is a foam aerated with egg whites or albumen and containing cooked sugar, glucose syrup, and honey in varying proportions. Nougat may be white and firm, like the venerable classic nougats Montelimar and torrone. Or it may be soft and very light, as in some American candy bars. It may contain chocolate, coffee, or other flavorings. Some nougat formulas intentionally induce crystallization to create a short, tender texture; in other formulas the confection is left uncrystallized to provide chewiness. A wealth of dry inclusions may be used in nougat, among them candied and dried fruit or seeds, but the most ubiquitous inclusions are nuts—usually almonds, pistachios, and hazelnuts. Once finished, nougat may be deposited in a slab, sandwiched between wafer papers, or cut into individual portions or bars and dipped partially or fully in chocolate. Given all of the variables of texture, flavor, inclusions, and finishing techniques, the possible variations are nearly endless.

technique

CLASSIC NOUGAT

The method for classic nougat Montelimar or torrone differs slightly from the basic albumen method. Rather than cooking all of the sugars together and adding them to the whipping albumen, the sugars are cooked in two separate batches: the first contains only the honey and is cooked to a relatively low temperature (approximately 120°C/248°F). This low-cooked honey is added to the already whipping albumen and both are whipped to aerate and stabilize the foam. This step is identical to making an Italian meringue in a pastry kitchen. After thoroughly aerating the albumen and the low-cooked honey mixture, a second batch of sugar—consisting of the sugar and glucose syrup—is cooked. This batch is cooked to a higher temperature, ranging from 130° to 155°C/266°

to 311°F, depending on the desired firmness of the finished product. The higher the temperature the sugars reach, the less water they contain, and the harder the nougat will be. The high-cooked sugar is then streamed into the whipping albumen-honey mixture, and the resulting nougat mixture is whipped until it begins to cool. After whipping, an optional ingredient like fondant or confectioners' sugar may be added to induce crystallization, resulting in a short texture. A fat such as cocoa butter is usually added to shorten the texture of the nougat, and inclusions (toasted nuts and dried or candied fruit) are mixed in.

There are several advantages to taking the extra step of cooking two batches of sugar for nougat production. First, honey, being acidic, inverts sugar if the

two are combined during cooking. When the honey is cooked separately, there is less inversion of the sugar, and therefore less stickiness, browning, and softness in the finished nougat. Therefore, cooking sugars in two batches is essential when making a hard nougat such as torrone. Another advantage is that the flavor and color of the honey is less damaged by lower cooking, resulting in a fresher, more delicate flavor and lighter color. Finally, by adding the lower-cooked honey during aeration, it is possible to aerate and stabilize the albumen more effectively, which results in a lighter finished product. Following the two-stage cooking method, it is possible to produce nougat with brilliant white color, fresh flavor, and excellent firm texture.

The technique for using albumen as a confectionery aerator is virtually identical whether the confectioner uses fresh egg whites, dried egg whites, or a combination of the two. In all cases, syrup is cooked to remove water and increase the concentration of sugars. The sugars in the syrup may be sucrose with the addition of glucose syrup as a doctoring agent, or honey or other sugars may be added as well. The temperature to which the syrup is cooked determines the water content, and therefore the firmness of the finished product. As the sugars cook, the egg whites are whipped to soft-peak consistency. The hot syrup is streamed into the meringue to stabilize and pasteurize it. The foam is then whipped to continue aerating it as it cools. Inclusions are optional and are usually mixed in by hand after whipping.

Whether making marshmallow, divinity, or nougat, the basic method for aerated confections using albumen is essentially the same.

1. **IF DRIED ALBUMEN IS USED, HYDRATE IT WITH WATER OR ADD IT TO EGG WHITES TO HYDRATE. IF FRESH EGG WHITES ALONE ARE USED, THIS STEP IS NOT NECESSARY.** Dried albumen must be rehydrated prior to use. This may be done using water or it may be done using fresh egg whites. In either case, it is important to avoid forming lumps of albumen when combining it with the water. The best method for avoiding lumps is to add a small amount of liquid to the powder and mix it to form a moist paste. Once the paste is formed, slowly add the remaining cold liquid while stirring to maintain a smooth texture. Allow hydrating albumen to soak for fifteen minutes or longer before use.

2. **BEGIN TO COOK THE SWEETENERS TO THE REQUIRED TEMPERATURE.** Any time sugar is cooked, the object is to dissolve it and then to remove water, leaving behind the desired concentration of sugar. The higher the temperature to which the sugar is cooked, the more water is removed, and the firmer the finished product will be. When cooking sugar for any confection, care must be taken to cook the sugar accurately to the desired temperature. The firmness of the finished candy will be substantially influenced by a temperature difference in the sugar of only one or two degrees.

3. **AS THE SWEETENERS APPROACH THE REQUIRED TEMPERATURE, BEGIN TO WHIP THE ALBUMEN TO AERATE.** When aerating with albumen, it is important to have the egg whites whipped to a medium-peak foam before adding the hot syrup. If the egg whites are not sufficiently aerated prior to adding the sugar, the mixture will never achieve the volume, light texture, and light color desired. To ensure good volume in the finished product, always begin whipping the whites several minutes before the sugar reaches the desired temperature. It is common practice to add a small amount of granulated sugar to the whites in order to increase their stability prior to the addition of the syrup, making them less likely to collapse as the hot syrup is added.

4. **STREAM THE COOKED—AND STILL HOT—SUGARS INTO THE WHIPPING EGG WHITES.** The hot sugar syrup should be added to the whipping whites as quickly as the whites will accept the syrup without collapsing. This is especially important for avoiding excessive caramelization when using high-boiled syrups, such as those used to make hard nougats. In a high-boiled syrup, the sugar continues browning in the saucepan as it is added to the whites. Although the syrup should be added reasonably quickly, dumping it in all at once would deflate the whites, resulting in a dense, low-volume product.

5. **CONTINUE WHIPPING TO FURTHER AERATE THE MIXTURE.** The mixture should continue to be whipped after all of the hot syrup has been added, in order to allow the sugar to begin to cool and to further aerate the confection. Continue whipping at room temperature, but in the case of hard nougat, heat may need to be applied by means of a heat gun or a propane torch. The heat will drive off more moisture and allow for longer whipping time, which will aerate the mixture more fully and create a lighter texture in the finished product.

6. **MIX IN INCLUSIONS, FAT, AND FLAVORING AS NEEDED.** The inclusions, flavoring, and fat should be added while the candy mix is still supple. The fat is added after whipping. If it is added sooner, it destabilizes the foam and causes loss of volume. The inclusions and flavors, however, can be added while the mixture is still on the mixer, or folded in by hand, depending on the equipment and facilities available.

7. **DEPOSIT AS DESIRED.**

TOP, LEFT: *Nougat's aeration is achieved by streaming cooked sugar into egg whites as they are whipped (see step 4 of the technique).* RIGHT: *Once the nougat is fully whipped, a variety of inclusions such as nuts, seeds, and dried fruits can be folded in (see step 6 of the technique).*

BOTTOM, LEFT: *The finished nougat is spread into frames to create even layers for later portioning and finishing.*

The technique for making aerated confections using gelatin is similar to the method used with albumen, except for differences in the way the aerator is handled. In both methods, sugar and glucose syrup are cooked to remove water and concentrate the sugar content. When gelatin is used, the cooked sugar is allowed to cool undisturbed until it reaches approximately 100°C/212°F. Once the sugar has cooled to this temperature, the hydrated, melted gelatin is added, and the mixture is whipped together. The gelatin traps the air that the whip incorporates and creates a stable foam. Gelatin is commonly used in marshmallow production but not in the production of nougat or divinity.

1. **HYDRATE THE GELATIN IN COLD WATER.** Gelatin must be hydrated before it is used so that it melts fully when heated. If it is not fully hydrated, it will not melt properly and will leave granules of hard gelatin in the finished product. When gelatin is used for confectionery applications, it is usually hydrated in a minimum amount of cold water so as not to add too much moisture to the finished product, which would soften it and reduce its shelf life. The water should be cold so that the gelatin uniformly absorbs the water rather than being softened and partially melted by it. In order to be certain that all the gelatin hydrates in the small amount of water, take care that the gelatin is evenly distributed in the water.

2. **COOK THE SWEETENERS TO THE DESIRED TEMPERATURE.** See step 2 in Whipped Aerated Albumen Technique and Theory, page 358.

3. **POUR THE COOKED SWEETENERS INTO A MIXING BOWL AND ALLOW TO COOL UNDISTURBED UNTIL THE STEMPERATURE FALLS TO 100°C/212°F.** Gelatin is damaged by exposure to high temperatures (see page 317), so the sugars must be allowed to cool to just under 100°C/212°F in order that the gelatin aerates the mixture as it should. Pouring the sugar into the mixing bowl to cool it prevents carryover cooking, cools the sugar more quickly, and warms the mixing bowl so that the mixture will remain malleable for whipping.

4. **MELT THE GELATIN OVER A WATER BATH.** The gelatin should already be melted when it is added to the sugar to ensure that it is fully incorporated and leaves no hard granules in the finished candy. Gelatin should always be melted over a water bath to avoid damaging it from high heat or scorching.

5. **ADD THE MELTED GELATIN TO THE SWEETENERS.** The melted gelatin is stirred into the hot sugar mixture to distribute it well.

6. **USING A MIXER, WHIP ON HIGH SPEED TO THE DESIRED DENSITY.** The mixture should be whipped on high speed to best incorporate air and to create a stable foam before the gelatin cools excessively. Some formulas for aerated confections indicate the specific gravity at which the product should be removed from the machine. (See Specific Gravity, page 362.) If no specific gravity is given, whip the mixture until it is well aerated and has reached approximately 45°C/113°F.

7. **DEPOSIT WHILE WARM.** Once gelatin cools, it begins to form a gel. Then it can no longer be aerated, nor will it be malleable enough for depositing in slabs or molds. It is therefore imperative to deposit the cooled gelatin while it is well over 30°C/86°F, at which point it begins to set.

TOP, LEFT: *The texture of marshmallow is achieved by aerating a combination of cooked sugar syrup and gelatin (see step 6 of the technique).* RIGHT: *The aerated confection is spread onto a sheet pan to set.*

BOTTOM, LEFT: *The layer of marshmallow should be made as smooth as possible for even portioning and appearance.* RIGHT: *Portioned marshmallows are dredged in starch to keep them from sticking together once packaged.*

SPECIFIC GRAVITY

Specific gravity is an expression of the weight of a substance compared to the weight of water. The unit of measure for specific gravity is weight divided by volume—grams per milliliter, for example—but is commonly expressed as a number without units. Water has a specific gravity of 1.000. (At 4°C/40°F, water weighs 1.000 g/mL. For confectionery purposes, however, temperature need not be considered when measuring specific gravity.) Substances heavier than water have a specific gravity greater than 1.000; those lighter than water have a specific gravity of less than 1.000. Marshmallow with a specific gravity of 0.40 weighs 40 percent as much as an equal volume of water. When aerated confections are being made, it is desirable to produce consistent results rather than a denser product one time and a lighter product the next.

To this end, formulas for aerated products often provide the specific gravity to which the mixture should be whipped. If each batch has the same specific gravity, the finished candy always has the same density and texture.

Measuring specific gravity in a kitchen is a quick and simple procedure: use a small bowl or container of about 250 mL/about 8.8 oz for this procedure, although the size is not critical.

1. Tare the container on a scale. Fill the container to the top with water.

2. Weigh the water and record the weight. Empty the container.

3. Fill the same container with the substance to be measured (marshmallow, in the present example). Again, fill the container exactly to the top. Be careful not to trap air pockets in the marshmallow.

4. Weigh the material and record the weight.

5. Divide the weight of the material by the weight of the water. The result is the specific gravity of the material.

Example: The water in the cup weighs 250 g/9 oz. The marshmallow in the same cup weighs 100 g/3.5 oz. The weight of the marshmallow (100 g) divided by the weight of water (250 g) equals the specific gravity (0.40).

Specific gravity is used to determine when a whipped confection should be removed from the mixer. If the specific gravity is higher than the specification in the formula, the mixture is too dense and should be whipped longer. When the specific gravity matches the formula specification, the mixture has been properly aerated and should be removed from the mixer.

ALTERNATIVE AERATING TECHNOLOGY

Chemical aeration

While whipping is the most common method of aerating confections, confectioners also use chemical leaveners and even pressurized gas to make lightened candies. Baking soda is the most common chemical leavener used. Baking soda reacts with the acids present in sweeteners, such as honey, or those created by the Maillard reaction or caramelization of sugar. Peanut brittle is aerated this way, as is sponge candy. Baking soda has the effect of promoting Maillard browning, and consequently alters color and flavor.

Pressure aeration

Another technique for making aerated confections is to use pressurized gas, such as nitrous oxide. This can be accomplished on a small scale by using a cream whipper fitted with nitrous oxide cartridges—the same device used to dispense whipped cream. When making aerated chocolate like Milk Chocolate Soufflés (page 398), tempered chocolate is placed in the warmed canister; the canister is charged with pressurized gas and shaken vigorously. The aerated chocolate is then dispensed into a slab or molds and allowed to crystallize. The result is a mousselike degree of aeration trapped in tempered chocolate. This method creates a unique product, but without manufacturing equipment, it is likely to be impractical for anything other than very small-scale production.

FUNCTION OF INGREDIENTS IN AERATED CONFECTIONS

Aerators

All aerated confections are made according to the same principle: incorporating gas in a sugar mixture and stabilizing the aerated mixture before the gas can escape. Two primary ingredients commonly used as aerators in confections are gelatin and albumen. Soy protein is another confectionery aerator, but although it is used in mass production of nougats, it is not usually found in artisan confections. All of the aerators referred to here are proteins that trap air bubbles as the proteins are denatured during vigorous whipping. Stabilization of the foam is achieved either by high sugar content alone or through the addition of another stabilizer, such as gelatin.

ALBUMEN

Albumen is the mixture of proteins found in egg whites and is responsible for their capacity to create foam for meringues and confections. The terms *albumen* and *egg whites* are used interchangeably in this book in the discussion of methods. In confectionery either fresh egg whites or dried ones (albumen) may be used to aerate candies. Dried albumen may be used either alone or in combination with fresh egg whites. In addition to convenience, the advantages of using dried albumen alone are increased food safety and reduced water content. Fresh egg whites carry a more significant risk of salmonella contamination than dried whites and are approximately 90 percent water, so they add considerable moisture to the candy—usually an undesirable factor in both shelf life and firmness. Combining dried albumen with fresh egg whites increases the strength of the foam created when they are whipped and contributes less moisture to the finished product than fresh egg whites alone. If fresh egg whites are used, it is vital that they reach a sufficiently high temperature during processing to pasteurize them, which nearly always occurs when the hot syrup is added to the whipping whites. Albumen is used in making nougat and divinity and is occasionally used in combination with gelatin to make marshmallow.

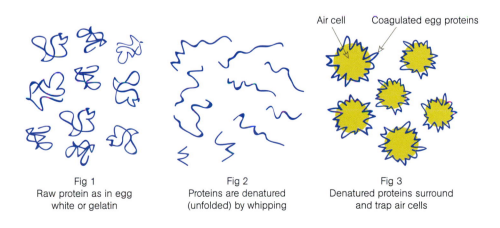

Fig 1
Raw protein as in egg
white or gelatin

Fig 2
Proteins are denatured
(unfolded) by whipping

Fig 3
Denatured proteins surround
and trap air cells

GELATIN

Gelatin is the aerator most often used in making marshmallow; it is not as light as albumen and yields a firmer, more elastic texture in finished confections. Gelatin not only aerates but also stabilizes confections by forming a gel when it sets; therefore gelatin is ideal for use in higher-moisture candies, like marshmallow, that would not hold their shape with albumen and sugars alone. Gelatin is damaged by excessive heat, so it should not be added to syrups at temperatures over 100°C/212°F. (For more information on gelatin, see page 317.)

CHEMICAL AERATORS

Baking soda, or sodium bicarbonate, is occasionally used as an aerator in confectionery, most notably in brittles and sponge candy. Baking soda reacts with the acidity of sugar, honey, and caramel to produce carbon dioxide, which aerates the candy, resulting in a delicate bite and—in the case of sponge candy—a uniquely light texture. Baking soda is always added at the end of cooking, immediately before depositing, in order to trap the gas generated.

Sweeteners

SUCROSE

Sucrose is used in virtually all aerated confections but is seldom the only sweetener present. As in all other confectionery, sucrose provides sweetness and bulk to aerated products; sucrose also stabilizes the foam that is the basis of aerated candies by setting to a firm consistency as it cools. Because of its tendency to crystallize if preventive steps are not taken, sucrose is not the only sweetener used in aerated confections. (For more information on sucrose, see page 2.)

GLUCOSE SYRUP

Glucose syrup is the second most frequently used sweetener in aerated confections; it acts as a doctoring agent, helping to prevent the crystallization of sugar. Glucose syrup may also contribute body, reduce sweetness, and alter flavor release, depending on the dextrose equivalent (DE) of the syrup used. Lower-DE glucose syrups provide a chewier texture, while higher-DE syrups make the product more tender. All of the characteristics of glucose syrups of varying DE levels—their sweetness, hygroscopicity, browning, and so on—apply to their use in aerated products. (See Characteristics of Glucose Syrups, page 4.)

HONEY

Honey has a long history of use in nougats and other aerated candies. Because invert sugar is its primary sugar component, honey aids in preventing crystallization, results in a tender bite, and contributes sweetness and flavor. Due to its hygroscopicity, honey is an effective humectant, helping to prevent finished confections from drying out. While this is an advantage for high-moisture confections such as marshmallow, it may be a disadvantage for low-moisture products such as hard nougat. Honey is high in reducing sugars, and therefore exhibits Maillard browning readily during high-temperature boiling, which affects both the flavor and the color of a finished product. Due to the acidity of honey, when it is boiled with sucrose, some inversion of the sucrose is inevitable; the more prolonged the boil, the more inversion occurs. Honey contributes more than just sweetness; it lends its unique flavor to everything it is used in. In addition, honeys from different sources each give their own individual flavor and color to the products in which they are used, and different varieties of honey may be matched to specific uses to create distinct flavor profiles. (For more information on honey, see page 6.)

INVERT SUGAR

Invert sugar can be useful in making aerated confections, as it exhibits all of the characteristics of honey except for the flavor, making it a good choice for products in which the sweetness, flavor release, hygroscopicity, and tenderness of honey are desired but the flavor of honey is not. (For more information on invert sugar, see page 4.)

Flavorings

Nougat, marshmallow, and divinity are almost always flavored with vanilla, either in extract form or by an infusion of the beans in the sugars during cooking. As already discussed, honey is a commonly used flavoring agent that has deep roots in the history of nougat making. Spices find use in aerated candies but are somewhat less commonly used than honey or extracts. If spices are used in a low-boiled sweet such as marshmallow, they should be added to the sugars at the beginning of cooking in order to infuse their flavors directly into the syrup. In high-boiled confections such as nougat, spices are likely to burn if they are cooked with the sugars, resulting in a bitter flavor, so they are better added when aeration begins. Fruit purées may be used in high-moisture aerated confections such as marshmallow, provided the purées are first reduced to remove much of the water. Using purées without first reducing them introduces too much water into the candy, softening it and raising its water-activity level, and thus shortening its shelf life. Due to their water content, purées are not appropriate for use in harder nougats. Extracts, natural flavors, and artificial flavors are all suited to flavoring aerated confections, depending on the results desired. Flavorings of this sort should be added near the end of whipping, when the mixture has begun to cool, to prevent them from flashing off volatile flavor components.

FAT

A small amount of fat is often added to nougat to shorten its texture, making the candy less chewy. Fat is almost never added to marshmallow and seldom to divinity. An ideal fat should set hard at room temperature, melt below body temperature, melt rapidly, and have a mild, pleasant flavor. In other words, the ideal fat to add to nougat is cocoa butter. However, because the high cost of cocoa butter, some confectioners use fractionated coconut fat or hydrogenated fats instead. These are acceptable substitutes in some regard, but they take a distant second place to cocoa butter because they melt at higher temperatures, contain trans fats, and lack flavor. Fat should be added to an aerated confection after whipping is complete, as fat destabilizes foam, and excessive handling after the fat has been added deflates the nougat, resulting in a dense texture.

INCLUSIONS

Traditional nougat contains nuts and often candied or dried fruit. Divinity is usually made with nuts and, occasionally, fruit. Only marshmallow is not often made with inclusions, although this is more of a tradition than a necessity. Inclusions in aerated confections provide contrasts of texture, color, and flavor—all of which increase interest in the confection. The guidelines for choosing inclusions for aerated confections are similar to those used for other candy: the inclusions must be low in moisture so that they will not spoil and must neither absorb moisture from the surrounding candy nor add moisture to it. Nuts, toasted or untoasted, and candied fruit and dried fruit are the inclusions most frequently used. Seeds, grains, and cereal may be used, provided they are low in moisture and can tolerate the heat and sheer force they will encounter when they are mixed into the warm aerated candy. Inclusions should be added in a manner that will not deflate the candy; they should be folded in by hand or mixed briefly in a mixer using a paddle attachment. Carefully selected inclusions in basic formulas allow the confectioner to create signature items and produce a great variety of confections, resulting in efficiency, market differentiation, and premium pricing.

DEFECTS IN AERATED CONFECTIONS

DEFECT	CAUSE	REMEDY
MARSHMALLOW		
HIGH SPECIFIC GRAVITY	Insufficient aeration	Whip longer
		Begin whipping while sugar is hotter
		Whip on high speed
	Sugar overcooked	Cook sugar to proper temperature
	Insufficient aerator used	Use correct amount of aerator
	Gelatin damaged by excessive heat	Allow sugar to cool to 100°C/212°F before adding gelatin
LOW SPECIFIC GRAVITY	Excessive aeration	Whip less
	Sugar undercooked	Cook sugar to proper temperature
SHORT SHELF LIFE; SPOILAGE	Excessive moisture	Cook sugar to proper temperature
		Use proper amount of water to hydrate gelatin or albumen
UNSPREADABLE	Gelatin has set	Remove from mixer at about 45°C/113°F; spread immediately
TOUGH TEXTURE	Insufficient aeration	Whip longer
		Begin whipping while sugar is hotter
		Cook sugar to proper temperature
		Whip on high speed
	Insufficient aerator	Use correct amount of gelatin
	Excessively strong gelatin used in formula	Use gelatin of correct bloom strength
	Gelatin damaged by excessive heat	Allow syrup to cool to 100°C/212°F before adding gelatin
	Excessive gelatin	Use correct amount of gelatin
DIVINITY		
DENSER THAN DESIRED	Insufficient aeration	Whip longer
		Whip on high speed
	Sugar overcooked	Cook sugar to proper temperature
	Insufficient aerator used	Use proper amount of egg white or albumen
SHORT SHELF LIFE; SPOILAGE	Excessive moisture	Cook sugar to proper temperature
		Use proper amount of water with gelatin or albumen

DEFECTS IN AERATED CONFECTIONS

DEFECT	CAUSE	REMEDY
NOUGAT		
DENSER THAN DESIRED	Insufficient aeration	Whip longer
		Whip on high speed
	Sugar overcooked	Cook sugar to lower temperature
	Nougat deflated during handling	Do not overmix inclusions into nougat
		Handle minimally after adding fat
CANNOT INCORPORATE INCLUSIONS	Nougat too cool	Add inclusions sooner, while nougat is warmer
	Inclusions too cool	Warm inclusions before adding
CANNOT INCORPORATE FAT	Nougat too cool	Add fat sooner, while nougat is warmer
	Fat added too quickly	Add fat in smaller increments
HARDER THAN DESIRED	Sugar overcooked	Cook sugar to correct temperature
SOFTER THAN DESIRED	Sugar undercooked	Cook sugar to correct temperature
EXCESSIVE BROWN COLOR	Sugar caramelized	Cook sugar to correct temperature
		Cook sugar as quickly as possible
		Add sugar to albumen as quickly as possible
		Whip longer
	Insufficient aeration	Whip on high speed
GRAININESS	Crystallized	Use sufficient doctoring agent
		Do not seed nougat with crystalline sugar
HONEYCOMB CRUNCH		
POOR VOLUME	Sugar too cool when baking soda added	Add baking soda when sugar is proper temperature
BROWN SPOTS IN CANDY	Unevenly incorporated baking soda	Sift baking soda before adding
		Stir vigorously while adding baking soda gradually
STICKY	Undercooked sugar	Cook sugar to proper temperature
	Poor storage conditions	Store protected from humidity
CHOCOLATE FROTH		
DENSE TEXTURE	Insufficient aeration	Use more gas pressure
STUCK IN BOTTLE	Chocolate setting in bottle	Maintain chocolate at maximum working temperature
		Warm bottle to 35°C/95°F before filling
		Dispense chocolate promptly

MARSHMALLOWS

yield: **234 PIECES**

Granulated gelatin	40 g	1.5 oz	2%
Water, cold	230 g	8 oz	13%
Sugar	680 g	24 oz	40%
Glucose syrup	340 g	12 oz	20%
Water	170 g	6 oz	10%
Honey	110 g	4 oz	7%
Invert sugar	110 g	4 oz	7%
Vanilla extract	20 g	1 oz	1%
BATCH SIZE	1700 g	60.5 oz	100%

Mixture of 1 part confectioners' sugar and 1 part cornstarch, sifted, for dusting	as needed

1. Hydrate the gelatin by stirring it into the cold water.

2. Combine the sugar, glucose syrup, water, honey, and invert sugar in a saucepan and cook to 122°C/252°F.

3. Pour the cooked sugar mixture into the bowl of a 12-qt planetary mixer with a whip attachment, but do not begin whipping. Allow the mixture to cool to 100°C/212°F.

4. While the sugar mixture cools, melt the hydrated gelatin over a water bath.

5. Mix the melted gelatin into the cooled sugar mixture. Whip on high speed for 8 minutes, or until well aerated. Add the vanilla extract.

6. Spread into a half-sheet pan lined with well-oiled parchment paper.

7. Place a piece of oiled parchment paper on top of the marshmallow. Flatten the top by hand until smooth. Alternatively, the marshmallow may be slabbed to 1-cm/½-in thickness for dipping in chocolate. Allow to set overnight.

8. Dust with the confectioners' sugar–cornstarch blend. Cut into squares, using the 22.5-mm strings on a guitar. Dust the pieces again and sift vigorously in tamis to remove excess starch.

NOTE: When the marshmallow mixture is properly whipped, the specific gravity should be below 0.40.

ANISE MARSHMALLOWS: Add 10 g/0.5 oz of ground anise while cooking the sugar. Add 30 g/ 1 oz of anise-flavored liqueur such as Pernod after fully whipping.

CHOCOLATE MARSHMALLOWS: Mix 90 g/ 3 oz of sifted cocoa powder into the marshmallow after fully whipping. Add 1 part cocoa powder to 3 parts confectioners' sugar– cornstarch blend for dusting.

CINNAMON MARSHMALLOWS: Add 10 g/ 0.5 oz of ground cinnamon to the sugar while cooking.

COFFEE MARSHMALLOWS: Add 50 g/2 oz of coffee extract at the end of whipping.

PASSION FRUIT MARSHMALLOWS: Add 70 g/3 oz of passion fruit purée, reduced by half, after fully whipping.

VARIOUS FLAVORED MARSHMALLOWS: Various manufactured flavors may be added at the end of whipping, either with or without accompanying colors.

PIPED MARSHMALLOWS

yield: **150 PIECES**

Granulated gelatin	15 g	0.5 oz	1%
Water, cold	60 g	2 oz	4%
Sugar	90 g	3 oz	7%
Dried egg whites	30 g	1 oz	2%
Water, cold	150 g	5 oz	9%
Sugar	600 g	21 oz	39%
Glucose syrup	300 g	11 oz	19%
Water	200 g	7 oz	13%
Honey	100 g	4 oz	6%
Vanilla extract	20 g	1 oz	1%
BATCH SIZE	1565 g	55.5 oz	100%

Mixture of 1 part confectioners' sugar and
1 part cornstarch, sifted, for dusting   as needed

1. Hydrate the gelatin by stirring it into the 60 g of cold water and let stand for 15 minutes.

2. Mix the 90 g of sugar and dried egg whites together. Whisk into the 150 g of cold water in the bowl of a 5-qt planetary mixer with a whip attachment, but do not begin whipping.

3. Combine the 600 g of sugar, glucose syrup, water, and honey in a saucepan. Cook to 112°C/234°F.

4. Begin whipping the egg white mixture on high speed.

5. Continue cooking the sugar mixture to 120°C/248°F. Remove from the heat, and slowly stream the hot sugar mixture into the whipping whites.

6. Continue whipping on high speed for 4 minutes or until well aerated.

7. While the whipping continues, melt the hydrated gelatin over a water bath. Add the gelatin to the whites and whip 2 minutes more, until stiff peaks form. Add the vanilla extract.

8. Place the marshmallow in a pastry bag fitted with a no. 4 French star tip. Pipe stars on lightly oiled parchment paper.

9. Dust the tops with the confectioners' sugar–cornstarch blend. Allow to set overnight.

10. Remove the finished pieces from the parchment paper and toss in the confectioners' sugar–cornstarch blend.

VARIATIONS: Add flavorings and colors as desired; pairings might include peppermint extract and red food coloring or spearmint flavoring and green food coloring. Add reduced fruit purées at the end of whipping. Add spices to the sugar while it cooks.

DIVINITY

yield: **90 PIECES**

Sugar	50 g	2 oz	3%
Dried egg whites	30 g	1 oz	1%
Fresh egg whites	50 g	2 oz	3%
Invert sugar	120 g	4 oz	7%
Sugar	600 g	21 oz	32%
Water	200 g	7 oz	11%
Glucose syrup	120 g	4 oz	7%
Vanilla extract	10 g	0.5 oz	1%
Salt	1 tsp	1 tsp	<1%
Premade fondant	50 g	2 oz	3%
Pecans, toasted, chopped	600 g	21 oz	32%
BATCH SIZE	1830 g	64.5 oz	100%

1. Mix the 50 g of sugar and dried egg whites together. Whisk into the fresh egg whites to hydrate.

2. Warm the invert sugar to about 60°C/140°F, until the crystals dissolve. Whisk the warm invert sugar into the egg white mixture. Pour into the bowl of a 5-qt planetary mixer with a whip attachment, but do not begin whipping.

3. Combine the 600 g of sugar, water, and glucose syrup in a saucepan. Cook to 112°C/234°F. Begin whipping the whites on high speed.

4. Continue cooking the sugar mixture to 125°C/257°F. Remove from the heat and slowly stream the hot sugar mixture into the whipping whites. Continue whipping on high speed for about 3 more minutes or until well aerated.

5. Add the vanilla extract and salt. Mix to combine.

6. Add the fondant and mix in thoroughly, for about 30 seconds. Do not overmix.

7. Remove the divinity from the mixer and blend in the pecans by hand.

8. Deposit into quenelles using a moistened spoon, or spread into a frame 12 × 12 × ½ in set on parchment paper. If using a frame, allow the divinity to crystallize until firm, then cut into pieces of the desired size and shape.

PET D'ANGE

yield: **150 PIECES**

SHORTBREAD ROUNDS

Shortbread Dough (page 376)	750 g	26 oz	100%
BATCH SIZE	750 g	26 oz	100%

MARSHMALLOW

Granulated gelatin	15 g	0.5 oz	<1%
Water, cold	60 g	2 oz	4%
Sugar	90 g	3 oz	7%
Dried egg whites	30 g	1 oz	2%
Water, cold	150 g	5 oz	9%
Sugar	600 g	21 oz	39%
Glucose syrup	300 g	11 oz	19%
Water	200 g	7 oz	13%
Honey	100 g	4 oz	6%
Vanilla extract	20 g	1 oz	1%
BATCH SIZE	1565 g	55.5 oz	100%

Dark chocolate, melted, tempered, for dipping and finishing	as needed

TO MAKE THE SHORTBREAD ROUNDS:

Roll the shortbread dough 2 mm/1⁄16 in thick. Cut into 150 rounds 30 mm/1 1⁄4 in, and bake at 177°C/350°F until lightly browned. Set aside and allow to cool completely.

TO MAKE THE MARSHMALLOW:

1. Hydrate the gelatin by stirring it into the 60 g of cold water.

2. Mix the 90 g of sugar and dried egg whites together. Whisk into the 150 g of cold water in the bowl of a 5-qt planetary mixer with a whip attachment, but do not begin whipping.

3. Combine the 600 g of sugar, glucose syrup, water, and honey in a saucepan. Cook to 112°C/234°F.

4. Begin whipping the egg white mixture on high speed.

5. Continue cooking the sugar mixture to 120°C/248°F. Remove from the heat, and slowly stream the hot sugar mixture into the whipping whites.

6. Continue whipping on high speed for 4 minutes or until well aerated.

7. While the whipping continues, melt the hydrated gelatin over a water bath. Add the gelatin to the whites and whip 2 minutes more, until stiff peaks form. Add the vanilla extract.

8. Place the marshmallow in a pastry bag fitted with a no. 4 round tip. Pipe a dome on top of each shortbread round. Allow to set for at least 1 hour, or up to overnight.

9. When completely set, dip each piece in the tempered dark chocolate. When the chocolate has set completely, use a paper cone to pipe a spiral of tempered dark chocolate onto each piece.

SHORTBREAD DOUGH

yield: **1515 G/53.5 OZ**

Butter	500 g	18 oz	33%
Sugar	250 g	9 oz	17%
Eggs	2 eggs	2 eggs	<1%
Egg yolks	2 yolks	2 yolks	<1%
Vanilla extract	15 g	0.5 oz	<1%
Flour, sifted	750 g	26 oz	50%
BATCH SIZE	1515 g	53.5 oz	100%

1. Cream the butter and sugar together thoroughly. Add the eggs, egg yolks, and vanilla extract in several additions, scraping down the side of the bowl after each addition.

2. Add the flour, mixing only to combine. Wrap the finished dough tightly in plastic wrap and chill thoroughly before use. The dough can be stored in the refrigerator for up to 1 week.

NOUGAT TORRONE

yield: **3 SHEETS (22 × 28 CM/8½ × 11 IN EACH)**

Sugar	50 g	2 oz	2%
Dried egg whites	10 g	0.5 oz	<1%
Fresh egg whites	100 g	3.5 oz	3%
Almonds, blanched	1100 g	39 oz	38%
Honey	450 g	16 oz	16%
Sugar	730 g	26 oz	25%
Glucose syrup	220 g	8 oz	8%
Water	200 g	7 oz	7%
Vanilla bean, split and scraped	1 bean	1 bean	
Cocoa butter, melted	40 g	1.5 oz	1%
BATCH SIZE	2900 g	103.5 oz	100%

1. Mix the 50 g of sugar and dried egg whites together. Whisk into the fresh egg whites to hydrate. Pour into the bowl of a 5-qt planetary mixer with a whip attachment, but do not begin whipping.

2. Toast the almonds. Place in a large stainless-steel bowl and keep warm in a 121°C/250°F oven until needed.

3. Bring the honey to a boil. Keep warm.

4. Combine the 730 g of sugar, glucose syrup, water, and vanilla bean and its seeds. Cook to 150°C/302°F. Add the warm honey to the sugar mixture. Begin whipping the whites on high speed.

5. When the sugar mixture reaches 155°C/311°F, remove from the heat. Remove the vanilla bean, and pour the hot sugar mixture into the whipping whites as rapidly as they will accept it without collapsing.

6. Move a propane torch constantly over the outside of the bowl to keep the nougat hot and to remove more water. Continue whipping, while applying the torch, for 2 more minutes. Caution: do not stop moving the torch for even 2 seconds or the nougat will burn.

7. Add the melted cocoa butter and continue whipping. The nougat will separate momentarily but will return to a smooth state within a minute.

8. Remove the bowl of toasted almonds from the warm oven and scrape the nougat into it. Using a wooden spoon or a gloved hand, mix the almonds into the nougat.

9. Divide the nougat among three wafer papers 22 × 28 cm/8½ × 11 in. Using an offset palette knife, spread as evenly as possible.

10. Place a second piece of wafer paper on top of each slab of nougat. Using a clean rolling pin, roll lightly to flatten the nougat and adhere the wafer paper to it.

11. Allow to cool completely or store overnight.

12. Break into irregular-size pieces. Protect from humidity to maintain hard texture.

    NOTE: If the nougat does not become smooth again after the cocoa butter is added, warm it through the bowl of the mixer with a propane torch or heat gun while it is whipping.

NOUGAT MONTELIMAR

yield: **22 PIECES**

Sugar	30 g	1 oz	2%
Dried egg whites	10 g	0.5 oz	<1%
Fresh egg whites	50 g	2 oz	3%
Sugar	380 g	13 oz	24%
Glucose syrup	120 g	4 oz	8%
Water	100 g	4 oz	6%
Vanilla bean, split and scraped	1 bean	1 bean	
Honey	230 g	8 oz	15%
Cocoa butter, melted	50 g	2 oz	3%
INCLUSIONS			
Almonds, blanched, toasted	200 g	7 oz	13%
Hazelnuts, toasted, skinned	70 g	3 oz	4%
Pistachios	100 g	4 oz	6%
Almonds, sliced, toasted	70 g	3 oz	4%
Dried pear, diced 6 mm/¼ in	50 g	2 oz	3%
Dried apricot, diced 6 mm/¼ in	50 g	2 oz	3%
Dried cherries, quartered	90 g	3 oz	6%
BATCH SIZE	1600 g	58.5 oz	100%

1. Mix the 30 g of sugar and dried egg whites together. Whisk into the fresh egg whites to hydrate. Pour into the bowl of a 5-qt planetary mixer with a whip attachment, but do not begin whipping.

2. Prepare all inclusions. The nuts may be left whole or lightly chopped, as desired. Place the inclusions in a large stainless-steel bowl and keep warm in a 121°C/250°F oven until needed.

3. Combine the 380 g of sugar, glucose syrup, water, and vanilla bean and its seeds in a saucepan and reserve.

4. Cook the honey to 108°C/226°F. Begin whipping the whites on high speed. Continue cooking the honey to 120°C/248°F.

5. When the honey reaches 120°C/248°F, immediately begin cooking the reserved sugar mixture on the highest heat.

6. Pour the hot honey into the whipping whites. Continue whipping on high speed as the sugar mixture cooks.

7. When the sugar mixture reaches 155°C/311°F, remove from the heat. Remove the vanilla bean and pour the hot sugar mixture into the whites as rapidly as they will accept it without collapsing. Continue whipping on high speed for 3 more minutes.

8. Add the melted cocoa butter and continue whipping. The nougat will separate momentarily but will return to a smooth state within a minute.

9. Remove the bowl of inclusions from the warm oven and scrape the hot nougat into it. Using a wooden spoon or a gloved hand, mix the inclusions into the nougat.

10. Place the nougat on a wafer paper 22 × 28 cm/8½ × 11 in and spread it out uniformly.

11. Place a second piece of wafer paper on top of the nougat. Using a clean rolling pin, roll lightly to flatten the nougat and adhere the wafer paper to it.

12. Allow to cool completely or store overnight.

13. Trim the edges of the nougat, making them square with the wafer paper, and cut the rectangle of nougat in half lengthwise.

14. Using a serrated knife or chef's knife, cut each half into 25-mm/1-in strips and then into bars 25 mm × 10 cm/1 × 4 in. Alternatively, cut into individual pieces of desired sizes.

   NOTE: If the nougat does not become smooth again after the cocoa butter is added, warm it through the bowl of the mixer with a propane torch or heat gun while it is whipping.

SOFT CHOCOLATE NOUGAT

yield: **180 PIECES**

Dark chocolate, melted, tempered, at 32°C/90°F	90 g	3 oz	6%
Cocoa butter, melted	30 g	1 oz	2%
Milk powder, pulverized in a blender	50 g	2 oz	4%
Cocoa powder	50 g	2 oz	4%
Confectioners' sugar	30 g	1 oz	2%
Egg whites	50 g	2 oz	3%
Glucose syrup	50 g	2 oz	3%
Glucose syrup	540 g	19 oz	34%
Sugar	470 g	17 oz	32%
Water	130 g	5 oz	9%
Vanilla extract	10 g	0.5 oz	1%
BATCH SIZE	1500 g	54.5 oz	100%

Dark chocolate, melted, tempered, for precoating and dipping		as needed

1. Combine the melted dark chocolate and cocoa butter. Keep warm.
2. Sift together the milk powder, cocoa powder, and confectioners' sugar. Set aside.
3. Combine the egg whites and the 50 g of glucose syrup in the bowl of a 5-qt planetary mixer with a whip attachment, but do not begin whipping.
4. Combine the 540 g of glucose syrup, the sugar, and the water in a saucepan. Cook to 112°C/234°F.
5. Begin whipping the egg white mixture on high speed. Continue cooking the sugar mixture to 118°C/245°F. Remove from the heat.
6. Stream the hot sugar mixture into the whipping whites.
7. Continue whipping for approximately 8 minutes, until the mixture has cooled to 50°C/120°F, or until the machine has slowed significantly.
8. Add the vanilla extract.
9. Remove the batch from the machine and mix in the reserved chocolate mixture by hand.
10. Mix in the sifted dry ingredients by hand.
11. Spread the nougat into a frame 12 × 12 × ½ in set on oiled parchment paper. Place a second piece of oiled parchment paper on top and, using a rolling pin, roll to make smooth. Allow to cool to room temperature.
12. Precoat one side of the nougat with the tempered dark chocolate. Cut into pieces 1 × 4 cm/½ × 1½ in. Dip each in the tempered dark chocolate. When the chocolate begins to set, use a dipping fork to mark the top of each piece.

NOTE: The dry ingredients in this nougat will cause it to crystallize and develop a short, tender texture 24 to 48 hours after it is deposited in the frame. While it can be cut and dipped on the day it is made, it requires 24 to 48 hours before it can be considered finished and ready for consumption.

NEW WORLD NOUGAT

yield: **APPROXIMATELY 160 SLICES**

Sugar	40 g	2 oz	2%
Dried egg whites	10 g	0.5 oz	1%
Fresh egg whites	60 g	2 oz	3%
Sugar	470 g	17 oz	23%
Glucose syrup	190 g	7 oz	9%
Water	130 g	5 oz	7%
Vanilla bean, split and scraped	1 bean	1 bean	
Honey	290 g	10 oz	14%
Cocoa butter, melted	80 g	3 oz	4%
INCLUSIONS			
Cocoa nibs	110 g	4 oz	6%
Dark rum	20 g	1 oz	1%
Sugar	20 g	1 oz	1%
Pumpkin seeds (pepitas)	220 g	8 oz	11%
Candied papaya, diced 6 mm/¼ in	360 g	13 oz	18%
BATCH SIZE	2000 g	73.5 oz	100%

1. Mix the 40 g of sugar and dried egg whites together. Whisk into the fresh egg whites to hydrate. Pour into the bowl of a 5-qt planetary mixer with a whip attachment, but do not begin whipping.

2. Prepare all inclusions. Moisten the cocoa nibs with the rum, mix in the sugar, and dry in a low oven. Dry the diced papaya in a low oven. Place all inclusions in a large stainless-steel bowl and keep warm in a 121°C/250°F oven until needed.

3. Combine the 470 g of sugar, glucose syrup, water, and vanilla bean and its seeds in a saucepan and reserve.

4. Cook the honey to 108°C/226°F. Begin whipping the whites on high speed. Continue cooking the honey to 120°C/248°F.

5. When the honey reaches 120°C/248°F, immediately begin cooking the reserved sugar mixture on the highest heat.

6. Pour the hot honey into the whipping whites. Continue whipping on high speed as the sugar mixture cooks.

7. When the sugar mixture reaches 155°C/311°F, remove from the heat. Remove the vanilla bean and pour the hot sugar mixture into the whipping whites as rapidly as they will accept it without collapsing. Continue whipping on high speed for 3 more minutes.

8. Add the melted cocoa butter and continue whipping. The nougat will separate momentarily but will return to a smooth state within a minute.

9. Remove the bowl of inclusions from the warm oven and scrape the hot nougat into it. Using a wooden spoon or a gloved hand, mix the inclusions into the nougat.

10. Divide the nougat into four 400-g/14-oz portions. Roll each into a 28-cm/11-in cylinder and place in 4 forms 28 × 4 × 4 cm/11× 1½ × 1½ in lined with wafer paper. Pack the nougat into the forms. Fold the wafer paper over to completely enclose the nougat. Allow to cool completely. Using a serrated knife, cut bar of nougat into slices 6 mm/¼ in thick.

NOTE: If the nougat does not become smooth again after the cocoa butter is added, warm it through the bowl of the mixer with a propane torch or heat gun while it is whipping.

HONEY ALMOND SOFT NOUGAT

yield: **182 PIECES**

Egg whites	50 g	2 oz	4%
Sugar	40 g	1 oz	2%
Almonds, sliced	150 g	5 oz	11%
Grand Marnier	20 g	1 oz	2%
Sugar	60 g	2 oz	4%
Glucose syrup	340 g	12 oz	27%
Sugar	340 g	12 oz	27%
Honey	150 g	5 oz	11%
Water	80 g	3 oz	6%
Vanilla bean, split and scraped	1 bean	1 bean	
Confectioners' sugar, sifted	50 g	2 oz	4%
Cocoa butter, melted	30 g	1 oz	2%
BATCH SIZE	1310 g	46 oz	100%
Dark chocolate, melted, tempered, for precoating and dipping	as needed		
Almonds, slivered, toasted, for finishing	as needed		

1. Mix the egg whites and the 40 g of sugar together. Pour into the bowl of a 5-qt planetary mixer with a whip attachment, but do not begin whipping.

2. Moisten the almonds with the Grand Marnier and toss with the 60 g of sugar. Toast in oven until golden. Place the toasted almonds in a large stainless-steel bowl and keep warm in a 121°C/250°F oven until needed.

3. Combine the glucose syrup, the 340 g of sugar, honey, water, and vanilla bean and its seeds in a saucepan. Cook to 115°C/239°F.

4. When the mixture reaches 115°C/239°F, begin whipping the egg whites on high speed.

5. When the sugar mixture reaches 125°C/257°F, remove the vanilla bean and pour the hot sugar mixture into the whipping whites as rapidly as they will accept it without collapsing. Continue whipping on high speed for 3 more minutes.

6. Add the confectioners' sugar, mix to combine, and add the melted cocoa butter. The nougat will separate momentarily but will become smooth again as whipping continues. Whip until smooth.

7. Remove the toasted almond mixture from the warm oven and scrape the hot nougat into it. Using a wooden spoon or a gloved hand, mix the almonds into the nougat.

8. Spread the nougat into a frame 30 × 30 × 1 cm/ 12 × 12 × ½ in. Allow to cool to room temperature.

9. Precoat one side of the slab with the tempered dark chocolate.

10. Using a caramel cutter, mark the nougat into ¾-in pieces. Cut the marked nougat with a chef's knife. Dip each piece in the tempered dark chocolate. When the chocolate begins to set, use a dipping fork to mark each piece with one diagonal mark. Finish with a sliver of toasted almond placed diagonally across the fork mark.

   NOTE: If the nougat does not become smooth again after the cocoa butter is added, warm it through the bowl of the mixer with a propane torch or heat gun while it is whipping.

PEANUT BUTTER SOFT NOUGAT

yield: **182 PIECES**

Milk powder, pulverized in a blender or crushed with a rolling pin	40 g	1.5 oz	2%
Confectioners' sugar	40 g	1.5 oz	2%
Peanut butter	210 g	7 oz	13%
Glucose syrup	60 g	2 oz	4%
Egg whites	40 g	1.5 oz	3%
Sugar	350 g	12 oz	24%
Glucose syrup	270 g	10 oz	20%
Molasses	130 g	5 oz	10%
Water	100 g	4 oz	8%
Vanilla extract	15 g	1 oz	2%
Peanuts, toasted, chopped	160 g	6 oz	12%
BATCH SIZE	1415 g	51.5 oz	100%
Milk chocolate, melted, tempered, for precoating and dipping	as needed		
Peanut halves, toasted, for finishing	as needed		

1. Sift together the milk powder and confectioners' sugar. Set aside.

2. Heat the peanut butter over a water bath until hot and fluid.

3. Combine the 60 g of glucose syrup and egg whites in the bowl of a 5-qt. planetary mixer with a whip attachment, but do not begin whipping.

4. Combine the sugar, the 270 g of glucose syrup, molasses, and water in a saucepan. Cook the mixture to 112°C/234°F. Begin whipping the egg white mixture on high speed.

5. Continue cooking the sugar mixture to 118°C/245°F.

6. Stream the hot syrup into the whipping whites.

7. Continue whipping for approximately 8 minutes, until the mixture has cooled to 50°C/120°F or until the machine has slowed significantly. Add the vanilla extract.

8. Remove the batch from the machine and mix in the peanut butter, using a wooden spoon.

9. Mix in the sifted dry ingredients using a wooden spoon.

10. Spread the nougat into a frame 12 × 12 × ½ in set on oiled parchment paper. Sprinkle with the toasted peanuts. Place a second piece of oiled parchment paper on top and, using a rolling pin, roll to make smooth. Allow to cool to room temperature.

11. Precoat the nut side of the nougat with the tempered milk chocolate.

12. Using a caramel cutter, mark the nougat into ¾-in squares, using a caramel cutter. Cut the marked nougat with a chef's knife. Dip each in the tempered milk chocolate. Before the chocolate sets, use a 2-prong dipping fork to make diagonal marks across each piece. Finish with half a toasted peanut.

NOTE: The dry ingredients in this nougat will cause it to crystallize and develop a short, tender texture 24 to 48 hours after it is deposited in the frame. While it can be cut and dipped on the day it is made, it requires 24 to 48 hours before it can be considered finished and ready for consumption.

CHOCOLATE NOUGAT

yield: **APPROXIMATELY 240 PIECES**

Sugar	40 g	2 oz	2%
Dried egg whites	10 g	0.5 oz	<1%
Fresh egg whites	60 g	2 oz	3%
Sugar	470 g	17 oz	23%
Glucose syrup	140 g	5 oz	7%
Water	130 g	5 oz	6%
Vanilla bean, split and scraped	1 bean	1 bean	
Honey	290 g	10 oz	15%
Dark chocolate, melted	100 g	3.5 oz	5%
Chocolate liquor, melted	100 g	3.5 oz	5%
INCLUSIONS			
Pistachios	200 g	7 oz	10%
Almonds, slivered, toasted	250 g	9 oz	12%
Dried cherries, quartered	250 g	9 oz	12%
BATCH SIZE	2040 g	73.5 oz	100%
Confectioners' sugar, sifted	as needed		
Cocoa butter, melted, for sealing	as needed		
Dark chocolate, melted, tempered, for finishing	as needed		

1. Mix the 40 g of sugar and dried egg whites together. Whisk into the fresh egg whites to hydrate. Pour into the bowl of a 5-qt planetary mixer with a whip attachment, but do not begin whipping.

2. Prepare all inclusions. The nuts may be left whole or lightly chopped, as desired. Place the inclusions in a large stainless-steel bowl and keep warm in a 121°C/250°F oven until needed.

3. Combine the 470 g of sugar, glucose syrup, water, and vanilla bean and its seeds in a saucepan and reserve.

4. Cook the honey to 108°C/226°F. Begin whipping the whites on high speed. Continue cooking the honey to 120°C/248°F.

5. When the honey reaches 120°C/248°F, immediately begin cooking the reserved sugar mixture on the highest heat.

6. Pour the hot honey into the whipping whites. Continue whipping on high speed as the sugar mixture cooks.

7. When the sugar mixture reaches 155°C/311°F, remove from the heat. Remove the vanilla bean and pour the mixture into the whites as rapidly as they will accept it without collapsing. Whip on high speed for 3½ more minutes.

8. Add the melted dark chocolate and chocolate liquor. Whip until smooth, about 30 seconds.

9. Remove the bowl of inclusions from the warm oven and scrape the hot nougat into it. Using a wooden spoon or a gloved hand, mix the inclusions into the nougat.

10. On a table dusted with sifted confectioners' sugar, form the nougat into a slab 25 mm/1 in thick. (It will be approximately 20 × 30 cm/ 8 × 12 in.) Allow to cool to room temperature.

11. Using a serrated knife or chef's knife, trim the edges of the slab, then cut the slab crosswise into strips 6 mm/¼ in wide. Lay the strips flat.

12. Lightly brush the tops of the strips with melted cocoa butter to seal them.

13. Cut pieces 4 cm/1½ in from each strip.

14. Dip each piece up to the top face in the tempered dark chocolate.

FRAPPE

yield: **APPROXIMATELY 1000 G/36 OZ**

Dried egg whites	100 g	3.5 oz	8%
Water, cold	100 g	3.5 oz	8%
Glucose syrup	500 g	18 oz	42%
Invert sugar	500 g	18 oz	42%
BATCH SIZE	1200 g	43 oz	100%

1. Whisk the egg whites into the cold water. Allow the mixture to rehydrate for about 30 minutes.

2. Combine the glucose syrup and invert sugar. Cook to 110°C/230°F.

3. Using a 5-qt planetary mixer, begin whipping the egg white mixture on high speed.

4. Continue cooking the glucose syrup mixture until the temperature reaches 116°C/240°F.

5. Stream the hot syrup into the whipping egg whites.

6. Continue whipping until the mixture has cooled to about 50°C/120°F.

7. Store at room temperature, tightly covered.

SLEEPING BEAUTIES

yield: **160 PIECES**

SOFT CARAMEL

Sugar	480 g	17 oz	30%
Evaporated milk	480 g	17 oz	30%
Heavy cream	200 g	7 oz	12%
Vanilla bean, split and scraped	1 bean	1 bean	
Glucose syrup	400 g	14 oz	26%
Butter	30 g	1 oz	2%
BATCH SIZE	1590 g	56 oz	100%

SOFT CHOCOLATE NOUGAT

Dark chocolate, melted, tempered, at 32°C/90°F	40 g	1.5 oz	6%
Cocoa butter, melted	20 g	1 oz	2%
Milk powder, pulverized in a blender	30 g	1 oz	4%
Cocoa powder	20 g	1 oz	2%
Confectioners' sugar	20 g	1 oz	2%
Egg whites	20 g	1 oz	2%
Glucose syrup	20 g	1 oz	2%
Glucose syrup	270 g	10 oz	37%
Sugar	240 g	9 oz	33%
Water	60 g	2 oz	9%
Vanilla extract	10 g	0.5 oz	1%
BATCH SIZE	750 g	29 oz	100%

Dark chocolate, melted, tempered, for precoating and dipping	as needed

TO MAKE THE SOFT CARAMEL:

1. Combine the sugar, evaporated milk, cream, and vanilla bean and its seeds in a saucepan. Bring to a boil, stirring constantly.

2. Add the glucose syrup. Continue cooking over medium heat, stirring, until the mixture reaches 110°C/230°F. Add the butter.

3. Cook until the mixture reaches 115°C/239°F, still stirring. Remove from the heat. Remove the vanilla bean and pour the hot mixture into a frame 12 × 12 × ¼ in set on oiled parchment paper.

TO MAKE THE SOFT CHOCOLATE NOUGAT:

1. Combine the melted dark chocolate and cocoa butter. Keep warm.

2. Sift together the milk powder, cocoa powder, and confectioners' sugar. Set aside.

3. Combine the egg whites and the 20 g of glucose syrup in the bowl of a 5-qt planetary mixer with a whip attachment, but do not begin whipping.

4. Combine the 270 g of glucose syrup, sugar, and water in a saucepan. Cook the mixture to 110°C/230°F.

5. Begin whipping the egg white mixture on high speed. Continue cooking the sugar mixture to 118°C/245°F.

6. Stream the hot syrup into the whipping whites. Continue whipping for approximately 8 minutes, until the mixture has cooled to 50°C/120°F, or until the machine has slowed significantly.

7. Add the vanilla extract.

8. Remove the batch from the machine and mix in the melted chocolate and cocoa butter by hand.

9. Mix in the sifted dry ingredients by hand.

10. Place a second frame 12 × 12 × ¼ in on top of the one containing the caramel. Spread the soft chocolate nougat into the frame. If necessary, use a rolling pin to flatten. Allow to cool to room temperature.

TO MAKE THE SLEEPING BEAUTIES:

1. Precoat the nougat side of the slab with the tempered dark chocolate.

2. Cut into pieces 1 × 4 cm/½ × 1½ in. Dip each in the tempered dark chocolate. Before the chocolate sets, use a 2-prong dipping fork to make diagonal marks across each piece.

NOTE: The temperature given for the fully cooked caramel, 118°C/245°F, is a very good estimate, but results may vary depending on the ingredients used. Always check caramels for consistency by hand during cooking.

HOT CHOCOLATES

yield: **160 PIECES**

CINNAMON MARSHMALLOW

Granulated gelatin	15 g	0.5 oz	2%
Water, cold	80 g	3 oz	13%
Sugar	240 g	9 oz	41%
Glucose syrup	120 g	4 oz	20%
Water	60 g	2 oz	10%
Honey	40 g	1.5 oz	7%
Invert sugar	40 g	1.5 oz	7%
Cinnamon, ground	1 tsp	1 tsp	<1%
Vanilla extract	10 g	0.5 oz	<1%
BATCH SIZE	607 g	22 oz	100%

GANACHE

Heavy cream	180 g	6 oz	25%
Glucose syrup	60 g	2 oz	7%
Crème de cacao	30 g	1 oz	5%
Butter, soft	20 g	1 oz	3%
Dark chocolate, melted, tempered, at 32°C/90°F	430 g	15 oz	60%
BATCH SIZE	720 g	25 oz	100%
Dark chocolate, tempered, for precoating and dipping	as needed		
White chocolate poodle curls (page 113), for finishing	as needed		

TO MAKE THE CINNAMON MARSHMALLOW:

1. Stir the gelatin into the cold water to hydrate.
2. Combine the sugar, glucose syrup, water, honey, invert sugar, and cinnamon and cook to 122°C/252°F.
3. Pour the sugar mixture into the bowl of a 5-qt planetary mixer with a whip attachment, but do not begin whipping. Allow the mixture to cool to 100°C/212°F.
4. While the sugar mixture cools, melt the gelatin over a water bath.
5. When the sugar mixture reaches 100°C/212°F, mix in the melted gelatin. Whip on high speed for 8 minutes, or until well aerated. Add the vanilla extract.
6. Spread the marshmallow into a frame 12 × 12 × ¼ in set on well-oiled parchment paper. Allow to cool fully before making the ganache.

TO MAKE THE GANACHE:

1. Combine the cream and glucose syrup in a saucepan. Bring to a boil.
2. Remove from the heat, add the crème de cacao, and allow to cool to 40°C/105°F.
3. Stir the butter into the melted dark chocolate, taking care that no lumps remain.

4. Pour the cooled cream mixture over the chocolate mixture. Using a spoon or spatula, stir in small outward circles to emulsify.

5. Stir outward in larger circles to spread the emulsion throughout the bowl, checking to see that all of the chocolate has melted. If necessary, heat the ganache over a hot water bath to melt the chocolate. The temperature of the ganache should not exceed 34°C/94°F.

6. Place a second frame 12 × 12 × ¼ in on top of the one containing the marshmallow. Spread the ganache over the marshmallow. Cover with plastic wrap and allow to crystallize overnight at room temperature.

TO MAKE THE HOT CHOCOLATES:

1. Precoat the ganache side of the slab with the tempered dark chocolate.

2. Using a 3-cm/1-in round praline cutter, cut pieces from the slab.

3. Dip the pieces in the tempered dark chocolate.

4. Finish each piece with a few white chocolate poodle curls.

NOTE: When the marshmallow is properly whipped, the specific gravity should be below 0.40.

SPONGE CANDY

yield: **TWO 4" HALF HOTEL PANS OF CANDY, APPROXIMATELY 150 PIECES**

Granulated gelatin	10 g	0.5 oz	20%
Water, cold	40 g	2 oz	80%
BATCH SIZE	50 g	2.5 oz	100%
CANDY			
Sugar	1370 g	48 oz	53%
Glucose syrup	740 g	26 oz	28%
Water	400 g	14 oz	15%
Honey	40 g	2 oz	2%
Baking soda, sifted	40 g	2 oz	2%
BATCH SIZE	2600 g	92 oz	100%
Milk chocolate, melted, tempered, for dipping (optional)		as needed	

1. Butter and flour 2 disposable half-hotel pans 10 cm/4 in deep.

2. Hydrate the gelatin in the cold water. Set aside.

3. Combine the sugar, glucose syrup, and water in a large saucepan. (A large saucepan will allow for the expansion that occurs when the baking soda is added.) Cook to 140°C/284°F. Add the honey and cook to 150°C/302°F.

4. Remove from the heat and allow to cool undisturbed for 5 minutes.

5. Add the hydrated gelatin and stir well to incorporate fully.

6. Vigorously stir in the baking soda, making sure it is well incorporated.

7. As the mixture rises, pour it into the prepared pans.

8. Let the candy cool, undisturbed, for at least 2 hours. If storing longer, wrap to protect from humidity.

9. Break or saw into pieces of the desired size and shape. Dip in the tempered milk chocolate if desired. If the pieces are left undipped, wrap to protect from humidity.

MILK CHOCOLATE SOUFFLÉS

yield: **140 PIECES**

SPECIAL EQUIPMENT REQUIRED

Gas-charged cream whipper canister			
Milk chocolate, melted, tempered, at 30°C/86°F	1000 g	34 oz	100%
BATCH SIZE	1000 g	34 oz	100%
Dark chocolate, melted, tempered, for precoating and dipping	as needed		

1. Warm the cream whipper canister and nozzle to approximately 32°C/90°F.
2. Put the milk chocolate in the canister. Close the lid and charge, according to manufacturer's instructions, with 2 or more gas charges.
3. Shake the canister vigorously for 1 minute.
4. Invert the canister and discharge the chocolate into a frame 12 × 12 × ¾ in set on parchment paper.
5. Spread the chocolate froth to make it level with the top of the frame. Adjust the frame size if necessary by moving the bars closer, to make a ½-in-thick slab.
6. Allow the chocolate to set until firm enough to handle.
7. Precoat one side of the slab with the tempered dark chocolate.
8. Cut into squares using the 22.5-mm strings on a guitar.
9. Dip the squares in the tempered dark chocolate. Before the chocolate sets, use a round dipping fork to make a circular mark on top of each piece.

11

Nuts have a long history of use in confectionery, and with good reason: they are a natural choice to provide flavor, textural contrast, and visual appeal to confections.

NUT CENTERS

Due to their low moisture content, nuts may be used in many different ways: as inclusions, either in centers or in chocolate itself; as decoration—left whole or positioned on top of centers and enrobed; as fillings, when ground into paste; or as adornments on the outside of candy, where they create visual interest. The large variety of nuts available adds to their versatility, with their wide range of flavors, textures, and shapes providing nearly limitless possibilities to the confectioner. While confections are not considered health food, nuts contain a large percentage of healthful monounsaturated, polyunsaturated, and omega-3 fatty acids, which make them a guilt-free pleasure.

NUT PASTES

Marzipan

A mixture of blanched almonds and sugar ground to a paste, marzipan has a long and nebulous history. Depending on the reference cited, its origins may lie in Germany, the Middle East, or Italy. Whatever its source, it is less important to the confectioner than the methods for making and using marzipan. While marzipan has not been extremely popular in the United States, some of this is no doubt due to Americans' exposure to a poor-quality product. The U.S. government does not recognize a standard of identity for marzipan, but all marzipan should be based on almonds. Confectioners may alter formulas as they see fit to create and market marzipan, but most agree that without almonds, the product simply is not marzipan. The marzipan formulas in this book contain 50 percent nuts on a dry-solids basis. Using fewer nuts is less expensive and makes the process easier but does not provide the full flavor found in marzipan containing more nuts. However, a marzipan that contains too many nuts—a quantity higher than 50 percent—is very prone to separation due to its high oil content.

Almond paste

Commercial almond paste is a mixture of equal parts almonds and sugar ground into a paste. Almond paste also contains bitter almond oil, which gives the paste its characteristic pungently sweet aroma. Almond paste is frequently used to make marzipan by combining it with glucose syrup, confectioners' sugar, and sometimes fondant. Marzipan made in this fashion is best suited to modeling rather than to confectionery work because of its very high sugar content and corresponding low percentage of nuts. Almond paste does, however, have practical applications in confectionery, as it is a convenient way to introduce ground almonds without having to start from scratch.

---

technique | theory | **MARZIPAN**

There are two general methods for producing marzipan: the German method and the French method. In the German method, the almonds are combined with sugar, cooked together, and then ground into a paste. This method is not commonly used by artisan confectioners. The method for the more applicable French marzipan is as follows:

1. **BLANCH THE NUTS IN BOILING WATER. ALLOW THEM TO SOAK FOR 5 MINUTES.** The nuts are blanched to hydrate them, facilitate the removal of the skins, if necessary, soften them for grinding, and pasteurize them. Using unblanched nuts is likely to result in separated marzipan due to insufficient water content. Although untoasted almonds do not have as much flavor as toasted almonds, they are traditionally used in order to make a lighter-colored marzipan, which may then be colored and painted more easily. Untoasted almonds also

provide greater resistance to rancidity, and therefore a longer shelf life, than toasted nuts do. The formulas in this book use both untoasted and toasted nuts. When toasted nuts are used, the temperature of the sugar used has been reduced to compensate for the moisture loss during toasting. Marzipan may be made using a variety of nuts in addition to almonds. Most often these nuts replace 50 percent of the almonds in the formula, but a higher percentage of other nuts may be used with success, depending on the fat content of the nut chosen. High-fat nuts, such as macadamias, are extremely likely to separate during grinding, and are better used in conjunction with almonds rather than in place of them.

2. **COARSELY CHOP THE NUTS.** Chopping the nuts after blanching exposes more surface area for the cooked sugar to adhere to and facilitates grinding.

3. **COOK SUGAR, GLUCOSE SYRUP, AND WATER TO THE DESIRED TEMPERATURE.** As always, the temperature to which sugar is cooked controls the moisture that remains in the syrup. (See Standard Wet-Sugar Cooking Technique and Theory, page 219.) Cooking the sugar to a high temperature results in marzipan that is firm but susceptible to separation. Conversely, cooking the sugar to a lower temperature makes for a softer marzipan that is less likely to separate.

4. **POUR THE COOKED SUGAR OVER THE CHOPPED NUTS IN A STAINLESS-STEEL MIXING BOWL. MIX TOGETHER LIGHTLY.** Mixing the sugar with the nuts ensures evenly distributed ingredients. Excessive stirring should be avoided, as it can cause crystallization of the sugar.

5. **POUR ONTO A MARBLE SLAB AND ALLOW TO COOL TO ROOM TEMPERATURE.** The marzipan is ground more efficiently when it has first cooled to room temperature. Grinding hot marzipan causes it to stick to the inside of the bowl.

6. **GRIND IN A FOOD PROCESSOR UNTIL THE DESIRED DEGREE OF SMOOTHNESS IS ACHIEVED.** The traditional tool for grinding marzipan is a mélangeur, or roller refiner. This is arguably still the best method, but very good quality marzipan can be made using powerful commercial food processors. Whatever machine is used, the nuts should be ground in increments that are not too large for the machine to handle. The marzipan should be ground until it forms a uniformly smooth dough.

7. **PRIOR TO USE, ALLOW TO COOL TO ROOM TEMPERATURE OR WRAP WELL AND STORE OVERNIGHT.** Immediately after grinding, the marzipan will be hot from the friction of the machine, and very soft due to the elevated temperature. It must cool completely before it can be used. When stored overnight, tightly wrapped, the marzipan will become firmer still.

LEFT: *A mixture of chopped nuts and sugar syrup cooling to room temperature on a marble slab (see step 5 of the technique).* CENTER: *Grinding marzipan to the desired consistency with a food processor (see step 6 of the technique).* RIGHT: *At room temperature, prepared marzipan can be rolled out or shaped and portioned as desired.*

REPAIRING SEPARATED MARZIPAN

Making marzipan is a relatively straightforward process with only one pitfall: fat separation. Although a solid, marzipan is a fat-in-water emulsion, just like ganache. Because fat is the dispersed phase of marzipan, if there is too much of it in relation to the continuous aqueous phase, the fat separates out of the marzipan. Excessive fat may be caused by nuts with an extremely high fat content or by cooking the sugar to too high a temperature, thus removing too much water from the emulsion. In all cases, separated marzipan is caused by too much fat in relation to water. (See emulsion diagrams, page 97.) The most common time for separation to occur is during grinding.

To repair separated marzipan, mix the marzipan with a small amount of liquid, usually either a spirit or syrup, to ensure low water activity and improved shelf life. In order to maintain flavor quality and a firm texture, the minimum amount of liquid possible should be added if the oil begins to separate. If separation is allowed to progress, it will require more liquid to re-emulsify the fat. As a result it will be very soft and will taste more like the liquor or syrup that was added than like almonds. In order to use this softened marzipan, a significant amount of confectioners' sugar will need to be worked into it, further diminishing the almond flavor. Therefore, a smaller amount of liquid added early in the separation process is a decidedly better solution than a larger amount of liquid added later.

Another method for making marzipan that is simpler than cooking sugar and grinding almonds is to begin with prepared almond paste and to mix it with confectioners' sugar, fondant, and glucose syrup. The advantages of this simplified method are saved labor and a guaranteed smooth texture. The disadvantages are the low percentage of nuts in the finished product and the strong aroma of bitter almonds from the almond paste, which some people find objectionable.

GIANDUJA

Gianduja (pronounced jon-DOO-ya) is another popular use of ground nuts in confectionery. Gianduja is quite simply nuts ground together with chocolate. When gianduja is manufactured, toasted nuts are refined to a size comparable to cacao, resulting in a product that is redolent of toasted nuts and just as smooth as chocolate, but slightly softer than chocolate due to the softening effect of the oil in the nuts. When gianduja is manufactured on a large scale, the nuts used are nearly always hazelnuts or almonds. Gianduja may be made using dark, milk, or white chocolate.

Even with commonly available equipment, it is possible for the artisan confectioner to make his or her own gianduja, and there are good reasons for doing so. Freshly made gianduja retains more of the aroma and flavor of freshly toasted nuts than its commercially available counterpart. When the artisan confectioner makes gianduja, he or she has total control over the product, including the flavor profile, color, sweetness, and relative firmness. The artisan confectioner can make gianduja that is a unique signature item not available from other sources by using ingredients not used in mass-produced gianduja.

LEFT: *Grinding the nuts until they release their oil is imperative to achieving the desired results (see step 2 of technique).* RIGHT: *Once the ground nuts and melted chocolate have been combined, the resulting smooth gianduja is tempered and molded as desired (see step 4 of technique).*

The procedure for making gianduja is simple, and the quantities of ingredients are flexible. To make a medium-consistency gianduja using dark chocolate, use a 1:1:1 ratio—that is, one part dark chocolate, one part roasted hazelnuts, and one part confectioners' sugar. If using milk or white chocolate, increase the amount of chocolate to approximately 1.25 parts, to ensure a similar texture. This ratio is highly variable, however. Because gianduja is a fat system, and not an emulsion, there is no danger of separation. Further, because gianduja contains virtually no moisture, high water activity—and therefore spoilage—is not a concern. The result is that the standard ratio for gianduja may be varied widely without creating much potential for failure. When a softer gianduja is desired, more nuts are ground into the mixture. When less sweetness is desired, the sugar may be decreased or eliminated; for flavor variations, nuts may be toasted to a greater or lesser degree, or different nuts may be used. This is where confectioners may use their own vision to create unique products.

As with marzipan, the ideal equipment to use for making gianduja is a mélangeur, or roller refiner. Good-quality gianduja can be made using a food processor, although it will never be as smooth as the product made with a refiner.

| technique | theory | **GIANDUJA** |

1. **TOAST THE NUTS TO THE DESIRED DEGREE.** The nuts for gianduja are always toasted to develop their flavor and to remove residual moisture. Allowing the moisture to remain in the nuts would have an adverse effect on the viscosity of the gianduja, just as moisture is detrimental to the viscosity of chocolate.

2. **USING A MÉLANGEUR OR FOOD PROCESSOR, GRIND THE NUTS WHILE HOT WITH ABOUT 25 PERCENT OF THE CONFECTIONERS' SUGAR TO AS FINE A CONSISTENCY AS POSSIBLE IN ORDER TO RELEASE THEIR OIL.** The nuts should be ground while hot to facilitate the release of the oils within them. The addition of a small amount of

confectioners' sugar helps them to be ground more efficiently. This step is crucial to the texture of the finished product, as it is at this point that the particle size of the nuts is reduced to make a smooth-textured product. While gianduja made in a processor will never be as smooth as that made using a mélangeur, whether in an artisan operation or a manufacturing plant. grinding the nuts until the oil has been released and the nuts reduced to a liquid state ensures the smoothest possible texture and best release of flavor from the nuts. It is not possible to overgrind the nuts in this step.

3. **ADD THE MELTED CHOCOLATE AND THE REMAINING CONFECTIONERS' SUGAR. PROCESS ONLY UNTIL THOROUGHLY MIXED.** Once the nuts have been satisfactorily ground, the remaining confectioner's sugar and the chocolate can be added and the entire mixture processed for a short time. Overprocessing at this point develops excessive heat, damaging the chocolate. Milk and white chocolates are particularly susceptible to damage from heat; milk and white giandujas become thick, viscous masses if they are overprocessed at this point.

4. **THE GIANDUJA MAY BE TEMPERED AND USED IMMEDIATELY OR STORED FOR LATER USE.** Although finished gianduja may be used immediately, it may also be stored for later use without any loss of quality.

GIANDUJA

It is important to remember that gianduja is a fat system that is high in cocoa butter; therefore it exhibits the same polymorphic characteristics as chocolate. The bottom line: like chocolate, gianduja must be tempered prior to use. The only difference between tempering gianduja and tempering chocolate is that because of the eutectic effect, gianduja requires a lower temperature and generally more time to form the desired seed crystals. Gianduja made in a food processor will also be of a thicker consistency than chocolate, so the easiest way to temper it is usually to put the entire batch onto a marble slab and agitate it generously until it is cooled to 27°C/80°F or below. At this temperature, after constant agitation, it is safe to assume that the gianduja is tempered. Because commercially purchased gianduja is much more fully refined than the processor-made product, it can be tempered more like chocolate: by tabling a portion at a time, and then using that portion to cool and seed the rest. Gianduja must be tempered for all the same reasons chocolate must be: to obtain a uniformly firm set, prevent bloom, provide more heat stability, and give the finished product a smooth mouthfeel free of large fat crystals.

By virtue of its low moisture content, gianduja has a long shelf life. Under proper storage conditions, it should not suffer loss of quality for three months. In addition to its extended shelf life, another unique characteristic of gianduja is that it does not require enrobing, due both to its low moisture content and to its resistance to moisture migration. A gianduja confection left exposed to air will not dry out as would a ganache, nor will it become soft, as would a caramel. Confectioners frequently take advantage of this trait by cutting gianduja confections and leaving the sides exposed for visual appeal.

GIANDUJA NUT PASTE METHOD

Gianduja may also be produced using commercial nut pastes. The advantage of using these products is that they are very finely ground, which ensures a smooth texture in the finished gianduja. Hazelnut paste and praline paste are two pastes commonly used for making gianduja. With a 1:1 praline paste, one part chocolate combined with two parts praline paste will result in a 1:1:1 gianduja. In the case of praline paste, the gianduja will have a noticeable pleasant caramel flavor due to the presence of caramelized sugar. The use of nut pastes is a convenient way to make a smooth-textured gianduja with less labor than if whole nuts are used. When using a paste, simply mix the chocolate with it, and temper the gianduja as usual.

CHOCOLATE-COATED NUTS

Dragées

The dragée method is the handwork predecessor to panning. (See page 70.) The French word *dragée* means "dredged." Here the centers are dredged first in caramel and then in chocolate. Rather than relying on mechanical rotation of pans to distribute the coatings, the coatings are applied by vigorous stirring in bowls. The precoat is a thin layer of caramel, which provides flavor and inhibits fat migration. The caramel is applied by cooking a sugar solution to the thread stage, then adding the untoasted nuts to the syrup. With vigorous stirring the syrup crystallizes, leaving a thin coating of crystals on the nuts. Once the sugar is crystallized, the nuts are returned to the heat and stirred constantly as the sugar caramelizes and the nuts toast. When each nut is coated with a thin varnish of shiny, smooth caramel, a small amount of butter is added and the nuts are poured onto oiled marble and separated by hand to cool. Tempered chocolate is applied to the nuts in stages, and stirred vigorously in a bowl. After the final coat of chocolate, a light dusting of cocoa powder and/or confectioners' sugar is used as a finish, as it is not practical to burnish dragées to the high shine that can be obtained from mechanical panning.

Like panning, the dragée technique is most successfully used for round, smooth nuts. It may also be applied to nontraditional centers, such as coffee beans, spice seeds, and cocoa nibs, to create unique products.

LEFT: *Once the sugar syrup has reached the thread stage, the desired centers, in this case almonds, are added to it and vigorously stirred to induce crystallization (see step 2 of the technique).* CENTER: *The crystal-coated almonds are heated to toast the nuts, melt the sugar crystals, and form a thin layer of caramelized sugar around them (see step 3 of the technique).* RIGHT: *Tempered chocolate is added to the cooled, caramel-coated almonds and stirred vigorously to form a chocolate layer. This process can be repeated as many times as is desired (see step 9 of the technique).*

1. **COMBINE SUGAR WITH WATER IN A LARGE SAUCEPAN OR COPPER KETTLE. COOK THE SUGAR TO THE THREAD STAGE (112°C/234°F).** The sugar for the dragée technique is always cooked without the addition of any type of doctoring agent so that it will crystallize after the nuts are added. Cooking the sugar to the thread stage ensures that the syrup will be supersaturated upon cooling and so will crystallize when it is stirred. The sugar should simply coat the nuts but not be caramelized at this stage. Caramelization will occur on the nuts when the nuts themselves toast later in the process.

2. **ADD THE UNTOASTED NUTS, REMOVE FROM THE HEAT, AND STIR VIGOROUSLY UNTIL THE SUGAR CRYSTALLIZES, COATING THE NUTS WITH A SKIN OF SUGAR CRYSTALS.** Untoasted nuts are used for dragéeing because they will toast during the dragée process. When the concentrated sugar syrup is removed from the heat and the nuts are added, the syrup cools, making it supersaturated. Stirring the syrup with the nuts in it causes the syrup to crystallize rapidly, creating a skin of sugar crystals on the outside of the nuts. This skin becomes the caramel coating after further cooking.

3. **RETURN TO MODERATE HEAT. COOK, STIRRING CONSTANTLY, UNTIL THE SUGAR MELTS AND CARAMELIZES FULLY AND THE NUTS ARE TOASTED.** Moderate heat is the best way to ensure that the sugar crystals melt and caramelize evenly and that the nuts toast simultaneously. It is important during this step to stir constantly and to monitor the heat to prevent hot spots that can scorch the nuts. It is a common error to stop cooking too early. The nuts should remain on the heat until the sugar is completely melted, forming a smooth caramel coating on each piece.

4. **ADD BUTTER TO THE NUT MIXTURE. STIR UNTIL THE BUTTER MELTS AND COATS THE NUTS.** The addition of butter provides flavor and helps prevent the caramel from picking up moisture from the air as it cools, but the primary purpose of adding butter is to make the nuts easier to separate into individual kernels after cooking. The layer of fat prevents the nuts from sticking together, forming one large agglomerate of caramelized nuts. Too much butter added at this stage will prevent the chocolate from hardening properly when it is added.

5. **POUR THE CARAMELIZED NUTS ONTO AN OILED MARBLE SLAB.** A stone slab draws heat quickly from the hot nuts, cooling them.

6. **AS THE NUTS ARE COOLING, SEPARATE THEM INTO INDIVIDUAL KERNELS USING GLOVED FINGERS.** As the nuts cool, they must be separated into individual kernels so that they can be coated with chocolate. This is best accomplished by hand, using gloves both for sanitation and to protect the fingers from the heat of the caramel.

7. **ALLOW THE NUTS TO COOL TO ROOM TEMPERATURE.** Once separated, the nuts must cool to room temperature in order for the chocolate to set on them. The nuts can hold heat inside even after they appear to be properly cooled. It is best to err on the side of allowing extra time, perhaps as long as an hour, for the nuts to cool so that the chocolate will set quickly when it is added.

8. **REFRIGERATE THE NUTS BRIEFLY TO CHILL THEM SLIGHTLY.** Chilling the nuts slightly causes the chocolate to set efficiently when it is added, reducing the time that must be spent stirring. Overchilling is likely to cause condensation on the nuts, dissolving the caramel and diminishing the quality. Refrigeration for 5 to 10 minutes is all that should be necessary.

9. **PLACE THE CARAMEL-COATED NUTS IN A LARGE STAINLESS-STEEL BOWL. POUR A SMALL QUANTITY OF TEMPERED CHOCOLATE ONTO THEM. STIR VIGOROUSLY UNTIL THE CHOCOLATE SETS AND THE NUTS ARE SEPARATED INTO INDIVIDUAL KERNELS.** The stainless-steel mixing bowl takes the place of a panning machine. In the dragée technique, the tumbling action of the nuts comes from manual stirring rather than from the rotation of a motorized pan. The chocolate used for dragéeing is tempered—unlike that used for panning—so that it will set quickly. Stirring must continue until the chocolate has set to the point at which the nuts are no longer in a mass but have again separated into individual kernels.

10. **POUR THE NUTS ONTO A SHEET PAN AND REFRIGERATE FOR 5 MINUTES.** The nuts are chilled slightly after each addition of chocolate so that the next layer of chocolate will set quickly with a minimum of stirring.

11. **REPEAT STEPS 9 AND 10 UNTIL THREE ADDITIONS OF CHOCOLATE HAVE BEEN PUT ON THE NUTS. AFTER THE THIRD ADDITION, SIFT COCOA POWDER, CONFECTIONERS' SUGAR, OR A COMBINATION OF THE TWO ONTO THE NUTS.** Three coats of chocolate are usually sufficient to cover the nuts with a layer of chocolate, but more can be added as desired. Unlike panned nuts, dragées are not polished to a high shine using glazes and polish but are finished more rustically with cocoa powder or confectioners' sugar.

LEFT: *Once the inclusions are mixed with tempered chocolate, the rochers are portioned out onto a sheet pan to set. Rochers can vary greatly depending on the chocolate and the inclusions used.*
RIGHT, LEFT TO RIGHT: *White chocolate, dark chocolate, and milk chocolate rochers with various inclusions*

ROCHERS

Rochers are clusters of nuts bound together by chocolate. Because they may be made using any type of chocolate and any type of nuts—whole or chopped—the variations are nearly endless. Other types of inclusions, such as cereals, seeds, or dried fruits, may be introduced for variety, provided they are extremely low in moisture.

technique	ROCHERS

1. Moisten the nuts with spirit or syrup, and sprinkle them with sugar if desired.

2. Toast the nuts to the desired degree in oven, turning them occasionally to ensure even toasting.

3. Allow the nuts to cool completely to room temperature.

4. Add other inclusions, such as cereal, seeds, or dried fruit, to the nuts.

5. Warm the nut mixture to about 28°C/82°F.

6. In a small bowl, coat small increments of the nut mixture with just enough chocolate to cover them.

7. Spoon the mixture out in small clusters onto parchment paper. Allow to set.

When making rochers, the prepared nuts, warmed to about 28°C/82°F, are coated with a thin film of tempered chocolate. Then, before the chocolate sets, the salpicon is spooned or dropped out onto pans in the desired size and allowed to set. Rochers are simple to make, may have any number of flavor profiles, and are crisp and delicious. However, there are a few common pitfalls to avoid. When making rochers, it is helpful to coat only a small quantity of nuts at a time. If too much of the mixture is prepared at once, the chocolate will begin to set before the entire mixture can be deposited, and the finished product will not have a smooth, shiny coat. Warming the toasted nuts to 28°C/82°F provides more working time to help prevent this defect. The other difficulty in rocher production lies in maintaining a consistent size and proper shape as the confections are deposited. They should be perfect little mounds with some height to them rather than irregular, flat patties.

RANCIDITY AND SHELF LIFE

While there is much to recommend the use of nuts in confectionery, they are not without their challenges. Expense is a consideration for any professional, and nuts are among the most expensive ingredients a confectioner uses. Nuts also present shelf-life concerns, not through moisture content or water activity but through the instability of the fats they contain. Nut oils are susceptible to rancidity from a variety of causes, so handling, storage, and freshness are prime concerns when dealing with products that contain nuts. Factors contributing to rancidity include enzymatic action and exposure to heat, oxygen, light, and the metals used in processing. Nuts placed on the surface of a confection are more susceptible to rancidity than those that are enrobed. This is due to their exposure to oxygen. For the same reason, the more finely nuts are chopped or ground, the more likely it is they will become rancid. Further, toasted nuts will always become rancid more readily than unroasted ones, due to the break-down of fatty acids during roasting. Nuts should be purchased in small quantities that allow for quick product turnover and should be stored tightly sealed in a cool, dry environment to retard the onset of rancidity. All nut products should be tasted prior to use to ensure their freshness and should be rejected if rancid flavors are detected. Toast nuts close to the time they are to be used in order to avoid the off flavors brought on by rancidity.

FAT MIGRATION

Another hurdle in the use of nuts with chocolate is the incompatibility of their oils with cocoa butter. The result of this incompatibility is fat migration, which causes bloom and softened chocolate. In simple terms, when nuts are used in making a center, the fat contained in them, which is largely liquid at room temperature, tends to migrate through the chocolate, while the cocoa butter in the chocolate migrates into the nut center, until an equilibrium of fat is reached. The consequence is the formation of fat bloom on the outside of the confection and a chocolate coating that no longer exhibits proper snap due to the softening effect of the nut oil. This process takes time to occur and is more of a concern to large-scale manufacturers than it is to artisan confectioners. Manufacturers of mass-produced confections have ex-tended storage requirements; artisan confectioners do not typically require as long a shelf life for his or her products. Even so, certain centers that contain a high percentage of ground nuts may exhibit drops of nut oil on the outside of the chocolate within hours of enrobing. Although these oil droplets are usually reabsorbed into the chocolate within a day, the choco-late will develop fat bloom within a short period of time.

There are steps the confectioner can take to minimize fat migration. The first is to under-stand and recognize the problem and to base the production of nut centers on a reasonably quick turnover. The damage from fat migration takes time to become evident, so ensuring that the product is consumed before it is damaged is the best form of prevention. To help delay the onset of fat migration, seal the centers prior to enrobing them in chocolate. The material used for sealing may be either a glaze based on a vegetable gum or a hydrogenated solid fat that creates a barrier to the migration. Both of these solutions are used in large-scale manufacturing, but may not be practical or desirable to the artisan confectioner. The most practical preventive measures for artisan confectioners are a well-tempered chocolate coat-ing, which creates a solid barrier to the nut oil, and a chocolate coating thicker than might be used on other centers, to retard fat migration. In addition, milk chocolate rather than dark chocolate can be a practical choice for enrobing nut centers; milk chocolate is less dramati-cally affected by fat migration—because it is relatively soft—and is less likely to exhibit fat bloom, due to the butterfat it contains.

EUTECTICS

For confectioners, a eutectic is a mixture of fats with a lowered melting point: the softening effect of the combined fats is more pronounced than would be predicted from simply combining the two and averaging their melting points. When combined with cocoa butter, many fats and oils create eutectics. The butterfat in milk chocolate forms a eutectic with cocoa butter that makes milk chocolate softer than dark chocolate and causes it to have a lower working temperature. The nut oil present in gianduja has the same effects on cocoa butter. One of the most pronounced examples of a eutectic effect comes from the combination of coconut fat or palm-kernel fat with cocoa butter. Both coconut and palm-kernel fats are tropical fats; a more accurate term is lauric fats, named for their chemical makeup. When a lauric fat is combined with cocoa butter, the eutectic effect is dramatic. When coconut fat with a 33°C/92°F melting point is combined with cocoa butter, which melts at around 34°C/93°F, the resulting mixture melts well below the temperature of either of the component fats, with the exact melting temperature dependent on the ratio of fats. Confectioners take advantage of this phenomenon to create centers called meltaways. The resulting compound fat melts quickly when these products contact the palate, spreading the flavor and releasing the aromatics of the center. Often meltaways are combined with nut pastes to rapidly release the nut flavor. With these products, the transition from a solid to a liquid state happens so quickly that it is possible to feel the heat being absorbed from the mouth. This is the reason that centers of this description actually leave a cool feeling on the palate as they rapidly melt.

Other factors that affect fat migration are the variety of nut used (higher-fat nuts cause more migration), the form of nut used (the more finely ground the nut, the more fat is released), and the temperature at which the product is stored (cooler temperatures retard migration). Freezing of confections all but stops fat migration while the product is frozen, and is a good option, provided procedures are followed to prevent the formation of condensation and subsequent sugar bloom. (See Freezing Confections, page 46.) Even nuts on the outside of chocolate can cause fat migration, but it is much less likely to be noticed because the nuts themselves disguise any bloom that occurs, and their texture masks the softening of the chocolate.

DEFECTS IN CONFECTIONS WITH NUT CENTERS

DEFECT	CAUSE	REMEDY
MARZIPAN		
GRAINY TEXTURE	Marzipan not ground finely enough	Grind finer in the processor
OIL SEEPING FROM MARZIPAN	Separation of oil	Add liquid during grinding
		Cook sugar to lower temperature
		Use nuts with a lower fat content
EXCESSIVELY SOFT MARZIPAN	Sugar not cooked to a high enough temperature	Cook sugar to a higher temperature in order to remove more water
	Too much liquid added during grinding	Add less liquid during grinding
GIANDUJA		
GRAINY TEXTURE	Nuts not ground finely enough	Grind nuts finer
	Gianduja not tempered, causing large fat crystals when set	Cool and agitate well before depositing
OVERLY VISCOUS	Excessive processing, resulting in heat damage	Do not process excessively after the chocolate is added
	Too much confectioners' sugar in formula	Reduce confectioners' sugar in formula
	Insufficient cocoa butter in chocolate	Use chocolate with sufficient cocoa butter content
TOO SOFT WHEN SET	Excessive nuts in formula	Use lower proportion of nuts in formula
	Gianduja not tempered	Cool and agitate well before depositing
TOO HARD WHEN SET	Insufficient nuts in formula	Use higher proportion of nuts in formula
	Insufficient grinding of nuts to release oil	Grind nuts finer to release oil before adding the chocolate
OFF FLAVORS	Rancidity in nut oil	Use fresh nuts
		Store nuts properly
		Do not allow reactive metals to contact nuts during handling
	Over-roasting of nuts	Roast nuts to proper doneness
ROCHERS		
ROCHERS NOT SHINY OR SMOOTH	Working with chocolate that has begun to set	Work with smaller amounts of rocher mixture at a time
		Warm the nuts to 29°C/85°F before adding chocolate
		Do not warm nuts over 32°C/90°F when mixing with chocolate
	Chocolate not tempered	Temper chocolate prior to mixing with nuts
OTHER NUT CENTERS		
BLOOM; DROPLETS OF OIL ON SURFACE; SOFTENED CHOCOLATE	Fat migration	Seal centers prior to enrobing
		Use a thicker coat of chocolate
		Be certain chocolate coating is well tempered
		Use milk chocolate coating

MARZIPAN

yield: **APPROXIMATELY 125 PIECES**

Almonds, whole, untoasted	430 g	15 oz	43%
Sugar	340 g	12 oz	34%
Water	120 g	4 oz	12%
Glucose syrup	110 g	4 oz	11%
BATCH SIZE	1000 g	35 oz	100%

1. Blanch the almonds in boiling water in a saucepan. Return to a boil. Cover, remove from the heat, and allow to soak for 5 minutes. Drain.

2. Coarsely grind the nuts in a food processor.

3. Combine the sugar, water, and glucose syrup in a saucepan. Cook to 118°C/245°F, following the Standard Wet-Sugar Cooking Technique and Theory (see page 219).

4. Pour the hot syrup over the chopped nuts in a stainless-steel bowl. Mix together lightly.

5. Pour the syrup-coated nuts onto an oiled marble slab. Allow to cool to room temperature.

6. Grind half of the batch at a time in a food processor until it reaches the desired fine consistency. (This may take 10 minutes or more.) If the marzipan separates during the grinding process, add a small quantity of liquid, such as spirit or boiled syrup, to restore the emulsion.

7. Combine the ground batches of marzipan. Allow to cool to room temperature, roll, and use as desired. (Marzipan may be made up days in advance.)

CASHEW MARZIPAN: Replace half the almonds with cashews. Cook the sugar to 120°C/248°F.

HAZELNUT MARZIPAN: Replace half the almonds with hazelnuts. Cook the sugar to 115°C/239°F.

PISTACHIO MARZIPAN: Replace half the almonds with skinned pistachios. Cook the sugar to 122°C/252°F.

PORT WINE MARZIPAN: Cook the sugar with 2 g/1 tsp of ground cinnamon and one split, scraped vanilla bean. Cook the sugar to 135°C/275°F. Remove the vanilla bean prior to grinding. Slowly stream about 80 g/3 oz of port wine into the nuts during grinding. (The exact amount of port will vary, depending on the desired consistency.)

TOASTED ALMOND MARZIPAN: Lightly toast the almonds prior to blanching. Cook the sugar to 114°C/237°F.

TOASTED HAZELNUT MARZIPAN: Replace half the almonds with toasted hazelnuts. Cook the sugar to 114°C/237°F.

WALNUT MARZIPAN: Replace half the almonds with walnuts. Cook the sugar to 116°C/240°F.

TOASTED HAZELNUT MARZIPAN

yield: **110 PIECES**

Toasted Hazelnut Marzipan (Variation, page 413)	1x formula	1x formula
Dark chocolate, melted, tempered, for precoating	as needed	
Hazelnuts, toasted, for finishing	80 nuts	80 nuts
Dark chocolate, melted, tempered, thinned, for dipping (see Note)	as needed	

1. Roll the marzipan into a rectangle approximately 18 × 30 cm/7 × 12 in, 1 cm/½ in thick.

2. Precoat one side of the slab with the tempered dark chocolate.

3. Using a round praline cutter, cut the marzipan.

4. Garnish each piece with a toasted hazelnut, point up. Secure the hazelnut with a dot of the tempered dark chocolate.

5. Dip the pieces in the thinned dark chocolate.

   NOTE: See Thinning Technique and Theory, page 64.

TOASTED ALMOND AND CHERRY MARZIPAN

yield: 110 PIECES

Dried cherries, finely chopped	120 g	4 oz
Toasted Almond Marzipan (Variation, page 413)	1x formula	1x formula
Dark chocolate, melted, tempered, for precoating and securing almond halves	as needed	
Almonds, toasted, halved	110 halves	110 halves
Dark chocolate, melted, tempered, thinned, for dipping (see Note)	as needed	

1. Mix the dried cherries into the marzipan.

2. Roll the marzipan into a rectangle approximately 18 × 30 cm/7 × 12 in, 1 cm/⅜ in thick.

3. Precoat one side of the slab with the tempered dark chocolate.

4. Using a 30-mm/1-in round cutter, cut slender crescent moons out of the marzipan.

5. Garnish each piece with half a toasted almond, secured with a dot of the tempered dark chocolate.

6. Dip the pieces in the thinned dark chocolate.

   NOTE: See Thinning Technique and Theory, page 64.

WALNUT MARZIPAN

yield: **110 PIECES**

Walnut Marzipan (Variation, page 413)	1x formula	1x formula
Dark chocolate, melted, tempered, for precoating, dipping, and finishing	as needed	
Walnut pieces, toasted, for finishing	110 pieces	110 pieces

1. Roll the marzipan into a rectangle approximately 18 × 30 cm/7 × 12 in, 1 cm/⅜ in thick.

2. Precoat one side of the slab with the tempered dark chocolate.

3. Using an oval praline cutter, cut the marzipan.

4. Dip the pieces in the tempered dark chocolate.

5. When the chocolate begins to set, garnish each piece with a sliver of walnut.

LUNAS

yield: **150 PIECES**

Port Wine Marzipan (Variation, page 413)	1x formula	1x formula
Dark chocolate, melted, tempered, for precoating and dipping	as needed	
White chocolate, melted, tempered, for finishing	as needed	

1. Roll the marzipan into a rectangle approximately 18 × 30 cm/7 × 12 in, 1 cm/½ in thick.

2. Precoat one side of the slab with the tempered dark chocolate.

3. Using a 30-mm/1-in round cutter, cut slender crescent moons out of the marzipan.

4. Dip the pieces in the tempered dark chocolate.

5. When the chocolate has set, filigree each piece with four stripes of white chocolate across the center.

TRIUMVIRATES

yield: **100 PIECES**

Hazelnut Gianduja (page 413)	530 g	19 oz	67%
Hazelnuts, toasted or dragéed	270 g	9 oz	33%
BATCH SIZE	800 g	28 oz	100%
Dark chocolate, melted, tempered, and well thinned, for dipping (see Notes)	as needed		

1. Temper the gianduja by tabling until it begins to thicken.
2. Transfer the gianduja to a pastry bag fitted with a no. 4 round tip. Pipe out slightly rounded domes of gianduja 19 mm/¾ in in diameter.
3. Immediately place 3 toasted hazelnuts, points up, on top of each dome.
4. Dip the domes in the thinned dark chocolate.

   NOTES: Gianduja may be made from fresh nuts or praline paste or may be purchased. For thinning chocolate, see Thinning Technique and Theory, page 64.

HAZELNUT GIANDUJA

yield: **1500 G/54 OZ**

Hazelnuts, toasted	500 g	18 oz	33%
Confectioners' sugar	500 g	18 oz	33%
Dark chocolate, melted, tempered, at 32°C/90°F	500 g	18 oz	33%
BATCH SIZE	1500 g	54 oz	100%

1. Grind the toasted hazelnuts with a small amount of the confectioners' sugar in a food processor until liquefied.

2. Add the remaining confectioners' sugar and the melted dark chocolate. Mix in the food processor just until homogeneous.

3. Temper the gianduja for immediate use, or store for future use.

MILK CHOCOLATE OR WHITE CHOCOLATE GIANDUJA: Increase the quantity of chocolate to 625 g/22 oz.

PRALINE GIANDUJA: Replace the hazelnuts and confectioners' sugar with 1000 g/35 oz of praline paste.

PRINCESSE

yield: **225 BARS**

Pistachios, chopped	190 g	7 oz	14%
Praline paste	840 g	30 oz	62%
Cocoa butter, melted	330 g	12 oz	24%
BATCH SIZE	1360 g	49 oz	100%

Milk chocolate, melted, tempered, for precoating and enrobing	as needed	

1. Sift the dust from the chopped pistachios and reserve.
2. Combine the praline paste with the melted cocoa butter. Stir in the chopped pistachios.
3. Temper the mixture by tabling on a marble slab until it is cooled to room temperature and well agitated but still fluid.
4. Spread into a frame 12 × 12 × ½ in set on parchment paper. Allow to crystallize until set, about 20 minutes.
5. Precoat one side of the slab with the tempered milk chocolate.
6. Cut the slab into 25-mm/1-in strips.
7. Place the strips precoated side down on an icing screen over a piece of parchment paper.
8. Enrobe the strips by ladling the tempered milk chocolate over them. Vibrate to remove excess chocolate.
9. Remove the strips from the screen before they set and place them on parchment paper.
10. When the chocolate begins to set, use a dipping fork to make wave patterns on the bars.
11. Lightly sift some of the reserved pistachio dust onto the bars before the chocolate fully sets.
12. Cut immediately, using the 15-mm strings on a guitar.

PEANUT BUTTER CUPS

yield: **200 CUPS**

Foil cups lined with milk chocolate (see page 87)	200 cups	200 cups	
FILLING			
Peanut butter	710 g	25 oz	71%
Confectioners' sugar	190 g	7 oz	19%
Cocoa butter, melted	100 g	3.5 oz	10%
Salt	½ tsp	½ tsp	<1%
BATCH SIZE	1000 g	35.5 oz	100%
Milk chocolate, melted, tempered, for capping	as needed		
Peanut halves, toasted, for finishing	200	200	

TO PREPARE THE FOIL CUPS:

Line cups with the tempered dark chocolate following the procedure on page 87.

TO MAKE THE FILLING:

1. Combine the peanut butter, confectioners' sugar, cocoa butter, and salt. Mix until homogeneous.

2. Adjust the temperature of the mixture to 28°C/82°F before filling the cups.

3. Fill the chocolate-lined foil cups to within 3 mm/⅛ in of the tops.

4. Vibrate the cups to level the filling.

5. Cap the filled cups using the tempered milk chocolate and a paper piping cone.

6. When the chocolate begins to set, garnish each cup with a toasted peanut half.

   NOTE: This filling is also appropriate for shell molding.

CRUNCHY CUPS: Make a croquant of 200 g/7 oz of caramelized sugar mixed with 200 g/7 oz of peanuts. Pour onto marble to cool, chop into 3-mm/⅛-in pieces. Mix with the filling.

SESAME SQUARES

yield: **156 SQUARES**

Lemon juice	¼ tsp	¼ tsp	<1%
Sugar	50 g	2 oz	4%
Sesame seeds, untoasted	100 g	3.5 oz	7%
Dark chocolate, melted, tempered, at 32°C/90°F	150 g	5 oz	11%
Milk chocolate, melted, tempered, at 30°C/86°F (see Note)	800 g	29 oz	60%
Tahini	220 g	8 oz	16%
Sesame seeds, toasted	30 g	1 oz	2%
BATCH SIZE	1350 g	48.5 oz	100%
Dark chocolate, melted, tempered, for dipping	as needed		

1. Rub the lemon juice into the sugar.

2. In a saucepan, caramelize the sugar over direct heat while stirring constantly.

3. Add the sesame seeds. Continue stirring over heat until the mixture is softened, and the seeds are toasted.

4. Pour the sesame croquant onto an oiled marble slab. Spread as thinly as possible and allow to cool until completely brittle. Use a rolling pin to crush the croquant into individual seeds.

5. Mix the crushed seeds with the tempered dark chocolate.

6. Roll the chocolate-sesame mixture between sheets of heavy plastic to form a square slightly larger than 30 × 30 cm/12 × 12 in. Trim the slab to 30 × 30 cm/ 12 × 12 in. Set up a frame 12 × 12 × ½ in around the perimeter of the slab.

7. Mix the tempered milk chocolate with the tahini (see Note). Spread into the frame containing the chocolate-sesame slab. Sprinkle with the toasted sesame seeds. Allow to crystallize at room temperature until set, about 20 minutes.

8. Cut into squares, using the 22.5-mm strings on a guitar.

9. Dip up to the top face in tempered dark chocolate.

   NOTE: It is important that the milk chocolate be tempered before it is mixed with the tahini.

TRIFECTIONS

yield: **180 PIECES**

WHITE CHOCOLATE GIANDUJA

Almonds, very lightly toasted	230 g	8 oz	13%
Confectioners' sugar	140 g	5 oz	7%
White chocolate, melted, tempered, at 30°C/86°F	230 g	8 oz	13%

MILK CHOCOLATE GIANDUJA

Almonds, toasted	230 g	8 oz	13%
Confectioners' sugar	140 g	5 oz	7%
Milk chocolate, melted, tempered, at 30°C/86°F	230 g	8 oz	13%

DARK CHOCOLATE GIANDUJA

Hazelnuts, toasted	230 g	8 oz	13%
Confectioners' sugar	170 g	6 oz	8%
Dark chocolate, melted, tempered, at 32°C/90°F	230 g	8 oz	13%
BATCH SIZE	1830 g	64 oz	100%
Dark chocolate, melted, tempered, for precoating	as needed		

TO MAKE THE WHITE CHOCOLATE GIANDUJA:

1. Grind the very lightly toasted almonds with a small amount of the confectioners' sugar in a food processor until liquefied.

2. Add the melted white chocolate and the remaining confectioners' sugar. Mix just until homogeneous.

3. Temper the white gianduja by tabling vigorously on a marble slab until it is cooled to room temperature and well agitated, about 5 minutes.

4. Spread into a frame 10 × 12 × ³⁄₁₆ in set on a heavy plastic sheet. Smooth the gianduja level with the frame.

TO MAKE THE MILK CHOCOLATE GIANDUJA:

1. Repeat steps 1 through 3 above, using the ingredients for milk chocolate gianduja.

2. Place a second frame 10 × 12 × ³⁄₁₆ in on top of the one containing the white chocolate layer. Take care that the white chocolate gianduja has set before spreading the milk chocolate gianduja on top of it.

TO MAKE THE DARK CHOCOLATE GIANDUJA:

1. Repeat the process using the ingredients for dark chocolate gianduja.

2. Allow the 3 layers of gianduja to crystallize.

TO MAKE THE TRIFECTIONS:

1. Remove the layered gianduja from the frame by running a paring knife around the edge. Invert the slab so the white chocolate side is up.

2. Spread a layer of the tempered dark chocolate onto the white chocolate gianduja. Texture with an icing comb before it sets.

3. Allow the chocolate to just set. Immediately, before the chocolate becomes too brittle, cut into bars using the 15-mm and 30-mm strings on a guitar.

4. Separate the pieces immediately.

JFB's

yield: 156 PIECES

Sliced almonds	220 g	8 oz	15%
Kirschwasser	30 g	1 oz	2%
Sugar	30 g	1 oz	2%
Praline paste	660 g	23 oz	44%
Dark chocolate, melted, tempered, at 32°C/90°F	330 g	12 oz	22%
Dried cherries, finely chopped	220 g	8 oz	15%
BATCH SIZE	1490 g	53 oz	100%
Dark chocolate, melted, tempered, for precoating and dipping	as needed		
Milk chocolate, tempered, for coating	as needed		

1. Moisten the almonds with the kirschwasser in a stainless-steel bowl. Sprinkle with the sugar. Toast in the oven until golden brown. Allow to cool to room temperature. Coarsely chop the almonds.

2. Combine the praline paste and the tempered dark chocolate. Mix in the dried cherries and the chopped almonds.

3. Temper by tabling on a marble slab until cooled to room temperature and well agitated but still fluid.

4. Spread into a frame 12 × 12 × ½ in set on parchment paper. Allow to set.

5. Precoat one side of the slab with the tempered dark chocolate.

6. Spread a 3-mm/⅛-in layer of the milk chocolate on top of the slab. Using a paper cone, immediately filigree thin parallel lines of tempered dark chocolate over the milk chocolate.

7. Working quickly, before the chocolate sets, run a paring knife back and forth, perpendicular to the filigree, to create a feathered effect.

8. Allow the chocolate to just set. Immediately, before the chocolate becomes too brittle, cut into squares, using the 22.5-mm strings on a guitar.

9. Dip each piece to the top face in the tempered dark chocolate.

   NOTE: It is vital to work quickly when applying the top surface of milk and dark chocolate. If necessary, cut the slab in half and work with only half at a time in order to finish before the chocolate sets.

MINT MELTAWAYS

yield: **180 PIECES**

Dark chocolate, melted, tempered, at 32°C/90°F	1040 g	37 oz	77%
Coconut fat, melted	310 g	11 oz	23%
Peppermint oil	10 drops	10 drops	<1%
BATCH SIZE	1350 g	48 oz	100%
Confectioners' sugar, sifted, for finishing	as needed		

1. Combine the melted dark chocolate, coconut fat, and peppermint oil.

2. Temper the mixture by tabling it on a marble slab until cooled to room temperature and well agitated but still fluid.

3. Spread into a frame 12 × 12 × ½ in set on parchment paper. Allow to crystallize until set, about 20 minutes.

4. Dust one side of the slab with the sifted confectioners' sugar.

5. With the dusted side down, cut the slab into rectangles, using the 15-mm and 30-mm strings on a guitar.

6. Dredge each piece in the sifted confectioners' sugar. Shake off excess.

   NOTE: The quantity of the peppermint oil may be increased or decreased as desired.

PRALINE MELTAWAYS

yield: **180 PIECES**

Milk chocolate, melted, tempered, at 30°C/86°F	830 g	29 oz	62%
Coconut fat, melted	210 g	7 oz	15%
Praline paste	310 g	11 oz	23%
BATCH SIZE	1350 g	47 oz	100%
Cocoa powder, sifted, for finishing	as needed		

1. Combine the melted milk chocolate, praline paste, and coconut fat.

2. Temper by tabling on a marble slab until cooled to room temperature and well agitated but still fluid.

3. Spread into a frame 12 × 12 × ½ in set on parchment paper. Allow to crystallize until set, about 20 minutes. Dust one side of the slab with the sifted cocoa powder.

4. With the dusted side down, cut the slab into rectangles, using the 15-mm and 30-mm strings on a guitar.

5. Dredge each piece in the sifted cocoa powder. Shake off excess.

PEANUT BUTTER MELTAWAYS

yield: **180 PIECES**

Milk chocolate, melted, tempered, at 30°C/86°F	880 g	31 oz	65%
Coconut fat, melted	200 g	7 oz	15%
Peanut butter, warmed to approximately 36°C/97°F	270 g	10 oz	20%
BATCH SIZE	1350 g	48 oz	100%
Confectioners' sugar, sifted, for finishing	as needed		

1. Combine the melted milk chocolate, coconut fat, and peanut butter.
2. Temper by tabling on a marble slab until cooled to room temperature and well agitated but still fluid.
3. Spread into a frame 12 × 12 × ½ in set on parchment paper. Allow to crystallize until set, about 20 minutes.
4. Dust one side of the slab with the sifted confectioners' sugar.
5. With the dusted side down, cut the slab into rectangles, using the 15-mm and 30-mm strings on a guitar.
6. Dredge each piece in the sifted confectioners' sugar. Shake off excess.

ALMOND DRAGÉES

yield: **APPROXIMATELY 800 PIECES**

Sugar	280 g	10 oz	14%
Water	90 g	3 oz	5%
Almonds, blanched, untoasted	930 g	32 oz	46%
Butter	40 g	1 oz	2%
Chocolate, melted, tempered, for coating	650 g	23 oz	32%
Cocoa powder	20 g	1 oz	1%
BATCH SIZE	2010 g	70 oz	100%

1. Combine the sugar and water in a wide saucepan. Cook to the thread stage, about 110°C/230°F. (See Stages of Sugar Cooking, page 217.)

2. Remove from the heat and add the almonds. Stir vigorously off the heat until the almonds fully crystallize and separate into individual sugar-coated nuts.

3. Return the pan to the heat. Cook the almonds, stirring constantly, until the sugar has caramelized and the almonds are toasted. Moderate the heat to ensure good caramelization without scorching.

4. Add the butter. Stir to coat the almonds evenly.

5. Pour the coated almonds onto an oiled marble slab. Separate them as they cool.

6. When the nuts have cooled to room temperature, refrigerate them for 5 minutes before proceeding.

7. Place the lightly chilled almonds in a large stainless-steel bowl. Add a third of the tempered chocolate, and stir vigorously until the chocolate sets and the almonds again separate into individual nuts.

8. Refrigerate the nuts for 5 more minutes. Repeat with another third of the chocolate.

9. Repeat the refrigeration and chocolate-coating cycle one more time.

10. After the third addition of chocolate, sift the cocoa powder over the nuts. Stir to coat evenly. Shake off excess.

CORIANDER DRAGÉES: Use the same technique with the following: 100 g/3.5 oz of sugar, 30 g/1 oz of water, 100 g/3.5 oz of coriander seeds, 20 g/0.75 oz of butter, 200 g/7 oz of tempered chocolate, and 20 g/0.75 oz of cocoa powder.

HAZELNUT OR MACADAMIA DRAGÉES: Replace the almonds with untoasted hazelnuts or macadamias.

ROCHERS

yield: **150 PIECES**

Slivered almonds	500 g	17 oz	90%
Kirschwasser	30 g	1 oz	5%
Sugar	30 g	1 oz	5%
BATCH SIZE	560 g	19 oz	100%
Chocolate, melted, tempered	as needed		

1. Toss the almonds with the kirschwasser in a stainless-steel bowl to moisten. Sprinkle with the sugar and toss together to mix.

2. Spread the nuts in a single layer on a sheet pan. Toast until golden. They will require turning to toast evenly.

3. Allow the nuts to cool to room temperature.

4. Working with only about 50 g/1.75 oz of the nut mixture at a time, put the mixture into a small bowl or cup that has been prewarmed to 28°C/82°F. Add enough of the tempered chocolate to just coat the nuts and, before the chocolate begins to set, spoon small mounds of the salpicon onto parchment paper.

5. Repeat until all the nut mixture is used.

   NOTE: The bowl and the chocolate must be warm to prevent the chocolate from setting prematurely. Work with a small amount of the mixture at a time, and work quickly, keeping the bowl, mixture, and chocolate near the optimal working temperature for the variety of chocolate used.

MACADAMIA GINGER ROCHERS: Replace the almonds with 500 g/17 oz of chopped toasted macadamias and 100 g/4 oz of finely chopped crystallized ginger.

TOASTED COCONUT MILK CHOCOLATE ROCHERS: Toast shredded coconut until golden. Allow to cool to room temperature. Make salpicon using milk chocolate.

STRAWBERRY BLONDES

yield: **170 PIECES**

Sliced almonds	200 g	7 oz	13%
Triple sec liqueur	20 g	1 oz	1%
Sugar	20 g	1 oz	1%
Cornflakes cereal	80 g	3 oz	5%
Dried strawberries, chopped	200 g	7 oz	13%
Dehydrated strawberry powder	20 g	1 oz	1%
White chocolate, melted, tempered, at 30°C/86°F	980 g	35 oz	66%
BATCH SIZE	1520 g	55 oz	100%
Dehydrated strawberry powder, for finishing	as needed		

1. Toss the almonds with the triple sec in a stainless-steel bowl to moisten. Sprinkle with the sugar and toss together to mix.

2. Spread the almonds in a single layer on a sheet pan. Toast until golden. The almonds will require turning in order to toast evenly.

3. Allow the nuts to cool to room temperature.

4. Gently mix the toasted almonds with the cereal, dried strawberries, and 10 g/0.5 oz of the strawberry powder. If the dried strawberries clump together, gently separate them, distributing them evenly throughout the mixture

5. Mix the tempered white chocolate with the remaining 10 g/0.5 oz of strawberry powder.

6. Working with only about 50 g/1.75 oz of the nut mixture at a time, put the mixture into a small bowl or cup that has been prewarmed to 28°C/82°F. Add enough of the tempered white chocolate blend to just coat the nuts. Before the chocolate begins to set, spoon small mounds of the salpicon onto parchment paper.

7. To finish, sift a small amount of the dehydrated strawberry powder over each mound.

8. Repeat until all the nut mixture is used.

   NOTE: The bowl and the chocolate must be warm to prevent the chocolate from setting prematurely. Work with a small amount of the mixture at a time, and work quickly, keeping the bowl, mixture, and chocolate near the optimal working temperature for white chocolate (30°C/86°F).

BARK

yield: **700 G/25 OZ**

Milk, dark, or white chocolate, melted, tempered	700 g	25 oz	100%
INCLUSIONS			
Dried fruit, toasted nuts, seeds, etc.	as needed		
BATCH SIZE	700 g	25 oz	100%

1. Spread the chocolate on a piece of parchment paper 41 × 61 cm/16 × 24 in. If desired, swirl, layer, or marble more than one variety of chocolate.

2. Apply room-temperature inclusions before the chocolate sets.

3. Allow to set completely and break into pieces.

MENDIANTS: Using a pastry bag or paper cone, pipe quarter-size discs of tempered chocolate onto a sheet pan lined with parchment paper. Apply inclusions to each piece before the chocolate sets.

APRICOT HONEY NUTS

yield: **120 PIECES**

Honey	600 g	21 oz	37%
Heavy cream	300 g	11 oz	19%
Glucose syrup	75 g	3 oz	5%
Slivered almonds, toasted	200 g	7 oz	12%
Pine nuts, toasted	180 g	6 oz	11%
Dried apricots, diced 3 mm/⅛ in	140 g	5 oz	9%
Pistachios, chopped	100 g	4 oz	7%
BATCH SIZE	1595 g	57 oz	100%
Dark chocolate, melted, tempered, for precoating and dipping	as needed		
Dried apricot diamonds, for finishing	as needed		

1. Combine the honey, cream, and glucose syrup in a saucepan.
2. Cook to 125°C/257°F.
3. Remove from the heat and mix in the almonds, pine nuts, apricots, and pistachios.
4. Pour the mixture into a frame 12 × 12 × ½ in set on oiled parchment paper. Allow to cool to room temperature.
5. Precoat one side of the slab with the tempered dark chocolate.
6. Cut into diamonds, 18 mm/¾ in on each side, using a sharp chef's knife.
7. Dip each piece in the tempered dark chocolate. Garnish with a dried apricot diamond.

WALNUT BON BONS

yield: **120 PIECES**

Milk chocolate, melted, tempered, for lining molds	as needed		
ALMOND FILLING			
Premade fondant	190 g	7 oz	19%
Almond paste	230 g	8 oz	23%
Sugar	110 g	4 oz	11%
Heavy cream, warm	240 g	8 oz	24%
Walnuts, toasted, finely chopped	230 g	8 oz	23%
BATCH SIZE	1000 g	35 oz	100%
Dark chocolate, melted, tempered, for stippling and capping molds	as needed		

TO PREPARE THE MOLDS:

1. Polish the interiors of the molds. Using a dry brush, stipple the molds with the tempered dark chocolate.

2. Line the molds with the tempered milk chocolate using the shell-molding technique. (See page 77.)

TO MAKE THE ALMOND FILLING:

1. Blend the fondant and almond paste in a food processor until the mixture is homogeneous.

2. In a heavy saucepan, caramelize the sugar until amber using the dry method. (See page 222.)

3. Add the warm cream slowly while stirring over low heat.

4. Add the almond paste mixture and continue stirring over low heat until incorporated.

5. Add the walnuts. Stir to incorporate.

6. Allow to cool to 28°C/82°F, or lower, before using.

7. Using a disposable pastry bag with a small opening cut in the tip, fill the lined molds with the cooled filling to within 3 mm/⅛ in of the tops.

8. Cap the molds using the tempered dark chocolate. Allow the tops to crystallize at room temperature. Then refrigerate the filled molds until the chocolate pulls away from the inside of the molds, approximately 20 minutes.

9. Place a piece of stiff cardboard over each mold and invert the mold to release the finished confections.

TURTLES

yield: **100 PIECES**

Pecans, almonds, or cashews, toasted	500 nuts	500 nuts	
Sugar	380 g	13 oz	30%
Evaporated milk	380 g	13 oz	30%
Heavy cream	160 g	6 oz	14%
Vanilla bean, split and scraped	½ bean	½ bean	
Glucose syrup	320 g	11 oz	24%
Butter	20 g	1 oz	2%
Salt	1 tsp	1 tsp	
BATCH SIZE	1260 g	44 oz	100%
Dark chocolate, melted, tempered, for finishing	as needed		

1. On a sheet pan lined with parchment paper, lay toasted nuts out in groups of 5 to resemble the head and legs of a turtle.

2. Combine the sugar, evaporated milk, cream, and the half vanilla bean and its seeds in a saucepan. Bring to a boil, stirring constantly.

3. Add the glucose syrup and continue cooking over medium heat, while stirring, until the mixture reaches 110°C/230°F. Add the butter.

4. Cook while stirring until the mixture reaches 115°C/239°F (see Note). Add the salt, remove from the heat, and remove the vanilla bean.

5. Using a fondant funnel, deposit the caramel onto the center of each group of nuts to bind them together. Allow to cool to room temperature.

6. Using a disposable pastry bag with a small opening cut in the tip, pipe the tempered dark chocolate on top of each turtle, directly over the caramel. Or, if desired, dip each turtle in the tempered dark chocolate, covering it completely.

NOTE: The temperature given for fully cooked caramel, 115°C/239°F, is a very good estimate, but results may vary depending on the ingredients used. Always check caramel for consistency by hand during cooking.

COCONUT SQUARES

yield: **182 PIECES**

Water	75 g	3 oz	5%
Invert sugar	75 g	3 oz	5%
Salt	1½ tsp	1½ tsp	< 1%
Desiccated coconut	450 g	16 oz	30%
Glucose syrup	420 g	15 oz	28%
Sugar	240 g	9 oz	17%
Water	165 g	6 oz	11%
Frappe (page 389)	60 g	2 oz	4%
BATCH SIZE	1485 g	54 oz	100%
Dark chocolate, melted, tempered, for dipping	as needed		
Desiccated coconut, for finishing	as needed		

1. Combine the 75 g of water, invert sugar, and salt in a saucepan. Bring to a boil. Pour the hot sugar water over the coconut and allow to hydrate for 30 minutes.

2. Combine the glucose syrup, sugar, and 165 g of water in a saucepan. Heat to 115°C/239°F.

3. Mix half of the coconut with the sugar mixture. Combine well.

4. Add the frappe to the coconut-sugar mixture and mix well. (If the frappe has been in storage, warming it slightly makes this step easier.)

5. Add the remaining half of the coconut. Mix until homogeneous.

6. Spread into a frame 12 × 12 × ⅜ in set on oiled parchment paper. Put another piece of oiled parchment paper on the top, and flatten the mixture with a rolling pin. Allow to cool to room temperature.

7. Precoat one side of the slab with the tempered dark chocolate. Using a 20-mm/ ¾-in caramel cutter, mark the slab into 20-mm/¾-in squares. Cut using a sharp, oiled chef's knife.

8. Dip each piece in the tempered dark chocolate. Before the chocolate sets, use a 3-prong dipping fork to mark each piece with a wave pattern. Garnish with a pinch of desiccated coconut.

PISTACHIO HOMAGE

yield: **156 SQUARES**

PISTACHIO GIANDUJA

Dark chocolate, melted, tempered, at 32°C/90°F	300 g	11 oz	40%
Pistachio paste	300 g	11 oz	40%
Confectioners' sugar, sifted	150 g	5 oz	20%
BATCH SIZE	750 g	27 oz	100%

PISTACHIO MARZIPAN

Pistachios, peeled	250 g	9 oz	22%
Almonds	250 g	9 oz	22%
Sugar	390 g	14 oz	34%
Water	140 g	5 oz	11%
Glucose syrup	130 g	5 oz	11%
BATCH SIZE	1160 g	42 oz	100%

Dark chocolate, melted, tempered, for precoating and dipping	as needed
Cocoa butter, melted	as needed
Pistachio halves, for finishing	156 halves

TO MAKE THE PISTACHIO GIANDUJA:

1. Combine the tempered dark chocolate, pistachio paste, and confectioners' sugar in a stainless-steel bowl. Mix until homogeneous.

2. Temper the gianduja by tabling on a marble slab until cooled to room temperature and well agitated, about 5 minutes.

3. Spread the gianduja into a frame 12 × 12 × ¼ in set on parchment paper. Allow to crystallize until set, about 20 minutes.

4. Invert the slab and precoat the bottom with tempered dark chocolate. Turn the slab right side up again and return the slab to the frame. Place a second frame 12 × 12 × ¼ in on top of the one containing the gianduja.

TO MAKE THE PISTACHIO MARZIPAN:

1. Blanch the pistachios. Blanch the almonds and allow them to soak in the hot water for 5 minutes.

2. Using a food processor, grind the nuts together coarsely.

3. Cook the sugar, water, and glucose syrup to 122°C/250°F. Pour the hot syrup over the chopped nuts. Mix lightly and pour onto an oiled marble slab.

4. When cooled to room temperature, use a food processor to grind the nuts into a fine-textured marzipan. Allow the marzipan to cool to room temperature before proceeding.

TO MAKE THE PISTACHIO HOMAGE:

1. Brush the gianduja slab lightly with the melted cocoa butter.
2. Roll the marzipan onto the gianduja to make a layer 6 mm/¼ in thick. Texture the marzipan with a ribbed rolling pin.
3. Spray the top lightly with cocoa butter to seal and prevent drying.
4. Cut into squares, using the 22.5-mm strings on a guitar.
5. Dip up to the top face in the tempered dark chocolate.
6. Garnish with a pistachio half placed diagonally across the top of each piece. (Affix the nut with a very small dot of chocolate.)

COCOMELS

yield: **110 BARS**

SOFT CARAMEL

Sugar	480 g	17 oz	30%
Evaporated milk	480 g	17 oz	30%
Heavy cream	200 g	7 oz	12%
Vanilla bean, split and scraped	1 bean	1 bean	
Glucose syrup	400 g	14 oz	26%
Butter	30 g	1 oz	2%
Salt	1 tsp	1 tsp	<1%
BATCH SIZE	1590 g	56 oz	100%

COCONUT FILLING

Water	50 g	2 oz	5%
Invert sugar	50 g	2 oz	5%
Salt	1 tsp	1 tsp	<1%
Desiccated coconut	300 g	11 oz	31%
Glucose syrup	280 g	10 oz	28%
Sugar	160 g	6 oz	16%
Water	110 g	4 oz	11%
Frappe (page 389)	40 g	1.5 oz	4%
BATCH SIZE	990 g	36.5 oz	100%

Dark chocolate, melted, tempered, for precoating and dipping	as needed
Sweetened shredded coconut, for finishing	as needed

TO MAKE THE SOFT CARAMEL:

1. Combine the 480 g of sugar, evaporated milk, cream, and vanilla bean and its seeds in a saucepan. Bring to a boil, stirring constantly.

2. Add the 400 g of glucose syrup and continue cooking over medium heat, while stirring, until the mixture reaches 110°C/230°F. Add the butter.

3. Still stirring, cook until the mixture reaches 115°C/239°F (see Note). Add the salt. Remove from the heat and remove the vanilla bean. Pour the caramel into a frame 12 × 12 × ¼ in set on oiled parchment paper. Allow to cool to room temperature.

TO MAKE THE COCONUT FILLING:

1. Combine the 50 g of water, invert sugar, and salt. Bring to a boil. Pour the hot sugar water over the coconut and allow to hydrate for 30 minutes.

2. Combine the 280 g of glucose syrup, 160 g of sugar, and 110 g of water in a saucepan and heat to 115°C/239°F.

3. Mix half of the coconut mixture with the sugar mixture. Combine well.

4. Add the frappe to the coconut-sugar mixture and mix well. (If the frappe has been in storage, warming it slightly makes this step easier.)

5. Add the remaining half of the coconut. Mix until homogeneous.

6. Place a second frame 12 × 12 × ¼ in on top of the one containing the caramel. Spread the coconut mixture onto the caramel. Place a sheet of oiled parchment paper on top and flatten the mixture with a rolling pin. Allow to cool to room temperature.

TO MAKE THE COCOMELS:

1. Precoat the caramel side of the slab with the tempered dark chocolate.

2. Cut into rectangles 19 × 38 mm/¾ × 1½ in, using a chef's knife.

3. Dip each piece in the tempered dark chocolate. Before the chocolate sets, use a 3-prong dipping fork to mark each piece with a wave pattern. Garnish with a few shreds of sweetened coconut.

NOTE: The temperature given for fully cooked caramel, 115°C/239°F, is a very good estimate, but results may vary depending on the ingredients used. Always check caramel for consistency by hand during cooking.

12

The composite candy bar is very much an American invention, and more than one company has built an empire on the production and sale of these products.

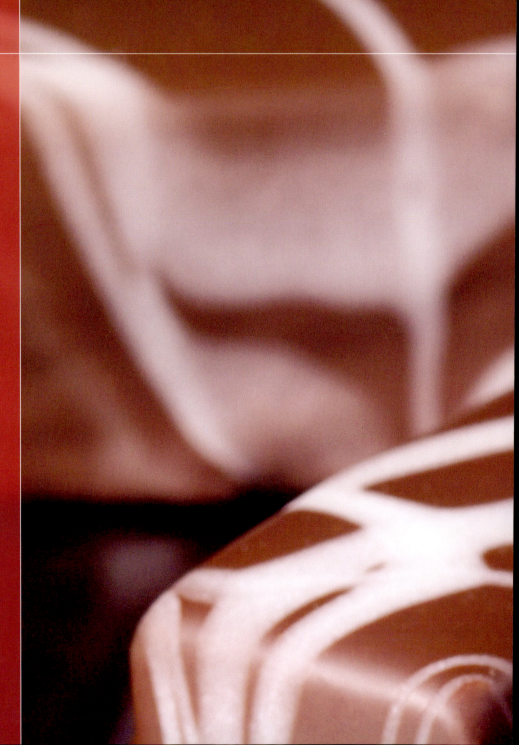

CANDY BARS

Mass-produced candy bars are deeply ingrained in American culture; both the bars and their names are well known to anyone who grew up in the U.S. Many of the most familiar layered bars came into existence in the early years of the twentieth century, when candy making was being transformed from a local artisan pursuit to a regional and national manufacturing concern. While today's layered candy bar is best known as a grocery- or convenience-store commodity, it is yet another area in which artisan confectioners can capitalize on the advantages they hold over manufacturers. Artisans can create truly singular pieces that are not only fresh and made with the highest-quality ingredients but are also unique items that manufacturers could never consider making; a mass-production candy maker could not accept the increased production costs, abbreviated shelf life, and narrower market that are facts of the artisan confectioner's life.

Producing layered candy bars on a small scale does not necessarily require formulas different from those for any other type of confectionery; in fact, the artisan can often create composite bars very efficiently by simply layering together two or more of the centers he or she is already producing. When inclusions are added, flavors adjusted, and special touches added to adorn them, bars can become important signature items that make a confection shop unique and impart cachet that helps to attract and maintain customers.

BALANCE IN BAR FORM

Making artisan layered candy bars requires a working understanding of each of the centers involved and how the centers and inclusions may interact. One layer impacts another in terms of moisture migration, fat migration, sensitivity to heat, and ease of cutting and handling. All this must be considered in light of the flavors and textures each center brings to the finished bar.

The best composite candy bars are a study of contrasting and complementary flavors, textures, and colors. If one component of a bar is very soft and sweet—like a white chocolate ganache—others should provide contrasting flavors such as the tartness of fruit or the bitter edge of a dark caramel and should balance the soft texture with crunch, chewiness, or another contrasting mouthfeel. Contrasting colors add considerable visual interest to bars that are designed to be eaten in more than one bite. When properly formulated and constructed, a bar should have elements that work together so that the finished product is neither too sweet nor too chewy, too firm, too tart, or too rich; all the components must work together to create precisely the desired balance.

Creating a perfectly balanced composite bar that has a shelf life appropriate for an artisan product is a great challenge. When selecting centers and inclusions to use in a bar, the artisan confectioner must consider how each flavor, texture, and color may affect the others during the life of the bar, which may be several weeks after it is first enrobed. The two main challenges to shelf life when multiple centers are used together are moisture migration and fat migration.

MOISTURE MIGRATION

Moisture migration will quickly ruin incompatible water-containing centers layered side by side in a candy bar. All of the moisture migration in an enrobed layered bar will be internal; that is, the movement of water will be from the center or inclusion with the higher free-water content into the center or inclusion with the lower free-water content. The unhappy result of moisture migration is the diminished quality of each center or inclusion: one is drier than it should be because it has lost moisture and the other wetter than it should be because it has picked up moisture. Further, moisture migration into noncrystalline sugar-based centers will induce those centers to crystallize, inexorably altering their texture. When a high-moisture center like ganache is layered with a center that is hygroscopic, like soft caramel, the caramel absorbs moisture from the ganache, unless steps are taken to prevent it. The same is true when inclusions that are likely to absorb moisture, such as cereals or baked cookie dough, are used with a high-moisture center like ganache. Combinations like these will last only hours or days before the inclusions soften and the quality becomes unacceptable. While the best practice is to simply avoid these combinations, moisture migration can be limited or prevented by placing a layer of fat between two incompatible parts of a bar. In the case of the caramel and ganache combination, brushing the caramel with a film of cocoa butter before pouring on the ganache will greatly prolong the life of the bar. In the case of the hygroscopic inclusions, coating them with a thin film of cocoa butter before incorporating them into the center will help to preserve their integrity. The method is helpful but imperfect as a moisture barrier; because most inclusions have a large surface area and are porous, they often do not receive the cocoa butter coating evenly or completely. For more information on moisture migration, see page 43.

A simple way to avoid moisture-migration issues within a composite confection is to choose a center that is a fat system. Gianduja, chocolate, or meltaways, although they contain no water, do not pick up free water from the atmosphere or from other centers. Fat systems can be paired with any type of center or inclusion without causing or suffering from moisture migration. Fat systems, however, are invariably vulnerable to fat migration.

FAT MIGRATION

Fat migration between incompatible fat-based systems will rapidly diminish the desired textural contrast between the centers, and fat migration into a chocolate shell will not only soften the chocolate—ruining its texture—but will result in fat bloom on the exterior of the bar. Fat migration occurs mainly from the use of nut-based centers, particularly those in which the nuts are finely ground, releasing much of their oil. It is not uncommon for a confection containing a ground-nut filling to exhibit fat bloom within two weeks of enrobing. Creating an additional layer of fat between the two fat systems can slow fat migration; brushing on cocoa butter before enrobing will slow the migration of the fat into the chocolate, and other barriers such as shellacs or gum Arabic solutions are highly effective at retarding or preventing fat migration. For the artisan confectioner, making fine-quality centers that have a high percentage of nuts, and therefore a high percentage of oil, fat migration is a reality that must be faced. The best solution, when possible, is to simply not make products too far in advance so that they are always fresh. Then there is not time for the product to diminish in quality from fat migration. (For more information on fat migration, see page 43.)

CHARACTERISTICS OF CENTERS

Ganache

Ganache is a high-moisture center that contributes water to any hygroscopic element that it contacts. For this reason it should not be coupled with hygroscopic inclusions like cereals, farinaceous products, or bits of toffee and should only be used with hygroscopic centers if a layer of fat intervenes. Ganache can be easily paired with other high-moisture centers such as marzipan, in which the free-water levels are nearly equal. Ganache cannot tolerate heat without coming out of temper, thus ruining its texture; any centers that are hot when deposited must be applied and allowed to cool before they are layered with ganache.

Butter ganache

Butter ganache is a relatively low-moisture center that contributes water only minimally to moisture migration. Not only does butter ganache have a low water-activity level (A_w), it is a water-in-fat emulsion, so the water it does contain is locked in a matrix of fat, preventing migration. The fat in butter ganache is not as prone to fat migration as are the oils in nuts, and therefore it does not as a rule adversely affect other fat-based centers or chocolate. Butter ganache cannot tolerate high heat and must be deposited only after layers that are deposited hot have cooled.

Noncrystalline sugar centers

Noncrystalline sugar confections are the most hygroscopic of all centers. They readily pick up moisture from any source they contact, including centers with higher A_w, inclusions, or even the atmosphere. Once they pick up moisture, they gradually crystallize, destroying their quality. Noncrystalline sugar centers should only be combined with fat systems that contain no moisture unless great care is taken to protect them from damage. They must often be deposited while very hot; they should therefore be allowed to cool fully before they are layered with centers that are sensitive to heat, like gianduja or ganache.

Crystalline sugar centers

In spite of their high sugar content, crystalline sugar centers like fudge are not particularly hygroscopic. Crystalline centers resist moisture because the sugar they contain is in a crystalline—rather than amorphous—state. In fact, crystalline centers have a tendency to *lose* moisture to hygroscopic centers or inclusions, not to absorb it. Such centers are usually deposited while warm, and they give off further heat as they continue to crystallize. (See Latent Heat of Crystallization, page 89.) They must be allowed to cool completely before they are layered with centers like gianduja or ganache that cannot tolerate heat.

Marzipan

Marzipan has the potential to participate in both moisture migration and fat migration when it is used as a part of a composite candy bar. Due to its relatively high water-activity level, marzipan loses moisture to hygroscopic centers like noncrystalline sugar. In addition, the oil from the nuts in marzipan migrates into chocolate, ruining its texture, although the damage does not occur nearly as quickly as that caused by the nut oils in gianduja. Marzipan is not particularly sensitive to heat, and so it is not damaged when hot centers are poured directly onto it during layering.

Chocolate, gianduja, and meltaways

As fat systems, chocolate, gianduja, and meltaways neither give off moisture to neighboring centers nor pick it up. Because of this, they can be easily and successfully paired with hygroscopic centers like caramels, or with high-moisture centers like ganache. Gianduja, chocolate, and meltaways are ideal for creating a crisp layer in a candy bar when they are mixed with inclusions that might get soggy if combined with a center containing water. The disadvantage of fat systems is fat migration; gianduja in particular is a great source of fat migration from the oil in the nuts. Fat systems are very sensitive to heat; they must be deposited only after hot centers have fully cooled or they will melt and come out of temper.

Jellies

With their relatively low A_w, jellies tend to be somewhat hygroscopic. However, the binding agents they contain prevent most moisture migration from penetrating beyond the surface. Therefore jellies can be coupled with high-moisture centers like ganache without suffering any substantial damage. Jellies must be deposited while hot, and therefore they must be allowed to cool before they are layered with heat-sensitive centers. As a consequence, jellies are not well suited to use in shell-molded bars; they would melt the chocolate shell.

Aerated centers

The hygroscopicity of aerated centers varies greatly depending on moisture content. A low-moisture nougat like torrone has a great tendency to pick up water from the surrounding environment, while marshmallow, with its higher A_w, is not as susceptible to moisture migration. The form of sugar in a nougat also influences the hygroscopicity; a tender nougat in which the sugar has crystallized is less likely to attract moisture than will a chewy nougat. Any nougat containing a large amount of honey is hygroscopic due to honey's natural affinity for water.

Inclusions

Inclusions are used in order to provide textural and flavor contrast and visual interest. When properly used, inclusions such as nuts create a very pleasant crisp texture. Dried fruit contributes bright, fresh bursts of flavor, along with vibrant color and rich texture, and cereals or farinaceous products add delicate crispness and their own flavors. Most inclusions are somewhat prone to moisture migration; if possible it is advisable to add them to either a low-moisture center or a fat system.

CHARACTERISTICS OF INCLUSIONS

Nuts and seeds

These popular and versatile inclusions are fairly resistant to moisture migration; they do not get soggy quickly in centers like nougat or marzipan that contain water. They are, however, high in fat and can therefore be responsible for considerable fat migration, particularly when they are chopped or finely ground.

Dried fruit

While dried fruit is hygroscopic, its low A_w means that it is compatible with most confectionery centers, making it an ideal inclusion in confections. It does not lose quality in ganache, as more hygroscopic inclusions do, and it doesn't exude excess water that would soften nougats. These qualities, coupled with its bright colors and fresh flavors, make dried fruit a popular inclusion for artisan confectioners.

Cereals and farinaceous products

Breakfast cereals and farinaceous products like pretzels, crackers, and shortbread can make excellent inclusions in candy bars, contributing a delicate crispness as well as flavor. These products require careful use, however; they are hygroscopic and soften quickly if they are exposed to moisture. While it is possible to coat these inclusions with a thin layer of fat in order to protect them, it remains an imperfect solution to the problem of moisture migration; cereals and farinaceous products tend to soften in spite of this precaution. In order to preserve their texture, these inclusions are best added to fat systems such as gianduja, chocolate, or meltaways.

Rework

There are few limits to the confectionery remnants that can be chopped and used as an inclusion in a candy bar. As long as confectionery rework is shelf stable, it can be incorporated into other candies. Many different types of rework can be used as inclusions: hard candy, sponge candy or toffee, nougat, marshmallow, and so on. When using rework inclusions, the confectioner must consider each inclusion in light of its moisture content, hygroscopicity, sensitivity to heat, and tendency to promote fat migration and employ the inclusion accordingly.

ASSEMBLING COMPOSITE CANDY BARS

There are two main methods of assembling layered candy bars, each with its own distinct advantages: shell molding and slabbing. Candy bar molds provide the confectioner with the option of using fillings that would be too soft to handle as a slab and afford greater textural contrast in the bar. Caramel-based centers and those based on ground nuts are popular options for shell molding. Molds can also be used to create bars in unique shapes and provide a high-gloss finish and near perfect uniformity.

Bars that are created in slabs allow the confectioner to use centers such as soft caramels or jellies that must be hot when deposited. In addition, forming and cutting a slab is more efficient than making many individual confections, and not having to buy the molds to begin with makes slabbing an economical choice.

The same general techniques and precautions that apply to shell molding individual pieces apply to using candy bar molds as well. (See page 77.) Clean, polished molds and optimally tempered chocolate are of vital importance in order to be successful. The filling to be used—of whatever type—must be of the proper texture and temperature when it is deposited in the molds.

Every filling for a shell-molded bar must be slightly fluid when it is deposited. This is true even for fillings that will be very firm when the bar is in its final form. If the filling is not somewhat fluid, it will not level out in the mold, and won't make an even layer, nor will it allow a small, even headspace for sealing the mold with chocolate. (See page 78.) Fillings that are too stiff when deposited frequently cause incomplete sealing of the bottom of the mold, creating a vector for moisture migration, oxidation, and leakage.

Temperature is equally important when filling lined candy bar molds. Any filling to be deposited into a lined mold must be below 30°C/86°F. Fillings above this temperature will cause the chocolate lining to come out of temper. The results are difficulty in unmolding the finished pieces and the formation of fat bloom. Exceptionally cold fillings should also be avoided, but this is seldom an issue, as confectionery fillings do not require refrigeration and so would rarely be chilled under any circumstance.

Order of the layers

Once the flavor profile, materials, and assembly technique for a bar have been selected, the logistics of assembling the bars must be determined. Generally, it is sensible to have the firmer or crisper layers on the bottom of the finished bar. In addition, flavor, color, and mouthfeel may influence the order of the layers. Whenever possible, it is preferable to deposit one layer directly onto another one, as opposed to pouring them separately and stacking them after each has set. Pouring layers directly onto one another provides better adhesion between the layers and a more uniform bar. Regardless of the order in which the strata will ultimately appear, the confectioner must consider the order in which the centers may be successfully assembled. If, for instance, a caramel layer is to be combined with a heat-sensitive layer such as gianduja, the caramel must be deposited and cooled before the gianduja can be applied. That makes it necessary to sometimes assemble layers out of order or entirely upside down. Ultimately, this makes no difference, as once cooled, the slab can be inverted to create the desired effect.

Precoating

Slabs of composite candy bars are precoated in the same manner as any other slab of center (see page 65) and for all of the same reasons: to seal the bar completely so that it has an acceptable shelf life and to make it easier to handle during enrobing. Of course, when using an enrober that has a bottoming function, it is not necessary to precoat the slab by hand. As always, the chocolate used for precoating should be the same type in which the bar will be enrobed.

Cutting

While some bars lend themselves to cutting on a guitar, many require the use of knives, and different types of bars are best cut with different styles of knives. Some bars respond well to a serrated knife, while others require a sharp chef's knife. Whatever is used, the goal is to cut straight, vertical sides and to leave corners that are square, not rounded. When cutting particularly soft centers, a brief period of refrigeration—approximately 5 minutes—firms the center enough to allow it to be cut cleanly.

Enrobing

Because bars are large, it is generally better to enrobe them with chocolate rather than to dip them using forks. The technique for enrobing the precoated cut bars is as follows:

1. **PLACE BARS PRECOATED** side down on an icing screen over a piece of parchment paper.

2. **USE A LADLE** to pour tempered chocolate over several bars.

3. **VIBRATE THE SCREEN** lightly to remove excess chocolate.

4. **USE AN OFFSET PALETTE KNIFE** to remove each bar from the screen. It is vital that the bars be removed before the chocolate sets.

5. **PLACE THE BARS** on a piece of clean parchment paper on a flat surface.

6. **FINISH AS DESIRED.**

7. **ALLOW TO CRYSTALLIZE FULLY**—preferably overnight—before wrapping.

TOP, LEFT: *Adding inclusions to the frame.* RIGHT: *Pouring hot caramel over the inclusions in the frame.*

BOTTOM, LEFT: *Each layer is added to the frame as quickly as temperatures permit.* RIGHT: *Precoating the slab.*

TOP, LEFT: *Cutting the bars.* RIGHT: *Hand-enrobing the cut candy bars.*

BOTTOM, LEFT: *Using a dipping fork to make decorative waves on the finished bars.* RIGHT: *Applying garnish to the bars.*

The following table illustrates the practical applications of various centers as they are likely to affect the artisan confectioner in the production and storage of composite candy bars.

CHARACTERISTICS OF CENTERS USED IN CANDY BARS

CENTER	AFFECTED BY MOISTURE MIGRATION[1]	AFFECTED BY FAT MIGRATION	SENSITIVE TO HIGH HEAT	TEMPERATURE WHEN DEPOSITED	CUTS CLEANLY WHEN COLD
BUTTER GANACHE	S	S	Y	Room temperature	Y
CHOCOLATE	N	Y	Y	Warm	N
FONDANT	Y	N	N	Warm	Y
FUDGE	Y	S	N	Warm	Y
GANACHE	Y	N	Y	Warm	Y
GIANDUJA	N	Y	Y	Warm	Y
HARD CANDY	Y	N	N	Hot	N
JELLIES	S	N	N	Hot	Y
MARZIPAN	S	S	N	Room temperature	Y
MELTAWAY	N	Y	Y	Warm	Y
NOUGAT	Y	N	N	Warm to hot[2]	Y
SOFT CARAMEL	Y	N	N	Hot	Y
TOFFEE	Y	N	N	Hot	N
INCLUSIONS					
CEREAL/FARINACEOUS PRODUCTS	Y	N	N	Room temperature	Y
CONFECTIONERY REWORK[3]					
DRIED FRUIT	Y	N	N	Room temperature	Y
NUTS	N	Y	N	Room temperature	Y

Y = Yes N = No S = Slightly

1. Whether a center absorbs or exudes water depends on its A_w. (See Water Activity of Confections table, page 42.)
2. The temperature for depositing nougats depends on the type of nougat. Hard nougats must be hotter than soft nougats when deposited.
3. Confectionery rework when used as an inclusion has the same characteristics the product has when it is used as a center.

SALT AND PEPPER BARS

yield: **120 BARS**

SALTED CARAMEL

Sugar	820 g	29 oz	30%
Evaporated milk	820 g	29 oz	30%
Heavy cream	340 g	12 oz	12%
Vanilla bean, split and scraped	1 bean	1 bean	
Glucose syrup	680 g	24 oz	25%
Butter	50 g	2 oz	2%
Salt	1 tsp	1 tsp	< 1%
Fleur de sel	40 g	1 oz	1%
Cocoa butter spray	as needed		
BATCH SIZE	2750 g	97 oz	100%

PEPPER GANACHE

Heavy cream	350 g	12 oz	27%
Glucose syrup	90 g	3 oz	7%
Black pepper, ground	20 g	0.75 oz	2%
Brandy	70 g	3 oz	7%
Butter, very soft	40 g	1 oz	2%
Dark chocolate, melted, tempered, at 32°C/90°F	700 g	25 oz	55%
BATCH SIZE	1270 g	44.75 oz	100%
Dark chocolate, melted, tempered, for enrobing	as needed		
Black pepper, ground, for finishing	as needed		
Fleur de sel, for finishing	as needed		

TO MAKE THE SALTED CARAMEL:

1. Combine the sugar, evaporated milk, 340 g of cream, and vanilla bean and its seeds in a saucepan. Bring to a boil, stirring constantly.

2. Add the 680 g of glucose syrup and continue cooking over medium heat, while stirring, until the mixture reaches 110°C/230°F. Add the 50 g of butter.

3. Cook while stirring until the mixture reaches 115°C/239°F (see Note). Add the salt, remove from the heat, remove the vanilla bean, and pour the caramel into a frame 12 × 24 × ⅜ in set on oiled parchment paper.

4. Sprinkle the fleur de sel over the entire surface of the caramel immediately.

5. Allow to cool to room temperature, about 1 hour.

6. Spray with cocoa butter spray to protect from moisture.

7. Place another frame 12 × 24 × ¼ in on top of the one containing the caramel.

TO MAKE THE PEPPER GANACHE:

1. Combine the 350 g of cream, 90 g of glucose syrup, and pepper in a saucepan. Bring to a boil. Remove from the heat and add the brandy.
2. Allow to cool to 40°C/105°F.
3. Stir the 40 g of butter into the tempered dark chocolate, taking care that no lumps of butter remain.
4. Pour the cooled cream mixture over the tempered chocolate mixture.
5. Using a spoon or spatula, stir in vigorous small circles outward to emulsify.
6. Stir outward in larger circles to spread the emulsion throughout the bowl, checking to see that all of the chocolate has melted. If necessary, heat the ganache over a hot water bath to melt the chocolate. The temperature of the ganache should not exceed 34°C/94°F.
7. Pour the ganache immediately into the frame on top of the salted caramel. Cover with plastic wrap and allow to crystallize overnight.

TO COMPLETE THE SALT AND PEPPER BARS:

1. Remove the frames from the slab.
2. Precoat the caramel side of the slab with the tempered dark chocolate.
3. Cut into bars 19 mm × 8 cm/¾ × 3 in. Enrobe in the tempered dark chocolate. Before the chocolate sets, use a 3-prong dipping fork to make diagonal waves on top of each bar. Garnish each bar with a sprinkle of freshly ground black pepper and fleur de sel.

   NOTE: The temperature given for fully cooked caramel, 115°C/239°F, is a very good estimate, but results may vary depending on the ingredients used. Always check caramel for consistency by hand during cooking.

Salt and Pepper Bars

PASSION HAZELNUT BARS

yield: **120 BARS**

TOASTED HAZELNUTS

Hazelnuts, granulated	680 g	24 oz	76%
Sugar	100 g	4 oz	12%
Brandy	100 g	4 oz	12%
BATCH SIZE	880 g	32 oz	100%

GIANDUJA

Praline paste	780 g	28 oz	67%
Dark chocolate, melted	390 g	14 oz	33%
BATCH SIZE	1170 g	42 oz	100%

PASSION FRUIT GANACHE

Heavy cream	200 g	7 oz	12%
Glucose syrup	140 g	5 oz	9%
Passion fruit purée, reduced (see Note)	200 g	7 oz	12%
Butter, very soft	60 g	2 oz	3%
White chocolate, melted, tempered, at 30°C/86°F	1040 g	37 oz	64%
BATCH SIZE	1640 g	58 oz	100%

Dark chocolate, melted, tempered, for precoating and enrobing	as needed
Granulated hazelnuts, toasted, for finishing	as needed

TO PREPARE THE TOASTED HAZELNUTS:

Combine the hazelnuts with the sugar and brandy. Toast in a 175°C/350°F oven until golden brown. Allow to cool completely.

TO MAKE THE GIANDUJA:

1. Combine the praline paste and the melted dark chocolate.
2. Add the toasted hazelnut mixture. Table to temper.
3. Spread the gianduja into a frame 12 × 24 × ¼ in. Allow to crystallize until set.
4. Place another frame 12 × 24 × ¼ in on top of the one containing the gianduja.

TO MAKE THE PASSION FRUIT GANACHE:

1. Combine the cream and glucose syrup in a saucepan. Bring to a boil. Remove from the heat and add the reduced passion fruit purée.
2. Allow the mixture to cool to 40°C/105°F.
3. Stir the butter into the tempered white chocolate, taking care that no lumps of butter remain.
4. Pour the cooled cream mixture over the white chocolate mixture.

5. Using a spoon or spatula, stir in vigorous small circles outward to emulsify.

6. Stir outward in larger circles to spread the emulsion throughout the bowl, checking to see that all of the chocolate has melted. If necessary, heat the ganache over a hot water bath to melt the chocolate. The temperature of the ganache should not exceed 34°C/94°F.

7. Pour the ganache immediately into the frame on top of the gianduja. Cover with plastic wrap and allow to crystallize overnight.

TO COMPLETE THE PASSION HAZELNUT BARS:

1. Remove the frames from the slab.

2. Precoat the gianduja side of the slab with the tempered dark chocolate.

3. Cut into bars 19 mm × 8 cm/¾ × 3 in. Enrobe in the tempered dark chocolate. When the chocolate begins to set, garnish each bar with a diagonal line of toasted granulated hazelnuts. Pipe a line of the tempered dark chocolate on either side of the hazelnuts.

NOTE: Passion fruit concentrate should be reduced by half. Natural-strength passion fruit purée should be reduced by three quarters.

SENSEI BARS

yield: **120 BARS**

BASE LAYER

Lemon juice	½ tsp	½ tsp	< 1%
Sugar	100 g	4 oz	17%
Sesame seeds, untoasted	200 g	7 oz	29%
Butter, very soft	50 g	2 oz	8%
Dark chocolate, melted, tempered, at 32°C/90°F	300 g	11 oz	46%
BATCH SIZE	650 g	24 oz	100%

SESAME GIANDUJA

Milk chocolate, melted, tempered, at 30°C/86°F	800 g	28 oz	78%
Tahini	220 g	8 oz	22%
BATCH SIZE	1020 g	36 oz	100%

GREEN TEA GANACHE

Heavy cream	250 g	9 oz	24%
Glucose syrup	80 g	3 oz	8%
Green tea powder (matcha)	10 g	0.5 oz	1%
Cocoa butter, melted	30 g	1 oz	3%
White chocolate, melted, tempered, at 30°C/86°F	680 g	24 oz	64%
BATCH SIZE	1050 g	37.5 oz	100%

Milk chocolate, melted, tempered, for enrobing	as needed
Green tea powder (matcha), for finishing	as needed

TO MAKE THE BASE LAYER:

1. Rub the lemon juice into the sugar.

2. In a saucepan, caramelize the sugar over direct heat while stirring constantly.

3. Add the sesame seeds. Continue stirring over heat until the mixture is softened and the seeds are toasted.

4. Pour the sesame croquant onto an oiled marble slab. Spread as thinly as possible and allow to cool. Use a rolling pin to break the croquant into individual seeds.

5. Stir the butter into the tempered dark chocolate, taking care that no lumps of butter remain.

6. Mix the crushed seeds into the dark chocolate mixture.

7. Roll the base-layer mixture between sheets of heavy plastic to form a rectangle slightly larger than 30 × 61 cm/12 × 24 in. Trim to 30 × 61 cm/12 × 24 in. Set up a frame 12 × 24 × ½ in around the perimeter of the slab.

TO MAKE THE SESAME GIANDUJA:

1. Combine the tempered milk chocolate and tahini.

2. Spread into the frame containing the base-layer mixture. The gianduja will not come to the top of the frame. Allow to crystallize at room temperature until set, approximately 30 minutes.

TO MAKE THE GREEN TEA GANACHE:

1. Combine the cream, glucose syrup, and green tea powder in a saucepan. Bring to a boil. Remove from the heat, cover, and let steep for 5 minutes.

2. Allow to cool to 40°C/105°F.

3. Add the melted cocoa butter to the tempered white chocolate. Pour the cooled cream mixture over the white chocolate mixture.

4. Using a spoon or spatula, stir in vigorous small circles outward to emulsify.

5. Stir outward in larger circles to spread the emulsion throughout the bowl, checking to see that all of the chocolate has melted. If necessary, heat the ganache over a hot water bath to melt the chocolate. The temperature of the ganache should not exceed 34°C/94°F.

6. Pour the ganache immediately into the frame on top of the gianduja. Spread the ganache into an even layer. Cover with plastic wrap once it is firm and allow to crystallize overnight.

TO COMPLETE THE SENSEI BARS:

1. Remove the frame from the slab.

2. Cut the slab into bars 19 mm × 8 cm/¾ × 3 in. Enrobe in the tempered milk chocolate. When the chocolate begins to set, use a dipping fork to make a wave pattern on top of each bar. Finish by lightly sifting green tea powder over the tops of the bars.

Sensei Bars

SOL FOOD BARS

yield: **120 BARS**

TOMATO JELLY

Water	320 g	11 oz	12%
Sundried tomatoes	80 g	3 oz	3%
Apple compote (see Note)	230 g	12 oz	13%
Glucose syrup	750 g	27 oz	28%
Sugar	90 g	3 oz	3%
Pectin	20 g	1 oz	1%
Sugar	750 g	27 oz	28%
Glucose syrup	350 g	12 oz	12%
Citric acid solution (1 part citric acid to 1 part water)	30 g	1 oz	<1%
BATCH SIZE	2620 g	97 oz	100%

BALSAMIC AND LEMON THYME GANACHE

Heavy cream	180 g	6 oz	17%
Lemon thyme	5 g	0.25 oz	< 1%
Milk	as needed		
Glucose syrup	60 g	2 oz	6%
Balsamic vinegar	60 g	2 oz	6%
White chocolate, melted, tempered, at 30°C/86°F	700 g	25 oz	71%
Salt	1 tsp	1 tsp	< 1%
BATCH SIZE	1005 g	35.25 oz	100%

Dark chocolate, melted, tempered, for precoating and enrobing	as needed
Maldon salt, for finishing	as needed

TO MAKE THE TOMATO JELLY:

1. Place the water and sundried tomatoes in a small saucepan. Bring to a simmer and cook, covered, for 5 minutes.
2. Remove from the heat, cover, and let steep for 10 minutes.
3. Purée the tomato mixture in a food processor until smooth.
4. Combine the tomato purée, apple compote, and the 180 g of glucose syrup in a saucepan.
5. Mix together the 90 g of sugar and the pectin. Whisk into the tomato mixture.
6. Bring the mixture to a boil, stirring constantly.
7. Add the 750 g of sugar and return to a boil while stirring.

8. Add the 350 g of glucose syrup, and continue cooking over low heat, stirring, until the batch reaches 106°C/223°F, or 75° Brix. This takes approximately 8 minutes of gentle boiling.

9. Add the citric acid solution and pour the jelly into a frame 12 × 24 × ⅜ in set set on oiled parchment paper.

10. Allow to set until cooled completely, about 1 hour. May be left overnight if desired.

11. Place another frame 12 × 24 × ¼ in on top of the one containing the tomato jelly.

TO MAKE THE BALSAMIC AND LEMON THYME GANACHE:

1. Combine the cream and lemon thyme in a saucepan and bring to a boil. Remove from the heat, cover, and let steep for 5 minutes.

2. Strain the infused cream through premoistened cheesecloth. Wring the lemon thyme in the cheesecloth to extract the maximum amount of flavor possible.

3. Return the cream to 180 g by adding milk.

4. Add the 60 g of glucose syrup to the flavored cream mixture. Bring to a boil.

5. Remove from the heat, add the balsamic vinegar, and allow to cool to 40°C/105°F.

6. Pour the cooled cream mixture over the tempered white chocolate. Add the salt.

7. Using a spoon or spatula, stir in vigorous small circles outward to emulsify.

8. Stir outward in larger circles to spread the emulsion throughout the bowl, checking to see that all of the chocolate has melted. If necessary, heat the ganache over a hot water bath to melt the chocolate. The temperature of the ganache should not exceed 34°C/94°F.

9. Pour the ganache immediately into the frame on top of the cooled tomato jelly. Spread the ganache into an even layer. Cover with plastic wrap and allow to crystallize overnight.

TO COMPLETE THE SOL FOOD BARS:

1. Remove the frames from the slab.

2. Precoat the jelly side of the slab with the tempered dark chocolate.

3. Cut into bars 19 mm × 8 cm/¾ × 3 in. Enrobe in the tempered dark chocolate. Before the chocolate sets, use a 3-prong dipping fork to make a diagonal waves on top of each bar. Garnish with the Maldon salt.

NOTE: Apple compote is available commercially under such trade names as Superpomme. If you wish to make the apple compote, peel, core, and slice apples. Cook with a little sugar and minimum water to make applesauce. Spread the sauce in a hotel pan and place it in a low oven to continue removing water, until the mixture is the consistency of thick applesauce. Purée prior to use.

KITCHEN SINK BARS

yield: **120 BARS**

INCLUSIONS

Mini pretzels	300 g	11 oz	29%
Peanuts, dry roasted, salted	430 g	15 oz	42%
Dried cranberries	300 g	11 oz	29%
BATCH SIZE	1030 g	37 oz	100%

SOFT CARAMEL

Sugar	680 g	24 oz	30%
Evaporated milk	680 g	24 oz	30%
Heavy cream	280 g	10 oz	13%
Vanilla bean, split and scraped	1 bean	1 bean	
Glucose syrup	570 g	20 oz	26%
Butter	40 g	1 oz	1%
Salt	1 tsp	1 tsp	< 1%
BATCH SIZE	2250 g	79 oz	100%

PEANUT BUTTER GIANDUJA

Milk chocolate, melted, tempered	570 g	20 oz	65%
Peanut butter, warmed to 27°C/80°F	320 g	11 oz	35%
BATCH SIZE	890 g	31 oz	100%

Milk chocolate, melted, tempered, for precoating and enrobing	as needed
Pretzel salt, for finishing	as needed

TO PREPARE THE INCLUSIONS:

Place the pretzels in a frame 12 × 24 × ⅜ in set on oiled parchment paper. Sprinkle the peanuts and dried cranberries over the pretzels.

TO MAKE THE SOFT CARAMEL:

1. Combine the sugar, evaporated milk, cream, and vanilla bean and its seeds in a saucepan. Bring to a boil, stirring constantly.

2. Add the glucose syrup and continue cooking over medium heat, while stirring, until the mixture reaches 110°C/230°F. Add the butter.

3. Cook while stirring until the mixture reaches 115°C/239°F (see Notes). Add the salt. Remove from the heat, remove the vanilla bean, and pour the caramel over the inclusions, spreading evenly to cover.

4. Allow to cool for 1 to 2 minutes. Place a piece of oiled parchment paper on top of the caramel, and use a rolling pin to roll the caramel out into an even layer. Allow to cool completely.

5. Place another frame 12 × 24 × ¼ in on top of the one containing the caramel.

TO MAKE THE PEANUT BUTTER GIANDUJA:

1. Combine the melted, tempered milk chocolate and peanut butter in a stainless-steel bowl.

2. Table slightly on a stone to temper, but leave fluid.

3. Spread the gianduja into the frame on top of the caramel (see Notes). Allow to crystallize until set.

TO COMPLETE THE KITCHEN SINK BARS:

1. Remove the frames from the slab.

2. Precoat the gianduja side of the slab with the tempered milk chocolate.

3. Cut into bars 19 mm × 8 cm/¾ × 3 in. Enrobe in the tempered milk chocolate. When the chocolate begins to set, use a dipping fork to make diagonal waves on top of each bar. Garnish with the pretzel salt.

NOTES: The temperature given for fully cooked caramel, 115°C/239°F, is a very good estimate, but results may vary depending on the ingredients used. Always check caramel for consistency by hand during cooking.

If a smoother surface is desired on the finished bars, turn the caramel slab over when it is completely cool and spread the peanut butter gianduja on the side with the inclusions.

Kitchen Sink Bars

GINGER CARAMEL PEAKS

yield: 56 BARS

CARAMEL CREAM FILLING

Lemon juice	¼ tsp	¼ tsp	< 1%
Sugar	570 g	20 oz	57%
Heavy cream, hot	290 g	10 oz	29%
Butter	140 g	5 oz	14%
BATCH SIZE	1000 g	35 oz	100%

GINGER GANACHE

Heavy cream	350 g	12 oz	29%
Ginger, peeled, sliced thin	70 g	3 oz	7%
Milk	as needed		
Glucose syrup	110 g	4 oz	10%
Butter, soft	50 g	2 oz	5%
Dark chocolate, tempered, at 32°C/90°F, chopped	570 g	20 oz	49%
BATCH SIZE	1150 g	41 oz	100%

Dark chocolate, melted, tempered, for lining and sealing the molds	as needed	

TO PREPARE THE MOLDS:

Line 8 peaked molds with the tempered dark chocolate. (See Shell-Molding Technique and Theory, page 77.)

TO MAKE THE CARAMEL CREAM FILLING:

1. Rub the lemon juice into the sugar.
2. In a saucepan, caramelize the sugar over direct heat while stirring constantly.
3. Add the hot cream slowly while stirring over low heat.
4. Stir in the butter until melted and combined.
5. Allow to cool to room temperature.

TO MAKE THE GINGER GANACHE:

1. Combine the cream and ginger in a saucepan and bring to a boil. Remove from the heat, cover, and let steep for 5 minutes.
2. Strain the infused cream through premoistened cheesecloth. Wring the ginger in the cheesecloth to extract the maximum amount of flavor possible.
3. Return the cream to 350 g by adding milk.
4. Add the glucose syrup to the flavored cream. Bring to a boil.
5. Pour the hot cream mixture over the chopped dark chocolate and let sit for 1 minute to allow the chocolate to melt.
6. Using a spoon or spatula, stir the mixture in vigorous small circles in the center of the bowl until it emulsifies.

7. Stir outward in larger circles to spread the emulsion throughout the bowl, checking to see that all of the chocolate has melted. If necessary, heat the ganache over a hot water bath to melt the chocolate. The temperature of the ganache should not exceed 34°C/93°F.

8. Pour into a hotel pan, allowing the ganache to cover the bottom of the pan in a thin layer.

9. Allow to rest at room temperature until the ganache reaches 25°C/77°F or slightly lower. It should be of a thick but fluid consistency.

TO COMPLETE THE GINGER CARAMEL PEAKS:

1. If necessary, warm the caramel to 27°C/80°F. Using a disposable pastry bag with a small opening cut in the tip, pipe the caramel into the prepared molds. Fill only the base of the peaks. Allow the caramel to cool to room temperature.

2. Using a disposable pastry bag with a small opening cut in the tip, pipe the ganache into the molds to within 3 mm/⅛ in of the top. Tap the molds to level the contents, and allow to crystallize completely at room temperature.

3. Seal the molds with the tempered dark chocolate. (See Shell-Molding Technique and Theory, page 77.) Refrigerate the sealed molds for about 15 minutes, until the chocolate pulls away from the inside of the molds.

4. Place a piece of stiff cardboard over each mold and invert to release the finished bars.

ESPRESSO CARAMEL CRUNCH BARS

yield: **120 BARS**

CARAMEL

Sugar	680 g	24 oz	30%
Evaporated milk	680 g	24 oz	30%
Heavy cream	280 g	10 oz	12%
Vanilla bean, split and scraped	1 bean	1 bean	
Glucose syrup	570 g	20 oz	25%
Butter	40 g	1 oz	1%
Salt	1 tsp	1 tsp	< 1%
Coffee extract	60 g	2 oz	2%
BATCH SIZE	2310 g	81 oz	100%

HAZELNUT GIANDUJA/SPONGE CANDY

Hazelnuts, toasted	440 g	16 oz	34%
Confectioners' sugar	440 g	16 oz	33%
Dark chocolate, melted	440 g	16 oz	33%
BATCH SIZE	1320 g	48 oz	100%
Sponge Candy (page 397), chopped into 6-mm/¼-in pieces	700 g	24 oz	100%
BATCH SIZE	700 g	24 oz	100%
Dark chocolate, melted, tempered, for precoating and enrobing	as needed		
Instant coffee crystals, for finishing	as needed		

TO MAKE THE CARAMEL:

1. Combine the sugar, evaporated milk, cream, and vanilla bean and its seeds in a saucepan. Bring to a boil, stirring constantly.

2. Add the glucose syrup and continue cooking over medium heat, while stirring, until the mixture reaches 110°C/230°F. Add the butter.

3. Cook while stirring until the mixture reaches 115°C/239°F (see Note). Add the salt and coffee extract and remove from the heat, remove the vanilla bean, and pour the caramel into a frame 12 × 24 × ¼ in set on oiled parchment paper.

4. Allow to cool to room temperature, about 1 hour.

5. Place another frame 12 × 24 × ⅜ in on top of the one containing the caramel.

TO MAKE THE HAZELNUT GIANDUJA/SPONGE CANDY:

1. Grind the toasted hazelnuts with a small amount of the confectioners' sugar in a food processor until liquefied.

2. Add the remaining confectioners' sugar and the melted dark chocolate. Mix just until homogeneous.

3. Temper the gianduja by tabling; mix in the chopped Sponge Candy. If necessary, rewarm the gianduja lightly to prevent excessive thickening.

4. Spread the mixture immediately into the frame on top of the caramel. Allow to crystallize until completely set.

TO COMPLETE THE ESPRESSO CARAMEL CRUNCH BARS:

1. Precoat the gianduja side of the slab with the tempered dark chocolate.

2. Cut into bars 19 mm × 8 cm/¾ × 3 in using a chef's knife. Enrobe in the tempered dark chocolate. Before the chocolate sets, use a 3-prong dipping fork to make waves on the surface of each bar. Garnish with a sprinkle of the instant coffee crystals.

NOTE: The temperature given for fully cooked caramel, 115°C/239°F, is a very good estimate, but results may vary depending on the ingredients used. Always check caramel for consistency by hand during cooking.

Espresso Caramel Crunch Bars

CARAMEL SHORTBREAD BARS

yield: **6 BARS**

SHORTBREAD BASES	6	6	
Shortbread Dough (page 376)	1400 g	49 oz	100%
CARAMEL			
Lemon juice	10 g	0.5 oz	1%
Sugar	570 g	20 oz	57%
Heavy cream, warm	290 g	10 oz	28%
Butter	140 g	5 oz	14%
BATCH SIZE	1010 g	35.5 oz	100%
Dark chocolate, melted, tempered, for lining and sealing molds	as needed		
Cocoa butter, melted	as needed		

TO MAKE THE SHORTBREAD BASES:

1. Roll the shortbread dough into a rectangle 23 × 30 cm/9 × 12 in, 3 mm/⅛ in thick.

2. Bake in a 163°C/325°F oven until just beginning to brown, about 15 minutes. Remove from the oven.

3. Cut into 6 rectangles 2.5 × 11.5 cm/¾ × 4½ in each. Return to the oven and bake until evenly light browned, about 6 minutes.

4. Remove from the oven, set aside, and allow to cool completely.

TO PREPARE THE MOLDS:

Line 6 candy bar molds with the tempered dark chocolate. (See Shell-Molding Technique and Theory, page 77.)

TO MAKE THE CARAMEL:

1. Rub the lemon juice into the sugar.

2. In a saucepan, caramelize the sugar over direct heat while stirring constantly.

3. Add the warm cream slowly while stirring over low heat.

4. Remove from the heat and stir in the butter until melted and combined.

5. Allow to cool to room temperature.

6. Using a disposable pastry bag with a small opening cut in the tip, pipe the cooled caramel into the lined molds, leaving space for the shortbread and the chocolate for sealing the molds.

TO COMPLETE THE CARAMEL SHORTBREAD BARS:

1. Brush the baked and cooled shortbread with melted cocoa butter.

2. Place the shortbread bases on top of the caramel in the molds, with the cocoa butter side against the caramel.

3. Seal the molds with the tempered dark chocolate. (See Shell-Molding Technique and Theory, page 77.) Allow the bars to crystallize at room temperature for 15 minutes.

4. Refrigerate the sealed molds for about 20 minutes, until the chocolate pulls away from the inside of the molds.

5. Place a piece of stiff cardboard over each mold and invert to release the finished bars.

BOURBON STRATOSPHERES

yield: **100 BARS**

BOURBON CORDIALS

Sugar	740 g	26 oz	57%
Water	260 g	9 oz	20%
Bourbon, warm	300 g	11 oz	23%
BATCH SIZE	1300 g	46 oz	100%

PECAN GIANDUJA GANACHE

Pecans, toasted	350 g	12 oz	28%
Confectioners' sugar	170 g	6 oz	14%
Dark chocolate, melted, tempered	350 g	12 oz	28%
Heavy cream	290 g	10 oz	23%
Glucose syrup	90 g	3 oz	7%
BATCH SIZE	1250 g	43 oz	100%

Dark chocolate, melted, tempered, thinned slightly with cocoa butter, for precoating and enrobing (see Note)	as needed
Dark chocolate, untempered, for adhering	as needed

TO MAKE THE BOURBON CORDIALS:

1. Prepare starch molds using a 25-mm/1-in hemispherical imprinter. Take care that the starch is very well dried. (See Starch-Molding Technique and Theory, page 90.)

2. Combine the sugar and water in a saucepan and cook to 119°C/246°F. Clean the sides of the saucepan while cooking. Remove any impurities from the surface of the syrup.

3. Remove the syrup from the heat. Gently blend in the warm bourbon. Take care that it is well mixed in, but do not overagitate.

4. Funnel the warm syrup into the prepared starch molds. Sift a layer of dry starch on top of the molds to completely cover them.

5. Allow to set undisturbed for 4 to 5 hours. Turn the pieces over to ensure even crystallization. (This step is optional but recommended.)

6. Leave the cordials overnight to crystallize in the starch.

7. Remove the cordials from the starch. Use a clean, dry pastry brush to remove excess starch.

TO MAKE THE PECAN GIANDUJA GANACHE:

1. Grind the toasted pecans with a small amount of the confectioners' sugar in a food processor until liquefied.

2. Add the remaining confectioners' sugar and melted dark chocolate. Mix just until homogeneous.

3. Temper the gianduja by tabling, bringing it to 29°C/85°F.

4. Combine the cream and glucose syrup in a saucepan and bring to a boil. Remove from the heat and allow to cool to 40°C/105°F.

5. Pour the cream mixture over the tempered gianduja. Using a spoon or spatula, stir in vigorous small circles outward to emulsify.

6. Stir outward in larger circles to spread the emulsion throughout the bowl, checking to see that all of the chocolate has melted. If necessary, heat the ganache over a hot water bath to melt the chocolate. The temperature of the ganache should not exceed 34°C/93°F.

7. Spread into a frame 12 × 24 × ¼ in set on a heavy plastic sheet. Cover with plastic wrap and allow to crystallize overnight.

TO COMPLETE THE BOURBON STRATOSPHERES:

1. Remove the frame from the ganache and peel the plastic from the slab.

2. Precoat one side of the slab with the tempered, thinned dark chocolate.

3. Cut into strips, using the 30-mm strings on a guitar. Cut the strips into 83-mm/ 3-in bars.

4. Adhere 3 bourbon cordials to each bar with dots of the melted untempered dark chocolate.

5. Enrobe each bar in the tempered, thinned dark chocolate.

NOTE: See Thinning Technique and Theory, page 64.

MORELLO BARS

yield: **120 BARS**

CHERRY JELLY

Cherry purée	350 g	12 oz	19%
Apple compote (see Note)	200 g	7 oz	11%
Glucose syrup	160 g	6 oz	9%
Sugar	80 g	3 oz	5%
Pectin	20 g	1 oz	2%
Sugar	660 g	23 oz	36%
Glucose syrup	310 g	11 oz	16%
Citric acid solution (1 part citric acid to 1 part water)	30 g	1 oz	2%
BATCH SIZE	1810 g	64 oz	100%

GANACHE

Heavy cream	190 g	7 oz	14%
Glucose syrup	80 g	3 oz	6%
Kirschwasser	120 g	4 oz	8%
Butter, very soft	50 g	2 oz	4%
White chocolate, melted, tempered, at 30°C/86°F	920 g	33 oz	68%
BATCH SIZE	1360 g	49 oz	100%

Dark chocolate, melted, tempered, for precoating and enrobing	as needed
White chocolate poodle curls (see page 113), for finishing	as needed

TO MAKE THE CHERRY JELLY:

1. Combine the cherry purée, apple compote, and the 160 g of glucose syrup in a saucepan.

2. Mix together the 80 g of sugar and the pectin. Whisk into the purée mixture.

3. Bring to a boil, stirring constantly.

4. Add the 660 g of sugar and return to a boil while stirring.

5. Add the 310 g of glucose syrup and continue cooking over low heat while stirring until the batch reaches 106°C/223°F, or 75° Brix. This takes approximately 8 minutes of gentle boiling.

6. Add the citric acid solution and pour the jelly into a frame 12 × 24 × ½ in set on oiled parchment paper. The jelly will fill the frame about halfway.

7. Allow to cool to room temperature, at least 1 hour.

TO MAKE THE GANACHE:

1. Combine the cream and the 80 g of glucose syrup in a saucepan. Bring to a boil, remove from the heat, and add the kirschwasser.

2. Allow to cool to 40°C/105°F.

3. Stir the butter into the tempered white chocolate.

4. Pour the cream mixture over the white chocolate mixture.

5. Using a spoon or spatula, stir in vigorous small circles outward to emulsify.

6. Stir outward in larger circles to spread the emulsion throughout the bowl, checking to see that all of the chocolate has melted. If necessary, heat the ganache over a hot water bath to melt the chocolate. The temperature of the ganache should not exceed 34°C/94°F.

7. Pour immediately into the frame on top of the jelly.

8. Cover with plastic wrap and allow to crystallize overnight.

TO COMPLETE THE MORELLO BARS:

1. Remove the frame from the slab.

2. Precoat the jelly side of the slab with the tempered dark chocolate.

3. Cut into bars 19 mm × 8 cm/¾ × 3 in, using a chef's knife. Dip in the tempered dark chocolate. Before the chocolate sets, use a 3-prong dipping fork to make waves on the surface of each bar. Garnish with white chocolate poodle curls.

NOTE: Apple compote is available commercially under such trade names as Superpomme. If you wish to make the apple compote, peel, core, and slice apples. Cook with a little sugar and minimum water to make applesauce. Spread the sauce in a hotel pan and place it in a low oven to continue removing water, until the mixture is the consistency of thick applesauce. Purée prior to use.

Morello Bars

STRAWBERRY TEMPTRESS BARS

yield: **120 BARS**

NOUGAT

Egg whites	70 g	3 oz	5%
Sugar	50 g	2 oz	4%
Sugar	450 g	16 oz	32%
Glucose syrup	450 g	16 oz	32%
Honey	200 g	7 oz	14%
Water	100 g	4 oz	7%
Vanilla bean, split and scraped	1 bean	1 bean	
Confectioners' sugar, sifted	60 g	2 oz	4%
Cocoa butter, melted	40 g	1 oz	2%
BATCH SIZE	1420 g	51 oz	100%

STRAWBERRY JELLY

Strawberry purée	440 g	16 oz	20%
Apple compote (see Note)	250 g	9 oz	11%
Glucose syrup	200 g	7 oz	9%
Sugar	100 g	4 oz	5%
Pectin	25 g	1 oz	1%
Sugar	825 g	29 oz	35%
Glucose syrup	390 g	14 oz	17%
Lemon juice	60 g	2 oz	2%
BATCH SIZE	2290 g	82 oz	100%

CHOCOLATE ALMOND CRISP

Sliced almonds	400 g	14 oz	44%
Kirchwasser	30 g	1 oz	3%
Sugar	50 g	2 oz	5%
Butter, melted	40 g	1.5 oz	4%
Dark chocolate, melted, tempered, at 32°C/90°F	400 g	14 oz	44%
BATCH SIZE	920 g	32.5 oz	100%
Dark chocolate, melted, tempered, for enrobing	as needed		
White chocolate, melted, tempered, for drizzling	as needed		

TO MAKE THE NOUGAT:

1. Combine the egg whites and the 50 g of sugar in the bowl of a 5-qt planetary mixer with a whip attachment, but do not begin whipping.
2. Combine the 450 g of sugar, 450 g of glucose syrup, honey, water, and vanilla bean and its seeds in a saucepan.

3. Cook until the mixture reaches 115°C/239°F. Begin whipping the egg whites on high speed.

4. When the sugar mixture reaches 128°C/262°F, remove from the heat. Remove the vanilla bean and pour the hot sugar mixture into the whites as rapidly as they will accept it without collapsing. Continue whipping on high speed for 3 minutes longer.

5. Add the 60 g of confectioners' sugar, mixing only to combine.

6. Stream in the melted cocoa butter. The nougat will separate momentarily but will return to a smooth state within a minute.

7. Spread into a frame 12 × 24 × ¼ in set on a silicone mat.

8. When a skin forms on the nougat, smooth the top, using gloved hands.

9. Place another frame 12 × 24 × ¼ in on top of the one containing the nougat.

TO MAKE THE STRAWBERRY JELLY:

1. Combine the strawberry purée, apple compote, and the 200 g of glucose syrup in a saucepan.

2. Mix together the 100 g of sugar and the pectin. Whisk into the purée mixture.

3. Bring the mixture to a boil while stirring constantly.

4. Add the 825 g of sugar and return to a boil while stirring.

5. Add the 390 g of glucose syrup, and continue cooking over low heat while stirring until the batch reaches 106°C/223°F, or 75° Brix. This takes approximately 8 minutes of gentle boiling.

6. Add the lemon juice, and pour immediately into the frame on top of the nougat.

7. Allow to cool to room temperature, at least 1 hour.

TO MAKE THE CHOCOLATE ALMOND CRISP:

1. Moisten the almonds with the kirschwasser. Toss with the 50 g of sugar.

2. Toast in an oven at 175°C/350°F until golden. Remove from the oven and allow to cool to room temperature. Crush the cooled almonds lightly with a rolling pin.

3. Stir the butter into the melted dark chocolate.

4. Add the crushed almonds, mixing to combine.

5. Roll the chocolate-almond mixture between sheets of heavy plastic to form a rectangle slightly larger than 12 × 24 in. Trim to 30 × 61 cm/12 × 24 in.

TO COMPLETE THE STRAWBERRY TEMPTRESS BARS:

1. Turn the nougat-jelly slab over so that the nougat side is facing up.

2. Spray the nougat lightly with cold water. Remove one sheet of plastic from the chocolate layer, and invert that layer onto the nougat. Roll lightly with a rolling pin to adhere. Peel the other plastic sheet off. Allow the chocolate to set.

3. Turn the slab over again so that the chocolate side is facing down.

4. Cut into bars 19 mm × 8 cm/¾ × 3 in, using a chef's knife. Enrobe in the tempered dark chocolate. When the chocolate begins to set, drizzle the bars with the tempered white chocolate. Tap the bars lightly on the table to smooth the chocolates.

NOTE: Apple compote is available commercially under such trade names as Superpomme. If you wish to make the apple compote, peel, core, and slice apples. Cook with a little sugar and minimum water to make applesauce. Spread the sauce in a hotel pan and place it in a low oven to continue removing water, until the mixture is the consistency of thick applesauce. Purée prior to use.

CARASCHMALLOW BARS

yield: **120 BARS**

SOFT CARAMEL

Sugar	680 g	24 oz	30%
Evaporated milk	680 g	24 oz	30%
Heavy cream	280 g	10 oz	14%
Vanilla bean, split and scraped	1 bean	1 bean	
Glucose syrup	570 g	20 oz	25%
Butter	40 g	1 oz	1%
Salt	1 tsp	1 tsp	< 1%
BATCH SIZE	2250 g	79 oz	100%

MARSHMALLOW

Gelatin	20 g	0.75 oz	2%
Water, cold	120 g	4 oz	12%
Sugar	380 g	13 oz	39%
Glucose syrup	190 g	7 oz	21%
Water	100 g	4 oz	12%
Honey	60 g	2 oz	6%
Invert sugar	60 g	2 oz	6%
Vanilla extract	15 g	0.5 oz	2%
BATCH SIZE	945 g	33.25 oz	100%

CRISPY RICE LAYER

White chocolate, melted, tempered, at 30°C/86°F	400 g	14 oz	63%
Butter, melted	40 g	1.5 oz	6%
Crisped rice cereal, warm	190 g	7 oz	31%
White chocolate, melted, untempered for adhering	as needed		
BATCH SIZE	630 g	22.5 oz	100%

Dark chocolate, melted, tempered, for enrobing and finishing	as needed

TO MAKE THE SOFT CARAMEL:

1. Combine the 680 g of sugar, evaporated milk, cream, and vanilla bean and its seeds in a saucepan. Bring to a boil, stirring constantly.

2. Add the 570 g of glucose syrup and continue cooking over medium heat, while stirring, until the mixture reaches 110°C/230°F. Add the butter.

3. Cook while stirring until the mixture reaches 115°C/239°F (see Note). Add the salt, remove from the heat, remove the vanilla bean, and pour the caramel into a frame 12 × 24 × ¼ in set on oiled parchment paper.

4. Allow to cool to room temperature.

5. Place another frame 12 × 24 × ¼ in on top of the one containing the caramel.

TO MAKE THE MARSHMALLOW:

1. Hydrate the gelatin by stirring it into the cold water.

2. Combine the 380 g of sugar, 190 g of glucose syrup, water, honey, and invert sugar in a saucepan and cook to 122°C/252°F.

3. Pour the cooked sugar mixture into the bowl of a 5-qt planetary mixer with a whip attachment, but do not begin whipping. Allow the mixture to cool to 100°C/212°F.

4. While the sugar mixture cools, melt the hydrated gelatin over a water bath.

5. Mix the melted gelatin into the cooled sugars. Whip on high speed for 8 minutes, or until well aerated. Add the vanilla extract.

6. Spread immediately into the frame on top of the caramel layer. Allow to set overnight.

TO MAKE THE CRISPY RICE LAYER:

1. Combine the tempered white chocolate and the melted butter.

2. Fold in the cereal.

3. Spread a thin layer of the untempered white chocolate on the caramel layer in the frame. This will help affix the cereal layer to the caramel.

4. Spread the cereal mixture on top of the white chocolate-caramel layer.

5. Cover the cereal layer with parchment paper. Use a rolling pin to spread the cereal to the edges of the caramel in an even layer 9 mm/⅜ in thick.

6. Allow to set completely.

TO COMPLETE THE CARASCHMALLOW BARS:

1. Remove the frames from the slab.

2. Precoat the crispy side of the slab with the tempered dark chocolate.

3. Cut into bars 19 mm × 8 cm/¾ × 3 in. Enrobe in the tempered dark chocolate. When the chocolate begins to set, use a paper cone to pipe tempered dark chocolate lines diagonally across each bar.

NOTE: The temperature given for fully cooked caramel, 115°C/239°F, is a very good estimate, but results may vary depending on the ingredients used. Always check caramel for consistency by hand during cooking.

Caraschmallow Bars

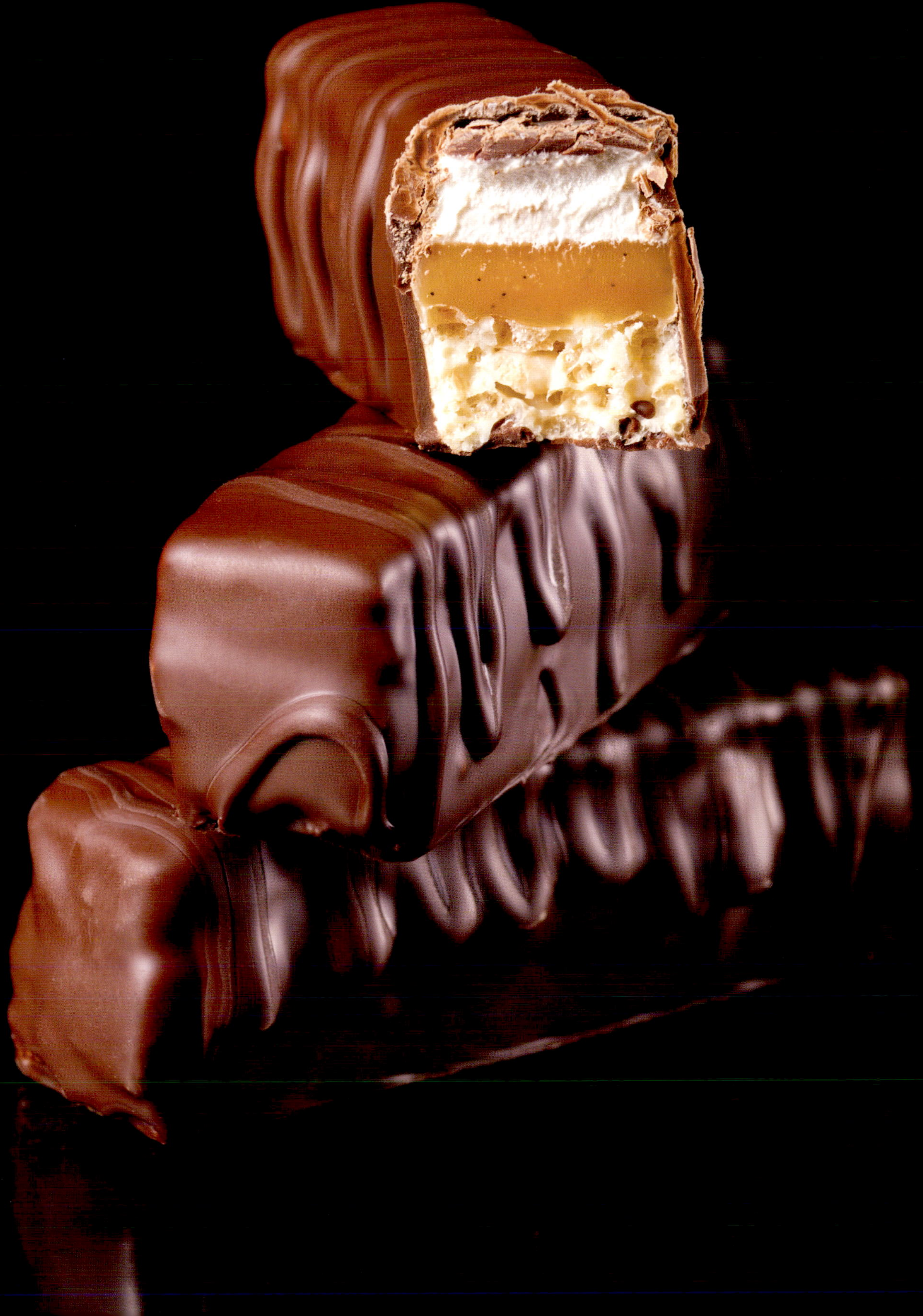

MERINGUE ANTOINETTES

yield: **120 PIECES**

ESPRESSO MERINGUE

Sugar	190 g	7 oz	55%
Egg whites	100 g	4 oz	32%
Cream of tartar	¼ tsp	¼ tsp	< 1%
Coffee extract	10 g	0.5 oz	13%
BATCH SIZE	300 g	11.5 oz	100%

HAZELNUT GIANDUJA

Hazelnuts, toasted	250 g	9 oz	28%
Confectioners' sugar	250 g	9 oz	28%
Dark chocolate, melted, tempered, at 32°C/90°F	250 g	9 oz	28%
Butter, soft	150 g	5 oz	16%
BATCH SIZE	900 g	32 oz	100%

Dark chocolate, melted, tempered, for enrobing	as needed
Red interference color, for brushing	as needed

TO MAKE THE ESPRESSO MERINGUE:

1. Combine the sugar, egg whites, and cream of tartar in the bowl of a 5-qt planetary mixer with a whip attachment and mix until thoroughly combined.
2. Place the bowl over a pot of barely simmering water and slowly stir the mixture until it reaches 60°C/140°F to dissolve the sugar.
3. Transfer the mixture to the mixer and begin whipping on high speed.
4. Continue whipping the egg white mixture until stiff peaks form, about 4 minutes. Add the coffee extract. Mix to combine.
5. Transfer the mixture to a piping bag fitted with a no. 2 round tip. Pipe into fingers 19 mm × 8 cm/¾ × 3 in on a piece of parchment paper.
6. Dry the fingers in an 82°C/180°F oven for 2 hours or in an oven warmed by the pilot light overnight. Remove from the oven and allow to cool completely at room temperature.

TO MAKE THE HAZELNUT GIANDUJA:

1. Grind the toasted hazelnuts with a small amount of the confectioners' sugar in a food processor until liquefied.
2. Add the remaining confectioners' sugar and tempered dark chocolate. Mix just until homogeneous.
3. Temper the gianduja by tabling it on marble to below 85°C/185°F.
4. Combine the gianduja with the butter in the mixing bowl of a 5-qt planetary mixer fitted with a paddle. Mix until well aerated.

TO COMPLETE THE MERINGUE ANTOINETTES:

1. Transfer the mixture to a piping bag fitted with a no. 2 round tip. Pipe two parallel cylinders down the length of the dried meringue fingers. Allow to crystallize until set, about 1 hour.
2. Dip the bars in the tempered dark chocolate. When the chocolate has set completely, finish by lightly brushing the finished bars with red interference color.

MINT MADNESS BARS

yield: **120 BARS**

MINT MELTAWAY

Dark chocolate, melted, tempered, at 32°C/90°F	860 g	30 oz	45%
Coconut fat, melted	280 g	10 oz	15%
Peppermint extract	1 Tbsp	1 Tbsp	< 1%
Peppermint Flake (page 247), finely chopped	750 g	27 oz	40%
BATCH SIZE	1890 g	67 oz	100%

WHITE CHOCOLATE MELTAWAY

White chocolate, melted, tempered, at 30°C/86°F	800 g	28 oz	80%
Coconut fat, melted	200 g	7 oz	20%
BATCH SIZE	1000 g	35 oz	100%

Dark chocolate, melted, tempered, for precoating and enrobing	as needed

TO MAKE THE MINT MELTAWAY:

1. Combine the tempered dark chocolate, 280 g of coconut fat, and peppermint extract in a stainless-steel bowl.

2. Temper by tabling on marble until cool and tempered but still fluid. Mix with the chopped Peppermint Flake.

3. Spread into a frame 12 × 24 × ½ in. The layer will be thin and will not nearly reach the top of the frame. Allow to set completely.

TO MAKE THE WHITE CHOCOLATE MELTAWAY:

1. Combine the tempered white chocolate and 200 g of coconut fat in a stainless-steel bowl.

2. Temper by tabling on marble until cool and tempered but still fluid. Spread into the frame containing the mint meltaway and spread evenly. Allow to set completely.

3. Table the remaining mint meltaway mixture until tempered but still fluid. Spread into the mold and spread evenly over the white chocolate layer. Allow to set completely.

TO COMPLETE THE MINT MADNESS BARS:

1. Precoat the mint meltaway-flake side of the slab with the tempered dark chocolate.

2. Temper by tabling on marble until cool and tempered but still fluid. Cut into bars 19 mm × 8 cm/¾ × 3 in, using a chef's knife. Enrobe in the tempered dark chocolate.

3. When the chocolate begins to set, use an empty airbrush to create decorative ripples in the surface of the chocolate.

COCOMEL BARS

yield: **120 BARS**

CARAMEL

Sugar	680 g	24 oz	30%
Evaporated milk	680 g	24 oz	30%
Heavy cream	280 g	10 oz	13%
Vanilla bean, split and scraped	1 bean	1 bean	
Glucose syrup	570 g	20 oz	26%
Butter	40 g	1 oz	1%
Salt	1 tsp	1 tsp	< 1%
BATCH SIZE	2250 G	79 OZ	100 %

COCONUT FILLING

Water	100 g	4 oz	6%
Invert sugar	100 g	4 oz	6%
Salt	2 tsp	2 tsp	< 1%
Desiccated coconut	600 g	21 oz	30%
Glucose syrup	560 g	20 oz	28%
Sugar	320 g	11 oz	15%
Water	220 g	8 oz	11%
Frappe (page 389)	80 g	3 oz	4%
BATCH SIZE	1980 g	71 oz	100%

Dark chocolate, melted, tempered, for precoating and enrobing	as needed	
Shredded coconut, for finishing	as needed	

TO MAKE THE CARAMEL:

1. Combine the 680 g of sugar, evaporated milk, cream, and vanilla bean and its seeds in a saucepan. Bring to a boil, stirring constantly.

2. Add the 570 g of glucose syrup and continue cooking over medium heat, while stirring, until the mixture reaches 110°C/230°F. Add the butter.

3. Cook while stirring until the mixture reaches 115°C/239°F (see Note). Add the 1 tsp of salt, remove from the heat, remove the vanilla bean, and pour the caramel into a frame 16 × 24 × ¼ in set on oiled parchment paper. Allow to cool to room temperature.

4. Place another frame 16 × 24 × ¼ in on top of the one containing the caramel.

TO MAKE THE COCONUT FILLING:

1. Combine the 100 g of water, invert sugar, and 2 tsp of salt in a saucepan. Bring to a boil. Pour the mixture over the coconut and allow to hydrate for 30 minutes.

2. Combine the 560 g of glucose syrup, sugar, and 220 g of water in a saucepan and cook to 112°C/234°F. Mix half the coconut with the sugar mixture. Combine well.

3. Add the frappe to the coconut-sugar mixture and mix well. (If the frappe has been in storage, warming it slightly makes this step easier.)

4. Add the remaining half of the coconut. Mix until homogeneous. Allow to cool to room temperature.

5. Spread the mixture into the frame on top of the caramel. Place a piece of oiled parchment on top, and use a rolling pin to smooth the coconut filling. Cool to room temperature.

TO COMPLETE THE COCOMEL BARS:

1. Precoat the caramel side of the slab with the tempered dark chocolate.

2. Cut into bars 19 mm × 8 cm/¾ × 3 in. Enrobe in the tempered dark chocolate. Before the chocolate sets, use a 3-prong dipping fork to make diagonal waves on each bar. Garnish with shredded coconut.

NOTE: The temperature given for fully cooked caramel, 115°C/239°F, is a very good estimate, but results may vary depending on the ingredients used. Always check caramel for consistency by hand during cooking.

PEANUT BUTTER GOODNESS BARS

yield: **120 BARS**

PEANUT BUTTER NOUGAT

Milk powder, crushed	80 g	3 oz	4%
Confectioners' sugar	80 g	3 oz	4%
Peanut butter	350 g	12 oz	16%
Glucose syrup	100 g	4 oz	5%
Egg whites	60 g	2 oz	3%
Vanilla extract	20 g	1 oz	1%
Sugar	580 g	21 oz	27%
Glucose syrup	450 g	16 oz	21%
Molasses	220 g	8 oz	11%
Water	180 g	6 oz	8%
BATCH SIZE	2120 g	76 oz	100%

CARAMEL

Sugar	680 g	24 oz	21%
Evaporated milk	680 g	24 oz	21%
Heavy cream	280 g	10 oz	8%
Vanilla bean, split and scraped	1 bean	1 bean	
Glucose syrup	570 g	20 oz	18%
Butter	40 g	1.5 oz	< 1%
Salt	1 tsp	1 tsp	< 1%
Peanuts, toasted	970 g	34 oz	30%
BATCH SIZE	3220 g	113.5 oz	100%

Milk chocolate, melted, tempered, for precoating and enrobing	as needed
Peanuts, toasted, chopped, for finishing	as needed

TO MAKE THE PEANUT BUTTER NOUGAT:

1. Sift together the milk powder and confectioners' sugar.

2. Heat the peanut butter over a water bath until it is hot and fluid.

3. Combine the 100 g of glucose syrup, egg whites, and vanilla extract in the bowl of a 5-qt planetary mixer with a whip attachment. Mix until just combined, but do not begin whipping.

4. Combine the 580 g of sugar, the 450 g of glucose syrup, molasses, and water in a saucepan. Cook the mixture to 112°C/234°F.

5. Begin whipping the egg white mixture on high speed. When the sugar mixture reaches 122°C/252°F, remove from the heat.

6. Stream the hot syrup into the whipping whites. Continue whipping on high speed for 4 minutes.

7. Remove the whipped whites from the mixer. Using a wooden spoon, fold in the dry ingredients.

8. Add the melted peanut butter and mix well.

9. Spread the nougat into a frame 12 × 24 × ⅜ in set on oiled parchment paper. Allow to cool completely.

10. Place another frame 12 × 24 × ⅜ in on top of the one containing the nougat.

TO MAKE THE CARAMEL:

1. Combine the 680 g of sugar, evaporated milk, cream, and vanilla bean and its seeds in a saucepan. Bring to a boil, stirring constantly.

2. Add the 570 g of glucose syrup and continue cooking over medium heat, while stirring, until the mixture reaches 110°C/230°F. Add the butter.

3. Cook while stirring until the mixture reaches 115°C/239°F (see Note). Add the salt, remove from the heat, remove the vanilla bean, and add the peanuts. Stir to combine.

4. Spread the mixture immediately into the frame on top of the peanut butter nougat. Allow to cool to room temperature.

TO COMPLETE THE PEANUT BUTTER GOODNESS BARS:

1. Precoat the caramel side of the slab with the tempered milk chocolate. Cut into bars 19 mm × 8 cm/¾ × 3 in, using a chef's knife.

2. Enrobe each bar in the tempered milk chocolate. Before the chocolate sets, use a 3-prong dipping fork to make diagonal waves on each bar. Garnish with chopped toasted peanuts.

NOTE: The temperature given for fully cooked caramel, 115°C/239°F, is a very good estimate, but results may vary depending on the ingredients used. Always check caramel for consistency by hand during cooking.

Peanut Butter Goodness Bars

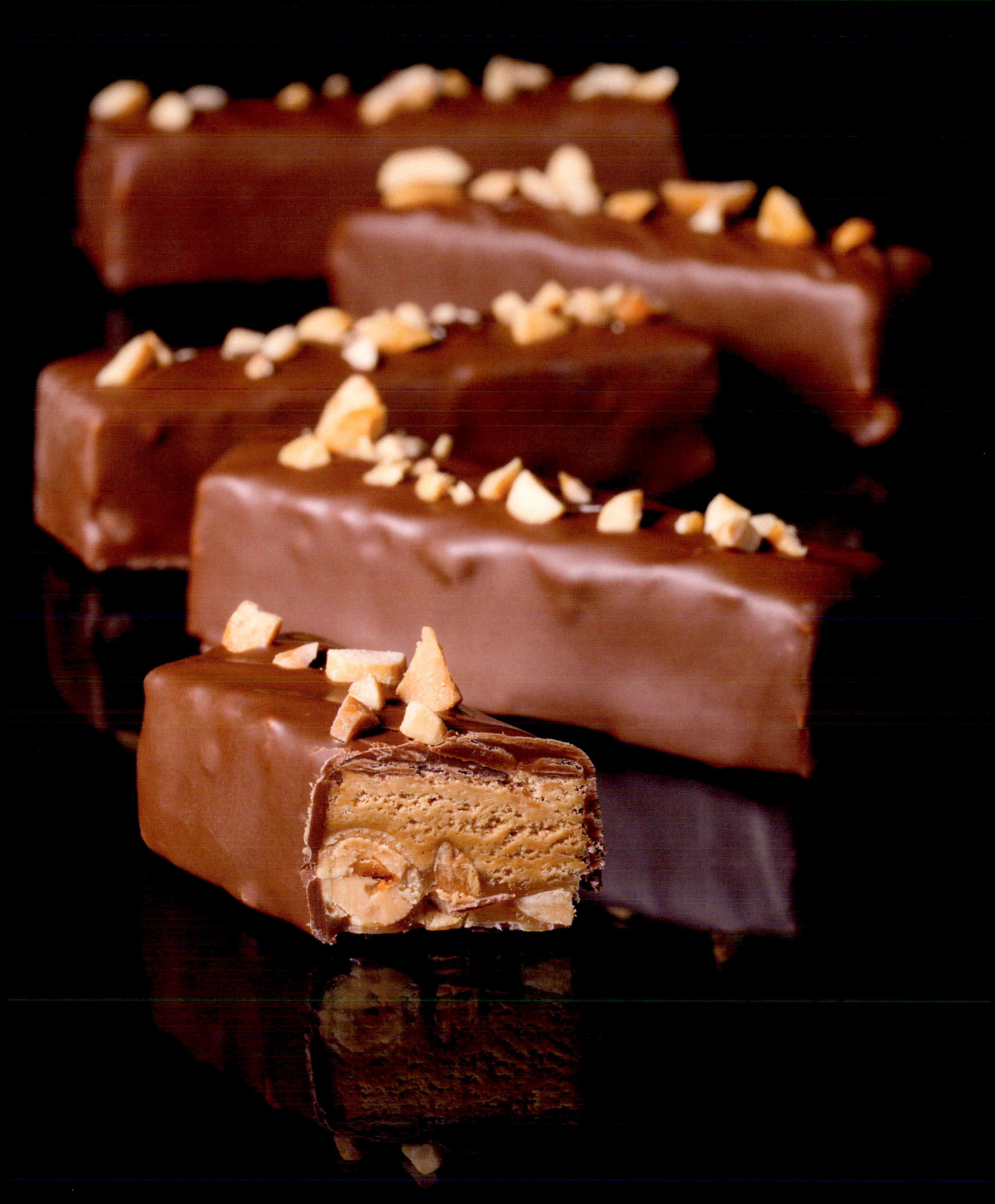

BIMINI BARS

yield: 36 BARS

COCONUT FILLING

Water	50 g	2 oz	5%
Invert sugar	50 g	2 oz	5%
Salt	1 tsp	1 tsp	<1%
Glucose syrup	280 g	10 oz	28%
Sugar	160 g	6 oz	17%
Water	110 g	4 oz	11%
Desiccated coconut	300 g	11 oz	31%
Frappe (page 389)	40 g	1 oz	3%
BATCH SIZE	990 g	36 oz	100%

RUM GANACHE

Heavy cream	140 g	5 oz	27%
Milk	40 g	1 oz	6%
Glucose syrup	50 g	2 oz	11%
Dark chocolate, unmelted, tempered, chopped	250 g	9 oz	50%
Dark rum	40 g	1 oz	6%
BATCH SIZE	520 g	18 oz	100%

Dark chocolate, melted, tempered,
for lining and sealing molds · · · · · as needed

TO PREPARE THE MOLDS:

Line 6 candy bar molds with tempered dark chocolate. (See Shell-Molding Technique and Theory, page 77.)

TO MAKE THE COCONUT FILLING:

1. Combine the 50 g of water, invert sugar, and salt in a saucepan. Bring to a boil.

2. Combine the 280 g of glucose syrup, sugar, and 110 g of water in a saucepan and cook to 112°C/234°F.

3. Mix half the coconut with the sugar mixture. Combine well.

4. Add the frappe to the coconut-sugar mixture and mix well. (If the frappe has been in storage, warming it slightly makes this step easier.)

5. Add the remaining half of the coconut. Mix until homogeneous. Allow to cool to room temperature.

6. Press 25 g/1 oz of the coconut mixture into the cavity of each mold, leaving room for the rum ganache layer as well as for sealing. Set aside.

TO MAKE THE RUM GANACHE:

1. Combine the 140 g of cream, milk, and glucose syrup in a saucepan. Bring to a boil.

2. Pour the hot cream mixture over the chopped dark chocolate and let sit for 1 minute to allow the chocolate to melt.

3. Using a spoon or spatula, stir in vigorous small circles outward to emulsify.

4. Stir outward in larger circles to spread the emulsion throughout the bowl, checking to see that all of the chocolate has melted. If necessary, heat the ganache over a hot water bath to melt the chocolate. The temperature of the ganache should not exceed 34°C/93°F.

5. Stream in the rum, stirring until the mixture is homogeneous.

6. Pour the ganache into a hotel pan, covering the bottom of the pan with a thin layer. Place plastic wrap directly on the surface of the ganache. Allow to cool to 27°C/80°F.

TO COMPLETE THE BIMINI BARS:

1. Transfer the ganache to a pastry bag fitted with a no. 2 round tip, and pipe the ganache on top of the coconut, leaving 2 mm/1/16 in at the top of the molds for sealing. Tap the molds on the table to level the contents.

2. Allow the ganache to set completely, then seal the molds with the tempered dark chocolate. (See Shell-Molding Technique and Theory, page 77.) Allow the bars to crystallize at room temperature for 15 minutes.

3. Refrigerate the sealed molds for about 20 minutes, until the chocolate pulls away from the inside of the molds.

4. Place a piece of stiff cardboard over each mold and invert to release the finished bars.

APPENDICES AND GLOSSARY

Appendix A: Sugar Densities

DEGREES BRIX OR % BY WEIGHT OF SUCROSE	SPECIFIC GRAVITY	DEGREES BAUME	DEGREES BRIX OR % BY WEIGHT OF SUCROSE	SPECIFIC GRAVITY	DEGREES BAUME
0.0	1.00000	0.00	32.0	1.13861	17.65
1.0	1.00389	0.56	33.0	1.14347	18.19
2.0	1.00779	1.12	34.0	1.14837	18.73
3.0	1.01172	1.68	35.0	1.15331	19.28
4.0	1.01567	2.24	36.0	1.15828	19.81
5.0	1.01965	2.79	37.0	1.16329	19.81
6.0	1.02366	3.35	38.0	1.16833	20.89
7.0	1.02770	3.91	39.0	1.17341	21.97
8.0	1.03176	4.46	40.0	1.17853	21.97
9.0	1.03586	5.02	41.0	1.18368	22.50
10.0	1.03998	5.57	42.0	1.18887	23.04
11.0	1.04413	6.13	43.0	1.19410	23.57
12.0	1.04831	6.68	44.0	1.19936	24.10
13.0	1.05252	7.24	45.0	1.20467	24.63
14.0	1.05677	7.79	46.0	1.21001	25.17
15.0	1.06104	8.34	47.0	1.21538	25.70
16.0	1.06534	8.89	48.0	1.22080	26.23
17.0	1.06968	9.45	49.0	1.22625	26.75
18.0	1.07404	10.00	50.0	1.23174	27.28
19.0	1.07844	10.55	51.0	1.23727	27.81
20.0	1.08287	11.10	52.0	1.24284	28.33
21.0	1.08733	11.65	53.0	1.24844	28.86
22.0	1.09183	12.20	54.0	1.25408	29.38
23.0	1.09636	12.74	55.0	1.25976	29.90
24.0	1.10092	13.29	56.0	1.26548	30.42
25.0	1.10551	13.84	57.0	1.27123	30.94
26.0	1.11014	14.39	58.0	1.27703	31.97
27.0	1.11480	14.93	59.0	1.28286	31.97
28.0	1.11949	15.48	60.0	1.28873	32.49
29.0	1.12422	16.02	61.0	1.29464	33.0
30.0	1.12898	16.57	62.0	1.30059	33.51
31.0	1.13378	17.11	63.0	1.30657	34.02

DEGREES BRIX OR % BY WEIGHT OF SUCROSE	SPECIFIC GRAVITY	DEGREES BAUME	DEGREES BRIX OR % BY WEIGHT OF SUCROSE	SPECIFIC GRAVITY	DEGREES BAUME
64.0	1.31260	34.53	83.0	1.43434	43.91
65.0	1.31866	35.04	84.0	1.44112	44.38
66.0	1.32476	35.55	85.0	1.44794	44.86
67.0	1.33090	36.05	86.0	1.45480	45.33
68.0	1.33708	36.55	87.0	1.46170	45.80
69.0	1.34330	37.06	88.0	1.46862	46.27
70.0	1.34956	37.56	89.0	1.47559	46.73
71.0	1.35585	38.06	90.0	1.48259	47.20
72.0	1.36218	38.55	91.0	1.48963	47.66
73.0	1.36856	39.05	92.0	1.49671	48.12
74.0	1.37496	39.54	93.0	1.50381	48.58
75.0	1.38141	40.03	94.0	1.5196	49.03
76.0	1.38790	40.53	95.0	1.51814	49.49
77.0	1.39442	41.01	96.0	1.52535	49.94
78.0	1.40098	41.50	97.0	1.53260	50.39
79.0	1.40758	41.99	98.0	1.53988	50.84
80.0	1.41421	42.47	99.0	1.54719	51.28
81.0	1.42088	42.95	100.0	1.55454	51.73
82.0	1.42759	43.43			

Shell Molding Operation Layout

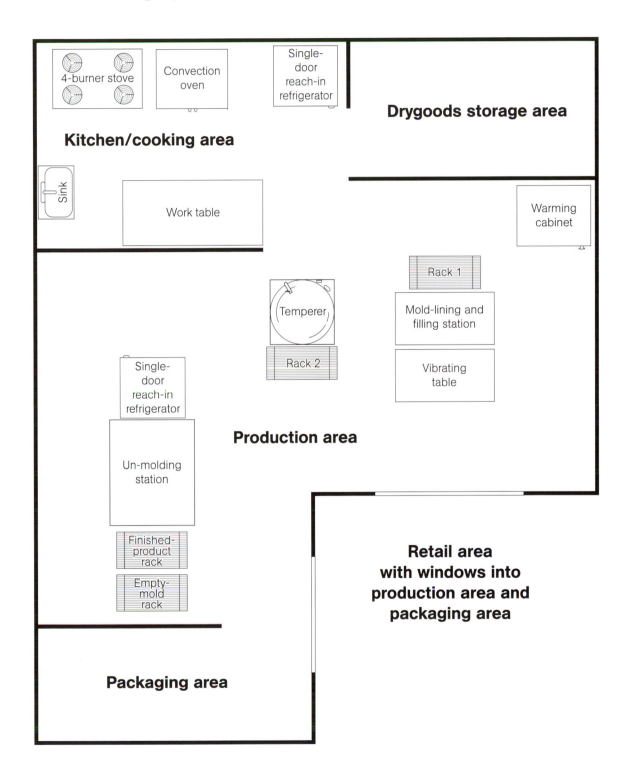

Enrobing Operation Layout

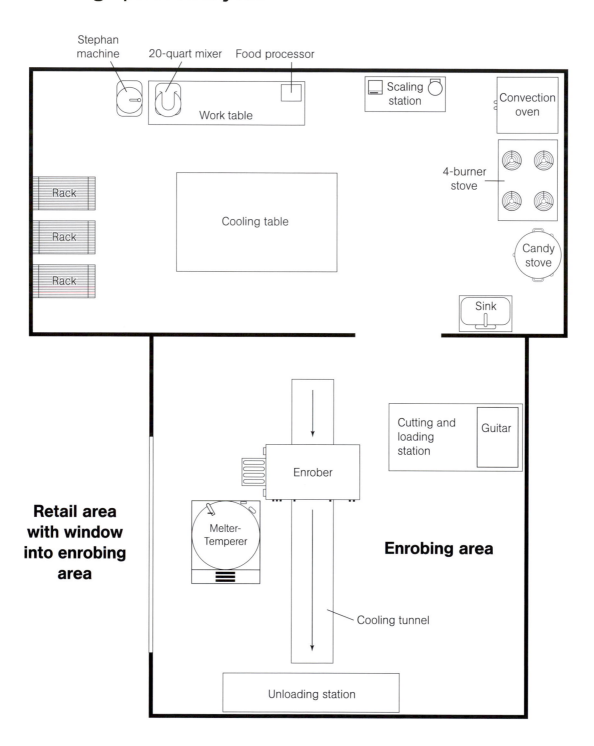

Stephan machine

20-quart mixer

Food processor

Work table

Scaling station

Convection oven

4-burner stove

Rack

Rack

Rack

Cooling table

Candy stove

Sink

Cutting and loading station

Guitar

Enrober

Retail area with window into enrobing area

Melter-Temperer

Enrobing area

Cooling tunnel

Unloading station

Panning Operation Layout

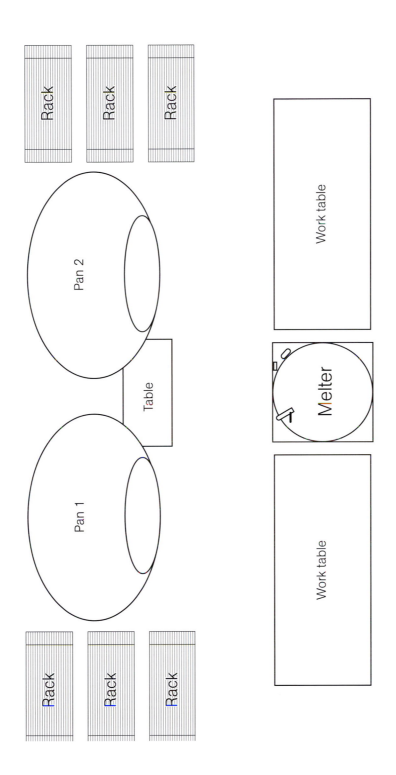

Glossary

AGAR: A powerful binding agent derived from sea vegetables. It produces a thermoreversible gel. *See* Thermoreversible.

AGGLOMERATE: A cluster of particles packed together.

AGITATE: To move with an irregular, rapid, or violent action, usually in order to induce crystallization of fats or sugars. This is often accomplished through tabling a mixture—working it on a smooth stone surface—or stirring it in a bowl.

ALKALIZATION: *See* Dutch processing.

AMINO ACIDS: The building blocks of proteins. Amino acids are essential components of the Maillard reaction.

AMORPHOUS: Noncrystalline. Hard candies are examples of sugars in a noncrystalline state.

ANHYDROUS: Free of water.

AQUEOUS PHASE: The portion of an emulsion that is water based. May be either the dispersed or continuous phase of the emulsion. *See* Dispersed phase and Continuous phase. Artificial flavor: A flavor that is manufactured from sources other than spices, fruits, vegetables, plants, poultry, or meat, as defined by the FDA.

AW: The symbol for the relative activity of water in a substance. *See* Water activity.

BAUMÉ: A scale of measurement of density expressed in degrees. It is sometimes used to describe sugar content. Baumé is measured with a saccharimeter, a densimeter calibrated on the Baumé scale.

BLOOM (CHOCOLATE): The gray cast, spots, or streaks that appear on poorly handled chocolate. *See* Fat bloom and Sugar bloom.

BLOOM (GELATIN): The process of hydrating gelatin prior to use.

BLOOM STRENGTH: A measurement of the strength of gelatin that describes the relative strength of the gel it forms. Higher bloom numbers correspond to stronger gelatins. Approximate measurements typically range from 100 to 300.

BOILING STARCHES: Acid-modified starches used in the production of starch jellies. Also known as thin boiling starches.

BOUND WATER: Water that is chemically bound to other substances, such as sugars. Bound water does not contribute to water activity. *See* Water activity.

BRITTLES: Amorphous sugar confections flavored through Maillard browning and typically made with nuts. Brittles usually contain a lower percentage of dairy products than toffee.

BRIX: A scale of measurement of sugar concentration in a solution. A Brix measurement is performed with a refractometer and is expressed in degrees. A reading of 1° Brix is equivalent to 1 percent sugar in solution.

CACAO: Botanical name relating to the agriculture of the South American evergreen Theobroma cacao and its products up to fermentation of the cacao bean.

CARAMELIZE: To brown sugar by exposing it to heat. Caramelization produces flavors and colors similar to those produced in the Maillard reaction, but it is a distinctly different reaction.

CHOCOLATE LIQUOR: The liquid produced when cocoa beans are ground into a paste, releasing the cocoa butter. Also a legally allowable name for unsweetened chocolate.

COATING CHOCOLATE: "Chocolate" in which most or all of the cocoa butter has been replaced with another type of fat. Coating chocolate generally requires little or no tempering.

COCOA: The term used to describe products resulting from cacao agriculture after the fermentation of beans (e.g., cocoa beans, cocoa butter, and cocoa powder). Also a legally allowable name for cocoa powder.

COCOA BUTTER: The fat found in cocoa beans.

COLD FLOW: The tendency of a center to ooze and change shape when held at room temperature. Taffy exhibits cold flow and must therefore be wrapped to hold its shape. Caramels should not exhibit cold flow and should therefore keep their shape after they are cut.

COLLOID: A substance consisting of suspended particles that are too small to be viewed with an ordinary light microscope.

CONFIT: From the French for "preserved." Used to refer to partially candied citrus peels.

CONTINUOUS PHASE: The phase of an emulsion that contains the droplets of the dispersed phase. (*See* Dispersed phase.) The continuous phase may be either fat or water, depending on the type of emulsion.

CONVERSION: The breakdown of starch, through hydrolysis, into various saccharides during the production of glucose syrup.

CORDIALS: Chocolates with a liquid center.

CORN SYRUP: Glucose syrup that is converted from cornstarch.

COUVERTURE: The European designation for chocolate containing at least 32 percent cocoa butter. The term has no legal standing in the United States.

CRIOLLO: The variety of cocoa bean that is generally regarded as being of the highest quality.

CRYSTALLINE: Sugar or fat that is not amorphous but has a highly ordered molecular structure. Fudge and fondant both contain crystalline sugar.

CRYSTALLIZE: To transform from the amorphous state to the crystalline state.

DE: Dextrose equivalence. Specification used to describe how much the starch molecule has been broken down into simpler sugars in a glucose syrup. DE affects flavor, viscosity, browning, and many other aspects of glucose syrup.

DENATURE: To unfold or uncoil protein molecules as a result of exposure to heat, acid, or mechanical agitation.

DENSIMETER: An instrument that measures the density of a syrup by floating in the syrup. Saccharimeters and hydrometers are examples of densimeters.

DEPOSIT: To place a quantity of a material for confectionery centers in a form or shape where it will set. Artisan confectioners may deposit centers using a piping bag, a fondant funnel, or by spreading into a frame.

DEW POINT: The temperature to which air must be chilled in order for the humidity to condense into water droplets.

DEXTROSE: A monosaccharide; one half of the sucrose molecule. Although sometimes referred to as glucose, in this book the term dextrose is used to distinguish glucose from glucose syrup. Dextrose is less sweet than sucrose.

DEXTROSE EQUIVALENCE: *See* DE.

DISACCHARIDE: Two single sugar molecules chemically bonded together. Sucrose is a disaccharide.

DISPERSED PHASE: The portion of an emulsion that is in droplets. A dispersed phase may be either the aqueous phase or the fat phase.

DISSOLVED SOLIDS: The total quantity of sugars dissolved in a solution.

DOCTORING AGENT: An ingredient added to sugar to prevent crystallization. Examples of doctoring agents are glucose syrup, organic acids, and invert sugar.

DRAGÉE: A rudimentary panning technique accomplished without a panning machine. *See* Panning. Often involves two steps of caramelization followed by coating with chocolate. From the Middle French, meaning literally "dredged."

DRY METHOD: Putting granulated sugar over direct heat without the addition of water to melt and caramelize it. The dry method may be used only for making caramel, not for cooking sugar to any intermediate stage such as soft ball, and so on.

DUTCH PROCESSING: A method by which cacao is treated with an alkali; may be carried out at various stages of manufacturing.

EMULSIFY: To convert into a mixture of two incompletely compatible liquids in which one of the liquids, in the form of fine droplets, is dispersed in the other.

EMULSION: A mixture of immiscible ingredients (i.e., fat and water) in which droplets of one substance are suspended within the other.

ENGROSS: In panning, to build up layers of the sugar or chocolate coating. *See* Panning.

ENZYME: A protein that is a catalyst, causing specific reactions in specific substances. For example, the enzyme invertase causes the inversion of sucrose.

EQUILIBRIUM RELATIVE HUMIDITY: *See* ERH.

ERH: Equilibrium relative humidity. An expression of water activity. ERH is the relative humidity that would be necessary for a substance to neither gain moisture from nor lose moisture to the surrounding environment.

EUTECTIC: A combination of fats that results in a product with a lower melting point than would be predicted by the solid fat index (SFI). Lauric fat combined with cocoa butter creates a eutectic that results in meltaways.

FAT BLOOM: Chocolate due to improper crystallization of cocoa butter. Fat bloom is caused mainly by improper tempering or storage of chocolate.

FAT MIGRATION: The movement of incompatible fats to create equilibrium; for example, when nut oil migrates through chocolate, softening it.

FAT SYSTEM: A system of solid particles within fat. Chocolate and nut pastes are examples of fat systems.

FAT-IN-WATER EMULSION: An emulsion in which the fat phase is dispersed in the continuous aqueous phase. *See* Aqueous phase and Continuous phase.

FATTY ACIDS: The long chains attached to the glycerol backbone making up triglycerides (fats). The breakdown of fatty acids is called rancidity and can cause off flavors.

FERMENTATION: The breakdown of sugars and other substances by yeasts and bacteria. In cacao production, fermentation of the beans produces the flavor precursors for chocolate flavor.

FONDANT: Sugar, water, and glucose syrup that is supersaturated and agitated to induce crystallization.

FOOT: A large flat spot on the bottom of chocolate-dipped confections due to excessive accumulation of chocolate around the base. Large feet are defects in dipped confections.

FORASTERO: The highest-yielding commercial variety of cacao.

FORCE-SETTING: Causing a substance to set by exposing it to cooler than usual temperatures. Chocolate or ganache that is force-set will form unstable fat crystals and produce inferior results.

FORM V: The stable form of cocoa butter crystal that can be produced during tempering.

FRACTIONATED FAT: Fat that has been chilled in order to isolate certain narrow melting ranges.

FRAPPE: An aerator added to some types of confectionery, including fudge and saltwater taffy. Frappe usually has a base of albumen or gelatin and sugars.

FREE WATER: Water that is not chemically bound to another substance and is therefore available for chemical or enzymatic reactions, bacteria, molds, and so on. Water activity is a measurement of free water.

FRUCTOSE: A monosaccharide that together with dextrose makes up sucrose. Fructose is sweeter than sucrose.

FUDGE: A crystalline confection similar to fondant, but containing fats, dairy products, and flavoring.

GANACHE: A mixture of chocolate with a water-containing ingredient, most commonly cream. Cream-based ganache is a fat-in-water emulsion.

GEL: A colloidal dispersion of solids that trap water. For example, jellies are gels created using various hydrocolloids.

GELATIN: A hydrocolloid protein mixture derived from animal collagen that creates a thermoreversible gel. Used in the production of gummy jellies. *See* Thermoreversible.

GELATINIZATION: The swelling of starches when heated in the presence of moisture, due to the absorption of water.

GIANDUJA: Chocolate that contains a finely ground nut paste.

GLASS: A noncrystalline solid. Hard candy and brittles are examples of glass.

GLUCOSE: Another name for dextrose. The name glucose syrup is often shortened to glucose, creating the potential for confusion.

GLUCOSE SYRUP: An aqueous solution of saccharides obtained from edible starch. Glucose syrup may be made from any edible starch. The name of the source starch may be used in place of the word glucose. For example, corn syrup is glucose syrup made from cornstarch.

GRAINED: Crystallized.

GUITAR: A wire cutter for confectionery use.

HALOPHILIC: Requiring a salty environment to thrive.

HIGH-METHOXYL (HM) PECTIN: Pectin that has not been chemically modified. It requires a high sugar content and relatively low pH to form a gel.

HUMECTANT: An ingredient that tends to keep products moist due to its hygroscopicity. Invert sugar is an excellent humectant.

HYDROCOLLOIDS: Gelling agents that form a three-dimensional network, trapping water and forming a gel.

HYDROGENATED FAT: Fat that has had additional hydrogen added to its structure during manufacture to make it more saturated, raising its melting point and increasing its resistance to rancidity.

HYDROLYSIS: The process of breaking the chemical bonds in starch or sugar to make shorter saccharide chains. The hydrolysis of sucrose into fructose and dextrose is called inversion.

HYDROMETER: An instrument that measures the specific gravity of a syrup by floating in the syrup. A hydrometer is usually calibrated in grams per milliliters.

HYDROPHILIC: The quality of being chemically attracted to water.

HYGROSCOPIC: The tendency to pick up water from the surrounding atmosphere. Amorphous sugar is hygroscopic.

HYSTERESIS: A delay in the action of a system. For example, agar can be considered as exhibiting hysteresis when it sets at about 40°C/105°F but, once gelled, melts only at about 85°C/185°F.

IMPRINTER: A tool used to make impressions in starch beds when starch molding. Imprinters are usually made of plaster shapes glued to a wooden board or stick.

INCLUSION: An added ingredient that remains discrete in the finished product.

INFUSION: The process by which an aromatic ingredient is steeped in a mixture and then removed, leaving only the essence of its flavor behind.

INVERSION: The hydrolysis of sucrose into dextrose and fructose. Inversion is accomplished mainly by acids or the enzyme invertase, but other factors, such as minerals and heat, can influence inversion.

INVERT SUGAR: Sucrose that has been hydrolyzed into fructose and dextrose. Invert sugar is usually purchased in a cream form containing approximately 20 percent water.

INVERTASE: The enzyme used to invert sucrose in order to soften centers and improve shelf life.

JACKET: The outside of a batch of hard candy that contains the colors and creates the striped appearance. The jacket is wrapped around a sugar core for decorative purposes.

LACTOSE: The sugar found in dairy products. Lactose is very low in sweetness and readily participates in Maillard browning.

LATENT HEAT OF CRYSTALLIZATION: The heat released when a substance crystallizes. Latent heat of crystallization can cause chocolate to bloom if it is not released as the cocoa butter crystallizes.

LAURIC FAT: Fat high in lauric acid. Lauric fat is incompatible with cocoa butter and creates a dramatic eutectic effect when combined with it. Coconut and palm kernel fats are examples of lauric fats.

LIPASE: A fat-degrading enzyme that causes rancidity.

LOW-METHOXYL (LM) PECTIN: Chemically modified pectin that does not require a high sugar content in order to form a gel. LM pectin requires the presence of calcium in order to gel.

MAILLARD BROWNING: Nonenzymatic browning as a result of the Maillard reaction.

MAILLARD REACTION: A browning reaction involving amino acids and reducing sugars that results in colors and flavors that greatly resemble caramelization.

MALTOSE: A disaccharide made up of 2 dextrose molecules.

MANUFACTURED FLAVORS: Flavors created by mixing organic chemicals. Manufactured flavors may be classified as "natural" or "artificial," depending on the sources of the chemicals used.

MARZIPAN: A confection of ground almonds and sugar. Marzipan may also be made using a portion of variety nuts in addition to almonds.

MÉLANGEUR: A refiner used for reducing the particle size of mixtures such as marzipan and gianduja.

MELTING RANGE: The temperature range at which fats begin to turn from a solid to a liquid state.

MICRON: One millionth of a meter.

MILK CRUMB: A mixture of chocolate liquor, sugar, and milk solids that is sometimes used as an ingredient in milk chocolate. Milk chocolate made using milk crumb often exhibits caramel flavor notes.

MOISTURE MIGRATION: The movement of moisture from areas of higher concentrations to areas of lower concentration. Depending on its ERH and the environment, a center may lose moisture to the atmosphere or may gain moisture from the atmosphere. See ERH.

NATURAL FLAVORS: Manufactured flavors made with chemicals extracted from spices, fruits, vegetables, plants, poultry, or meat, through allowable processes, including fermentation, hydrolysis, and distillation.

NONCRYSTALLINE: In an amorphous or glass state. *See* Amorphous; Glass.

NONENZYMATIC BROWNING: Browning that is not caused by the action of enzymes. Maillard browning and caramelization are two primary examples of nonenzymatic browning.

NOUGAT: An aerated confection usually employing albumen as an aerator. Many styles of nougat exist; nougat Montelimar is one of the most famous.

ORGANOLEPTIC: Those properties that are perceived by the senses, as opposed to those that are measured with instruments.

OSMOPHILE: An organism that is able to thrive in environments with high osmotic pressure, such as syrups with high percentages of sugar.

OSMOPHILIC: Growing under conditions of high osmotic pressure, such as a sugar syrup with a high dissolved solids content.

OSMOSIS: The diffusion of water through a semipermeable membrane. It is through osmosis that the water in the cells of fruit is replaced with sugar syrup when candying fruit.

OSMOTIC PRESSURE: The pressure of water moving across a semipermeable membrane. The higher the sugar content in syrup, the higher the osmotic pressure. Osmotic pressure lowers the water activity level of a substance. Most bacteria and fungi cannot thrive in an environment with a high osmotic pressure.

PANNING: The process of building up layers on centers by tumbling the centers in revolving pans. The layers may consist of chocolate or sugar, depending on the type of panning.

PÂTE À GLACER: French term describing coating chocolate.

PECTIN: A hydrocolloid extracted from fruit and used as a binding agent in confectionery.

PH: Measurement of the relative acidity/alkalinity of a substance. A measurement of pH 7 is neutral; a pH lower than 7 is acidic; and a pH higher than 7 is alkaline.

POLYMORPHIC: Capable of setting in a number of different forms. Cocoa butter is polymorphic; it may set in several different crystal forms.

POLYSACCHARIDE: Molecules made up of thousands of single sugars chemically bonded together. Starches are examples of polysaccharides, as is agar.

PRALINE: A crystalline confection most frequently made with brown sugar and pecans. Pralines are popular throughout the southern United States.

PRALINÉ: From the French for "sugar coated." A European term denoting a confectionery center dipped in chocolate. A praliné is usually a finished chocolate-coated one-bite confection.

PRALINE PASTE: A paste made with hazelnuts and caramelized sugar. Praline paste may be purchased in formulas with various ratios of nuts to sugar.

PRECRYSTALLIZE: To temper; to seed chocolate with enough stable cocoa butter crystals to induce it to set properly.

PROTEASE ENZYMES: Enzymes that degrade proteins. Frequently found in tropical fruits, protease enzymes can inhibit the binding capability of gelatin.

RANCIDITY: Degradation of fats due to breaking of fatty acid chains. Rancidity may be caused by oxygen, enzymes, light, heat, or metals. Rancidity can cause off flavors.

REDUCING SUGARS: Sugars that react with amino acids in the

MAILLARD REACTION: Lactose, dextrose, and fructose are all examples of reducing sugars; sucrose by itself is not.

REFINER: A machine that uses rollers to reduce the particle size of mixtures such as marzipan and gianduja. *See* Mélangeur.

RESIDENCE TIME: The time required at correct temperature for chocolate to form seed crystals during tempering.

REWORK: The scraps from a batch of confectionery that cannot be sold. A certain amount of rework can be incorporated into many confectionery batches to recoup the loss from the scrap.

ROCHER: Toasted nuts bound with chocolate and spooned into individual portions.

SACCHARIMETER: An instrument that measures the density of a syrup in degrees Baumé by floating in the syrup.

SALPICÓN: A mixture of solid particles bound with a thick liquid. In rochers the nuts and the liquid chocolate form a salpicón.

SATURATED SOLUTION: A syrup that cannot dissolve any more sugar without being heated; that is, it is holding the maximum amount of sugar that it can at a given temperature.

SEED: To introduce crystals in order to induce crystallization. When tempering chocolate, the confectioner seeds it with Form-V cocoa butter crystals; fudge is often seeded with a bit of fondant.

SFI: Solid fat index. A measure of the percentage of fat that is solid at a given temperature. Fats with a higher SFI are harder than fats with a lower SFI.

SLABBED: Describes a center that is spread out to uniform thickness in a frame or pan to be cut after it has set.

SPECIFIC GRAVITY: A measurement of density. Aerated centers, such as marshmallow, can be measured for specific gravity, to ensure their consistency; specific gravity applied to syrups measures their sugar content.

STABLE CRYSTALS: Form-V cocoa butter crystals. Stable crystals tend not to transform and cause bloom.

STARCH MOLDS: Beds of dry starch imprinted with shapes (or molds) into which a center is funneled. Starch molds are used for making liquor cordials as well as molding jellies and fondants.

STOVING: Holding jellies, usually starch jellies, at an elevated temperature in beds of starch to allow them to dry slightly resulting in a higher dissolved-solids content.

SUCROSE: Common sugar obtained from sugar cane or sugar beets. Sucrose is a disaccharide consisting of one molecule of fructose bonded to one molecule of dextrose.

SUGAR BLOOM: The gray cast, spots, or streaks that appear on poorly handled chocolate. Sugar bloom is caused by exposure to excessive humidity or moisture, and it is a result of the sugar on the surface of the chocolate dissolving, and then recrystallizing in larger, visible crystals.

SUPERSATURATED: Describes a syrup that is holding more sugar than it could have dissolved at that temperature. All noncrystalline sugar confections are supersaturated solutions.

TABLING: Working a mixture on a tabletop, usually a flat stone or marble slab, to remove heat and induce crystallization. Tabling is one method of agitation. *See* Agitate.

TEMPER: To precrystallize chocolate; to introduce enough stable cocoa butter crystals to cause the rapid crystallization of the rest of the cocoa butter.

TEMPERED: Chocolate that has been properly precrystallized.

TERROIR: The environmental conditions, including soil and climate, that affect the properties of agricultural products such as cocoa beans.

THEOBROMA CACAO: The tree that produces cacao beans, from which chocolate is made.

THERMOREVERSIBLE: Describes a gel that, once set, can be rewarmed to liquefy and will once again gel upon cooling. Agar and gelatin form thermoreversible gels.

TOTAL WATER CONTENT: The total amount of free water plus bound water in a system. *See* Bound water.

TRIGLYCERIDE: A glycerin backbone with three chains of fatty acids attached. Fats are triglycericdes.

TRINITARIO: A hybrid variety of cocoa beans bred from Forastero and Criollo beans.

UNSTABLE CRYSTALS: Cocoa butter crystals that will transform during storage, resulting in bloom. In cocoa butter, an unstable crystal is any form of cocoa butter crystal lower than Form V.

VISCOSITY: A measure of fluidity. High-viscosity fluids do not flow easily; low-viscosity fluids do.

WATER ACTIVITY: A measure of the amount of water available for chemical or enzymatic reactions or for biological use. The water-activity level of a substance is always compared to that of pure water, which has a water-activity level of 1.00.

WATER-IN-FAT EMULSION: An emulsion in which the aqueous phase is the dispersed phase. *See* Aqueous phase; Dispersed phase.

REFERENCES

Publications

Alexander, R. J. *Sweeteners: Nutritive.* St. Paul, Minn.: Eagan Press, 1998.

Almond, Steve. *Candyfreak: A Journey Through the Chocolate Underbelly of America.* Chapel Hill, N.C.: Algonquin Books, 2004.

Beckett, S. T., ed. *Industrial Chocolate Manufacture and Use.* Oxford, UK: Blackwell Science Limited, 1999.

Beckett, Stephen T. *The Science of Chocolate.* Cambridge, UK: Royal Science of Chemistry Publishing, 2000.

Chandan, Ramesh C. *Dairy-Based Ingredients.* St. Paul, Minn.: Eagan Press, 1997.

Edwards, W. P. *The Science of Sugar Confectionery.* Cambridge, UK: Royal Science of Chemistry Publishing, 2000.

Harris, Norman E., Silvio Crespo, and M. S. Peterson. *A Formulary of Candy Products.* New York: Chemical Publishing Co., Inc., 1998.

Jackson, E. B., ed. *Sugar Confectionery Manufacture.* New York: Aspen Publishers, Inc., 1999.

Mathewson, Paul R. *Enzymes.* St. Paul, Minn.: Eagan Press, 1998.

McGee, Harold. *On Food and Cooking: The Science and Lore of the Kitchen.* New York: Scribner, 1997.

Minifie, Bernard W. *Chocolate, Cocoa, and Confectionery.* New York: Aspen Publishers, Inc., 1999.

Presilla, Maricel E. *The New Taste of Chocolate: A Cultural and Natural History of Cacao with Recipes.* Berkeley, Calif.: Ten Speed Press, 2001.

Pyler, Ernst J. *Baking Science and Technology.* Kansas City, Mo.: Sosland Publishing Co., 1998.

Richmond, Walter. *Choice Confections: Manufacturing Methods and Formulas.* Glen Rock, N.J.: Manufacturing Confectioners Publishing Co., 1997.

Skuse, E. *Skuse's Complete Confectioner.* London: Kegan Paul Limited, 2004.

Stauffer, Clyde E. *Fats and Oils.* St. Paul, Minn.: Eagan Press, 1996.

Thomas, David J., and William A. Atwell. *Starches.* St. Paul, Minn.: Eagan Press, 1999.

Web Sites

CANDY HISTORY AND INFORMATION

http://www.hungrymonster.com/FoodFacts/Food_Facts.cfm?Phrase_vch=Candy&fid=6986

http://www.foodtimeline.org/foodcandy.html#marshmallows

FOOD AND DRUG ADMINISTRATION

STANDARDS OF IDENTITY FOR CACAO PRODUCTS:

http://www.accessdata.fda.gov/scripts/cdrh/cfdocs/cfcfr/CFRSearch.cfm?CFRPart=163%20

STANDARDS OF IDENTITY FOR DAIRY PRODUCTS:

http://www.accessdata.fda.gov/scripts/cdrh/cfdocs/cfcfr/CFRSearch.cfm?CFRPart=131

STANDARDS OF IDENTITY FOR SWEETENERS:

http://www.accessdata.fda.gov/scripts/cdrh/cfdocs/cfcfr/CFRSearch.cfm?CFRPart=168

STANDARDS OF IDENTITY FOR TREE NUT AND PEANUT PRODUCTS:

http://www.accessdata.fda.gov/scripts/cdrh/cfdocs/cfcfr/CFRSearch.cfm?CFRPart=164

FDA WATER ACTIVITY:

http://www.fda.gov/ICECI/Inspections/InspectionGuides/InspectionTechnicalGuides/ucm072916.htm

CHOCOLATE COMPANIES

SCHARFFEN BERGER

http://www.scharffenberger.com/

GUITTARD

http://www.guittard.com/

EQUIPMENT AND SUPPLIES

J.B. PRINCE CO.

http://www.jbprince.com/

PASTRY CHEF CENTRAL

http://pastrychef.com/

ALBERT USTER IMPORTS

http://www.auiswiss.com/

TOMRIC SYSTEMS

http://tomric.com/

INDEX

Page numbers in *italics* indicate recipe illustrations